# Urban Rules and Processes

# Urban Rules and Processes

Historic Lessons for Practice

Besim S. Hakim

EmergentCity Press

*To Malak, Noor, Ayah, and Zeena*

ISBN: 978-0-9683184-5-4

Library of Congress Control Number: 2019948472

Copyright © 1985 to 2019 by Besim S. Hakim

Formatting and cover design by Guglielmo Minervino

Published by EmergentCity Press, 2019
Available from Amazon.com

Cover: A street in the village of Sidi Bou Sa'id, Tunisia. Photo dated July, 2005 by Bojan Stankovski who granted permission to use it on the cover.

# Contents

Introduction ............................................................. vii

**Part I: Historic Precedence** ........................................ 1

1 - Mediterranean Urban/Building Rules ....................... 3
2 - Julian of Ascalon's 6th-c Treatise ............................ 37
3 - Nature of Rules in Islamic Law ............................... 87
4 - Effects of Local Customs ....................................... 93
5 - Case of 19th-c Northern Nigeria .......................... 119
6 - Further Studies Needed ....................................... 159

**Part II: Recycling Lessons** ..................................... 173

7 - Framework for Recycling ..................................... 175
8 - Recycling Experiences of Process and Form ......... 183
9 - Nature of Islamic Urbanism and its Lessons ........ 199
10 - Reviving the Rule System .................................. 245
11 - Applying Lessons in Abiquiu, New Mexico ........ 257
12 - Neighborhood Test Design ................................ 277

**Part III: Generative Processes** ............................... 295

13 - Generative Processes and its Components .......... 297
14 - Applying Generative Process in Al-Ain .............. 317
15 - Eco-Urbanism for Iraqi Cities ............................ 329

**Appendices** .......................................................... 343
Acknowledgements ................................................. 379

# Introduction

After submitting the final manuscript of *Arabic-Islamic Cities* to the US Copyright Office in January 1979, while living in Arizona, I started the slow process of finding a suitable publisher. One must remember that during that time there was no email or access to the Internet and all correspondence was by snail mail. Finally I signed a publishing agreement with Kegan Paul International, London, UK in October 1983. This was shortly after I started teaching at King Faisal University in Dammam. A major consideration and emphasis in my work is how to learn from the heritage of historic urbanism, in terms of the underlying processes and the resulting built form. An attempt was made to articulate this aspect in Appendix 4, titled "Notes on the benefits of the traditional experience" in the book *Arabic-Islamic Cities: Building and Planning Principles*. This part of my research was further developed by designing a six-part framework for the purposes of identifying aspects of the traditional experience worthy of re-cycling. My time was spent on teaching and research, the latter activity initially concentrated on the possibilities of the six-part framework. The findings of the research was presented in conferences and public lectures and published in conference proceeding and peer reviewed journals. These are all documented in my detailed Curriculum Vitae that is available in the Appendices of this book.

This book contains fifteen chapters grouped in three parts. Each chapter was edited for the purposes of the book and the content of each one determined its location in the structure of the book. The first part of six chapters lays out the evidence available to me of the nature of the historic precedence. It presents the rules and processes that were operational in the societies located in the Near East and surrounding the Mediterranean basin, as well as in some regions of Sub-Sahara Africa. Local customs influenced the manner in which the overarching system was adjusted to shape its implementation at the local level. Part II is comprised of six chapters and addresses a) the question of how to identify the underlying features of the traditional/historic experience that are useful as lessons to learn from, and b) present a framework, mentioned above, that covers issues related to the procedures of the building process, and those that are related to the organizational system and built form. The application of how to recycle the lessons pointed out in the framework is discussed in detail in chapters 8 and 9. This is followed by a discussion of how in general terms to revive the rule system, applicable in many regions, with particular attention to the Maghrib countries of North Africa. Chapter 11 applies the lessons of process to a proposal for a housing project in Abiquiu, New Mexico. Followed by chapter 12 that demonstrates the application of the generic lessons inherent in the traditional physical organizational system and planning to a neighborhood test design. Part III of the book presents the underlying generative processes that comprise the backbone of the manner in which the procedures of building activity took place in traditional / historic societies in most locations and cultural settings. It is a dynamic process that has attributes of complex adaptive systems and sustainability. Three case studies are presented, two in chapter 13 and the third in chapter 14. Chapter 15 uses the concept of eco-urbanism as an overarching theme, that includes generative processes and its components, by recommending principles and policies for repairing and re-building Iraqi cities and towns after many years of war. The content of this last chapter is useful and applicable to other countries that underwent similar traumas.

The appendices contain a brief introduction to four of my books, a postscript to *Arabic-Islamic Cities* written in June 2008, and a detailed Curriculum Vitae for current and future researchers that will enable them to trace down information and publications.

*Besim S. Hakim*
September 2019

# Part I: Historic Precedence

This part presents the historical precedence of the rules and processes that were operational in the societies located in the Near East and surrounding the Mediterranean basin, as well as in some regions of Sub-Sahara Africa. Local customs influenced the manner in which the overarching system was adjusted to shape its implementation at the local level. Part I is comprised of six chapters:

1 - Mediterranean Urban/Building Rules ............ 3

2 - Julian of Ascalon's 6th-c Treatise ............ 37

3 - Nature of Rules in Islamic Law ............ 87

4 - Effects of Local Customs ............ 93

5 - Case of 19th- c Northern Nigeria ............ 119

6 - Further Studies Needed ............ 159

2

# Chapter 1

# Mediterranean Urban / Building Rules

## 1 - Origins and diffusion

Byzantine and Islamic codes have direct roots in practices and customary laws in the ancient civilisations of the Near East, but they evolved separately. Their diffusion in the vast territories surrounding the Mediterranean basin demonstrates their look-alike impacts on the built environment due to overlapping similarities in the two system of rules particularly because of common goals and intentions underlying the rules and the specific codes. There is no evidence that clearly demonstrates how the Byzantine system influenced its Islamic counterpart (Lemerle, 1971).[2] On the contrary the evidence suggests that Islamic rules and codes evolved from existing practices in the region, particularly in the Arabian Peninsula, during the 7th century when Islam emerged. This is corroborated by a number of the Prophet's sayings and deeds regarding matters related to land use, its distribution, and various aspects of the construction process. He especially emphasized practices that were compatible with Islamic values (Hakim, 1986).

As for Byzantine codes, the treatise of Julian of Ascalon from Palestine, written during the period 531–533 CE, is the oldest source specifically written for construction and design rules that have so far been discovered. Its use became widespread in the Byzantine Empire when it was incorporated in the *Book of the Eparch* of Constantinople during the reign of Emperor Leon VI (886–912 CE). Subsequently, in 1345 CE, it was incorporated in the *Hexabiblos* of Armenopoulous in Thessaloniki (Hakim, 2001).[3] This widened its influence in the Balkan countries, and earlier in other regions that were under the control of the Byzantines, such as southern Italy.

Although Julian's treatise was composed during the same years of the compilation of the *Corpus Juris Civilis* on orders of the Emperor Justinian I (527–565 CE), its stipulations were firmly rooted in the customary practices in the broader area of Bilad al-Sham, which included Palestine. In fact, the original treatise's title rendered in English is: ‹From the treatise of architect Julian of Ascalon on the laws, or conventions, in Palestine› (Hakim, 2001). One of the sources that pre-dates Julian and is firmly embedded in practices of the Near East region is the *Syro-Roman Lawbook*, dating to about 468 CE (Hakim, 2001).[4]

This brief discussion is to establish the common roots of the two systems of codes that spread to the whole Mediterranean regions via the Byzantines and Muslims. Figures 1a–d are base maps for the years 528, 830, 998, and 1360 CE respectively that have been used to locate various treatises which included rules for the built environment attributed to the Byzantine and Islamic cultures.

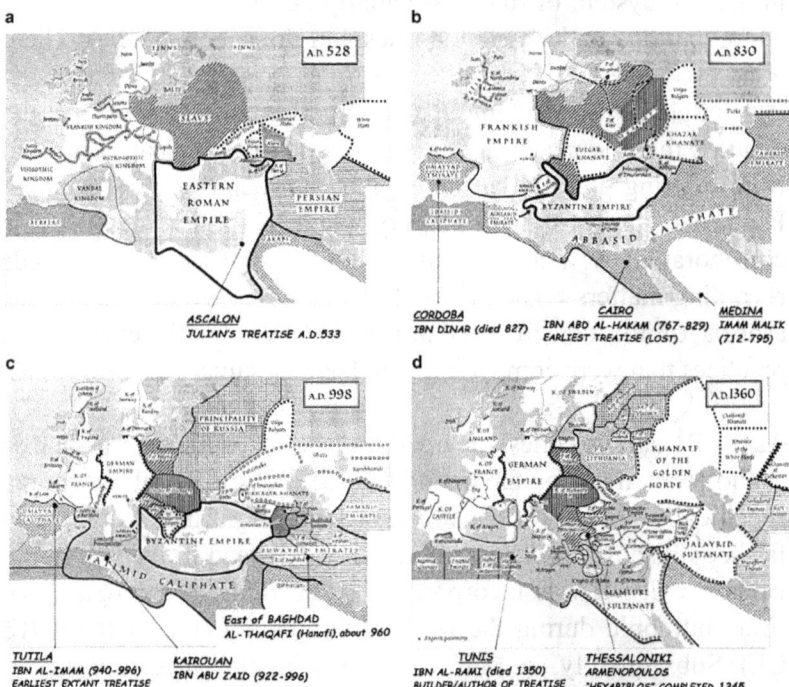

**Figure 1.** Maps showing dates and location of treatises and the authors that wrote about rules for the built environment. The base maps are from Colin McEvedy, *The Penguin Atlas of Medieval History*, Penguin Books, UK, 1961.

Map 528 CE (Figure 1a) shows the frontiers of the Eastern Roman/Byzantine Empire and the location of Ascalon 5 years before Julian's treatise was completed.

Map 830 CE (Figure 1b) shows the frontiers of the Byzantine Empire and the territories governed by Islamic dynasties. Medina, located in the Arabian Peninsula, was a major source for Islamic law through the teaching and writing of Imam Malik (712–795 CE). The earliest treatises on city, neighbourhood, and building construction were written during this period in Cairo and Cordoba, both directly influenced by Malik. They were the work of Ibn Abd al-Hakam (767–829 CE) from Cairo, and Ibn Dinar (d. 827 CE) from Cordoba. Both treatises are lost, but are cited by later authors.

Map 998 CE (Figure 1c) shows the location of Kairouan and Tutila and the work of Ibn Abu Zaid (922–996 CE) from the former and Ibn al-Imam (940–996 CE) from the latter. The treatise of Ibn al-Imam specifically addresses urban and construction topics and draws on works from Medina, Cairo, Cordoba, and Kairouan. It should be noted that all of these treatises are from the Maliki School of Law. The earliest known work on this subject from the Hanafi School of Law is by al-Murajja al-Thaqafi from the region east of Baghdad, as shown in the map.

Map 1360 CE (Figure 1d) shows the locations of Tunis and Thessaloniki. Ibn al-Rami, a master builder from Tunis (d. about 1350 CE), wrote a comprehensive treatise on building and urban codes and related customary laws of his region. He draws on previous and contemporary works and also on local opinions and practice, including his own. This treatise has been studied extensively by the present author and its rationale and main cases recorded and published (Hakim, 1986).[5] During this period in Thessaloniki, within the territory of the Byzantine Empire, a lawyer by the name of Armenopoulos compiled his large compendium on civil law in 1345 CE, known as the *Hexabiblos* (ie six books). Julian's treatise from 533 CE was included and comprises the bulk of Book 2 of this work. It is through this work by Armenopoulos that Julian's stipulations were further entrenched in the territories of the then shrinking Byzantine Empire, and especially in the Balkan countries and Greece were its influence continued well into the late 19th century and early years of the 20th century.[6]

Figure 2a is a sample page from the 1300s CE of a surviving copy of Julian's treatise. This copy was discovered in 1891 CE by a Swiss scholar as a part of the *Book of the Eparch*, attributed to the reign of Emperor Leon VI (886–912 CE). Figure 2b is a sample page from one of the four surviving copies of Ibn al-Imam's treatise from 10th century Tutila. It is generally known by the long title of: ‹Rules for abutting buildings and prevention of damages›. There are now three Arabic verifications and commentaries of this treatise published in 1996 in Saudi Arabia, 1999 in Morocco, and 2003 in Tunisia.[7]

**Figure 2.** (a) Sample page of an extant copy from the 14th century of Julian of Ascalon 6th century treatise. *Source*: Bibliotheque Publique et Universitaire, Geneva, Switzerland. (b) Sample page from one of the four extant copies of Ibn al-Imam's 10th century treatise from Tutila in northern Spain. *Source*: Bibliotheque Nationale d'Algerie, Alger.

## 2 - Content of Byzantine and Islamic codes: their similarities and differences

For the comparison the present study uses the treatises of Julian (written during the period 531–533 CE) to represent the Byzantine system, and Isa bin Musa al-Tutaili, known as Ibn al-Imam (940–996 CE) to represent the Islamic system. Ibn al-Imam was from Tutila, modern Tudela, Spain, about 50 miles northwest of Zaragoza. His treatise was influenced by the work of scholars from Medina in Arabia, Cairo, Cordoba, and Kairouan (Van Staevel, 2000).[8] First let us look at the similarities of these two treatises in terms of their underlying *goal*:

> The goal is to deal with change in the built environment by ensuring that minimum damage occurs to preexisting structures and their owners, through stipulating fairness in the distribution of rights and responsibilities among various parties, particularly those who are proximate to each other. This ultimately will ensure the equitable equilibrium of the built environment during the process of change and growth.[9]

The underlying assumed *intentions* that are evident by a careful study of these treatises are:
1. Change in the built environment should be accepted as a natural and healthy phenomenon. In the face of ongoing change, it is necessary to maintain an equitable equilibrium in the built environment.
2. Change, particularly that occurring among proximate neighbours, creates potential for damages to existing dwellings and other uses. Therefore, certain measures are necessary to prevent changes or uses that would (i) result in debasing the social and economic integrity of adjacent or nearby properties, (ii) create conditions adversely affecting the moral integrity of the neighbours, and (iii) destabilize peace and tranquillity between neighbours.
3. In principle, property owners have the freedom to do what they please on their own property. Most uses are allowed, particularly those necessary for a livelihood. Nevertheless, the freedom to act within one's property is constrained by preexisting conditions of neighbouring properties, neighbours' rights of servitude, and other rights associated with ownership for certain periods of time.
4. The compact built environment of ancient towns necessitates the implementation of interdependence rights among citizens, principally among proximate neighbours. As a consequence of interdependence rights, it becomes necessary to allocate

responsibilities among such neighbours, particularly with respect to legal and economic issues.
5. The public realm must not be subjected to damages that result from activities or waste originating in the private realm.

In addition to the intentions above, there is an additional generic rule in Ibn al-Imam's treatise:
> It is the right of a neighbour to abut a neighbouring existing structure, but he must respect its boundaries and its owner's property rights.

This is clearly an important additional right evident in most treatises written by Muslim scholars regardless of the School of Law to which an author belongs. This implies a host of necessary rules in dealing with common party walls (Hakim, 1986). The emphasis on abutting adjacent structures and on party wall although mentioned in Byzantine codes are not as elaborated as in their Islamic counterparts. Ibn al-Imam also addressed issues related to streets and the '*fina*'.[10] On the question of overlooking and views, Muslim societies were more concerned with preserving privacy from visual intrusions. Whereas Byzantine societies were especially concerned with the preservation of pleasant views such as of the sea, mountains, orchards, and public mural on walls. This is an example that clearly demonstrates how culture is encoded, or embodied, in the built form through codes. The following is a list of the issues and related cases that were addressed by Julian and Ibn al-Imam.

Julian addresses the following issues:
- *Land use*: including baths, artisanal workshops, and socially offensive uses.
- *Views*: for enjoyment and also those considered a nuisance.
- *Houses and condominiums*: involving acts that debase the value of adjacent properties, walls between neighbours, and condominiums in multi-storey buildings and those contiguous with porticos.
- *Drainage*: of rain and wastewater.
- *Planting*: of trees, shrubs, and other vegetation.

Ibn al-Imam addresses more issues:
- *Land use*: location of mosques, bakeries, shops, and public baths.

- *Streets*: open-ended streets, cul-de-sacs, '*fina*', projections on streets, servitude and access.
- *Walls*: abutting and sharing rights; ownership rights and responsibilities.
- *Overlooking*: visual corridors that compromise privacy generated by the location of doors, windows, openings, and heights.
- *Drainage and hygiene*: rain and wastewater drainage; responsibilities for cleaning septic tanks, and removal of garbage.
- *Planting*: of trees, and other vegetation.
- *Animals*: cattle, sheep, chicken, birds, and bees.

Figure 3 points out the underlying concepts and principles (*Qawa'id Fiqhiyah*) of Islamic law that governed the rationale for the processes of change and growth. The original Arabic version of these principles is included for reference. The English translation of the seven *Qawa'id* are:
1. the basis for action is the freedom to act,
2. stimulated and judged by the intentions for those actions,
3. which are constrained by the prevention of damages to others,
4. however, it is sometimes necessary to tolerate lesser damages so as to avoid greater ones,
5. older established facts must be taken into account by adjusting

قواعد فقهية

١- الأصل في الأشياء الإباحة   ٢- الأمور بمقاصدها (إنما الأعمال بالنيات)
٣- لاضرر ولاضرار   ٤- الضرر الأشد يزال بالضرر الأخف
٥- القديم يترك على قدمه   ٦- المعروف عرفاً كالمشروط شرطاً
٧- الأعراف قابلة للتغيير عبر الزمن

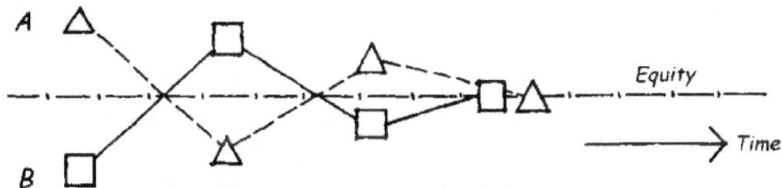

**Figure 3.** Principles of Islamic law (*Qawa'id Fiqhiyah*) that governed the rationale for the process of growth and change. The original Arabic version is included for reference. An important goal for these principles is to achieve equity between neighbours when expectations, demands, and needed change would create benefits to one owner to the detriment of his neighbour(s). Two owners (A and B) are illustrated. The effect of these principles over time tends to equitably harmonize the competing and sometimes conflicting demands of adjacent owners. Drawing by the author.

to their presence and conditions,
6. people's customs must be respected and followed,
7. however, time might change those customs and new solutions will be needed.

An important goal for these principles is to achieve equity between neighbours when expectations, demands, and needed change would create benefits to one owner to the detriment of his neighbour(s). Two owners (A and B) are illustrated in the diagram. The effect of these principles over time tends to equitably harmonize the competing and sometimes conflicting demands of adjacent owners.

Figure 4 portrays the conceptual representations of impacts on the local level (three geometric shapes denoting three settlements) by *proscriptive* meta-principles, and by *prescriptive* imposed laws.[11] The diagram on the left represents a settlement's ability to respond freely to local conditions and requirements, but is restrained by an overarching set of meta-principles. This would result in settlements that are diverse in their physical form and exhibit distinct identity. The diagram on the right represents how prescriptions from a central authority, which are usually far removed from a locality, can inhibit creative solutions to local problems. Over time the resulting settlements would tend to become similar to each other.[12]

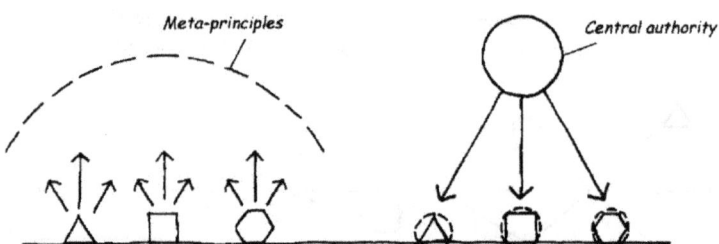

**Figure 4.** Conceptual representation of the impacts on the local level (three geometric shapes denoting three settlements) by *proscriptive* meta-principles, and by *prescriptive* imposed laws. The diagram on the left represents a settlement's ability to respond freely to local conditions and requirements, but restrained by an overarching set of meta-principles. This would result in settlements that are diverse in their physical form and exhibit distinct local identity. The diagram on the right represents how prescriptions from a top-down central authority, far removed from a locality, inhibits creative solutions to local problems. Over time the settlements would tend to become similar to each other. Drawing by the author.

Figure 5 shows the various uses and implications of the *'fina'*. Columns on both sides of the *Sabat* allow flexibility for sale and purchase of the room above the right of way. Figure 6 shows a typical sequence of the emergence of the fabric of a prototypical

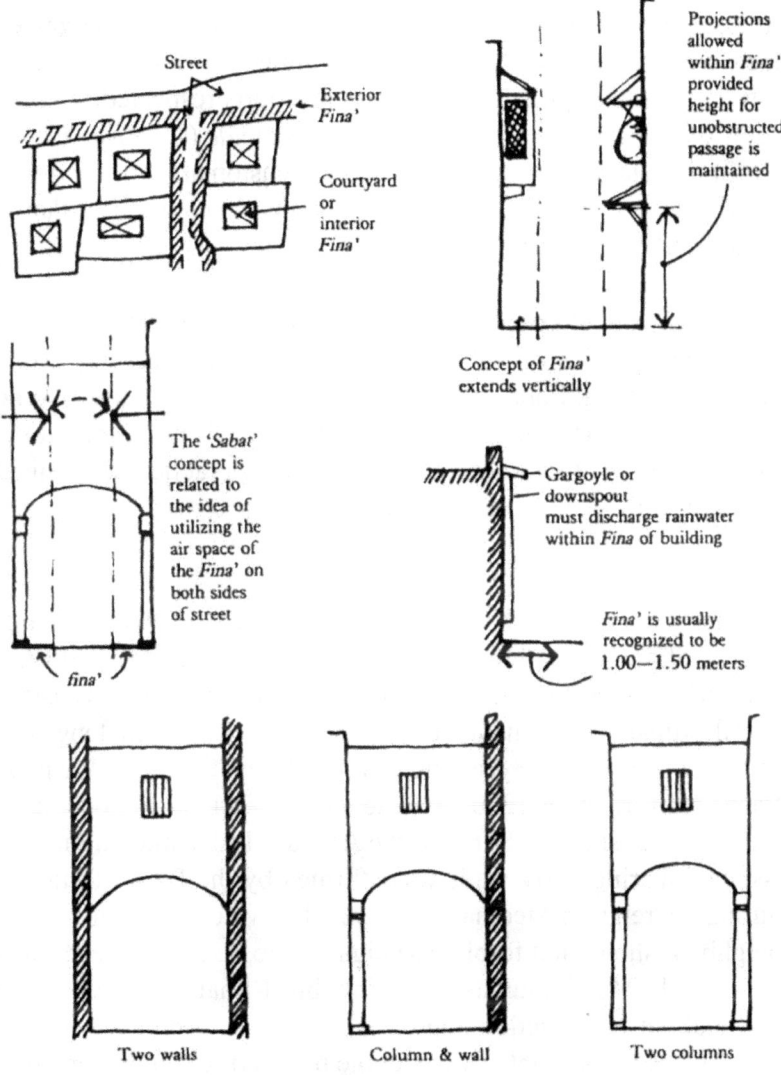

**Figure 5.** The *Fina* and *Sabat*. The diagram shows how the *Fina* is utilized. It is an invisible space about 1.00–1.50 m wide alongside all exterior walls of buildings – primarily alongside streets and access paths – and extends vertically alongside the wall of the building. The principle for the formation of the *Sabat* is shown as well as various methods for its support. Drawing by the author from Hakim, (1986).

traditional Islamic neighbourhood, following locally applied codes and customary practice. On site studies of sequences showing growth and change are essential for understanding how the codes worked and the nature of the accretion process.

It should be noted that both Byzantine and Islamic law recognized local customary practice. When determining the validity of a custom in a specific jurisdiction Byzantine courts respected the concepts of *consensus populi* and *longa consuetude* (J. de Malafosse, 1962). In Islamic law the local *Urf* (i.e. customary practice) was recognized as valid provided it did not clearly contradict Islamic values and law (Hakim, 1994).

## 3 - Examples of specific codes and their impacts
There are a number of codes related to the issues covered by Julian and Ibn al-Imam. Four codes have been selected that tended to be universal in their impact in shaping the built form of traditional towns in the Mediterranean. Local customary practice determined the final form and character of a place.

### 3.1 - Party walls
Buildings abutting each other on more than one side were a major feature of ancient and traditional towns dating back to 2000 BCE and earlier in the Near East. Julian recognized this age-old custom in Palestinian towns and addressed it in his treatise. The longevity of this custom in the Byzantine and post-Byzantine periods can be traced forward, over 1200 years, to a ruling in 1777 in documents found at the island of Syros in the Aegean. In Islamic culture the issue of sharing party walls was affirmed by the Prophet himself during his reign in Medina (622–632 CE), which translates as: 'A neighbour should not forbid his neighbour to insert wooden beams in his wall'. Muslim jurists, including Ibn al-Imam and others who wrote about construction and design codes to ensure that neighbours respect this right, always quote this saying. Implementation details for this stipulation were developed by jurists and are fully documented in Islamic jurisprudence literature.[13] Two aerial photos of traditional towns from North Africa and Greece demonstrate the impact of this stipulation (Figure 7a and b).

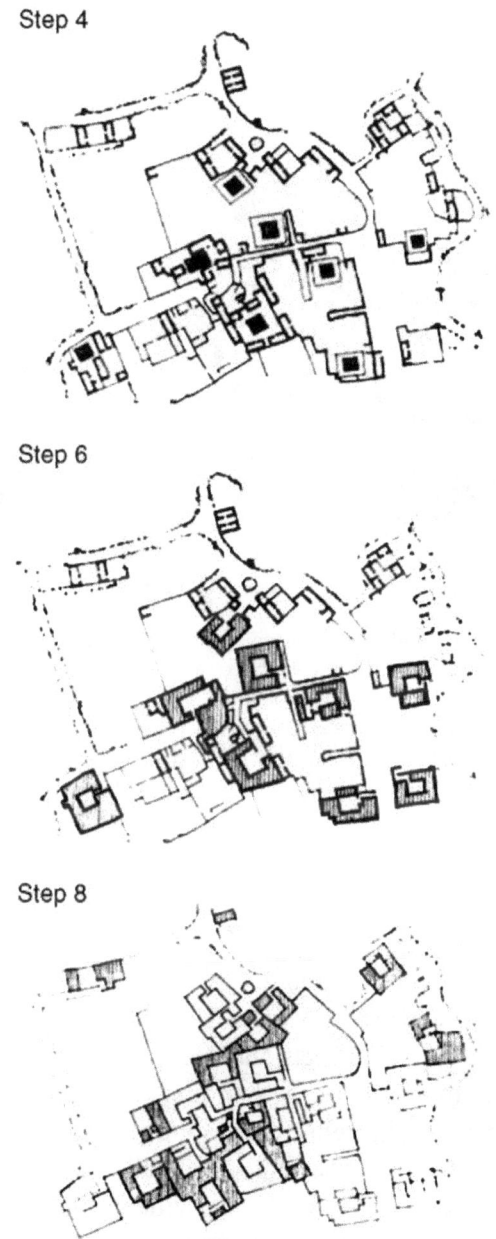

**Figure 6.** Simulated typical sequence of the emergence of a cluster of houses in a traditional Islamic neighbourhood setting. What is shown are only three steps from a sequence of eight. Step 4 shows the laying out of courtyards, step 6 the location and layout of rooms around the courtyard, and step 8 the final configurations. The simulation is described in the book by Howard Davis, *The Culture of Building*, New York, 1999, pp. 202–206.

Figure 7. (a) Sid Bou Sa'id, Tunisia. A village located about 12 miles north-east of Tunis the capital, and is about 400 feet above sea level. The air photo was taken in 1970, and was published in the author's book: *Sidi Bou Sa'id, Tunisia: A Study in Structure and Form* (1978). Courtesy Office de la Topographie et de la Cartographie, Tunis. (b) Pyrgi, village on the island of Chios, Aegean sea, Greece, whose origins date back to the mid-14th century. The air photo is of the northern half of the village, taken in 1934. Courtesy Ministry of Public Works, Aerial photos Department, Greece.

## 3.2 - *Fina* (syn: *Harim*)

This is an invisible space about 1.00–1.50 m wide alongside all exterior walls of a building which is not attached to other walls, and primarily alongside streets and access paths. It extends vertically alongside the walls of the building. The owner or tenant of the building has certain rights and responsibilities associated with his *fina*. Although Julian does not specifically mention it, its usage is clearly evident in Greek towns and villages that have survived since the post-Byzantine period, primarily from the post-1500s period. There is adequate evidence for this concept from pre-Islamic history in Arabia; the concept was thoroughly recognized by Muslim jurists and scholars in the extant literature of the Near East, North Africa, and pre-1500 Spain. It is a powerful concept and an effective tool that has done much to allow the articulation of the facades and thresholds along the public realm. Built-in benches near entrances, troughs for vegetation, high-level projections in the form of balconies and enclosed bay windows, and rooms bridging the public right-of-way (*sabat* – Arabic term – discussed below) were all possible due to implementing the various allowances of this concept. Maintenance of streets and private passageways, by keeping them clean and safe from obstructions, was also related to the responsibilities associated with using the *fina*. Figure 8a–d are examples from Tunisia, Greece, Italy, and Spain, respectively.

### 3.3 - Visual corridors
Views – from primary windows, balconies, and terraces of houses – of the sea, mountains, gardens, and orchards were considered important in Byzantine and later Greek culture. Accordingly, stipulations and codes were devised to protect these assets. Evidence of such codes exists since the Roman period and from the late 5th century Constantinople. Figure 9 shows the major consideration of views of the sea in Julian's treatise.

In Islamic culture, protection from visual intrusion into the private realm of houses was the paramount consideration. Views were appreciated when available, but they took second place to the blocking of visual corridors into the private realm. Figure 10 was developed using the treatise of Ibn al-Rami in Tunis from the early 14th century. The original codes do not specify dimensions but rather intentions for performance. The dimensions indicated in Figure 10 are interpretations of this author. To discourage overlooking neighbouring terraces, roof terraces in many traditional towns in the Muslim world would be screened by parapets. Bay windows towards the public realm, usually located at upper levels, would be screened by wooden lattices which allowed views of the outside but prevented those outside from seeing in.[14]

### 3.4 - *Sabat* (syn.: *Stegasto [Naxos]* and *Katastegia [Mykonos]*)
The configuration and possibility of bridging the public right-of-way emanates from the concept of the *fina*. It is a device that allows the creation of additional space attached to a building. Codes written by Muslim jurists clearly stipulate the legal rights associated with constructing *sabats*. In Figure 5 the *fina* is shown in

**Figure 8.** (a) A street in old Tunis, Tunisia. Note the steps for the house on the right are within the *fina*. Windows are above eye level, and the *sabats*. Photo taken by author in the mid-1970s. (b) A street in Amorgos town on the island of Amorgos, Greece. Note the steps to the houses on the right, the balconies on the upper level, and the upper level room projection are all within the *fina* space of the houses. Sketch by author after a photo in *Greek Island Villages* by Norman F. Carver Jr., 2001. (c) A street in Ostuni, Puglia region, Italy, near the Adriatic coast. Note the projecting lamp is high enough for traffic below it, and it is within the *fina* of the house. The *sabat* belongs to the house on the right. The arch, in the foreground, spanning the street is built to reinforce the stability of the walls implemented after agreement between owners of the houses across the street. Sketch by author after a photo in *Italian Hilltowns* by Norman F. Carver Jr., 1979. (d) A street in the village of Vejer de la Frontera, Cadiz province, Spain. The *Fina* on both sides of the street is cleaned by the residents. Photo by Bernard Rudofsky, early 1960s.

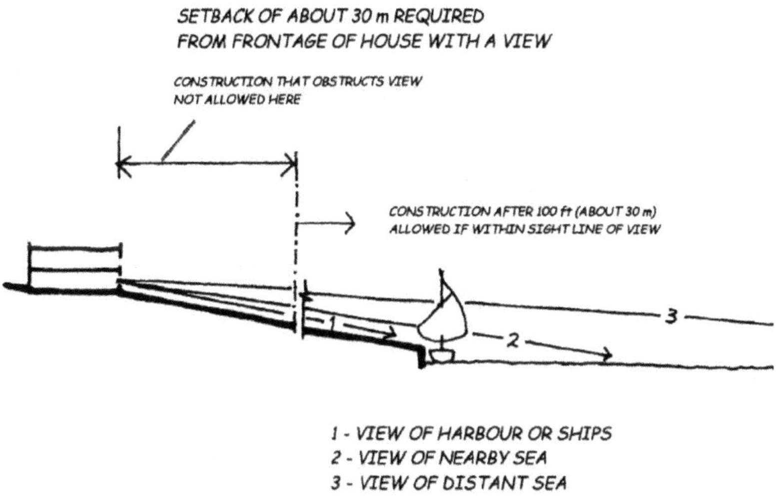

SETBACK OF ABOUT 30 m REQUIRED
FROM FRONTAGE OF HOUSE WITH A VIEW

CONSTRUCTION THAT OBSTRUCTS VIEW
NOT ALLOWED HERE

CONSTRUCTION AFTER 100 ft (ABOUT 30 m)
ALLOWED IF WITHIN SIGHT LINE OF VIEW

1 - VIEW OF HARBOUR OR SHIPS
2 - VIEW OF NEARBY SEA
3 - VIEW OF DISTANT SEA

**Figure 9.** Preserving the view of the sea, and the categorization of the type of sea views as stipulated in Julian of Ascalon's treatise from the early 6th century. Sketch by author from his published study of Julian's treatise.

section and an indication on how it merges from both sides of a street to form the *sabat*.

When buildings on both sides of a street are owned by the same person, then he can create a *sabat* by directly using the walls for support. When somebody else owns the building on the opposite side of the street, then the party who wants to build a *sabat* might decide to use columns for support abutting the opposite exterior wall. Or alternatively, both sides can be supported by columns that will then make the *sabat* marketable to the opposite neighbour at a future unknown time. Sometimes adjacent neighbours along the axis of the street might also decide to build *sabats*. This will result in continuous *sabats* abutting each other and forming a tunnel effect over the street. The question of height clearance for the right-of-way is addressed by Muslim jurists by stipulating that the clearance be high enough to allow the height of a rider of a beast of burden to pass unhindered. In certain regions the measure was a fully loaded camel. For example, in post-Islamic Toledo, the Spanish codes of the early 15th century prescribed that a knight with all his weapons be the measure for the clearance. One of the stipulations in Armenopoulos›s *Hexabiblos* (mid-14th century) specifies that any projections, such as balconies, must allow a clearance of 15 feet above the street level.

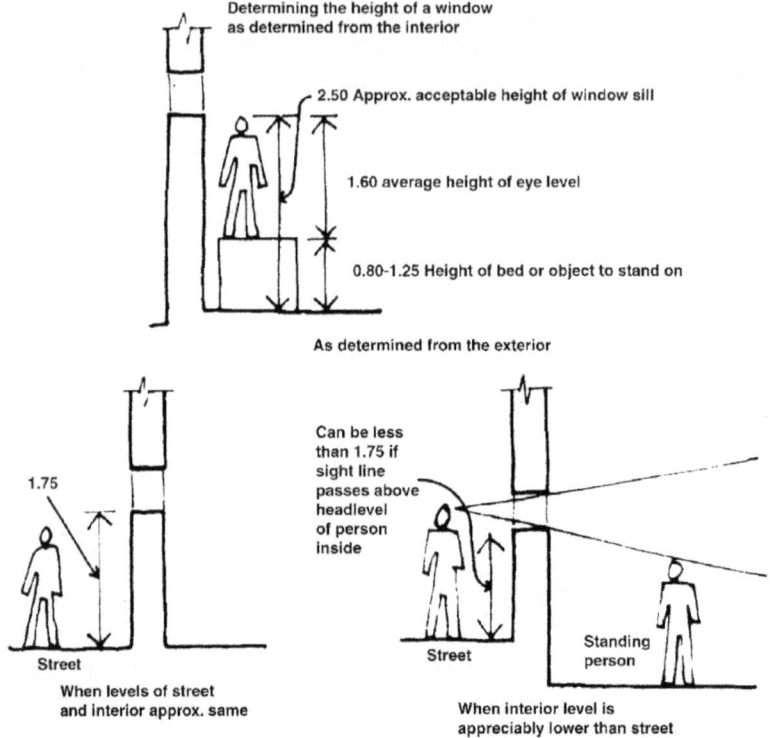

**Figure 10.** Determining the height of windows for the preservation of privacy in Islamic cities. The above sketch shows how to determine the height from the interior if the opening overlooks the private domain of the neighbours. The lower two sketches indicate how to determine the height of the window sills from the street so as to prevent looking into the interior. The original codes do not specify dimensions but rather intentions for performance. The dimensions shown are interpretations by the author. Sketches by the author from Hakim (1986).

There are other considerations to be aware of, which are not discussed in this study, related to the distribution of responsibilities among various parties whose decisions affected the built environment, the procedures that were followed in making those decisions, and the manner conflicts were addressed and resolved. There are numerous lessons for us to be learned from those considerations, particularly in viewing them as precedence and possibly models, for simplifying our procedures and patterns of responsibility allocations that in many instances are hindrances to achieving equity and quality in the built environment.

## 4 - Impact of codes on the traditional built environment

There are a very large number of examples from the southern and northern regions of the Mediterranean which demonstrate the impacts of the building and urban codes, briefly discussed above, on the built form qualities and characteristics of villages, towns, and cities. However, especially interesting is the phenomenon of towns in the Puglia and Calabria regions of southern Italy where a large number of towns exhibit astonishing similarities in their urban structure and form to those in North Africa. Yet the presence of the Muslims in those regions of Italy (excluding Sicily were Muslim rule lasted over two centuries) was of a temporary nature in the 9th and 10th centuries of the Common Era. We do find a scholar like Enrico Guidoni using the term 'Italian-Muslim town planning' to describe this phenomenon (Guidoni, 1979).

What processes and rules were followed in establishing towns in Puglia and Calabria?[15] Did the Muslims have enough time to establish their system of urban development in the various towns of this region that display urban structure and form similar to Islamic urbanism? Figure 11 are plans of six towns (not to the same scale), Figure 12 is the plan of Cisternino, and Figure 13 is a view of a typical street in Cisternino. All seven towns are from the Puglia region of Italy. They all display astonishing similarities to Islamic towns, especially apparent in the street system comprising of through streets and cul-de-sacs. My own suspicion is that Byzantine codes were well established in this region and were embedded in the local customary laws that were used in the development of these towns.[16] Extensive research of this question is necessary and waits to be undertaken.

In such towns as Toledo and in numerous towns and villages in southern Spain, the effects of the rules and codes, which have their roots in the Islamic period, are on display. Casares, a town in the Andalusia province about 80 miles southeast of Seville, is one such example. However to acquire a more complete picture the phenomenon of the transition and changes to the built environment in the Iberian Peninsula from Islamic to Christian control is important to investigate and is currently being studied by the present author. However, from a cursory investigation some evidence of the continuation of Islamic law and practice and also the influence of Roman/Byzantine laws has been found. This is par-

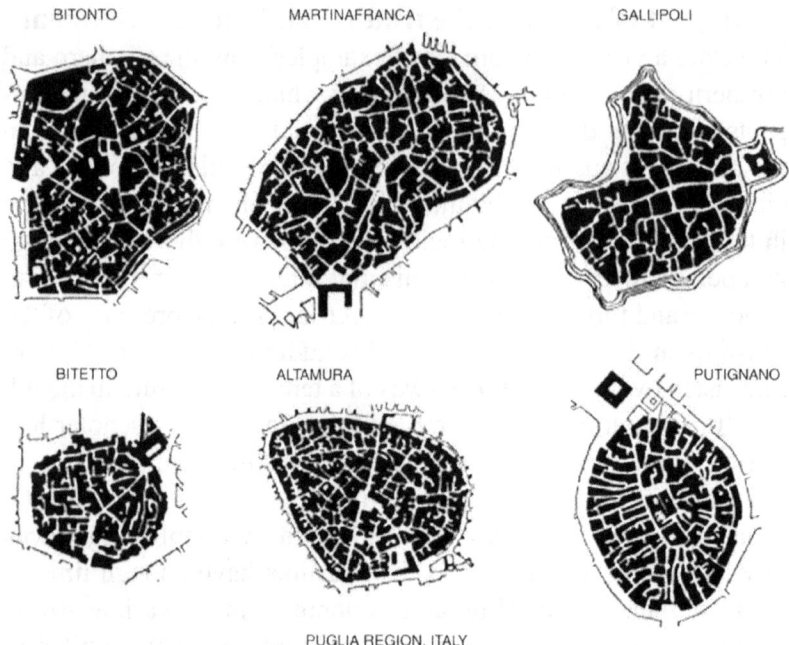

**Figure 11.** Six examples of traditional towns (not to the same scale) from the Puglia region located in the southeast part of the Italian peninsula. The Italian urban historian, Enrico Guidoni, made a study of the Islamic influence on towns in Sicily and southern Italy and his work was published in 1979 and 1984. This figure is from Guidoni (1979).

**Figure 12.** The plan of the core of the town of Cisternino in the Puglia region of southeast Italy. The drawing is from the mid-1960s. *Source*: Edward Allen, *Stone Shelters*, Cambridge, MA, 1969, p. 147.

**Figure 13.** A typical view of a street in Cisternino showing the impact of the *Fina* and other features discussed in this study. *Source*: Edward Allen, *Stone Shelters*, Cambridge, MA, 1969, p. 157.

ticularly evident in the codes of the Alarife institution, particularly from the available manuscripts written in Toledo and Cordoba that can be traced to the 15th century Common Era. The practices and impacts of Alarife institution continued in Andalusia well into the 19th century (Benito, 1986; Gonzalez, 1996).

Christian rulers also introduced concepts and specific stipulations that contradicted both Islamic and Byzantine laws. This was probably done to create a new identity for Christian rule via built form features in towns and cities, particularly considering the centuries of continuous Islamic rule. The results of such an investigation will illuminate theoretical issues related to urbanization in general, but more specifically to urban history in the Iberian Peninsula.

As for the Islamic world, we still find very large numbers of towns and cities that display the typical pattern that is based on the typology of courtyard buildings and the access system of through streets and cul-de-sacs. Granted, a number of cities in the Islamic world did not follow this pattern, choosing instead a different typology of buildings and urban morphology as evident in traditional towns of Yemen and the Southwestern region of Saudi Arabia. But therein lies the wisdom of the code system, which was responsive to different morphologies, because it was flexible, comprehensible, and easily implementable.

Customary laws and codes, with their distinct attributes, evolved in Greek towns and villages during the period of approximately 1500–1900, because of the lack of a central authority that imposed building standards at the local level. This has resulted in unique architectural and urban landscape features, still admired by visitors from all parts of the world. Unfortunately, this began to change when the central authority in Athens began to impose its central codes and standards for the whole country from about the first third of the 20th century. Uniformity and sameness began to creep in slowly; the process continues to this day. In the mid-1980s, on the island of Paros, Greece, it was observed that the concept of the *fina* was alive and well, as was the use of *sabats*. However, if local traditional rules and codes are not revived in places such as Paros, all will be lost in the coming decades.

## 5 - Lessons for contemporary and future practice

It is essential and instructive to understand the system and processes underlying the development of traditional towns and cities. Recent science can provide us with good analogies that clarify the phenomenon. John Holland's book contains useful insight (Holland, 1995). In Chapter 1 he explains what a Complex Adaptive System is and how it works by identifying Adaptive and Aggregate Agents. Individual agents behaviour is determined by a collection of rules that are a convenient way to describe agent strategies. These agents interact with each other according to rules that produce aggregation of agents at the next level and those may again be aggregated to add new hierarchal levels. Rules can change as experience is accumulated. This is precisely what occurs in traditional built environments as described earlier in the present article. What is also important to understand is that a complex adaptive system is non-linear and dynamic that creates unpredictable and diverse results within the framework of rules. Although multitudes of changes do occur, particularly at the micro level, overall coherence of the character and identity of the town or city is not compromised.[17]

In a recent study (Hakim and Ahmed, 2006) we have demonstrated how the traditional city in 19th century Northern Nigeria embodies the characteristics of a self-regulating and adaptive system. The self-regulating aspect is a result of the decisions and actions of specific individuals in starting new compounds or small farms. In doing so, they respond to existing conditions on adjacent properties by adjusting their planning and design decisions. Over time, changes and adaptations occur in compounds as their owners adjust and adapt to changes in neighbouring and contiguous compounds. The alignment of pathways and streets will be delineated and extended in response to the creation and/or changes of farm boundaries and compound walls.

Another important phenomenon that occurred in traditional towns is feedback. There are two types of feedback: negative and positive. It is the former that can handle random changes, and a way of reaching equilibrium and equitability. Positive feedback repeats the same action again and again and is associated with top-down prescriptive codes as evident in current zoning laws. The relationship between proximate neighbours depends on decisions affected by negative feedback, such as when a window from one house overlooks the private domain of another. The owner of the latter reacts by demanding that the window be sealed or removed. However, if the window was there before the new neighbour built his house, he must respond by laying out the house so that overlooking would not occur.

Emergent systems (see note 1 and note 17 at the end of this chapter), such as we find in traditional Mediterranean urbanism, depends on living within boundaries defined by rules. The system's capacity for learning, growth, and experimentation derives from its adherence to these rules. Another important property in a living dynamic system is its network pattern. Networks of communications generate feedback loops, and such systems learn from mistakes. Thus, a community can correct its mistakes, regulate, and organize itself, as explained above in the example of negative feedback.

It is extremely instructive for further understanding the underlying generative system and its codes that shaped traditional Mediterranean towns is to use the analogy of the human or animal embryo. The following insight is from Lewis Wolpert's book (Wolpert, 1991). He uses the term 'generative program' as a framework for explaining how a generative system works:

> The embryo does not contain a description of the animal to which it will give rise, rather it contains a generative program for making it. It is like a recipe and different from a descriptive program, and a complex form can come from a simple program that is essentially contained within the genes that control cell behaviour. There is no 'master builder' in the embryo. Each cell in the developing embryo has access to the same genetic information. A general principle of the embryonic organization is that 'small is beautiful'. There is no central government but rather, a number of small self-governing regions.

This is what occurs in a typical traditional built environment, that is, the cell referred to above is the agent or individual household, the embryo is the town under formation and once formed will continue to experience change and growth. The genetic information is the rules and codes that individuals follow without being dictated by a top-down authority. The small governing regions correspond to neighbourhoods in the town.

In a book by Virginia Postrel (Postrel, 1998), she asks in her introductory chapter: 'How we feel about the evolving future tells us who we are as individuals and as a civilization: Do we search for *stasis* – a regulated, engineered world? Or do we embrace *dynamism* – a world of constant creation, discovery, and competition?'

Mediterranean traditional urbanism and its associated generative processes, rules, and codes represent dynamic systems that allow creation and discovery and celebrate bottom-up decision-making processes. Current zoning codes, and recent attempts to replace them with form-based codes, are stasis in nature and are regulated, engineered, and mostly based on top-down decision-making structures. Yet it should be noted that form-based codes, such as the SmartCode, does provide advantages that are absent in current zoning codes.

Postrel's general principles for dynamist rules are remarkably similar to the principles of rules and associated decision-making processes found in most traditional built environments around the Mediterranean. Postrel's five principles are:
1. allow individuals (including groups of individuals) to act on their own knowledge;
2. apply to simple, generic units and allow them to combine in many different ways;
3. permit credible, understandable, enduring, and enforceable commitments;
4. protect criticism, competition, and feedback;
5. establish a framework within which people can create nested, competing frameworks of more specific rules.

In general therefore current types of coding, whether they are conventional zoning that dictate land use and enforce nominal prescriptive regulations for each use, or form-based codes that require adherence to very specific stipulations related to the form of the building or clusters of buildings are all top-down codes that are stasis in nature and cannot produce the dynamism discussed above.

On keeping rules simple, which was an essential attribute of Mediterranean codes, the book by Richard A. Epstein is very relevant (Epstein, 1995). He suggests seven simple rules that, in his estimate, will suffice to deal with about 95% of all possible situations facing the legal system in the US. His proposed rules are:
1. self-ownership, or autonomy,
2. first possession,
3. voluntary exchange,
4. protection against aggression,
5. limited privilege for cases of necessity,
6. taking property for public use on payment of just compensation, and
7. take and pay.[18]

Regarding the question of how the law can be made to act dynamically, J.B. Ruhl's proposals are worthy of consideration (Ruhl, 1996). He proposes to make rights-based common law, a system that is adaptive, a corner stone of the legal system in the US. The three positive features of common law that he cites are: (1) Common law changes slowly and incrementally because it is limited by the dimension of rights as exercised and enforced that allows it to evolve with society's needs. (2) The common law tackles issues as they come, keeps their components together because it is adaptive and decides issues in their context, thus avoiding incomprehensible outcomes.[19] (3) The common law operates at the component interaction level *vs* current legal practice that, more often than not, tackles problems abstractly. The result is that the common law, because of its evolutionary qualities, is focused more on system structure and process thus avoiding it to fall into stasis.

All of the above qualities of the common law are very similar to the legal structure and its associated processes found in traditional Mediterranean societies. It thus enforces the qualities of complex adaptive systems and its dynamic non-linear nature. It helps to self-regulate legal decisions and promotes the emergent qualities in the built environment discussed earlier because it is essentially a bottom-up system that responds to local micro conditions.

To further address the question: What are the lessons for contemporary and future practice? It should be remembered that modern towns and cities have employed many technologies that were absent in the past. Specifically the car and its requirements for street design and parking including multi-story parking structures, infrastructure technologies that include sewers, water, electricity, and communication lines. In addition, the contemporary city, at least since about the mid-20th century, has added various building types that did not exist in the past, such as airports, large hospitals, factories for numerous manufacturing processes, and so on. Therefore it is necessary to demarcate the city into sectors that would require control and management of infrastructure and buildings that are for public use and that require precision and technological know-how for their construction and maintenance, and the rest of most of the city that is dedicated to housing.

The lessons from the traditional Mediterranean experience, particularly its aspects of control, management, and coding, are primarily applicable to the housing sectors of contemporary and future towns and cities. The following essential principles, applicable to the habitat sectors of cities, need to be adopted and applied:
- Habitat, or housing, formation and its subsequent growth and change over time should be formed and designed to behave as a *Complex Adaptive System*.
- The system must also be *Self-Regulating*.
- The system must rely on feedback. *Negative Feedback* is what should occur during the process of self-regulation, as described earlier.
- The system must operate by a *Generative Program* and not a *Descriptive Program*.
- The generative program must be *non-linear* in nature, that is, it should rely on decisions that are informed by feedback.
- At the micro level *Agents* behave in *Adaptive* ways, and they form the next level of *Aggregate Agents* who in turn form another layer and so on. An agent could be an individual or a household.
- The *Responsibility* distribution between agents at various levels will require making changes to the current system of production and delivery, such as the role of the developer in assembling and sub-dividing land.

- The rules and codes should primarily be based on intentions for performance and therefore should be *Proscriptive* in nature. However, a minority of the codes might have to be *prescriptive*, particularly those related to technological elements such as the car and various infrastructure elements.
- The resulting system for habitat will be *Dynamic* in nature, which means that *Emergent* forms and configurations, particularly at the micro level, will be unpredictable. The resulting qualities of form will be unique to each location, thus enhancing the sense of place and identity at each micro level of the built environment. These unpredictable and sometimes surprising results will be evident from the level of the house design to the manner clusters of houses relate to each other, to the character of the public realm in streets, and to the level of a whole neighbourhood.

To summarize, the above principles are therefore anchored in the following keywords: Complex Adaptive System, Self-Regulation, Negative Feedback, Generative Program *vs* Descriptive Program, Non-Linearity, Adaptive Agents, Aggregate Agents, Responsibility Distribution, Simple Rules, Proscriptive *vs* Prescriptive, Dynamic *vs* Stasis, Emergent Form. See definitions in note 17.

Finally recent examples of attempts to work out alternatives to current practice in habitat production are highlighted. The work of Christopher Alexander comes to mind for theoretical constructs, and his built and unbuilt projects. This is amply documented in his recent four-volume book *The Nature of Order* (2002–2005). Volume 2 addresses process, and Volume 3 comprises many examples of built and unbuilt projects including a number of housing projects that attempt to recreate the underlying processes of traditional urbanism including the properties that are embodied in the list of keywords above.[20]

Leon Krier's Poundbury development, an extension of the city of Dorchester in Dorset, UK, is another example for attempting to re-create the character and sense of place of traditional towns and villages of that region. It is an example of a top-down structure of decision-making: from creating a general master plan to the manner in which the streets are laid out to the laying out the blocks for houses. The delegation for design of each building to a different architect, following a reasonably coherent code, is a process that is only partly similar to what occurred in traditional towns and has resulted in an environment with character and a sense of place. Needless to say that without Leon Krier overseeing the process at all its stages the results might not have been as successful. This is very different from development of traditional towns that did not have a master planner overseeing its development. However, Poundbury may be viewed as a first step experiment toward future attempts that will embody more of the principles that have been outlined above.

The SmartCode by Andres Duany *et al*, which is now in version 9.0, is rapidly being disseminated in the US via workshops, the Internet, and by other means. It is a model code that is designed to be adopted by local governments after changes are made to the code by using a process of calibration. The code is based on seven zones along a transect covering areas from the natural to the urban core and special districts. The implementation of the code requires a top-down structure and technical expertise due to its many provisions that are mostly prescriptive. Calibrating the code to a specific locality requires thorough technical understanding of how the code works and very sensitive reading of a locality's characteristics to make it locally friendly. As it relates to the lessons and attributes of traditional urbanism outlined above the code can be described as based on a descriptive program that relies on prescriptive stipulations. It is stasis in nature and does not foster unpredictable emergent form.

An attempt has been made recently by this author to incorporate various attributes of the processes that shaped traditional towns in a project sponsored and funded by the UNDP (United Nations Development Program) for revitalizing the historic sectors of the towns of Muharraq and Manama in Bahrain.[21] Briefly, a control, management and coding system has been developed that is based on a revival of the traditional system but adapted to the current structure of government in Bahrain. The proposed system embodies most of the principles and attributes of traditional towns that have been summarized above.

## 6 - Conclusion

We have seen from the material in this study how traditional towns located around the Mediterranean and beyond display individual uniqueness in their built form qualities and overall physical attributes including a strong sense of place. We also know from observation and research that residents develop a strong sense of attachment to their town and always remember with fondness the sense of place in and around their neighbourhoods later on in life when they are living elsewhere in 'modern' contemporary built environment settings.

The study also demonstrates and explains the typical coding system and its attributes that was used. What is remarkable, however, about this coding system and its related decision-making mechanism – particularly as it relates to building in sequence and the steps that are appropriate for each family and for each neighbourhood – is that it clearly replicates natural phenomenon and related processes of inception, growth, change, rejuvenation, decay, and re-birth. The phenomenon of *Emergence* that was discovered and elaborated on within the last two decades by scientists from different disciplines confirms that these traditional towns follow models of sustainable natural processes.

In the current awareness among concerned individuals and societies about global warming, sustainability, democracy, and the strive to achieve justice, equity, and quality in the built environment that the lessons of the model of traditional towns from around the Mediterranean and in countries that have followed a similar pattern of development, that we find inspiration and clear lessons to follow and implement now and in the future.

## Acknowledgements

Parts of this study were presented earlier at two conferences: (1) Congress for the New Urbanism, Council IV on Codes, held in Santa Fe, New Mexico, USA, October 2002. (2) La Ciudad en el Occidente Islamico Medieval, 1st Session: La Medina Andalusi, held at the Escuela de Estudios Arabes in Granada, Spain, November 2004.

## Notes

[1] ‹Emergence is what happens when an interconnected system of relatively simple elements self-organizes to form more intelligent, more adaptive higher-level behaviour. It is a bottom-up model; rather than being engineered by a general or a master planner, emergence begins at the ground level›. From book cover (Johnson, 2001).

[2] ‹The Arabs were not obsessed with taking over the cultural heritage of Antiquity at the time of their conquests› (p. 21), and ‹The two worlds were strangers to each other› (p. 27), (Lemerle, 1971).

[3] Julian›s treatise was included as a part of the *Book of the Eparch* in Constantinople, 377 years after it was written, and then 435 years later in 1345 CE, it was incorporated in the *Hexabiblos*, a span of 812 years after its authorship in Palestine.

[4] For details about this source, written in Syriac, see the work of Arthur Voobus. In his two-volume study of *The Syro-Roman Lawbook*, Stockholm, 1982, he indicates how much embedded is this compilation of codes in the ancient practices and laws of the Near East, including roots to Hammurabi's laws.

[5] Chapter 1: ‹Islamic law and neighborhood building guidelines›: 15–54.

[6] A case using a stipulation from Julian was found in a legal document dated October 1826 as a part of the local administration of the island of Naxos, Greece. This demonstrates the longevity of Julian's influence and how many of his stipulations became embedded as a part of local customary laws.

[7] The nature of these codes are not to be viewed as being similar to contemporary planning regulations that are written to enforce an adopted master plan. Traditional towns, that are the subject of this study, were conceived and implemented according to known concepts and customary practices of a particular region. However, the incremental process of growth and change required that they follow accepted customary practices and rules known within the locality. These rules were formalized within the legal literature to provide local courts a framework for making sound and equitable decisions when two or more parties face conflicts resulting from changes and adjustments to their immediate surroundings. It is from this legal literature that we can identify specific rules and codes that were applied in the built environment of traditional towns.

[8] For a detailed study of the sources that Ibn al-Imam utilized in writing his work, see Jean-Pierre Van Staevel's dissertation, 2000.

[9] Equitable equilibrium is a term used here to imply that fairness and justice must always be maintained between the rights of proximate neighbours to achieve harmony and good will.

[10] *Fina* is an invisible space of about 1.00–1.50 m wide alongside all exterior

walls of a building, primarily alongside streets and access paths. It extends vertically alongside the walls of the building and allows extensions to be built from upper levels such as balconies, awnings, and even rooms bridging a street called ‹*sabat*› (see Figure 8).

[11] *Proscription* is an imposed restraint synonymous with prohibition as in ‹Thou shalt not›, for example, you are free to design and manipulate your property provided you do not create damage on adjacent properties. *Prescription* is laying down of authoritative directions as in ‹Thou shalt›, for example, you shall setback from your front boundary by ($x$) meters, and from your side boundaries by ($y$) meters regardless of site conditions. Byzantine codes in many instances included specific numeric prescriptions, unlike their Islamic counterparts that tended not to include them.

[12] For examples from the past one can see how each town has distinct features and a sense of place unique to its built form. Whereas one can see the almost identical land use patterns and built form features in the thousands of communities that were built in the United States after World War II, that is, from about the early 1950s.

[13] Remarkable similarities have been found from the north of France in the 13th century. Probably due to the influence of Byzantine/Roman law, although the linkage has not yet been traced: *The Coutumes de Beauvaisis of Phillippe de Beaumanoir* completed in 1283. The County of Beauvais of the 13th century is located in the north of Paris. This book contains specific dynamic type of codes that are remarkably similar to the type of codes found in the 6th century Julian of Ascalon treatise on building and in Islamic codes from the Mid-East, North Africa and Spain. Consider this example from Chapter 24 on Customs (equivalent to the *Urf* in Arabic): *From article 706*: (But other building conventions are current in the bigger towns because the lots are narrower, for my neighbour may support his construction beams against my adjoining wall, whether I want him to or not, provided that the wall is strong enough for my house not to be in danger... continues). This clearly allows abutting of buildings together incrementally across the passage of time.

[14] Also from *The Coutumes de Beauvaisis of Phillippe de Beaumanoir* completed in 1283 (see note 13 above), the issue of privacy and overlooking is addressed as it was in Islamic codes. Example *from article 708*: (When someone makes his garden or yard in a private place where the neighbours cannot see in, and one of the neighbours wants to build next to it, you cannot prevent him from building, but you can prevent him from building a door or window which would spoil the privacy of the yard or garden; for some people would do it in bad faith to take away their neighbours' privacy. Therefore a person wanting light on that side must put in an opaque window, then there will be light and the neighbour's place will not be spoiled).

[15] My question does not apply to Sicily that was under Islamic rule for over two centuries (832–1056 CE).

[16] A Greek manuscript known as the ‹Procheiron Legum› was found in Soverato on the eastern shores of Calabria, about 30 km south of Cantanzaro. This was possibly authored during the reign of Emperor Basil II (976–1025 CE), and subsequently revised in the reign of the Norman King Roger II (1101–1154 CE). The author is unknown but as evident from its contents he compiled this treatise from the two official manuals of the Ecloga of Leon III (717–741 CE), and the Procheiros Nomos of Basil I (867–886 CE). See *Procheiron Legum* (eds.) F. Brandileone and V. Putoni, Instituto Storica Italiano, Rome, 1895. Remarkable similarities to the ‹Procheiron Legum› are evident in the contents of Julian of Ascalon›s treatise and in Islamic codes.

[17] The phenomenon of self-regulating and adaptive systems has been the focus of many disciplines for at least the last 50 years, such as in physics, biology, economics, and geography. It has been scrutinized by mathematics and has captured the imagination of social scientists whose interpretations brought the findings of these various disciplines, especially the life sciences, closer to urban planning and design. The following are brief definitions of the primary terms used to explain the phenomenon of *Emergence* – related to the term *Emergent Form* (the outcome that results from a bottom-up organization which follows its own set of rules that are often fairly simple). *Complex adaptive system* (a form of system containing many autonomous agents who self-organize in a co-evolutionary way to optimize their separate values). *Self-regulation* (When a complex adaptive system self-organizes itself it would need rules to follow during processes of change and growth. It thus forms such rules to follow, and they are generally few and simple). *Negative Feedback* (negative feedback tends to return the system to a balanced tranquil state where equity is maintained between adjacent neighbours). *Generative Program vs Descriptive Program* (a generative program is based on bottom-up rules that are understood and followed by various actors in a system. Their aggregate decisions create a unique emergent form. Whereas a descriptive program is one that is usually top-down directed and instructed where all actors follow the same rules regardless of their particular micro condition, resulting in a predictable outcome). *Non-linearity* (linear is a property of straight lines, of simple proportions, of predictability. Nonlinear on the other hand applies to systems that do unpredictable things, that cannot be exactly predicted and need to be approximated). *Agents and Aggregate Agents* (the basic elements of a Complex Adaptive System are agents. Agents are semi-autonomous units that seek to maximize their fitness by evolving over time. Agents scan their environment and develop schema. Schema are mental templates that define how reality is interpreted and what are appropriate response for a given stimuli. The term Aggregate Agents is used to refer to the aggregate result of decisions and acts by a number of agents).

[18] For a detailed discussion and the rational for these rules see Part II of Epstein's book, pp. 53–148. There are many similarities in the spirit and purpose of these rules to the Mediterranean rules and codes that were discussed earlier in this study.

[19] For a detailed study of an issue that was a part of common law practice in the UK see the excellent study by Howard Davis, The Future of Ancient Lights, *Journal of Architectural and Planning Research*, **6**(2), Summer 1989, 132–153. The doctrine of ancient lights was also practiced in the early history of the US but was finally struck down by the New York Supreme Court in the case of Parker *vs* Foote, 1838 (19 Wend. 309). Another study that describes the workings of the common law in London during the 13th to 15th centuries is by Diane Shaw, The construction of the private in medieval London, *Journal of Medieval and Early Modern Studies*, **26**(3), Fall 1996, 447–466. A more general study that also discusses similar issues in medieval urban England is by Vanessa Harding, Space, property, and propriety in urban England, *Journal of Interdisciplinary History*, **32**(4), Spring 2002, 549–569.

[20] For Alexander's work on neighbourhoods and related generative codes visit: http://www.livingneighborhoods.org/ht-0/bln-exp.htm. For Hakim's work on traditional Mediterranean towns and their codes visit: http://historiccitiesrules.com. Also, see Hakim, B. Generative processes for revitalizing historic towns or heritage districts, *Urban Design International*, 12 (2/3), 2007: 87–99.

[21] The article in *Urban Design International*, mentioned in note 20 contains a brief description of the Bahrain project. Work on that project by Hakim was completed at the end of February 2006.

## References

Benito, R.I. (1986) Normas sobre edificaciones en Toledo en el siglo XV, *Anuario de estudios medievales*, 16: 519–532.

Davis, H. (1989) The future of ancient lights, *Journal of Architectural and Planning Research*, 6(2): 132–153.

Epstein, R.A. (1995) *Simple Rules for a Complex World*. Cambridge, MA.

Gonzalez, J.P. (1996) *Pedro Lopez II, Maestro Mayor y Alarife de Cordoba (1478–1507)*. Cordoba.

Guidoni, E. (1979) La componente urbanistica Islamica nella formazione delle citta Italiane, in Gabrieli, F. and Scerrato, U. (eds.) *Gli Arabi in Italia*. Milano, pp. 575–597.

Hakim, B.S. (1986) *Arabic-Islamic Cities: Building and Planning Principles*, (2nd edn., 1988), London.

Hakim, B.S. (1994) The Urf and its role in diversifying the architecture of traditional Islamic cities, *Journal of Architectural and Planning Research*, 11(2): 108–127.

Hakim, B.S. (2001) Julian of Ascalon's treatise of construction and design rules from sixth-century Palestine, *Journal of the Society of Architectural Historians*, 60(1): 4–25.

Hakim, B.S. and Ahmed, Z. (2006) Rules for the built environment in 19th century Northern Nigeria, *Journal of Architectural and Planning Research*, 23(1): 1–26.

Hakim, B.S. (2007) Generative processes for revitalizing historic towns or heritage districts, *Urban Design International*, 12(2/3): 87–99.

Holland, J. (1995) *Hidden Order: How Adaptation Builds Complexity*. Cambridge, MA.

Johnson, S. (2001) E*mergence: The Connected Lives of Ants, Brains, Cities, and Softwar*e. New York.

Lemerle, P. (1971) *Le premier humanisme byzantin: Notes et remarques, enseignement et culture a Byzance des origins au X siecle*, Paris. English translation (1986) titled: *Byzantine Humanism*, Canberra, Australia.

de Malafosse, J. (1962) La loi et la coutume a Byzance, manifetations d'autorite et sources d'enseignement, *Etudes de droit contemporain*, Travaux et Recherches de l'Institut du droit compare de l'Universite de Paris, pp. 59–69.

Postrel, V. (1998) *The Future and its Enemies: The Growing Conflict over Creativity, Enterprise, and Progress.* New York.

Ruhl, J.B. (1996) Complexity theory as a paradigm for the dynamical law-and-society system: A wake-up call for legal reductionism and the modern administrative state, *Duke Law Journal*, 45(5): 849–928.

Van Staevel, J.-P. (2000) *Les usage de la ville: Discourse normative, habitat et construction urbain dans l'Occident musulman medieval (10–14 siecles)*, Dissertation, Universite Lyon II.

Wolpert, L. (1991) *The Triumph of the Embryo*. Oxford.

## Chapter 2

## Julian of Ascalon's 6th-c Treatise

Ascalon was a city on the Mediterranean coast of Palestine, 16 km north of Gaza. Its history extends from about 1370 B.C. to A.D. 1270, a continuous presence of over 2,600 years.[1] King Herod, who reigned between 37 and 4 B.C., adorned the city with fine public buildings, some of which have been excavated.[2] During the Byzantine period, Palestine was divided into three provinces (Figure 1). Ascalon was within the province named Palestina Prima, whose capital was Caesarea. A Byzantine consular governed each province until A.D. 536, when Emperor Justinian I promoted the governor at Caesarea to proconsul and gave him supervisory authority over the other two consulars.[3] In the fourth century, Ascalon became a bishopric. According to the acts of the Council of Constantinople in 536, the city had a bishop, an indication that at the time a sizable part of the population was Christian.

From the fourth to the sixth century A.D., building activity flourished in Syria and Palestine.[4] Economic growth was robust in the fifth century, due to the relative peace enjoyed by the eastern provinces of the Byzantine Empire.[5] A recent study by Georges Tate shows that in northern Syria there was constant growth between A.D. 270 and 550; it increased after 320, became more vigorous from 410 to 480, and reached a peak between 450 and 480; this was followed by a reduction from 480 to 550. Tate suggests that the pattern was basically the same throughout the region, with local variations.[6]

The export of olive products provided wealth to landowners, who also collected taxes and administered the surrounding rural areas.[7] In the case of Ascalon and nearby Gaza, the export of wine was

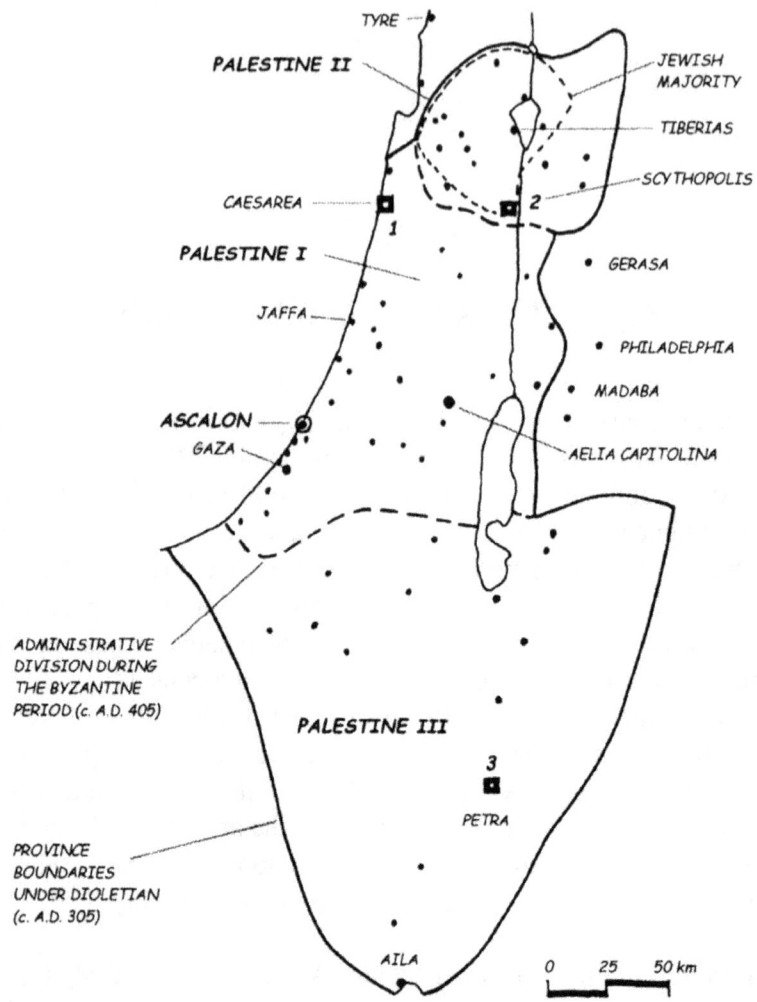

**Figure 1.** The province of Palestine was divided into three administrative sectors during the Byzantine period. Ascalon is in Palestine I, which had Caesarea as its capital. By author after map in E. Barnavi, ed., *A Historical Atlas of the Jewish People* (London, 1992).

also a chief economic activity.[8] Landowners lived in the cities to take part in social and political activities, and their presence was an important component of city life. According to A.H.M. Jones, "The city was a social phenomenon, the result of the predilection of the wealthier classes for the amenities of urban life."[9] In Ascalon, however, there was a tendency by the elites, notably the landowners, to move to newly built provincial estates nearby. In order to discourage the flight of the urban aristocracy, the local government

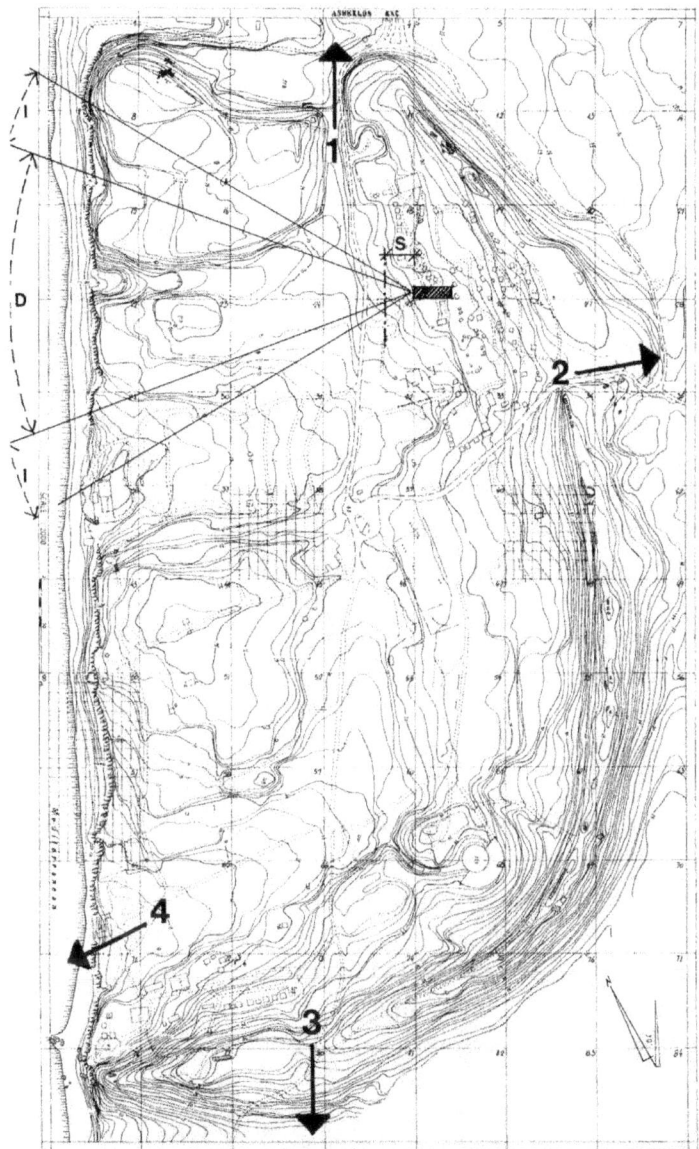

**Figure 2.** Plan of the site of Ascalon showing its general contours; the hatched rectangle represents the footprint of buildings and their setbacks (15 x 45 m) as discussed in case Hex. 13; the visual corridors (sight lines) show what constitutes a direct view (D) and indirect views (I). as explained in Hex. 47 and elaborated in Figure 9. Also shown is the minimum setback (S) of 100 feet (about 30 m) for allowing construction on the view side of a house with a view of the sea. The hatched footprint and the setback stipulation (S) represent the level of the basic units of incremental change in the built environment. The scale of the grid on the plan is 100 x 100 meters. The gates of the city are: (1) Jaffa gate; (2) Jerusalem (Aelia Capitolina) gate; (3) Gaza gate; and (4) gate toward the sea. Courtesy Ashkelon Excavations.

authority enacted laws designed to maintain and enhance the aesthetic beauty of the city, and for controlling change that could be detrimental.[10] The situation in Ascalon, together with the revival and codification of Roman law by the emperor in Constantinople, is the context for understanding the purpose of Julian's treatise. The excessively prescriptive nature of its stipulations should be viewed in light of the centralized structure of Byzantine government in the region.[11]

The period from the late fifth to the mid-sixth century, covering the reigns of the emperors Zeno (A.D. 474-491), Anastasius I (A.D. 491-518), Justin I (A.D. 518-527), and Justinian I (A.D. 527-565), is important for the study of the treatise. For example, Zeno's laws, particularly those related to the preservation of mountain views and the construction of new balconies facing the public realm, influenced related stipulations in Julian's work.

Ascalon was well known for its fine buildings and urban order, and this reputation continued well into the seventh century. In A.D. 636, Ascalon's city fathers accepted in peace the hegemony of the Arab Muslims, and there is evidence that the Arabs fully admired the city's beauty and architecture.[12] (See Figures 2 and 3 for the size, configuration, and topographic features of the city.) Many of the buildings comprising the housing stock were three or four stories high, as demonstrated by the prescriptions for such buildings in Julian's treatise and the evidence from contemporary depictions (Figure 4).[13] I have calculated an estimated area of 57 hectares (140 acres) for the city within its walls, with a gross density of approximately 270 persons/hectare (107 persons/acre).[14]

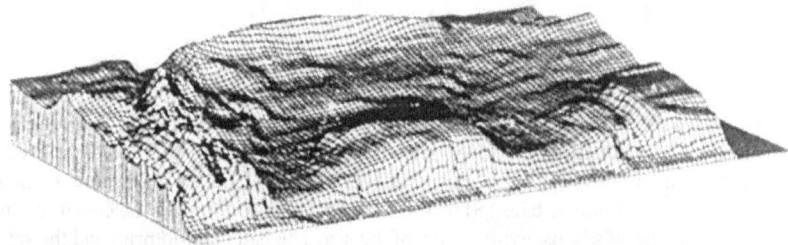

**Figure 3.** Ascalon, computer-generated bird's-eye view of the topography of the site from the northwest, fronting on the Mediterranean. Courtesy Ashkelon Excavations.

**Figure 4.** Mosaic image of Ascalon showing multistoried buildings flanking a round structure. This mosaic, among others, was discovered in the eighth-century Church of Saint Stephen at the site of the Byzantine town of Umm al-Rasas, 25 km southeast of Madaba, in Jordan. Photograph by Rami G. Khouri. Courtesy *Aramco World*.

## 1 - Julian of Ascalon

According to Mikhail Sjuzjumov, the only fact known about Julian is that he was an architect from Ascalon. Sjuzjumov infers this from the title of the treatise, which he renders in Russian and which translates into English as, "From the treatise of architect Julian of Ascalon on the laws, or conventions, in Palestine."[15] This title is corroborated by a recent French translation.[16] Sjuzjumov attempts to connect Julian to a family of architects by pointing to an inscription on an early-fifth-century church in Brad, northern Syria (commonly referred to in Arabic as Qasr al-Brad), which indicates that its architect is Julian.[17] On the other hand, Joseph Geiger mentions that the architect's name (Julian) is inscribed on two churches at Brad, on the road from Antioch to Chalcis in Syria, dating from A.D. 399 and 402. He tentatively suggests that this Julian may be the father or grandfather of our Julian. Geiger is not certain whether Julian of Ascalon was pagan or Christian, but he thinks that our Julian had a "modicum of classical upbringing," as evident from his writing style in "simple, unaffected and clear Greek."[18] He summarizes what is known about Julian: that he was an architect who lived in Ascalon, probably descended from a family of architects.

In the introduction of his treatise, Julian attempts to structure his work by using the four elements of fire, air, water, and earth, which indicates that he may have been interested in the theoretical aspects of the physical sciences.[19] The city of Ascalon was also the home of Eutocius, born there about A.D. 480, a contemporary of Julian's. Eutocius produced commentaries on Archimedes and Apollonius and is credited with making the latter's work accessible to scholars of his generation.[20]

## 2 - The historic context of the treatise

Scholars have situated the composition of Julian's treatise within the years A.D. 531-533.[21] Julian's legal perspective was greatly influenced by the law school at Beirut, a major center of Roman law studies during that period.[22] In fact, Justinian I had praised the school and invited two well known jurists from its faculty to participate in the compilation of the *Corpus Juris Civilis*.[23]

The conditional style used in most of Julian's stipulations has precedence in ancient Near Eastern laws and appears as far back as the laws of the Old Babylonian city-state of Eshnunna in the nineteenth century B.C., discovered in the outskirts of Baghdad, Iraq, in 1948.[24] These ancient conditional laws are usually grouped in three categories: laws of persons, of things, and of procedures.[25] Roman law followed a similar categorization, and it has been suggested that the earliest "Roman laws of the twelve tables" were influenced by Near Eastern contacts.[26]

Roman law in its classical period displayed a great deal of flexibility, particularly in its operation at the neighborhood level. Contracts between adjacent neighbors were based on the concept of servitude, or easement, in all its manifestations and were thereby responsive and sensitive to ongoing growth and change in the built environment. The system, as in ancient Near Eastern cities, relied on contracts between individual owners and was sensitive to conditions at the micro level of neighborhoods. As a result, the management of the built environment was from the bottom up and democratic in spirit.

Julian of Ascalon's treatise, though incorporating local customs, is basically a collection of rules designed to be applied from the top down; its stipulations are written in a manner that rendered them unable to respond sensitively to microconditions. In that sense they were prescriptive, whereas the procedures and implementation techniques of classical Roman law tended to be proscriptive.[27] This is convincingly demonstrated by Alan Rodger, for example, in reference to preserving an acceptable level of natural light within a house if a neighbor were to raise his building or add to it in a way that would decrease the level of light in the adjacent structure.[28]

Essentially, classical Roman law allowed freedom within the property of an individual owner, although this freedom was subject to proscriptive prohibitions. These restrictions could be overcome, however, using the mechanism of servitudes (*servitutes*), particularly the *jus altius tollendi* (the positive form), which gave the beneficiary the right to build higher, or the *servitus altius non tollendi* (the negative form), which imposed on the owner the obligation not to build higher than a certain limit.[29] The law and its mechanism could be applied in any location and would still be responsive to local conditions. This could not be said for the prescriptions in Julian's treatise. Its stipulations were designed for the city of Ascalon and other Palestinian cities of the period sharing a similar climate, topography, and tradition of building. Yet, even within a particular city, the stipulations could not have been responsive to microconditions.

The emperor Zeno published building regulations, written in Greek, for the capital, Constantinople.[30] They employed distances between buildings as prescriptive stipulations, and levied severe fines on homeowners, architects, and contractors who violated them. On 1 September 531, Emperor Justinian I imposed Zeno's law, with associated fines, on all cities of the Byzantine empire.[31] Documentary evidence dating from October 548 indicates that inspectors (*de discussoribus*) were sent to Palestine for the purpose of monitoring any violations in building activities. Julian's prescriptions were influenced by Zeno's stipulations for distances between buildings, particularly in order to maintain views of mountains and the sea and distances between balconies facing each other and overlooking the public realm.[32] Julian makes reference to Zeno in Hex. 51, "Concerning the vista of the mountain and sea," and in Hex. 32, "On balconies."[33]

Other legal sources predating Julian of Ascalon include the *Syro-Roman Lawbook*, which scholars date to the late fifth century A.D., more specifically to about A.D. 468.[34] Most of the stipulations in this lawbook address issues of personal law such as marriage and inheritance. Only two paragraphs (133 and 157) relate to the built environment. The former is about the responsibilities of owners for repair work in a multistory apartment building, addressing similar issues as those in Julian, Hex. 41 and 42. The latter covers roads, spaces between buildings, and drainage. Although Julian's stipulations are more specific than those in the *Syro-Roman Lawbook*, both documents treat similar concerns.[35]

Another way of looking at Julian's prescriptions is with reference to the German terms *Reichsrecht* and *Volksrecht*.[36] The first refers to a top-down system of laws that usually rely on specific measurements derived largely from the experience of the empire's capital; the laws apply to all the cities of the empire. The latter term refers to customary laws that have evolved locally and might also be recognized regionally; they are well understood by all individuals involved in the day-to-day activities related to construction.

The impact of customary laws on the built environment is from the bottom up; that is, the aggregate of local microdecisions affects the overall character at the neighborhood level, and aggregates of neighborhoods shape the overall character of the city. It seems to this writer that Julian of Ascalon's motivation was to incorporate both types of laws in his treatise.

The similarities between certain prescriptions in Julian of Ascalon's treatise and the Jewish law of the period were not due to direct borrowing but rather to earlier influences from Hellenistic and Roman laws on the one hand, and ancient Near Eastern laws and customs on the other. For instance, the concern to prevent damages was one of the primary considerations of ancient Near Eastern laws; it is evident as an important aspect of the Roman legal concept of *damnum infectum* (threatened damage).[37] In a study addressing this issue, Saul Lieberman argues that in the larger cities of Palestine, particularly the coastal cities with a mixed population, Byzantine authorities did not take into account Jewish law and judgments regarding buildings and hygiene.[38] He maintains that some Byzantine laws for cities became the custom of the land and were also binding on the Jews. Indeed, Jewish law accepted the law of the land.[39] Lieberman shows, for example, that in the city of Tiberias in the Galilee region, with a majority Jewish population, the glass industry was located outside the city limits, confirming one of Julian of Ascalon's stipulations (Hex. 19).

Another interesting observation by Lieberman is that only those stipulations and customs that had the force of law have reached us from Julian's treatise. Among them is the custom in Ascalon and Caesarea regarding the method of sharing expenses between owners of lower and upper levels in a multistoried apartment building (Hex. 42). According to Lieberman, there must have been other local customs that Julian documented in his treatise, but these were either lost or omitted from later laws.[40] If omitted, then this was most likely done by Byzantine authorities when they attached Julian's treatise to the *Book of the Eparch* in the early tenth century.[41]

## 3 - Diffusion of the treatise

Until 1893, Julian of Ascalon's treatise was known through the *Hexabiblos* of Armenopoulos.[42] Its compiler, Constantine Armenopoulos, was a fourteenth-century jurist; he is identified with a document signed by him in 1345, indicating his title as judge of Thessaloniki. The *Hexabiblos* (Six books) is a corpus of secular law that is also called the *Procheiron nomon* (Handbook of the laws) and dates to A.D. 1345. Armenopoulos used a number of known references, including the treatise of Julian of Ascalon. He organized the legal material into an easily usable manual that became very popular, transmitted in almost seventy manuscripts. In practice, the *Hexabiblos* served as a law code.[43]

Jules Nicole, a Swiss scholar born in Geneva in 1842, discovered *The Book of the Eparch* in 1891 at the Geneva University library. He attributed it to the period of Emperor Leo VI (A.D. 886-912), specifically to the second half of the emperor's reign. The manu-

**Figure 5.** Page from the manuscript Genevensis 23, fol. 381r. This page contains the cases identified by Armenopoulos in his Hexabiblos 2.4 as case numbers 16, 17, 18, 19, 20, and 21. Courtesy Bibliotheque Publique et Universitaire, Geneva.

script found by Nicole, however, dates from the fourteenth century and is written in cursive Greek (Figure 5). Nicole added a Latin translation and published it in Geneva in 1893 under the title *Le livre du prefet (Eparchicon biblion), Text grec du Genevensis 23* – "published for the first time by Jules Nicole with a Latin translation, notices, critiques and variants of the Genevensis 23 with the text of Julian of Ascalon."

Based on available evidence, Julian's treatise was disseminated as part of the *Book of the Eparch* in Constantinople, 377 years after it was written in Ascalon. In 1345, in Thessaloniki, it was included in Book Two of the *Hexabiblos*, a span of 812 years after its authorship. From then on, it spread wherever the *Hexabiblos* was adopted and used, particularly in Greece, where it survived well into the twentieth century, as well as in many Slavic countries.[44] In brief, Julian of Ascalon's treatise, written during the years A.D. 531-533, was resurrected at least two times, approximately 400 years apart, and its influence endured for about 1,400 years. It is because of its widespread impact and longevity within the eastern Mediterranean that the treatise is worthy of careful study.

### 4 - The organization of Julian's treatise
Julian chose the metaphor of the four elements of fire, air, water, and earth to structure his compilation. He begins with this statement: "There exist four elements: fire, air, water, and earth, and by virtue of their influence [on the construction of buildings] many misconceptions arise in people's minds. We therefore consider it expedient relative to the nature of these elements to include [in a treatise] a compendium of the situations that occur [due to the influence of these elements], explaining both the causes and incurred damages, and to offer appropriate solutions [...to avoid damage]."[45]

The first and second group of cases in Julian's treatise, namely, those related to fire and air, are preceded by a heading to that effect. However, the cases that belong to water and earth do not bear corresponding titles.[46] The latter might have been dropped or lost in the process of recopying that produced the extant copy of Genevensis 23 from the fourteenth century.

I have devised a different structure for analyzing Julian's treatise, more compatible with the underlying goal of his work. However, it is worthwhile to discuss briefly the framework he used, in order to demonstrate that the elements are generally redundant; it is their underlying philosophy, not discussed by Julian, that is most significant. The following brief discussion should clarify this point.

Empedocles (490-430 B.C.), the Greek philosopher, statesman, poet, religious leader, and physiologist, is known for the philosophy that assumes four eternally existing "roots." He believed that two forces, Love and Strife, interact to unite or separate the four elements. Strife acts to make an element withdraw itself from the others, creating imbalance, whereas Love leads them to mingle, achieving balance.[47] It is the state of balance, or in the case of the built environment, the state of equitable equilibrium, that is central to Julian's concerns and constitutes the rationale for his prescriptions.[48] A central preoccupation of his treatise deals with change in the built environment, which unleashes the opposing forces of Love and Strife; his prescriptions are designed to encourage Love to prevail. If this occurs, the damage in the built environment will be minimized; people's rights and responsibilities will be fairly allocated, facilitating the maintenance of an equitable equilibrium in the built environment during the processes of change and growth. In other words, when the force of Love prevails, the four elements will mingle together equitably, achieving a state of balance. Julian does not mention Empedocles' underlying philosophy of Love and Strife, but only the four elements. This is why the use of the four elements as a framework for the treatise creates difficulty in rationalizing the categorization of the cases presented; furthermore, it does not help to clarify the underlying purpose of his stipulations. Therefore, it is not surprising that Armenopoulos did not include, or even allude to, the four elements in his *Hexabiblos*; he might have thought they were redundant or did not add substance to the stipulations he copied from Julian's treatise.[49]

## 5 - Julian's goal and intentions

The goal of Julian's treatise is to deal with *change* in the built environment by ensuring that *minimum damage* occurs to preexisting structures and their owners, through stipulating fairness in the *distribution of rights and responsibilities* among various parties, particularly those who are proximate to each other. This ultimately will ensure the *equitable equilibrium* of the built environment during the process of change and growth.

Julian's intentions can be grouped in seven categories:

1. Change in the built environment should be accepted as a natural and healthy phenomenon. In the face of ongoing change, it is necessary to maintain an equitable equilibrium in the built environment.
2. Change, particularly that occurring among proximate neighbors, creates potential for damages to existing dwellings and other uses. Therefore, certain measures are necessary to prevent changes or uses that would (a) result in debasing the social and economic integrity of adjacent or nearby properties, (b) create conditions adversely affecting the moral integrity of the neighbors, and (c) destabilize peace and tranquility among neighbors.
3. In principle, property owners have the freedom to do what they please on their own property. Most uses are allowed, particularly those necessary for livelihood. Nevertheless, the freedom to act within one's property is constrained by preexisting conditions of neighboring properties, neighbors' rights of servitude, and other rights associated with ownership for certain periods of time.
4. The compact built environment of ancient towns such as Ascalon necessitates the implementation of interdependence among citizens, principally among proximate neighbors. As a consequence of interdependence, it becomes necessary to allocate responsibilities among such neighbors, particularly with respect to legal and economic issues.
5. It is desirable to maintain a built environment that will uplift the spirit of its inhabitants. Certain views should be preserved, especially those that give pleasure to the beholder or bear cultural significance. Making use of the bounties of nature within one's property, such as collecting rainwater and planting fruit trees and vineyards, should be encouraged.
6. The use of improved building materials and construction techniques should be encouraged, as their utilization will reduce the burden of preventive setbacks from property boundaries and thus maximize the potentials of the land.
7. The public realm must not be subjected to damages that re-

sult from activities or waste originating in the private realm, or from the placement of troughs for animals.

## 6 - Technical aspects of Julian's treatise
I have developed a framework of five categories, discussed below, to analyze the technical aspects of Julian's treatise:
- Land use (including baths, artisanal workshops, and socially offensive uses).
- views (both for enjoyment and those considered a nuisance),
- houses and condominiums (involving acts that debase the value of adjacent properties, walls between neighbors, and condominiums in multistory build ings and those contiguous with porticoes)
- drainage (of rain water and waste water).
- planting (of trees, shrubs, and other vegetation).

According to the author of *Le traité*, the cubit Julian of Ascalon uses is equivalent to 52.50 cm, and the footis 35 cm.[50] However, for simplifying conversions to the metric scale and for appreciating the metric equivalents cognitively, it is conve nient to assume the cubit to be 50 cm and the foot to be 30 cm.

## 6.1 - Land use
Land use in Julian's treatise refers to the control and prevention of potential damage that could result from proposed uses adjacent to or near existing dwellings.[51] The latter could be a single-story house or an apartment building (condominiums) of two, three, or more stories. In broad terms, the cases that Julian cites can be grouped in two subcategories. The first consists of proposed uses that can inflict damages to nearby existing buildings due to fire sparks, smoke, offensive odors, and vibrations that can harm adjacent walls. Under this category Julian includes private baths (as an addition to an existing building or as a new structure) and baking ovens, as well as pottery kilns, gypsum workshops, kilns for lime burning, and workshops for dyeing cloth, glassmaking, vegetable-oil making, rope making, and preparing marinades. The second subcategory includes socially undesirable uses-such as taverns, brothels, and stables - near an existing dwelling.

In both categories the approach, in principle, is to allow the proposed use if certain precautionary measures are taken. Modest distances between the use and the existing dwelling are specified as the usual remedy, as in the case of a bath, bakery, pottery kiln, or gypsum workshop. Longer distances are required for threshing floors and kilns for lime burning; glassmakers are not allowed to locate within a town. In the case of socially undesirable uses, the remedies range from locating doors so that they will not face the door of an existing dwelling, to prohibiting outside benches for clients of a tavern and troughs or stalls for animals near proposed buildings, on public streets and squares, and adjacent to public porticoes. Brothels are in principle prohibited in towns but might be allowed in a village, if its local customs do not oppose them.
The following examples offer detailed discussions on land use issues dealing with baths and artisanal workshops.

### *Prevention of damage due to fire sparks and smoke*
To design and communicate his prescriptions for the following cases, Julian envisages a schematic layout in plan form based on the cardinal points. The existing building is located at the center (the junction of the north/south and east/west axes), and the proposed uses are assumed to locate in any of the four cardinal directions on the sides of the existing building (Figure 6). It is interesting to note that although the coast of Palestine lies on a northeast/southwest axis, Julian chose to discuss his cases and stipulations based on the cardinal directions. This might have been for the purposes of clarity, but it was more probably due to the sixth-century view in Palestine that in fact the region was oriented in this way.

Julian usually assumes that the existing structure (Figure 6, A) is either one story (a single dwelling) or two, three, or more stories (an apartment/condominium building). He further assumes that each possibility may be with or without windows facing the proposed use. We have thus four possible conditions for the existing building (A), for each of which Julian proposes remedies in the form of setbacks from (A). In the case of a proposed *bath* facility (Hex. 13), the potential damage is predicted to be from the chimney or the stove that heats the water, which is usually in continuous use. The chimney emits smoke and occasionally sparks, and the prevailing wind can carry them to neighboring buildings. Be-

low are Julian's prescriptions to remedy this condition, along with the underlying rationale:
1. If (A) is an existing building of two or three stories with windows facing the proposed bath (Figure 6, B), and if (B) is to the south or west of (A), then a minimum of 20 cubits setback must be allowed. Julian's reasoning is that winds blow from the south and the west in winter, when windows of the neighboring dwelling are rarely opened and when the heat from the bath stove is dissipated and thinned out by the moist breeze. If (B) is to the north or east of (A), then a minimum of 30 cubits setback must be observed, because the prevailing wind blows primarily from the north and the east during summer, when windows are frequently opened and the proposed bath (B) may inflict damage on (A).
2. If (A) is an existing building of two or three stories with a blank wall facing the proposed bath (B), then the setbacks can be reduced to one-third of those specified above.
3. If (A) is a one-story building and is the same height as the proposed bath (B), with openings that face (B), then the setback distances can be one-third of those stipulated in 1 above, or the same as in 2.
4. If (A) is a one-story building, is the same height as the proposed bath (B), and has a blank wall facing (B), then the setback distances can be reduced to one-sixth of those specified in 1.

Julian indicates that the above stipulations are for locations within towns. Setbacks in villages can be reduced by one-half.

I have assumed the footprints for the existing building (A) and the proposed building (B) to be 15 x 15 meters. I have also equated 1 meter to approximately 2 cubits. Thus when a 30-cubit setback is stipulated between buildings (A) and (B), the total footprint of buildings and their setbacks is a rectangle of 15 x 45 meters (see map of Ascalon in Figure 2 to appreciate the scale of this footprint within the overall size of the town). This is an important observation, as it points out that interventions in the built environment are undertaken in small increments, and the aggregate of ongoing interventions is reflected in the overall character of the town.

In the construction of a *bakery* (Hex. 14), Julian assumes the exist-

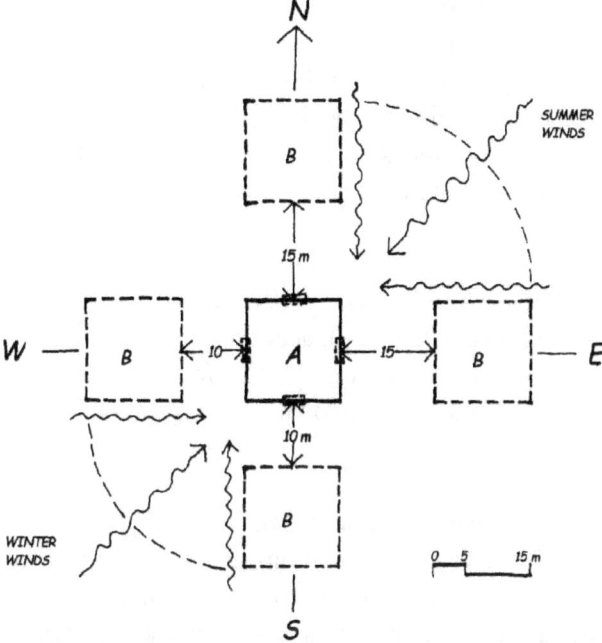

**Figure 6.** Julian of Ascalon's generalized plan for establishing and communicating his prescriptions. The existing structure (A) is imagined to be located at the junction of the cardinal points, and it could be one, two, three, or more stories, with or without openings toward a proposed structure (B). The latter's location can be on any of the four sides of (A). Setback dimensions relate to the case of the proposed bath (Hex. 13). Author.

ing building (A) to be either one, two, three, or more stories high. He neither concerns himself with openings facing the proposed bakery nor does he give a reason for this omission. He mentions, however, that bakeries usually operate during nighttime hours. He thus stipulates building the bakery on an elevated area if possible and observing, in towns, a setback of one-half of that specified for baths and, in suburbs or villages, one-half of the setback devised for urban areas (Hex. 13).

In the case of *pottery kilns* (Hex. 15), Julian specifies requirements only for villages, reflecting the custom that these workshops are commonly located in villages. He notes that they operate usually in summer months. The rationale for the setbacks is similar to that for baths but with shorter dimensions. In the case when an existing building (A) is two, three, or more stories high and has openings toward the proposed pottery kiln (B), a 20-cubit setback is required if (B) is to the north or east of (A); if (B) is to the south or west of (A), the setback is 12 cubits. If the existing building is one story with a blank wall facing the proposed kiln, the setback can be reduced to one-third of those dimensions. In the event that a proposed pottery kiln is to be located adjacent to another pottery kiln, the setback distances are more: 30 cubits for sites to the north and east of the existing kiln and 15 cubits for sites to the south and west.

Workshops of *glassmakers* (Hex. 19), glassblowers, and makers of axes and sickles (blacksmiths), according to Julian, are prohibited in towns due to the severe danger their fires pose. However, if they have to be located within the town boundaries, they must be sited in an uninhabited area.

### *Prevention of damage due to vibrations*
There is only one case that mentions the damage that might occur due to vibrations, and that is the case of *gypsum workshops* (Hex. 16). Although damage from this type of workshop can be caused by fire and smoke, for which setback distances are specified, vibrations from the grinding and pulverizing of gypsum can also harm adjacent walls. Accordingly, Julian specifies 6 cubits as the setback from an existing wall, to isolate the effect of the vibrations.

### *Prevention of damage due to odor*
Four cases discuss the problem of damages due to unpleasant odor. They are dealt with according to the level of their impact on the built environment. *Marinade preparation* (Hex. 22) produces a very strong and unpleasant odor that, according to Julian, travels long distances and remains in the air for a long time. In principle, such businesses should be prohibited from locating in towns and villages, but if they are necessary their minimum distance from an existing building should be 3 stadia (3 x 400 cubits = 1,200 cubits, or about 600 meters).

For *kilns for lime burning* (Hex. 17), a distance of 100 cubits (about 50 meters) should be observed from a building of two, three, or more stories, regardless of the orientation of the wind. There is no mention of the setback requirements from a one-story building. The distance can be reduced to one-half (50 cubits) if the existing nearby facility is a threshing floor.

Because *oil makers' workshops* (Hex. 20) pose a danger due to the spread of fire, and also produce a harmful odor that can cause illness, they are prohibited from locating beneath or adjacent to an inhabited part of a building. If they are to be located opposite an existing building, then a setback distance of 3.5 cubits is necessary between the doors of the two buildings.

Julian reminds us that the workshops of *rope makers and fullers* (wool washers) (Hex. 21) burn sulfur for fumigating and generate an offensive odor. Occasionally fire is used in the process, creating potential danger to neighboring properties. In this case, Julian does not specify setbacks but simply states the requirements that these workshops should be isolated and not allowed to be contiguous with any other structure. He also stipulates that if it is necessary to locate them in proximity to or contiguous with other structures, the owner of the workshop must provide written assurance to residents of adjacent houses that he will not use sulfur for fumigating purposes.

### *Socially undesirable uses*

The four following examples discusses uses that are socially undesirable near an existing dwelling. Julian starts this category with a proposed *house or warehouse* (Hex. 23) to be located adjacent to an existing building on flat terrain. He assumes that such a structure would not be a source of damage and suggests a 10-foot (about 6 cubits) setback from the existing building, allowing for windows and doors on any side of the proposed structure. He explains that if it is a warehouse, its door will be used only occasionally and thus should not be a source of nuisance.

When the proposed structure is a *stable* (Hex. 2 5), Julian does not specify the type of animal to be housed there, but he mentions oxen in a later case. His only stipulation is that the door of the stable should not be adjacent to or face the door of a dwelling; it can, however, be set back from its location across a street so that an oblique line of vision is created between the two doorways (Figure 7). There is no mention of a minimum setback for the proposed building, but one can assume from the previous case that it would be 5 cubits from an existing structure. It is interesting to

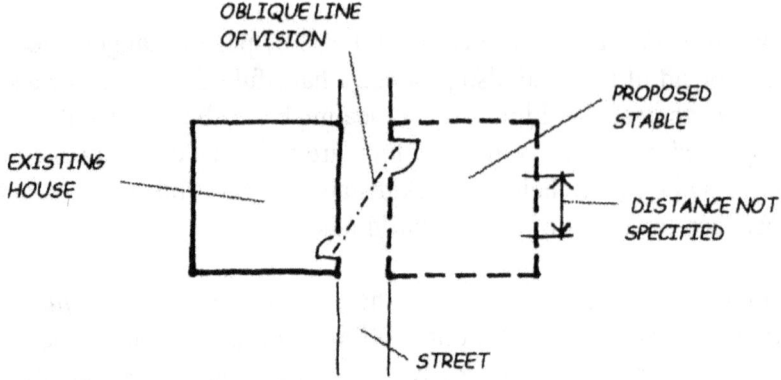

**Figure 7.** Location of the door for a proposed stable relative to the existing door of a house across the street (Hex. 25). Author.

note that Julian does not specify here a distance from the door of the stable to an adjacent door, or to the door of a dwelling on the opposite side of a street. This proscriptive approach is rarely used by Julian.[52]

When the proposed building is a *tavern* (Hex. 26), Julian's remedy for the location of the door is similar to the previous case. To prevent trouble, the owner of the tavern is not allowed to provide outside benches for his clients, or an outside straw mattress. Activities such as drinking and reclining must be confined within the building. In addition, troughs for animals are not permitted outside, even temporarily during construction. Julian's reason for this stipulation is the animals' unpleasant odor. Julian continues by explaining the principle of rights secured by a servitude and attached to an earlier use: if the tavern existed prior to the construction of an adjacent house, the owner of the house cannot challenge the continued use of the tavern. If both uses (tavern and house) have been there for a long time, and it is not clearly established which is older, then the owner of the house cannot lodge a complaint against the tavern owner or demand changes to its use. However, if the house existed before the tavern and the owner of the house had not lodged a complaint while residing in his house for ten years, or while absent for twenty years, then he loses his rights of servitude. Julian also indicates in this case that constructing another building nearby for the same use as the tavern or the stable is not allowed.

*Brothels* (Hex. 27) are not allowed in houses or taverns in towns. As for tavern owners in villages who might want to provide brothel services, the decision depends on the local customs of the particular village.[53]

In dealing with socially undesirable uses, Julian also reminds us that stalls for livestock are not allowed in public streets, squares, or privately co-owned passages in towns, due to the danger posed by animals such as oxen to passersby, as well as the unpleasant odors.

**Rules for land use derived from Julian's case studies**
1. Certain uses are prohibited in towns, such as glassmaking and blacksmithing. Others - for example, marinade preparation - are not allowed in towns or villages, but when necessary they should be placed at a distance of 1,200 cubits (600 meters) from the settlement. This dimension is equivalent to the width of the town of Ascalon, or approximately one-half its length.
2. Setbacks are prescribed to prevent sparks and smoke from reaching existing buildings.[54]
3. An elevated area is encouraged for certain uses, such as bakeries, to promote the dissipation of sparks and smoke away from existing buildings.
4. The orientation of the wind and consideration of periods of operation for specific types of workshops are used for determining setback requirements to prevent the transfer of fire and smoke. Although wind also facilitates the transfer of odor, Julian does not mention those implications.
5. Location of openings (primarily windows) on walls facing a source of potential damage increases the distance of setback requirements.
6. The height of an existing building affects the setback requirements. The higher the building, the wider is the set back between the building and any potential source of damage, such as from fire and smoke. A one-story building usually requires one-third of the setback for a building of two or more stories.
7. If an existing structure is two or more stories high with no windows facing a source of potential damage, the setback can be reduced to one-third of the distance required when there are windows in that direction. However, if the structure is of

one-story with no windows facing a source of potential damage, then the setback can be one-sixth of the required distance for a building of two or more stories with windows facing the source of potential damage.
8. Although most of Julian's design rules employ prescriptive standards, in a few cases he uses proscriptive stipulations, such as the case of locating the door of a stable (Hex. 25). In proscriptive stipulations, Julian does not specify dimensions.

## 6.2 - Views

Views for enjoyment and views causing a nuisance through overlooking are both addressed by Julian.[55] For the former, Julian preambles the case concerning the *vista of an area as seen from a house* (Hex. 47) by arguing that "the faculty of sight is the most acute of all the senses, manifesting itself over very long distances." He also acknowledges legal precedence concerning views and mentions three types that should not be obstructed by new construction: views of the sea; views of gardens, trees, and groves; and views of public paintings. He clearly establishes the parameters for defining a direct view from a house: there must be an

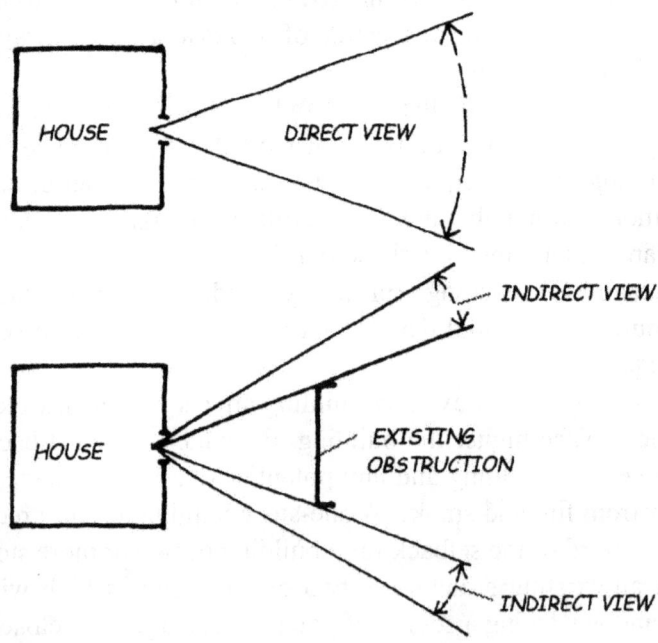

**Figure 8.** Clarification of direct and indirect views (sketches are in plan) (Hex. 47). Author.

unobstructed sight line from a window. An oblique view is considered indirect and cannot legally be used as a basis for challenging obstruction (Figure 8).

Julian maintains that legal precedence on views is vague and has been misunderstood by those who propose building on the sight line of a view (the visual corridor) from an existing house. He calls for the development of careful criteria; otherwise, he cautions, if every new building is challenged because of its potential to obstruct a view, the construction of houses, towns, and villages will be precluded altogether. Accordingly, Julian stipulates that the most pleasant views are direct sea views, defined as the view of a harbor, if there is one, or the view of anchored ships; and views of the nearby sea, understood to include the shoreline. In some cases, both types are combined, but they might be distinct. Distant views of the sea cannot be used to challenge new construction (Figure 9).

The case of the *vista of mountains or the sea* (Hex. 51) offers additional criteria to deal with the obstruction of such a view. Julian equates the pleasure derived from both types of views and accepts Zeno's stipulation that new construction should be allowed if a minimum setback of 100 feet (about 30 meters) is allocated to a house with a sea view (see Figure 9).[56] Julian's acceptance of Zeno's law leads to a certain inflexibility, making it difficult to respond to specific site conditions, particularly in places that slope gently toward the sea. On the other hand, by equating the value

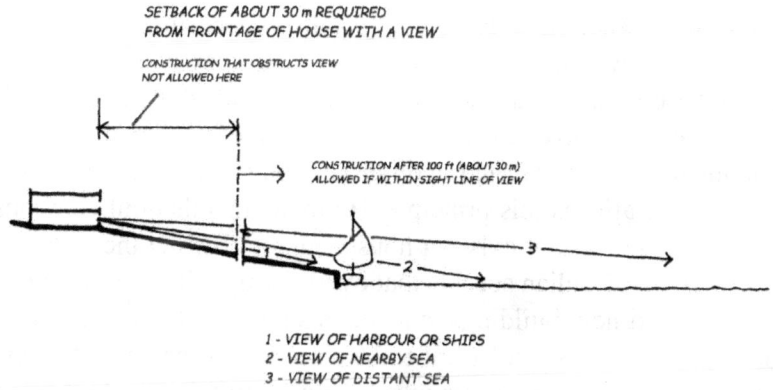

**Figure 9.** Three types of views discussed in the case Hex. 47. The diagram also shows the minimum setback requirements for allowing construction on the view side of a building (Hex. 51). Author.

59

of mountain and sea views, he has made his stipulation more inclusive than Papinian's, which only prohibits views of mountains from being obstructed.[57]

The owner of a house with a *view of a garden* (Hex. 48), or an area planted with trees, can demand that a new construction that might obstruct his view be placed at a minimum distance of 50 feet (about 15 meters). Julian does not mention the effect on the view of the height of the new building or the nature of the terrain between the existing and proposed buildings.

The third type of view that can be used legally to challenge new construction is the *view of a public painting* (Hex. 49). It is obvious from this case that paintings of historical or mythological scenes on exterior walls, whether walls of buildings or walls specially constructed for this purpose, were popular in Ascalon and other Palestinian cities during the sixth century, and that people enjoyed viewing them from their houses. However, Julian stipulates a condition for seeking to protect a view of a public painting: the person with such a view must appreciate and understand its significance, in which case he can demand a setback of 50 feet (about 15 meters) between his house and the new construction. This is the same distance stipulated for views of gardens.[58]

For views as a nuisance, the case of *overlooking the houses of others* (Hex. 50) sets the stage. Here Julian addresses a basic principle of whether existing dwellings can prevent the construction of nearby new houses, based on the fear that they would overlook the older houses' windows and doors and invade their owners' privacy. Julian clearly affirms that the owner of an existing house cannot stop new construction on these grounds, and mentions that precedence affirms this principle. He maintains that only envious or spiteful owners of existing houses might obstruct the rights of others to build. Julian accepts that overlooking will occur between existing and new buildings, and suggests that if the owner of an existing house does not want to be overlooked, he should create his own defensive measures in the form of curtains or shutters on his windows.

Despite this principle, Julian makes stipulations about *opening a window in a blank wall* (Hex. 33) and *constructing a balcony* (Hex. 32). In the former case, owner (A) has a window that faces the blank wall of an opposite neighbor (B) (distance not mentioned). If (B) wants to open a window for ventilation and/or light, he can do so, provided the proposed window sill is 3.5 cubits (about 1.75 meters) above the floor level of the room, that is, above eye level of a person standing in (B)'s room. (B) is thus prevented from overlooking (A)'s window. However, if (B) wants to build a window for looking out, he can do so only if the distance between the walls of (A) and (B) is 20 feet (about 6 meters) or more. Julian explains the reason for requiring this distance as a measure to discourage reciprocal invasion of privacy and thus to prevent the corruption of morals.

As for the latter case of constructing a balcony (Hex. 32), if an existing owner (A) of a window with a balcony that faces the public realm, such as a street or square, has a neighbor (B) across the street who wants to construct a balcony, then (B) should be allowed to do so, provided a minimum distance of 10 feet (about 3 meters) is maintained between the two balconies. This dimension affirms Zeno's law regarding such cases, even though it is half the distance established for the earlier case. Clearly, Julian does not want to contradict an established imperial stipulation. This case also affirms the principle of reciprocity: if (A) enjoys the view of the public realm from his balcony, then (B) should be allowed to build one and enjoy the same view.

**Rules for views derived from Julian's case studies**
1. What you can see determines the basis for preserving the view.
2. Direct views of a harbor, anchored ships, the shoreline, and mountains are considered the most enjoyable views and should be preserved.
3. Direct views of a garden with trees and of public paintings depicting popular historical or mythological scenes should be preserved.
4. In principle, the owner of an existing house cannot prevent the construction of a nearby house on the pretext that the occupants of the new house will be able to overlook him. The owner of the existing house, if he so desires, should use preventive measures to obstruct overlooking.

5. The principle of equitability between neighbors is used to determine the construction of windows or balconies for a house neighboring another that has one or both of those elements.
6. Setback requirements are the mechanism used for preserving views and for making it possible to add a window or a balcony.

### 6.3 - Houses and condominiums

The cases concerning houses and condominiums are grouped in three categories: acts that could debase the value of a neighbor's property; problems among neighbors due to shared walls; and issues of condominiums in multistory buildings.[59]

*Debasement of the value of adjacent properties*
*Increase in building height* (Hex. 28) concerns situations where the owner of one of two nearby structures wants to add one or more stories to his building. The fear is that such an addition could potentially diminish the value of the other building. Julian explains that two conditions have to be met when an existing two-story house (A) is near an existing house (B) whose owner wants to add another story: the two houses must appear to be of similar status in appearance and plot size; and a minimum distance of 10 feet (about 3 meters) must separate them. If both conditions are met, then the owner of (B) can add a second story to his house, thereby matching in appearance house (A) without diminishing its value. However, if there is a minimum space of 20 feet (about 6 meters) between two neighboring buildings, and if (A) is two, three, or more stories high, whereas (B) is a one-story building, then the owner of (B) can build additional stories to his house and can open windows facing (A) regardless of whether or not (A) has windows looking toward (B). In villages the minimum distances may be reduced by one-half.

The following two cases concern changes affecting the exterior wall of a two-story building, where (A) is the owner of the lower apartment and (B) the owner of the upper one. *Concerning opening or enlarging a door or window* by (A) (Hex. 29), the premise is that alterations by owner (A) to the lower part of a two-story exterior wall by opening and/or enlarging doors and windows might cause structural damage to the upper portion of (B)'s wall. Assuming (A)'s door and/or window is small and he wants to enlarge it or open a new one, Julian stipulates that (A) is not permitted to do so unless (B) has a window above the door or window of (A). The requirement then is that (A) may open a new door or window or enlarge the existing one, provided it is 6 fingers (about 10 cm) narrower on each side than the opening above; and (A) must notify (B) in writing of the changes to (A)'s wall and also assume full responsibility for any damage that may occur to (B)'s wall within a period of two months after the completion of the changes in (A)'s wall. (A) must in addition cover all expenses due to potential damage to the crossbeams and doorframes in (B)'s apartment (Figure 10).

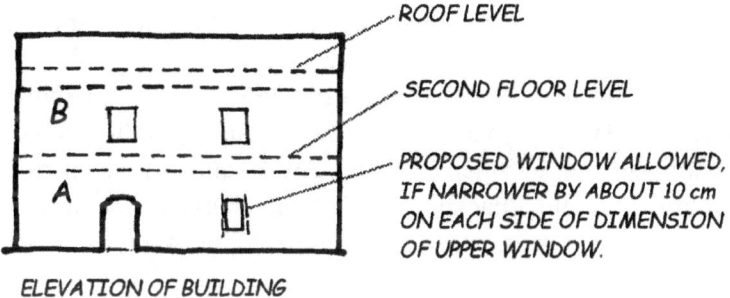

**Figure 10.** Stipulations for opening or widening a window or door on the lower level relative to an existing opening on the upper level of a two-story structure (Hex. 29). Author.

The second case deals with *replacing piers by columns* (Hex. 30). Replacing piers of exterior walls by columns, which are less space-consuming and more elegant, should not be prevented. In the case of (A)'s lower apartment, the only stipulation is that the diameter of the column that replaces the pier should be one-half of the diameter of the pier. If owner (B) of the upper apartment wants to replace his pier, he is allowed to do so only after installing a beam under the column to distribute the weight evenly on the lower portion of the wall. The beam must have a minimum thickness of 8 fingers (about 13 cm).

The case of an a*dditional door to a communal courtyard* (Hex. 31) addresses potential harm to tranquility and privacy that may result from an increase in traffic due to opening another doorway onto a communal courtyard. The additional door may open directly onto the courtyard or indirectly via a warehouse or workshop. Julian's remedy is based on the principle of maintaining the original levels of traffic, and thus stipulates that if a new door is desired it can replace the older one, which should be permanently sealed.

## *Walls between neighbors*

The first two cases (Hex. 83 and 85) concerning walls between neighbors address the rights and responsibilities of owner (B) whose property abuts a wall belonging to (A). In the first case, (B) undertakes to dig adjacent to (A)'s wall; in the second case, (B) wants to construct a wall adjacent to (A)'s wall. These are followed by three cases (Hex. 34, 35, and 36) that deal with the situation when (B), whose vacant lot is adjacent to (A)'s building, wants to construct a new building adjacent to or abutting the wall of (A)'s building. The last two cases (Hex. 37 and 38) address the situation when two existing buildings of the same height abut each other and (B) wants to add a penthouse to his roof either when (A) already has one, or when (A) does not. In all of these cases, it is permitted to build adjacent to or abutting an existing wall belonging to another owner, provided certain conditions are met.

In the case dealing with *excavations* (Hex. 85), (B) should allocate a distance of 6.5 cubits (3 .25 meters) from (A)'s wall before digging on his property. However, if (B) wishes to build a wall adjacent to (A)'s wall, then the level of the foundation for (B)'s wall should be higher than (A)'s foundation (Figure 11). In addition, if (B) digs a pit on his property (Hex. 83), he should not pile the soil against (A)'s wall. If necessary, however, he can keep it there for a few days, with (A)'s permission. This stipulation is designed to prevent the dug-out soil, particularly if it is wet, from damaging (A)'s wall. Should (A)'s wall have a berm facing (B)'s property, then (B) is not allowed, while working on his lot, to modify the berm in any way (Figure 12).

If (B) wishes to *construct a building on his vacant property that will abut an existing wall belonging to (A)'s building* (Hex. 34), a number of stipulations should be observed. If (A)'s wall encloses his courtyard, then (B) can abut this wall, hence use it structurally, and raise his new building to the height he desires. In this situation, (B) has to pay one half the cost of (A)'s wall (Figure 13). However

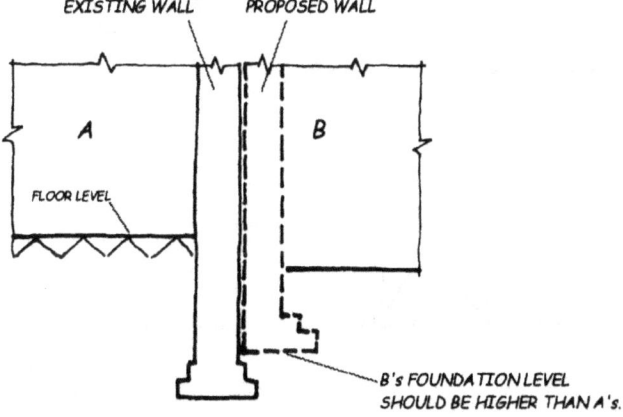

**Figure 11.** Treatment of the foundation of a proposed wall (B), adjacent to an existing wall (A) (Hex. 85). Author.

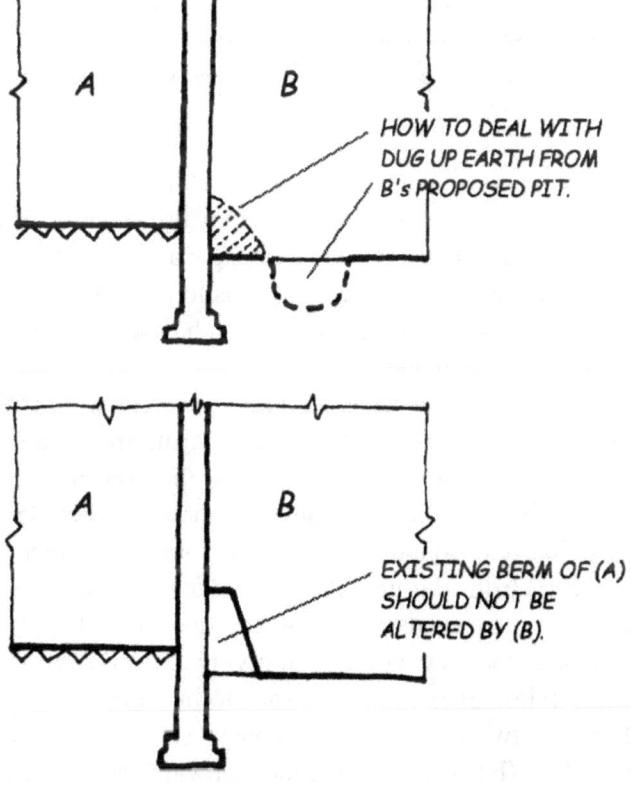

**Figure 12.** Stipulations for digging on one's property (B), when adjacent to the wall of a neighbor's house (A) (Hex. 83). Author.

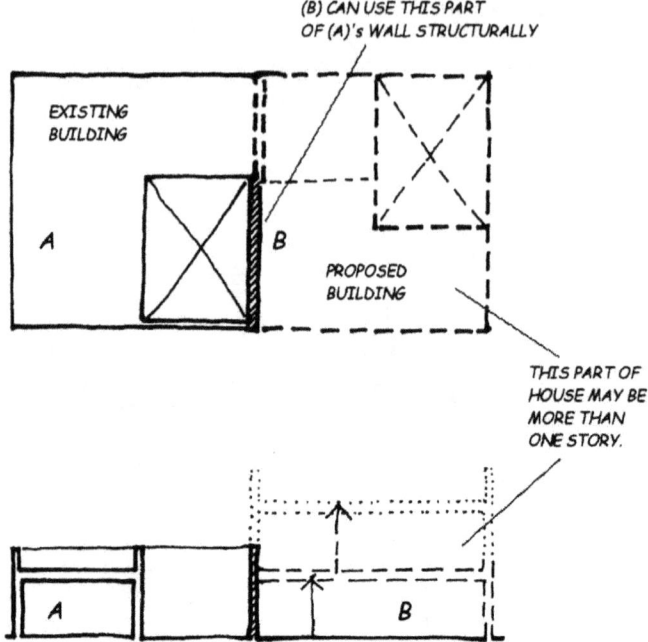

**Figure 13.** Abutting a proposed building to the existing wall of an adjacent building (first part of Hex. 34). Author.

if (A)'s wall is part of a building with more than one story, and (B) wants to make use of the wall, then he may do so only if his building is one story and if he abuts the existing wall without using it for structural purposes. In this event, (B) has to pay (A) one-third the cost of the wall. Estimation of costs in both cases is to be decided by an expert in these matters.

(B) wishes to build on his vacant lot and use (A)'s wall: if the wall encloses a room and has small windows in it, and if this configuration has existed for ten or more years, then (B) must set back from the wall by 3.33 cubits (about 1.66 meters) (Hex. 35). But if (A)'s room has additional windows on its other side, then he cannot prevent (B) from abutting his wall and using it for his new construction. These cases also relate to the possible situation where (A)'s rainwater spouts have been emptying onto (B)'s property for a long time (Hex. 36), and (B) wishes to build on his vacant lot. Here there are two stipulations to consider: if (A)'s wall has no windows, then (B) has to divert the rainwater spouts within his property so that no damage occurs to (A)'s wall; however, if (A)'s wall has windows, then (B) has to observe the 3.33 cubit setback.[60]

In the case of two existing buildings of the same height that abut each other (owned by A and B), if (B) wants to add a penthouse to his roof, Julian considers two conditions: when (A) has a penthouse (Hex. 37) and when (A) does not (Hex. 38). In the former situation, (B) cannot build a penthouse, because the addition, as Julian explains, would create a condition that would encourage squabbles between the neighbors. Julian stipulates that if (B) wants to build a penthouse that will be used frequently, then he must build a second story so that the level of the new roof will be at least 4.50 cubits (2.25 meters) above the level of (A)'s roof; the difference in the heights of the two roofs would thus be sufficient to prevent any potential conflict (Figure 14a). However, if (A) does not have a penthouse, (B) can build one on his roof, even if it is at the same level as (A)'s roof, provided he also builds a parapet wall at least 3 cubits (1.50 meters) high separating the two roofs. Should (A) in the future wish to add a penthouse, he must then reimburse (B) one-half the cost of the parapet wall (Figure 14b).

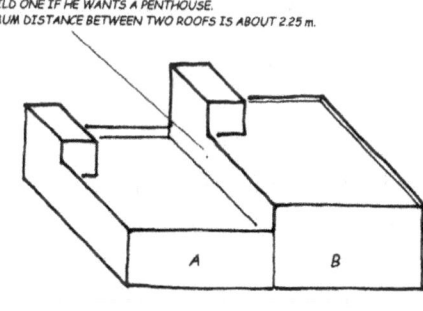

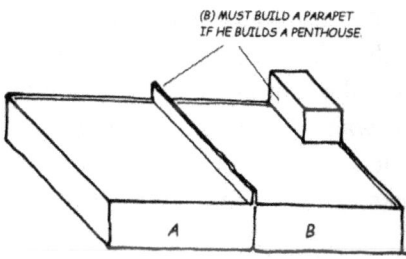

**Figure 14.** (a) When an existing building (A) has a penthouse, and the adjacent neighbor (B) proposes to build one (Hex. 37); (b) when an existing building (A) does not have a penthouse, and the adjacent neighbor (B) proposes to build one (Hex. 38). Author.

### Condominiums in multistory buildings

Julian addresses issues that confront owners of condominiums in multistory buildings of two, three, or more stories. They include issues surrounding distribution of construction costs of a new building among a number of individuals (Hex. 40 and 42), the use of roof terraces by those who do not own them (Hex. 39), the method of dividing the cost of repairs to the main entrance vestibule (Hex. 41), walls (Hex. 44), and public porticoes that are a part of multistory structures (Hex. 43). Catherine Saliou illustrates the stipulations in the case on *house building* (Hex. 40).[61] She demonstrates how the construction costs of a hypothetical building, described by Julian, are divided among the owners of each floor. Another illustration speculates on the construction details of the joints between walls and floors.[62] This case also establishes parties responsible for different parts of the building during the initial construction and for future maintenance and repairs. For example, maintenance of the exterior wall is the responsibility of the owner of the condominium enclosed by that portion of the wall. If a portion of the wall belonging to the lower condominium requires repair, then the owners of the upper floors have to arrange for their part of the wall to be supported on piles while the lower portion is repaired or rebuilt.

The case of *roof terraces* (Hex. 39) addresses their use by residents who are not the owners but who have access to them. A rental fee is paid to the owner depending on the use: for example, if the terrace is used for drying clothes or cooling bread, then the renter must pay the owner the equivalent of one-third the cost of the terrace. If, however, the residents will use the terrace for sleeping during the summer, then the payment is one-half its cost. The case also stipulates that if the top floor is smaller than the lower floors and has access to the roof of a lower condominium, and the owner of the top floor wants to pave, with marble slabs, the terrace that belongs to the lower floor, then he is also responsible for the cost of adding braces to strengthen the beams that will carry the extra weight.

Should the *entrance and the walls of the vestibule hall require repair* (Hex. 41), Julian stipulates that the owner of the adjacent condominium must pay one-half of the cost of repairs. The others must pay in proportion to the number of inhabitants in their apartments, and/or in conformance to any damage they have caused to the entrance and vestibule.

In the case titled *concerning stories* (Hex. 42), we find detailed stipulations regarding the apportionment of expenses for constructing a new multistory condominium and for its repairs during the life cycle of the building. Julian stipulates the same proportions as allocated in Hex. 40. However, when the building requires reconstruction due to its dilapidation, then the owner of each apartment is responsible for building his story up to the upper level, including the connection to it. If it is only the owner of the ground level condominium who has to undertake repairs (presumably in his exterior and interior load-bearing walls), three approaches regarding cost sharing are mentioned by Julian: the custom in Caesarea Maritima is that each owner is responsible for the repairs to his apartment; the custom in Ascalon is that the owners who are vertically contiguous must divide the cost equally between them; and Julian's preference (which he describes as a middle-of-the-road solution) is for owner of the lower unit to pay two-thirds of the cost and the upper neighbor one-third.

If the uppermost story under a flat roof requires repairs, its owner must cover the entire cost, but those residents who share his flat roof must assist him in the construction, for example in replacing and nailing the planks. Julian concludes this case by reminding the owners that they have the right to use all shared and individually owned porticoes (arcades) that are contiguous with their apartments, up to the center line of the walls that divide their apartment from their neighbor's. Julian also addresses the problem of cost sharing among neighbors who are horizontally contiguous.[63]

The last case in this series (Hex. 43) addresses *repairs needed to public porticoes* (arcades) that are contiguous with or located under apartments and provide covered access to shops on the ground level. The primary focus is on repairs of columns and epistyles (a column's upper crossbeam). The allocation of cost sharing is based on who benefits the most from the portico (Figure 15). Owners of shops on the ground level (A) should pay half, because porticoes accommodate their customers; owners on level (C) should pay the other half, because their apartments sit on the columns. In this configuration, owners on level (B) are exempt from any contribution to the cost of repairs since they do not benefit from the portico, and furthermore, it reduces their access to natural light. If, however, the portico requires repairs to its underside, then the owners on level (A) pay half the cost, owners on level (B) pay one-sixth because the portico shelters their apartments from the rain, and the owners on level (C) pay the remaining one-third. The public treasury pays for the cost of repairing or replacing columns damaged at their capitals, bases, or foundation stones.[64]

**Rules for houses and condominiums derived from Julian's case studies**
1. Acts of construction and/or changes in land or building use that would negatively impact adjacent properties by debasing their use or value must comply with stipulations designed to prevent such damages. These stipulations are based on one or more of the following considerations: setback requirements, maintaining the structural integrity of the building, and maintaining the initial level of traffic between the public and private realms.
2. In principle, it is allowed to build adjacent to or abutting an

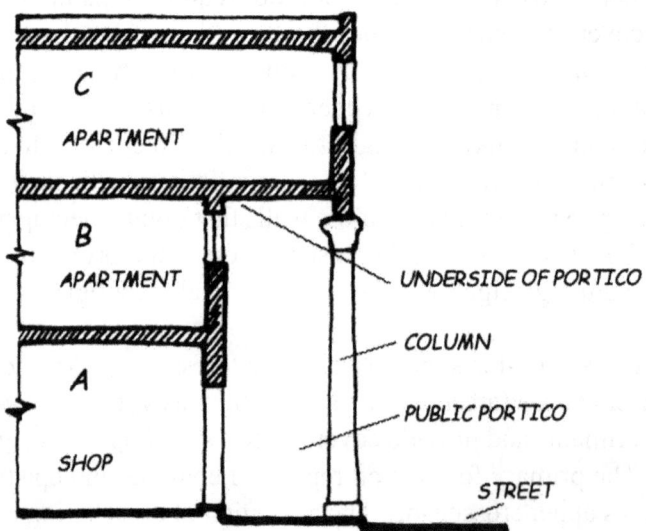

**Figure 15.** Julian's treatise apportions the expense of maintaining a shared public portico among owners (A), (B), and (C) (Hex. 43). By author after Saliou, *Le traite d'urbanisme de Julian d'Ascalon* (Paris, 1996)

existing wall belonging to another owner, provided certain stipulations, designed to address three potential situations, are observed: first, when excavating near an existing wall, where the foundation footings for a new wall are adjacent to the existing wall; second, when proposing to abut the existing wall for structural purposes, and how the expenses shall be equitably shared; and third, when two existing buildings of the same height abut each other and one of the owners wishes to build a penthouse on his roof.

3. Ownership rights and responsibilities of condominiums in multistory buildings address issues of initial and life-cycle construction costs; repairs of load-bearing walls, entrance vestibules, and public porticoes that are part of a building; and use of roof terraces by residents who do not own them. Specific stipulations for each of those conditions are included.[65]

## 6.4 - Drainage

In compact built environments such as sixth-century Ascalon, drainage of rain and waste water requires careful handling to avoid damage to foundations and to prevent health hazards.[66] In his attempt to classify his treatise according to the four elements of fire, air, water, and earth, Julian addressed such problems under the category of water in two subcategories: drainage of rainwater and drainage of waste water.

### *Drainage of rainwater*

This category deals with the *laying out of pipes for drainage* (Hex. 75), and assumes an existing building (A) adjacent to a vacant lot (B). The wall of the building that faces the lot has small windows and a rainwater pipe that drains onto lot (B). The horizontal part of the pipe on the ground should be 3.33 cubits (1.66 meters) from the wall. The owner of (A) is allowed access to the vacant lot to repair his rainwater pipe and/or windows. The owner of lot (B) should allocate the necessary setback from (A)'s wall for any planting that he undertakes. The setback requirements are stipulated in a case discussed below under Planting (Hex. 87). However, in the event that the owner of (B) wants to build on his property, he should then set back from (A)'s wall by 3.33 cubits (1.66 meters) (refer to cases Hex. 35 and Hex. 36). This would enable the owner of (A) to reconfigure the horizontal segment of his rainwater drainage pipe within the setback space so that no damages will occur to his wall.

In the following two cases (Hex. 76 and 77), Julian addresses changes that the owner of (B) might initiate. If there is a building or a wall (A) next to land belonging to owner (B) (Hex. 76), and the owner of (B) wants to *lay out water supply and/or drainage pipes* on his land, then he must set back from (A)'s building or wall by 1 cubit (0.5 meter). However, if there is no building or wall and if the property is a field, then the owner of (B) does not have to observe the setback and is free to design the layout of his pipes in any manner he wishes. In the second case (Hex. 77), an owner (B) wants to *build a cistern to collect rainwater* on his property, and there is an existing wall belonging to the adjacent neighbor (A). Owner (B) must then set back his cistern from (A)'s wall by 6.66 cubits (3.33 meters) to ensure that no damage occurs to the wall should the cistern overflow.

### *Drainage of waste water*

The first case concerns *constructing latrines and cesspools* (Hex. 78). If (B) wishes to build a latrine or a cesspool on his plot and the facility is enclosed by a stone wall of at least 1 cubit (0.5 meter) in thickness, then he should leave a distance of 3.33 cubits (1.66 meters) from neighbor (A)'s wall. If, however, the wall of the latrine or cesspool is built of stone and lined by bronze, then its thickness can be reduced to 0.5 cubit (0.25 meter). For cesspools without walls, the setback from the neighbor's property should be 6.50 cubits (3.25 meters). If neighbor (A)'s property is vacant, then half of the stipulated distances may be observed. A minimum distance between an existing latrine and a proposed one should be 2 cubits (1 meter).

The second case specifies *construction materials for a cesspool or underground sewage channel near a jointly owned wall* (Hex. 79). Should (B) want to build a cesspool or an underground sewage channel adjacent to a jointly owned wall with neighbor (A), then (B) should construct a wall 1.50 cubits (0.75 meter) thick with lime for the cesspool or underground sewage channel situated alongside the wall. This stipulation ensures that damage will not occur to the jointly owned wall.

The third case concerns *responsibilities and procedure for constructing or maintaining a sewer channel used by a number of parties* (Hex. 80). Julian stipulates the distribution of responsibilities among a number of owners who will share a privately constructed sewer channel from its inception at each house to its connection to the public sewer line. The requirement for the initial construction of the channel and for its maintenance and repairs are the same. Each owner is responsible for the cost and maintenance of the channel from its inception at his house to its connection to the channel emerging from the next house in line (Figure 16). The last owner (4 on the diagram) is responsible for a length equivalent to the average constructed by parties 1, 2, and 3. The cost and maintenance of the remaining length of sewer channel to the public sewer is divided equally among the parties.

The last case addresses the *draining of a cesspool located aboveground* (Hex. 82). If (A) has an aboveground cesspool, it should be drained or accessed for cleaning from (A)'s property. In the event that (A) has a legal right in the form of a servitude that permits his cesspool to drain onto neighbor (B)'s property, and (B)'s property is damaged in the process, then (A) is responsible for paying double the cost of damages to (B). The principle underlying these stipulations also applies to the drainage and collection of rainwater in cisterns. Waste-water drainage from houses is not allowed onto a public street, square, or portico, or to any part of the town or village, as this will create harm to the passersby.

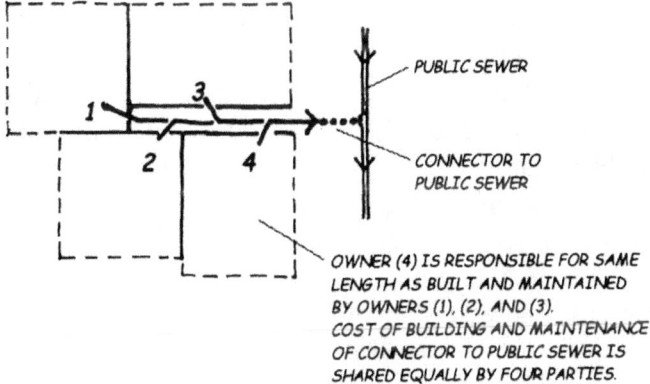

**Figure 16.** Responsibilities of four parties for constructing or repairing a sewer channel (Hex. 80). Author.

73

**Rules for drainage derived from Julian's case studies**
1. Drainage issues are viewed in two distinct categories: rainwater and waste water.
2. Damages to a neighbor's adjacent building or wall from the drainage of rain or waste water, or due to the collection of rainwater in a cistern, should be avoided and are subject to stipulations designed to prevent potential damages.
3. The absence of a neighboring building or wall allows complete freedom for the layout of water supply and/or drainage pipes on one's property.
4. The use of certain construction materials and techniques could compensate for setback stipulations from a neighbor's building or wall to prevent potential damages due to the construction of latrines and cesspools, resulting in a more efficient use of the property.
5. The responsibility for constructing and maintaining sewer channels is divided equitably among the owners.
6. Waste water is not allowed to drain from private properties onto any part of the public realm.

## 6.5 - Planting

The first case explains problems and *potential damages to nearby buildings and facilities caused by trees and shrubs* (Hex. 86).[67] The roots of trees spread toward walls and houses and can seriously damage underground waterlines and wall footings. Trees can also damage vineyards and facilitate access for burglars to upper-level windows. For all these reasons the following *setbacks must be observed from a neighboring house*: for (B) from an existing house (A), 3.33 cubits (1.66 meters) for shrubs, 6.5 cubits (3.25 meters) for vineyards, 10 cubits (5 meters) for apple, pomegranate, or other trees similar in size, and 20 cubits (10 meters) for fig, sycamore, Lombardy poplar, or other trees similar in size; no setback is necessary for vegetation not requiring deep planting, such as ivy, rosebush, or similar species (Hex. 87).[68]

The last case addresses the situation when (B) wants to *till and irrigate his land for crops* (Hex. 88). He can do so, provided he observes a setback of 3.33 cubits (1.66 meters) from an adjacent existing building. However, if (B) has full grown trees on his unimproved lot, and if he wishes to build a house, then the setback stipulations related to plant type do not legally apply, because he is building for himself, and it becomes his responsibility to decide the distances to protect his own house from any damages that might occur from plants on his property.

**Rules for planting derived from Julian's case studies**
1. In principle, a property owner is allowed to plant what he wishes within his property boundaries, provided such planting will not cause future damage to adjacent properties.
2. Setback requirements are stipulated for plant types, based on the principle that plants with longer roots, particularly trees, require larger distances from existing adjacent buildings.

## 7 - Conclusions
The underlying goal, intentions, and design rules comprise the essence of Julian of Ascalon's treatise. It should be noted that Julian also provided for situations not directly covered by any of these design rules: "All of the above are guiding principles, and should an unforeseen problem arise which I have not addressed in my text, then it should be resolved by using analogous resolutions."[69]

I have drawn five general conclusions from studying Julian's treatise:
1. *Stimulus for creating the treatise and significance of its author's skills.* The treatise seems to have been inspired by stimulus from Constantinople, where Emperor Justinian was undertaking major legal projects for the empire. This confirms the conclusion that commitment and encouragement from the highest governing authorities will motivate individuals to take their own initiative to participate in those efforts. Julian seems to have composed his treatise in conformity with Justinian's broader project, using his skills and insights as an architect, – an important fact, given that most legal stipulations related to building design and construction before and after Julian were not composed by architects.
2. *Intentions and their impact on the structure of the treatise.* In composing his treatise, Julian addressed an important and central concern of law, that is, the intent underlying the stipulations in his treatise. To deal with this question, he invoked the work of ancient Greek philosophers. He used Empedocles'

philosophy of four eternal roots: fire, air, water, and earth. Yet, because Julian's knowledge and comprehension of Empedocles' work was most likely incomplete, he did not refer to the underlying mechanism of Love and Strife that affects the intermingling of those roots when he articulated the intentions for his treatise.

3. *Maintaining equitability in the face of change.* This was one of Julian's central concerns in formulating the stipulations of his treatise. It is still a primary concern and should continue to be so in societies that value equitability. The threat to the built environment is caused by damage to one party by another's acts. Thus, changes in the built environment must be tempered to prevent or at least moderate such damage.

4. *Aspects of the built environment addressed by the treatise.* Land use, views, houses and condominiums, drainage, and planting constitute aspects of the normal uses of land and buildings related to economic activities and habitation that may also lead to conflicts due to incompatible adjacent uses. The question of views, particularly views of the sea, was important in Greek culture. People in Palestine during the Byzantine period shared the value of preserving such views. Thus, land use and views were the two significant aspects that impacted local conditions of urban design and architecture.

Julian's treatise does not address issues related to the design of public buildings; it concentrates on the private realm. Julian deals with two types of housing stock prevalent in Ascalon: the single or two-story house owned by one person or family, and the condominium multistory building, where each apartment was owned by an individual or family. Julian examines economic issues related to potential uses that might debase the value of adjacent or nearby properties, and ownership rights of walls between neighbors. Both concerns were of paramount importance to the people of Ascalon and elsewhere; they maintain their universal validity to this day.

Drainage issues relate to rainwater and waste water. Julian's attitude is that water from these two sources should be dealt with according to the source. As for planting within one's property, he considers this to be a positive activity that should be encouraged, but he addresses the potential damages that might result from the roots of plants and trees invading adja-

cent properties.
5. *Prescription vs. proscription.* This issue is rarely raised in studies of the history of construction codes or laws promulgated for construction or urban development. Yet the distinction between prescriptive and proscriptive stipulations has profound implications for their use and the outcome they generate in the built environment. Prescription is the laying down of authoritative rules or directions, usually associated with a central administration that has jurisdiction over the area where the rules will be imposed. It is a top-down mechanism designed by officials who may or may not be familiar with the area in question. Such stipulations, by their very nature, dictate absolute solutions to a problem regardless of the local conditions.

Proscriptive rules, on the other hand, tend to allow freedom of action and initiative within a framework of prohibitions – for example, the freedom to make changes to one's property provided no damage is inflicted on a neighbor. Due to their flexible framework, proscriptive codes tend to evolve over long periods of time and rely on accumulated experience. They are in part associated with customary laws, and the prohibitions they assume tend to overlap with the predominant (largely religious) value and ethical system of the community. Due to the community roots of proscriptive rules, they need to be viewed as a bottom-up system of self regulation, and thus democratic in spirit. Most of the stipulations in Julian's treatise are prescriptive, some more so than others. This is a major difference from earlier Roman laws on the built environment, which were more proscriptive. Jewish law during Julian's period also tended to be proscriptive. Later on Islamic law for the built environment was almost always proscriptive in nature. Refer to chapters 3, 4, and 5.

It is over fourteen centuries since the time of Julian's treatise. Despite its rigid prescriptive nature, we find that its influence survived well into the first decades of the twentieth century, within the former Byzantine cultural sphere. This longevity is not necessarily due to the adaptability of the treatise to changing conditions in various periods and geographic locations, but rather to the importance attached to the continuity of certain Byzantine traditions that per sisted well into the long period of Ottoman rule. Nevertheless, Julian's treatise is more than a regional document. As demonstrated in this study, it provides us with numerous lessons about building and urban codes in general, as well as with insights into the nature of those codes.

**Acknowledgements**

I would like to thank the individuals who translated various critical sources into English: Caterina Basba from Greek; Boris Iundin and Kirill Sereda from Russian; David Powers for arranging a translation from Hebrew. Thanks to Catherine Saliou for clarifying, by correspondence, aspects of her work related to Julian of Ascalon's treatise. I am also very grateful to the following libraries for the rare sources essential for this study: in London, The British Library, Library of the Institute of Classical Studies, University of London Library, University College Library; in Athens, the Gennadion Library; in Geneva, Bibliotheque Publique et Universitaire; in Albuquerque, University of New Mexico Library system, and particularly Randall Moorehead.

Individuals who introduced me to the treatise of Julian of Ascalon are acknowledged in my review of Catherine Saliou, *Le traite* (see n. 16), in the *Journal of Roman Archaeology* 11 (1998): 680-682. This study is dedicated to my sister Fayha and my brother Wisam.

**Notes**

[1] For a history of Ascalon, see W. J. Phythian-Adams, "History of Askalon" in *Palestine Exploration Fund*, Quarterly Statement, April 1921, 76-90; see also the article "Askalan" in *Encyclopedia of Islam*, new ed. (1960), 1: 710--711, and the article "Ashkelon" in *New Encyclopedia of Archaeological Excavations in the Holy Land*, ed. E. Stern (New York, 1993), I: 103-112.

[2] *Encyclopaedia Britannica*, CD-ROM, 1998 standard edition, s.v. "Ashqelon."

[3] Alexander P. Kazhdan, ed., *The Oxford Dictionary of Byzantium*, 3 vols. (New York and London, 1991), article "Palestine," 3: 1563-1564. The fol lowing quote clarifies the special place of Palestine in the eyes of Emperor Justinian I: "We are aware that Palestine is inhabited by a great and estimable people, and forms no inconsiderable part of Our Empire, both because of the amount of taxes which it pays, and by reason of its exceeding loyalty; that it includes cities of great renown; produces good citizens versed in all kinds of knowledge, as well as eminent among the priesthood; and that, finally (which is more important than everything else), Our Lord Jesus Christ,

... redeemed us in Palestine"; the Justinian Novel Title 4 within the Eighth Collection, from S. P. Scott, ed. and trans., *Corpus Juris Civilis (The Civil Law)*, 17 vols. in 7 books (Cincinnati, 1932; reprinted, New York, 1973), 17: 12-13.

[4] Mikhail Sjuzjumov, "O traktate Juliana Askalonita" (From the treatise of Julian of Ascalon), *Anticnaja Drevnosti Srednje Veka* 1 (1960): 3-34 (in Russian), 3.

[5] Averil Cameron, *The Mediterranean World in Late Antiquity* (London, 1993), 182.

[6] Georges Tate, *Les campagnes de la Syrie du nord I*, Institut Francais d'Archeologie du Proche-Orient, Bibliotheque Archeologique et Historique, 133 (Paris, 1992), quoted by Clive Foss in "The Near Eastern countryside in late antiquity: a review article," *Journal of Roman Archaeology*, supplementary ser., 14 (1995): 218-219.

[7] Hugh Kennedy, "From *Polis* to *Madina*: Urban Change in Late Antique and Early Islamic Syria," *Past & Present* 106 (February 1985): 23.

[8] Sjuzjumov, "O traktate," 4.

[9] Kennedy, "*Polis* to *Madina*," 23, quoting Jones.

[10] Sjuzjumov, "O traktate," 5.

[11] Hugh Kennedy, "From Antiquity to Islam in the Cities of al-Andalus and al-Mashriq," handout of lecture delivered at Massachusetts Institute of Technology, Cambridge, Mass., 9 October 1996.

[12] The Arabs referred to Ascalon, and sometimes to Damascus, as "the bride of al-Sham" (i.e., greater Syria); one of the Prophet's companions, Abdullah bin Omar, said: "There is a pinnacle for everything, and the pinnacle for al-Sham is Askalan"; cited by Yaqut al-Hamawi (d. A.D. 1228 ), entry on "Askalan," in his *Mu'jam al-Buldan* (Dictionary of cities and towns) (Beirut, 1979), 4: 122.

[13] Mosaics discovered in 1986 at the eighth-century Church of Saint Stephen at Umm al-Rasas, Jordan, depict images of numerous cities, including Ascalon and Gaza. Images of the latter two cities show buildings of three and four stories. Figure 4 is from a colored reproduction of this mosaic in R. G. Khouri, "Mosaic Country," *Aramco World* 38, no. 1 (1987): 34--40.

[14] This assumes that the population in Ascalon was about 15,000 people. If most of the housing stock was in two-story structures, then the estimate would yield a net density of approximately eight persons per two-story house, which is not unreasonable for walled cities during that period. It is also possible to assume a density of sixteen persons per four-story structure. The footprint of a typical building designed for housing is based on a dimension of 15 x 15 meters, and the net density is calculated by allocating 80 percent to the the footprint of the buildings and 20 percent for access, that is,

for streets and cul-de-sacs. In comparison, Caesarea, the capital, was 2 .25 times larger in area than Ascalon during the mid sixth century. It also had a semicircular plan, with a north/south axis of about 1,500 m and an east/west axis of 900 m. The area within the walls was about 127 hectares (314 acres).

[15] Sjuzjumov, "O traktate," 3 (see n. 4).

[16] Catherine Saliou, *Le traiti d'urbanisme de Julian d'Ascalon: Droit et archi tecture en Palestine au VI siecle* (Paris, 1996), 32. The French rendition of the treatise title is: "Tire de l'ecrit de Julien d'Ascalon, architecte: extrait des lois, ou coutumes, en usage en Palestine" (Drawn from the writing of architect Julian of Ascalon: extract of laws and customs used in Palestine).

[17] Sjuzjumov, "O traktate," 3 (see n. 4), referring to the work of G. Tchalenko, *Villages antiques de la Syrie du Nord*, vols. 1-3 (1955-1959), 1: 109.

[18] Joseph Geiger, "Julian of Ascalon," *Journal of Hellenic Studies* 112 (1992): 31-43. See p. 41 and notes 68 and 69 concerning Geiger's views that if the connection with the church builder Julian in northern Syria can be firmly established, then both Julians would be Christians. See p. 42 for information on Ascalon as a cultural center. Geiger refers to his article written in Hebrew, whose title he translates as "Greek intellectuals from Ascalon," *Cathedra* 60 (1991): 5-16.

[19] Geiger, "Julian," 42.

[20] Anton Heinen, "The role of Palestine in the transmission of the exact sciences from Hellenistic to Arab culture," in the proceedings of *The Third International Conference on Bilad al-Sham: Palestine, 19-24 April 1980*, vol. 2, *Geography and Civilization of Palestine* (Amman, 1984), 61-68.

[21] Contardo Ferrini, "Gli estratti di Giuliano Ascalonita" (Extracts from Julian of Ascalon), *Rendiconti Istituto Lombardo* II, 35 (1902): 613-622. Republished in *Opere di Contardo Ferrini I* (Milan, 1929), 443-452. The author argues that the dating of the composition of Julian's treatise must be before the publication of Justinian's Digest and revised Codes. The other view, by Scheltema, argues for a post-Justinian date, in H. J. Scheltema "The nomoi of Julianus of Ascalon," *Symbolae ad Jus et Historiam Antiquitatis Pertinentes Julio Christiano van Oven Dedicatae* (Leiden, 1946), 349-360. Geiger, "Julian," 41, settles for the treatise's composition within the dates of September A.D. 531 and December A.D. 533, and he is supported by N. van der Wal and J.H.A. Lokin, *Historiae juris Graeco-romani delineatio: Les sources du droit byzantin de 300 a 1453* (Groningen, 1985). Sjuzjumov, "O traktate," 6 (see n. 4), dates it to post-October A.D. 548.

[22] For a brief history of the Beirut law school, see the article by Shereen Khairallah, "The School of Law at Beirut," in Ihsan Abbas, Shereen Khairallah, and Ali Z. Shakir, eds., *Studies in History and Literature in Honour of Nicola A. Ziadeh* (London, 1992), 9-15. Khairallah frequently cites the study by Paul Collinet, *Histoire de l'Ecole de Droit de Beyrouth* (Paris, 1925).

²³ Code of Justinian (C. 11. 21. 1): "We decree that the city of Berytus, already renowned for its admirable qualities, . . ." from Scott, ed., *Corpus* (see n. 3), and from the introduction titled "The Whole Body of Law" in Alan Watson, ed. and trans., *The Digest of Justinian*, 2 vols. (Philadelphia, 1985; revised ed., 1998), 1, para. 7: "...in the most excellent civitas of Berytus, which might well be called the nurse of the law . . .." See also ibid., "The Confirmation of the Digest," para. 9.

²⁴ "If you wish to do this ..., then you must observe this ..."; briefly discussed in William W. Hallo, *Origins: The Ancient Near Eastern Background of Some Modern Western Institutions* (Leiden, 1996), 245.

²⁵ Ibid., 247.

²⁶ See the detailed study by Raymond Westbrook, "The Nature and Origins of the Twelve Tables," *Zeitschrift der Savigny Stiftung Für Rechtsgeschichte* 105 (1988): 74--121.

²⁷ Proscription is an imposed restraint synonymous with prohibition, as in "Thou shalt not," whereas prescription is the laying down of authoritative rules or directions, as in "Thou shalt." The former allows innovative solutions to occur in response to a local problem within the framework of prohibitions; the latter dictates solutions to a problem regardless of the conditions in a locality.

²⁸ Alan Rodger, *Owners and Neighbours in Roman Law* (Oxford, 1972), for a detailed analysis of this condition.

²⁹ Adolf Berger, "Encyclopedic Dictionary of Roman Law," *Transactions of the American Philosophical Society*, vol. 43, part 2 (1953), 333-808, 702; a servitude is a form of easement. "Servitutes were classified among *iura in re aliena* (i.e., rights over another's property). This right was vested in the beneficiary not as a personal one, but as a right attached to the immovable land or building) itself, regardless of the person who actually happened to own it." For a detailed analysis and discussion of the workings of the *altius tollendi* and *altius non tollendi*, see Rodger, *Owners*, 32.

³⁰ Zeno's laws were addressed to the prefect of Constantinople. They contained detailed stipulations regarding the construction of balconies, either made of wood planks or of the "Roman style." Those were recorded in the Code of Justinian (C. 8. 10. 11) and (C. 8. 10. 12. 5). For a French rendition, see Catherine Saliou's article: "La maison urbaine en Syrie aux epoques Romaine et Byzantine d'apres la documentation juridique," in *Les maisons dans la Syrie antique du III millinaire aux debuts de l'Islam*, Institut Français d'Archéologie du Proche-Orient (Beirut, 1997), 313-327.

³¹ Code of Justinian (C. 8. 10. 13), translated in Scott, *Corpus* (see n. 3), and mentioned by Sjuzjumov, "O traktate," 6 (see n. 4).

³² Sjuzjumov, "O traktate" (see n. 4), suggests that Julian, although from Ascalon, was in Constantinople in A.D. 548, and was sent back to Palestine

81

with a delegation of *de discussoribus* (inspectors) and asked to write a treatise about building rules for the cities of Palestine. This hypothesis is not mentioned by other scholars familiar with the treatise of Julian of Ascalon; they argue that Emperor Justinian I forbade reference to sources before his *Corpus Juris Civilis* effective 30 December A.D. 5 33 or very shortly thereafter, as indicated in para. 19 of the "Confirmation of the Digest" in Watson, *Digest* (see n. 23). Julian, on the other hand, mentions earlier sources in his treatise. *De discussoribus* is a form of the term *discussor* that is mentioned in the Code of Justinian 10.30 (Concerning Assessors). In Berger, "Dictio nary," 438 (see n. 29), *discussor* is defined as "an official in the later Empire who verified the accounts of expenditures for public buildings and the records connected with tax administration."

[33] Constantinos Armenopoulos, *Manual of Laws or the Hexabiblos*, ed. Gustav Ernst Heimbach (Leipzig, 1851 [in Greek and Latin]; reprint ed., Darmstadt, 1969). This *Hexabiblos* (Six books), a handbook of laws from fourteenth-century Thessaloniki, is discussed in this article under the subhead "Diffusion of the Treatise." The stipulations in Julian's treatise are cross-referenced by the numbers given in Book 2, part 4, of the *Hexabiblos* as Hex. followed by the number of the case-for example, Hex. 51, etc. Since the fourteenth century, Julian's stipulations have been known primarily through this handbook.

[34] *The Syro-Roman Lawbook*, trans. Arthur Voobus, Papers of the Estonian Theological Society in Exile, no. 39 (Stockholm, 1983), 60. In addition to this English translation, see the four volumes by A. Voobus, *The Synodicon in the West Syrian Tradition* (Louvain, 1975-1976).

[35] One reason for this similarity is the underlying force of customary law throughout the Near East. A study of similarities and differences between these two sources is necessary and would yield additional insights into Julian of Ascalon's treatise. Another useful study would be to trace the origins of some of the stipulations in Julian's treatise to ancient Greek and Roman laws. E.J. Owens included an appendix titled "Town planning and the law" in his book *The City in the Greek and Roman World* (London, 1991), 166-170, where he mentions that the laws addressed three areas: the relationship between state and individual and the responsibility of the individual to the community; relations between individuals and their neighbors; and ensuring the general health and well-being of citizens as well as the overall maintenance of the city and its services. Julian's treatise clearly deals with the second category of these relationships. Owens also cites numerous examples, such as, "at Athens, Hippias taxed overhanging balconies, and doors and shutters which opened outward on to the road" and, "in Rome laws established a minimum width of 2.90 m for urban streets precisely to allow for overhanging balconies." In an earlier study by E. J. Owens, "The Koprologoi at Athens in the fifth and fourth centuries B.C.," *Classical Quarterly* 33, no. 1 (1983): 44-50, the author indicates that laws from Piraeus and Pergamon were designed to

keep streets passable, to protect adjacent buildings, and to safeguard pedestrians. In the astynomic law at Pergamon, the removal of rubbish from streets was the responsibility of individual property owners and was privately organized. Householders were responsible for the cleanliness of the streets outside their property and up to a certain distance on either side. Another example is a law from Gortyn, on the island of Crete, which forbade the location of ovens and dung heaps within a certain distance of houses; a minimum distance of 10 feet is indicated.

[36] The popularity of these two terms must date back to the well-known German study by L. Mitteis, *Reichsrecht und Volksrecht in den ostlichen Provinzen des romischen Kaiserreichs* (Imperial and customary laws in the eastern provinces of the Roman empire) (Leipzig, 1891). I use the terms to refer to imperial laws or decrees (*Reichsrecht*), and to customary laws (*Volksrecht*).

[37] In Berger, "Dictionary," 424 (see n. 29), the term is defined as "a damage not yet done but threatening one's property by the defective state of a neighbor's property." Another, related statute concerned with the damage done to another's property is the *Lex Aquilia*, which sets general rules of liability for damage; Watson, *Digest*, 9.2 (see n. 23), and defined in Berger, 547-548. Thus, for example, the loss inflicted on the owner must be the result of a wrongful act (*damnum iniuria datum*). The original provisions of the *Lex Aquilia* were extended and became the *Actio legis Aquiliae*; according to one of its characteristic features, a defendent who denied his liability had to pay double damages if condemned. The stipulation of paying double damages is used by Julian in the case relating to an owner (A) who has a servitude to access and clean his cesspool from the neighbor (B)'s property. However, should damage occur to (B)'s property, then (A) has to pay (B) double the cost of those damages (Hex. 82).

[38] Saul Lieberman, title translated from Hebrew (Something about Julian of Ascalon's book-the law, Palestine and its customs), in *Tabriz* 40 (Jerusalem, 1971), 409-417.

[39] Ibid., 411.

[40] Ibid., 410, 416.

[41] The eparch of Constantinople was the governor of the city, successor of the late Roman urban prefect. He was considered supreme judge in the capital and its vicinity, second only to the emperor, and was the chief of police responsible for order, decoration, and ceremonial events in the capital. As head of the city police he had jurisdiction over prisons. His other functions included the control of commercial and industrial activities in the capital; Kazhdan, ed., *Dictionary of Byzantium*, 1: 705 (see n. 3).

[42] Heimbach, ed., *Hexabiblos*. This is the most accessible current edition, reprinted in 1969.

⁴³ Kazhdan, ed., *Dictionary of Byzantium*, 2: 902 (see n. 3).

⁴⁴ The *Hexabiblos* was compiled in 1345, but it was not until the mid-1700s that its influence began to spread in Greece and the Balkan countries, lasting in the former until about the 1940s. From N. J. Pantazopoulos, *Church and Law in the Balkan Peninsula during the Ottoman Rule* (Thessaloniki, 1967).

⁴⁵ This is a direct translation from Sjuzjumov, "O traktate," 18 (see n. 4). Words in brackets were added by Sjuzjumov to further explain Julian's intentions.

⁴⁶ Saliou, *Le traité* (see n. 16), added the missing headings to her translation of the treatise. She also added a fifth heading, Views. The actual cases, according to their numbering in the *Hexabiblos* of Armenopoulos and their sequence in Genevensis 23, are as follows: Fire: *Hexabiblos* 2.4: 13-22; Air: 23, 25-44; Water: 75-80, 82; Earth: 83, 85-88. The balance of the cases, according to their sequence in Genevensis 23, relate to "views": *Hexabiblos* 2.4: 47-51. Armenopoulos added stipulations from other sources and mixed them with Julian's, which explains why some numbers are missing.

⁴⁷ The information in this discussion is derived from two sources: M. R. Wright, ed., *Empedocles: The Extant Fragments* (New Haven, 1981), and from various articles in *Encyclopaedia Britannica* (see n. 2).

⁴⁸ I use the term *equitable equilibrium* to mean that the built environment needs to reach a state of equilibrium at any point in time, but it does so only when all concerned parties are equitably treated in the process.

⁴⁹ The roots of the concept of Love and Strife might be traced back to the doctrines of Zoroaster, the Iranian religious reformer (628-551 s.c.). The ancient Greeks saw in Zoroastrianism the archetype of the dualistic view of the world and of human destiny. Zoroaster is known to have instructed Pythagoras (580-500 s.c.) in Babylon. The latter's philosophy includes a set of ten pairs of contrary qualities. I believe three of these relate to certain aspects of Love and Strife: they are Good vs. Evil, Unity vs. Plurality, and At Rest vs. In Motion. Empedocles was a pupil of Pythagoras; he was also influenced by the ideas of Heracleitus (540-480 s.c.), who argued for the need for people to live in social harmony. Heracleitus's interpretation of the *logos* (reason, in Greek) is the underlying connection between opposites that define each other, such as health and disease, good and evil, and hot and cold. Essentially, his philosophy is based on the notion of a dynamic equilibrium that maintains an orderly balance in the world, a persistence of unity despite change. (f his synthesis is based on sources in *Encyclopaedia Britannica* [see n. 2]).

⁵⁰ Saliou, *Le traité* (see n. 16).

⁵¹ There are fourteen cases related to land use in the *Hexabiblos*. On baths and artisanal workshops, see Hex. 2.4: 13-22; on socially offensive uses, see Hex. 2.4: 23 and 25-27.

⁵² For definitions of *proscriptive* and *prescriptive*, see n. 27.

⁵³ For a detailed discussion of brothels in Palestine during the Byzantine period, see Claudine Dauphine, "Brothels, Baths and Babes: Prostitution in the Byzantine Holy Land," *Classics Ireland* 3 (1996): 47-72.

⁵⁴ In Hex. 18, Julian mentions that smoke dissipates at a distance of 6.5 cubits.

⁵⁵ There are seven cases related to views in the *Hexabiblos*. On views for enjoyment, see Hex. 2.4: 47-49 and 51; for views as nuisance, see Hex. 2.4: 50, 33 (window openings), and 32 (balcony construction).

⁵⁶ Emperor Zeno's (A.D. 474-491) laws regarding this issue can be found in the Code of Justinian (C. 8. 10. 12. 2a) and (C. 8. 10. 12. 4), as cited and discussed in Rodger, *Owners*, 35, 129, 132-140 (see n. 28).

⁵⁷ Rodger, *Owners*, 134--140 (see n. 28). Aemilius Papinianus (A.D. 140-212) was a Roman jurist who posthumously became the definitive authority on Roman law, possibly because his moral highmindedness was congenial to the world view of the Christian rulers of the postclassical empire; *Encyclopaedia Britannica*, 1998 ed., s.v. "Papinian" (see n. 2).

⁵⁸ Julian provides two examples of public paintings of significance: a painting of Achilles and one of Ajax. The former is "the principal Greek hero of the *Iliad*, and his popularity was retained well beyond late antiquity. This popularity can be explained by the search for the ideal warrior"; "Achilles," in Kazhdan, ed., *Dictionary of Byzantium*, 13-14 (see n. 3). Ajax was, "next to Achilles, the bravest of all Greeks in the Trojan war"; "Ajax," in *Lemprière Classical Dictionary of Proper Names mentioned in Ancient Authors Writ Large*, 3rd ed. (London, 1984), 26. It is clear that heroes from Greek mythology continued to be admired in Ascalon during the sixth century, despite the fact that a large portion of the population was Christian.

⁵⁹ There are seventeen cases related to houses and condominiums in the *Hexabiblos*. On acts that could debase the value of adjacent properties, see Hex. 2.4: 28-31; on walls between neighbors, see Hex. 2.4: 34--38 and 83, 85; on condominiums in multistory buildings and those contiguous with porticoes, see Hex. 2.4: 39-44.

⁶⁰ I am assuming that in this case (A) has to rechannel the rainwater spouts within the setback in such a way that his wall will not be damaged.

⁶¹ Saliou, *Le traité* (see n. 16), figs. 6a and 7.

⁶² Ibid., fig. 6b.

⁶³ In this case (Hex. 44), it is difficult to envision the configuration described by Julian, whether in Sjuzjumov or Armenopoulos. Saliou's attempt to configure this case in figure 10 of *Le traité* (see n. 16) is neither clear nor convincing.

⁶⁴ Although Julian does not provide the reason for the public treasury's involvement, one might assume that the columns were originally provided by,

or paid for by, the public treasury.

[65] Condominium buildings of two, three, or more stories, where each story was owned by one party, were one of the patterns of tenure in Ascalon and Caesarea, and possibly in other cities of Palestine and the Near East, during the sixth century and earlier.

[66] There are seven cases related to drainage in the *Hexabiblos*. On rainwater, see Hex. 2.4: 75, 76 (which also relates to waste water), and 77. On waste water, see Hex. 2.4: 78-80 and 82 (which also applies to rainwater).

[67] There are three cases related to planting in the Hexabiblos. On trees, shrubs, and other vegetation, see Hex. 2.4: 86-88.

[68] The approach based on distances from the boundary has early precedence in ancient Greek law. In 10.1.13 of the *Digest* (Watson, *Digest*; see n. 23), Gaius quotes a law that Solon passed at Athens in the sixth century B.C.: "If a man ...plants an olive tree or fig tree, nine feet away from the other man's land, other trees five feet away."

[69] This quote is from the last paragraph of Julian's treatise, as translated by Sjuzjumov, "O traktate," 34 (see n. 4).

# Chapter 3

# Nature of Rules in Islamic Law

The built environment of Muslim towns and cities was determined in the past largely by the manner in which responsibilities were allocated and individual behaviours were affected by the notion of rights. In the early period the predominant customary practices (*urf*) of the Arabian peninsula in particular and the Near East in general were assimilated by the early Muslims (Hakim, 1994). These practices were adapted and changed as necessary to bring them into conformity with the practice and experience in Medina following the *hijra* in 622 C.E. Through his statements and actions, the Prophet Muhammad affirmed customary practices that were consistent with Islamic values, and he clarified the purpose of other practices that he encouraged. Thus was established the basis for practices that subsequently were elaborated upon and expanded by Muslim jurists. In general, it can be said that there are more similarities than differences in the positions adopted by the various schools of Islamic law relative to the built environment.

It was the responsibility of the ruling authority to establish the primary mosque in a central location and to specify the location of the government building, treasury, market, defensive perimeter wall and its gates, and thoroughfares leading from the center of town to the city gates. In newly created towns, it also was the responsibility of the ruling authority to allocate land to tribes, ethnic groups, and extended families through a procedure known as *iqta*. The subdivision and management of these allocated lands was the responsibility of the tribal elders or representatives and not that of the ruling authority. Heads of households in turn were responsible for laying out the organization of the cluster and the design of their houses (Akbar, 1990, 1992).

When Muslims settled in existing towns, the above-mentioned responsibilities were allocated in a similar manner. In certain cases the existing urban fabric underwent changes due to the rights and responsibilities associated with the parties that controlled various sectors of the built environment. The sectors and facilities of the built environment that were used by the public were overseen by the *muhtasib*.

At the level of neighborhood formation, change in the urban environment was regulated by *qawa'id fiqhiyya*, overarching legal principles that formed the framework within which the Muslim community set out rules that people understood, respected, and followed in making decisions that affected the design of their houses and the manner in which those decisions affected adjacent buildings. Muslim jurists define the term *qa'ida* as a "general ruling that applies to its particulars," or "an overarching rule that applies to the various levels of a situation or a problem" (al-Zarka, 1989). All law schools agree that the five primary *qawa'id* constitute a framework within which other *qawa'id* fit, covering most issues addressed by the law (al-Sadlan, 1996). These five principles and their corollaries comprise a system in which a concept or decision related to any one of them is affected by, or affects, the others.

The five *qawa'id* that served as the basis upon which secondary principles and rules were established are:
1. Do not harm others and others should not harm you (*la darar wa-la dirar*);
2. Affairs are determined by their intent (*al-umur bi-maqasidiha*);
3. Certainty is not removed by doubt (*al-yaqin la yazul bi-l-shakk*);
4. Hardship brings relief (*al-mashaqqa tajlib al-taysir*);
5. Custom has the weight of law (*al-ada muhakkima*).

These five principles influenced the formation of the built environment by forming a set of overarching rules that set limits on behaviour (al-Burnu,1983).

With respect to the built environment, *la darar wa-la dirar* is the central and most influential principle (even though it is often listed as the second principle in legal texts). This principle is always applied to issues relating to decisions affecting the built environment.

Five additional rights and conditions that operated at the level of a single unit of the built environment (e.g., a house) affect decisions and actions:

1. Freedom to act, on the condition that harm is not inflicted on adjacent properties or facilities (Madkur, 1963). This freedom, known as *ibaha*, is defined as "freedom that is constrained by what is forbidden" or "permission to act as desired by the actor" (*al-idhn bi-ityan al-fi'l kayfa sha'a al-fa'il*; al-Jurjani,1983).
2. Precedence: realities on the ground created by earlier builders must be respected by those who follow. Thus a person who builds a new structure adjacent to or across from an existing structure must situate and design the new building—especially its windows and doors—so that no visual corridor is created between the two buildings (Hakim, 1986, 2007).
3. The person who builds first has the right to exercise "control over potential damage" (*hiyazat al-darar*) (Ibn Farhun, 1884). That is to say, the earlier building or facility exercises control over what a subsequent builder can do when building next to it.
4. A neighbour has the right to abut his building against the wall of an existing structure, provided no harm is done to the pre-existing wall or structure. Because houses were built around inner courtyards that provided light and air, this right facilitated the clustering of buildings adjacent to one another on more than one side.
5. Access to a structure is through a space called a *fina* (or *harim*) that is approximately 1–1.5 meters wide and runs alongside all exterior walls of a building. This space also extends vertically alongside the walls of the building. The owner or tenant of a building has the right to use the *fina* for temporary purposes provided such use does not impede traffic in the street, and he is responsible for keeping his part of the *fina* clean and safe from any obstructions and the accumulation of rainwater or snow. The vertically extended *fina* allows upper level projections in the form of balconies, enclosed bay windows, and rooms bridging the public right-of-way (called *sabat*). In the traditional literature we find that some Muslim scholars attribute these projections and the *sabat* to the right of *ihya al-*

*mawat*, in this case the utilization of dead space that would not harm the traffic underneath.

To summarize: It was the responsibility of the ruling authority to create the broad framework for the town or city. The decisions of the ruling authority affected city walls and gates; the location of the major mosque, the palace, and the central market area; and the general alignment of the primary streets connecting all of these structures. In other respects, the city emerged naturally as a result of the decisions and actions of its residents, who, when they built houses and other structures, responded to existing conditions on adjacent properties by adjusting their own design. Over time, changes occurred as the owners adapted to neighbouring and, especially, contiguous structures. The alignments of pathways and streets were delineated and extended in response to the creation of nearby structures and changes in them. In a word, the system was self-regulating and adaptive.

Islamic urbanization is governed at the local level by the principle of freedom, that is, that one may develop one's property without restrictions, subject to overarching proscriptive rules derived from normative principles based on Islamic values. The city emerges from decisions made by the various actors involved in the construction and renovation within their immediate built environment. In this respect, the emergence of the built environment resembles any organized complex system (Weaver, 1948). As N. J. Habraken has put it, "to use built form is to exercise some control, and to control is to transform ... A complex hierarchy of control patterns within a continuity of action emerges ... [C]ontrol thus defines the central operational relationship between humans and all matter that is the stuff of built environment" (Habraken,1998).

In order to understand the development of the built environment, it is necessary to think about process, to work inductively (reasoning from particulars to the general), and "to seek "unaverage" clues involving very small quantities, which reveal the way larger and more "average" quantities are operating" (Jacobs, 1961). The relationship between the owners of adjacent houses depends on decisions affected by negative feedback, as when a window in one house overlooks the private domain of an adjacent house: the owner of the adjacent house reacts by demanding that the window be sealed or removed; if the window existed before the new neighbour built his house, the new neighbour responds by designing his house in such a way that no visual corridor is created. In all living systems, feedback loops generated by networks of communication among its members make it possible for a community to correct mistakes and to regulate itself (Capra, 1996). These features of living systems help explain how the local built environment developed in the traditional Islamic city as residents interacted with one another. The emergence of the traditional Islamic city is best understood as a product of a system of rules that created boundaries that were observed by residents. The system's capacity to accumulate and internalize experience by growth and experimentation derives from its adherence to these rules (Johnson, 2001; Hakim, 2007).

## References

Abu Jayb, Sa'di, *al-Qamus al-fiqhi*, Damascus, 1982.

Akbar, Jamel, "Khatta and the territorial structure of early Muslim towns", *Muqarnas 6*, 1990, pp. 22-32.

---------------, *Imarat al-ard fil-Islam,* Jidda and Beirut, 1992.

Al-Burnu, Muhammad Sidqi b. Ahmad, *al-wajiz fi idah qawa'id al-fiqh al-kulliyya,* Beirut, 1983.

Capra, Frijof, *The Web of Life*, London and New York, 1996.

Al-Dirini, Fathi, *Nazariyyat al-ta'assuf fi sti'mal al-haqq*, Beirut, 1977.

Habraken, N.J. *The Structure of the Ordinary: Form and Control in the Built Environment*, ed. Jonathan Teicher, Cambridge, MA, 1998.

Hakim, Besim S., *Arabic-Islamic Cities: Building and Planning Principles*, London, 1986, 1988 (2nd Ed), 2008 (3rd Ed with Postscript).

---------------, "The *Urf* and its role in diversifying the architecture of traditional Islamic cities", *Journal of architectural and planning research*, 11/2, 1994, pp. 108-27.

---------------, and Zubair Ahmed, "Rules for the built environment in 19th century Northern Nigeria", *Journal of architectural and planning research*, 23/1, 2006, pp. 1-26.

---------------, "Generative processes for revitalizing historic towns or heritage districts", *Urban Design International*, 12/2-3, 2007, pp. 87-99.

----------------, "Law and the city", in *The city in the Islamic world*, ed. Salma K. Jayyusi, Leiden, 2008, 1:71-92.

Ben Hammush, Mustafa Ahmad, *Jawhar al-tamaddun al-Islami: Dirasat fi fiqh al-umran*, Beirut, 2006.

Al-Hathloul, Salih b. Ali, *al-Madina al-Arabiyya al-Islamiyya: Athar al-tashri fi takwin al-bi'a al-umraniya*, Riyadh, 1994.

Heinrichs, Wofhart P., "*Qawa'id* as a genre of legal literature", in *Studies in Islamic legal theory*, ed. Bernard G. Weiss, Leiden, 2002, pp. 365-84.

Ibn Farhun (d. 1397 C.E.), *Tabsirat al-hukkam*, Beirut, 1884 (with, in the margin, al-Kinani (d. 1340 C.E.), *Kitab al-aqd al-munazzam lil-hukkam*).

Jacobs, Jane, *The death and life of great American cities*, New York, 1961.

Johnson, Steven, *Emergence: The connected lives of ants, brains, cities, and software*, New York, 2001.

Al-Jurjani, Ali b. Muhammad (d. 1413 C.E.), *Kitab al-ta'rifat*, Beirut, 1983.

Madkur, Muhammad Sallam, *al-Hukm al-takhyiri aw Nazariyyat al-ibaha indal usuliyyin wal-fuqaha*, Cairo, 1963.

Al-Sadlan, Salih b. Ghanim, *al-Qawa'id al-fiqhiyya al-kubra wa-ma tafarra'a anha*, Riyadh, 1996.

Sharara, Abdul Jabbar Hamad, *Nazariyyat nafy al-darar fi al-fiqh al-Islami al-muqaran*, Tehran, 1997.

Weaver, Warren, "Science and complexity", *American Scientist*, 36, 1948, pp. 536-44.

Al-Zarqa, Mustafa Ahmad, *Sharh al-qawa'id al-fiqhiyya*, Beirut, 1989 (2nd Ed).

# Chapter 4

# Effects of Local Customs

## 1 - Introduction
What is the 'Urf' (custom)? The following are definitions put forward by a number of Muslim scholars:
- What is accepted by people and is compatible to their way of thinking and is normally adopted by those considered to be of good character – Al-Ghazali (d.1111A.D.).[1]
- Action or belief in which persons persist with the concurrence of the reasoning powrs and which their natural dispositions agree to accept as right – Al-Jurjani (d.1413 A.D.).[2]
- A habit or a way of doing things that is constantly repeated, and which settles well and is accepted by people considered of good character – Ali Haider (d.?).[3]
- What is customary to a people and which they follow in their sayings, acts and in what they reject – Abdul-Wahab Al-Khallaf (d. 1956 A.D.).[4]
- The habit (or custom) of a people in their sayings or acts – Mustafa Al-Zarka (born 1904 A.D.).[5]
- What is customary to a people and which they follow in their living pattern – Abdulaziz Al-Khayyat (born 1923).[6]

As evident in the latter three definitions the trend is for more open-endedness on the part of contemporary scholars. One reason for this is the fact that writing on the Urf as a distinct topic and theory is a recent phenomenon. One of the early treatises which is often cited by contemporary scholars is that by Ibn Abdin – who completed his treatise on Urf in late 1827. This is a very recent date considering the long history of Islamic jurisprudence. The later scholars realized that the Urf's status within the *Fiqh* (Islamic jurisprudence), is as complex as other areas in jurisprudence. As a result their definitions are guarded and open-ended .

The authors of the four well-known and extensive studies on Urf are listed chronologically:
- Mohammad Amin Effendi known as "Ibn Abdin," treatise dated 1827.[7]
- Ahmad Fahmi Abu-Sanah, treatise published 1949.[8]
- Mustafa Ahmad Al-Zarka, treatise as part of a book, published 1945, revised 3rd edition, 1952 includes comments on item 2.[9]
- Abdulaziz Al-Khayyat, treatise completed and published 1977.[10]

The first treatise written in the early 19th century and the latter three from mid to the start of the fourth quarter of the 20th century – a span of only 150 years.[11] The first section of this paper owes much to Al-Zarka and Al-Khayyat's treatises.

The second section of this paper discusses the implication of the Urf on building practice in the traditional Islamic city, and how the Urf contributed to the distinctiveness and character of each city through the details of its built form and architectonics. To the knowledge of the author this is the first attempt to do this, and because of it, this paper should be viewed as exploratory in nature. The ideas presented can, no doubt, be further scrutinized and developed.

Finally, in brief passages, lessons from the traditional Islamic city in terms of the workings of the Urf are presented. Those observations should be of interest and benefit to those involved in contemporary city planning and urban design in other cultures. The paper concludes with suggestions for further research.

## 2 - Urf in Islamic Jurisprudence (*Fiqh*)
Some scholars refer to the verse 7:199 in the Quran as the basis for sanctioning the Urf. The translation of the meaning of this verse is best rendered by this author as: *Take things at their face value and bid to what is customary [or accepted by local tradition], and turn away from the ignorant.*[12] Thus the Fuqaha saw in this Quranic verse a clear sanction for accepting the Urf, and it constituted the seed for a tree of knowledge which was later developed by them as

one of the pillars for interpreting and developing the law.

The main points and observations which are extracted from the literature are intended for their relevancy to building activity. Thus what is discussed below should be primarily viewed in light of the purposes of this paper.

The origin of a habit (*Ada*) is initiated at the individual level. For every act there must be an impetus or reason. This impetus could be external to the individual, or it could emanate from within. So if the person feels content with his act in response to the impetus (whether it is external or internal), and if it is repeated, then it becomes a habit (*Ada*). If others find this habit agreeable and repeat it by imitation and it spreads in the community, then it becomes a custom or Urf, i.e. the habit of the group or community. Therefore every Urf is a habit (*Ada*), but not every habit (*Ada*) is Urf.[13]

As with a habit or act in response to an impetus, we find the same applies in language. A group of people who share a common activity such as in the trades or professions develop a language composed of a vocabulary of terms to ease communication between members of that group. In some instances these specialized terms become known to that part of the larger conunumity who are interested or involved in aspects of that group's activities or concerns. The terms then become part of the local Urf.[14]

The Urf can be initiated by order of the local authority or by its encouragement.[15] Or it can be inherited from previous generations, as occurred with the perpetuation of certain pre-Islamic customs. Or it can evolve locally in response to certain conditions or changes in the milieu of the environment.

Habits (*Adat*: plural of *Ada*) and Customs (*A'raf*: plural of *Urf*) get embedded in people and become part of their being and culture. The Fuqaha recognized that to require people to abandon their customs is a very difficult and anguishing process.[16] Thus we find that an aspect of the human trait is resistance to changes in habits and customs.

It was recognized early on in Islam that not all habits and customs were good. Many would be offensive to Islamic values and teachings. Thus the necessity emerged in the eyes of the Fuqaha (plural of Faqih: a specialist in *Fiqh* or Islamic jurisprudence) to develop a theory or reasoning to deal with this situation, i.e. how to distinguish by logic and reason between acceptable habits and customs and those which needed to be rejected because of incompatibility with Islam. The ultimate purpose for the Fuqaha was to develop the necessary framework to help in formulating rational decisions and judgments when faced with questionable habits and customs.[17]

Essentially the Urf is viewed by the Fuqaha as related to: **Linguistic** and **Practical** (a way of doing something). And it can be designated as Public (*A'm*) Urf or Private (*Khas*) Urf. The former is that which is commonly followed by an established large community or by many communities. Whereas the latter is that which is followed locally by a small community or a specific group of people belonging to a trade or profession within a community.[18] These designations can be shown to interrelate as in Figure 1.

The legitimacy of the Urf - The Urf is viewed by the Shari'a (Islamic Law) as an important basis for rulings and judgments, particularly decisions and judgments based on the knowledge and understanding of a locality.

Legitimacy of the Linguistic Urf. It is accepted that the localized language and its vocabulary should be used as a basis for rulings, judgments and/or disputes. This is so even if certain Urf terms have different meanings in classical Arabic (from which some of the terms might be derived). Thus the Fuqaha acknowledge the *Fiqh* principle that: *The basis for truth is the proof of custom.*[19] This posture by the Shari'a has encouraged the legitimization of the local dialect or "slang" in adjudicating disputes and resolving conflict. In this way there was no reason to impose, for instance, the spoken classical Arabic in the courts of various regions of the Islamic world. This also meant that judges (*qadis*) had to be well versed in the nuance of the local language and the people's customs as a whole.

Legitimacy of the Practical Urf. The opinions and writings of Fuqaha clearly demonstrate that both branches of the practical urf

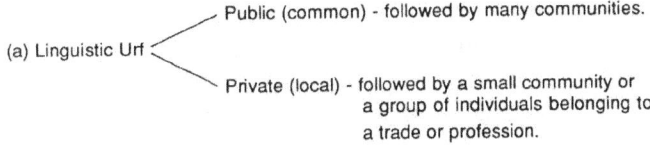

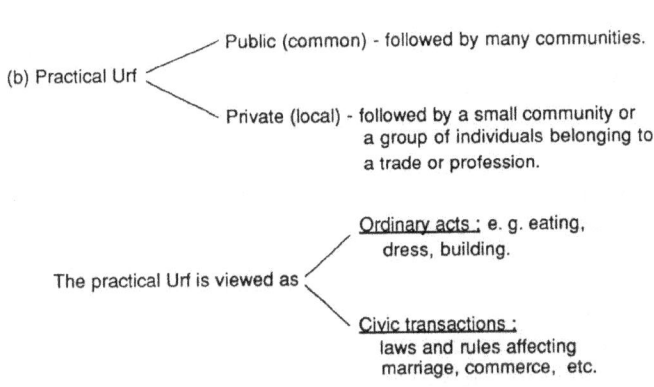

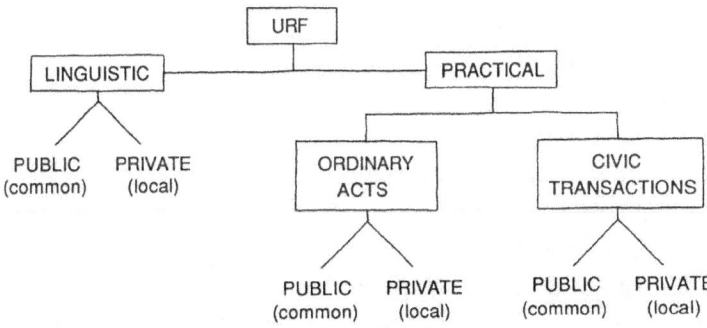

**Figure 1.** Designation of the Urf according to Fiqh scholars.

(i.e. ordinary acts and civic transactions) are used as a basis for decisions, rulings and judgments, provided that the particular Urf (which is used for such a basis) does not contravene any stipulation of the Shari'a. There is a well known *Fiqh* principle attributed to Sarkhasi: *That which is established by Urf is like that which is established by the texts.* Article 45 from the Majallat al-Ahkam al-Adliyah stipulates the principle: *Stipulating by the Urf is like stipulating by the texts.*[20]

The nature of a ruling which is based on the Urf can change if the Urf changes with time. Thus rulings must reflect the Urf as practiced and understood in a specific time and place. Therefore, a judgment based on a specific localized Urf is only implemented in that particular locality and cannot be emulated by another community with different customary conditions.[21]

For the Urf to have legitimacy it has to meet the requirements of all of the following conditions[22]:
- The Urf has to be popular and consistently followed by the majority in a community.
- The Urf has to be currently alive, and if it changes then it cannot be used for justifying or unjustifying previous decisions or acts. In other words the legitimacy of an Urf is constrained by its currency.
- When the Urf is used as a condition or as a basis for a judgment or a decision, it must not contravene a pre-existing stipulation or agreement, as this can void its legitimacy .
- The Urf must not by its use abolish or cancel a ruling from the texts or a principle of the Shari'a. This could occur in one of three situations:
    (a) It could collide with a specific Shari'a ruling from the Quran or Sunna.
    (b) It could contravene a general ruling from the texts
    (All written sources of the Shari'a).
    (c) It could differ with an opinion(s) derived by Ijtihad (Independent Reasoning).

For each of these three situations the Fuqaha have developed guidelines for determining the legitimacy of any kind of Urf – be it linguistic or practical and whether it is common or local.

The preceding text briefly explains how the Urf was viewed by the Fuqaha and its place in the Science of *Fiqh*. Implicitly it also indicates how it used to be implemented.[23]

## 3 - Implications on building practice
The implication of the above observations on building practice in the traditional Islamic city was direct and its manifestations evident in any city, particularly if viewed comparatively to other Islamic cities across space and time. Elsewhere this author has al-

luded to the Urf[24] but in this paper he will elaborate more on the implications and address its manifestation in built form. But first there are a number of observations and issues which need to be addressed before examples are presented.

At which scale of the built environment can we look for the manifestations of the Urf? On the whole the smaller the scale the more evident is the impact. Although in some instances we also find the effect on the larger scale. See the examples in Figures 3, 5, 6, 7, and 8.

Related to the first observation, the evidence indicates more prominence at a scale where individuals' decisions and building craftsmanship occurs. This is especially true in housing areas at the scale of the cluster and progressing down from that scale to more details.[25] Refer to Figures 3, 5, 6, 7, and 8.

The Urf is dynamic, i.e. it changes with time, but because of the conservative nature of people relative to their habits, the rate of change tended to be slow. In the traditional city the relative unchanging nature of building materials and technology converged with conservatism to minimize change in the Urf of building practice. Such as the persistent Urf of curving the corners of buildings to facilitate the movement of animals carrying a load. The use of pack animals continued until the advent of the car (see Figure 6).

Although there was much contact between urban centers in the ancient Islamic world which resulted in the transfer of ideas, such influences were manifest in private works of the wealthy classes and in public buildings controlled by individual patrons or the authority. Where Islamic law was operational on a day to day basis, such as in housing areas and the market places, influences from the outside, if any, were moderate. This was largely due to the respect accorded to the localized Urf.

The phenomenon of diversity within unity so apparent in traditional Islamic cities can be interpreted thus:
*Unity* was achieved by the initial concept of urban formation which the Arabs brought with them from Arabia to the various geographic regions whose people embraced Islam. This concept had a very

ancient history in the Near East region, and from the sketchy evidence available the same system with some modifications was followed during the Prophet's last ten years in Medina. His sayings regarding a number of issues which related to building activity reflected a process of reinforcing certain pre-Islamic building practices which were accepted as part of the localized Urf in Medina.[26] But because some of those customs were traced directly to the Prophet's sayings and deeds, they became enshrined as part of the Shari'a texts. They were thus legitimized on two levels: (a) they were part of the Sunnah (the Prophet's sayings and deeds), and (b) they were also localized Urf. It is at the level of their legitimacy as part of the Sunnah that they spread across the Islamic world and contributed to the process of unifying the character of Islamic cities[27] (see Figure 2).

*Diversity* was achieved due to the recognition by Islamic law of the localized Urf in both its forms: the linguistic and practical. The Shari'a recognized and protected the local vocabulary developed by those in the building trades. The terms which evolved locally had an influence in sustaining the continuity of specific local building practices and their peculiar characteristics. This was because a term from such a vocabulary tended to integrate the form and function of the physical component and its purpose as utilized

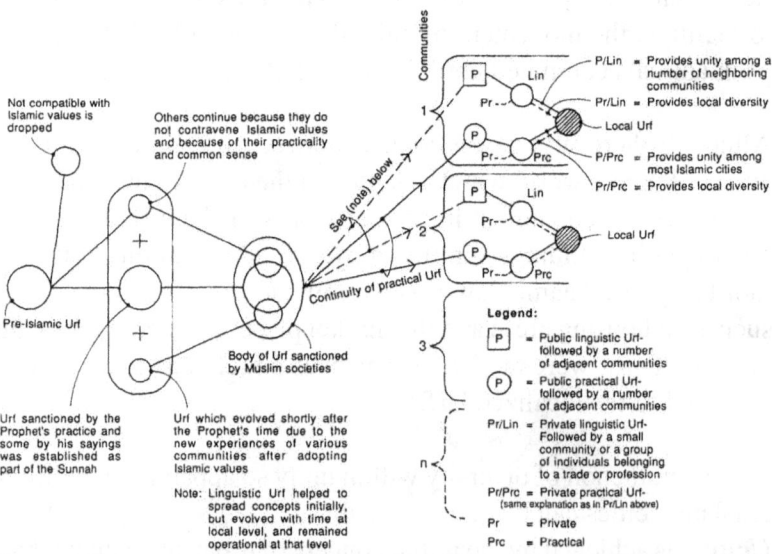

**Figure 2.** A conceptual diagram of the Urf's contribution to the phenomenon of unity and diversity in the built environment of traditional Islamic cities.

in that specific locality.[28] This continuity was also sustained by the conservative nature of traditional Islamic society (see Figure 3).

As for the practical Urf, Islamic law recognized the local peculiarity and ways of doing things of a group of individuals belonging to a specific trade or profession, as in the building trades. Thus the Urf of that trade in a particular locality was respected by the Shari'a. This occurred through the legitimization of decisions resulting from the Urf in cases of disputes or litigation. This state of

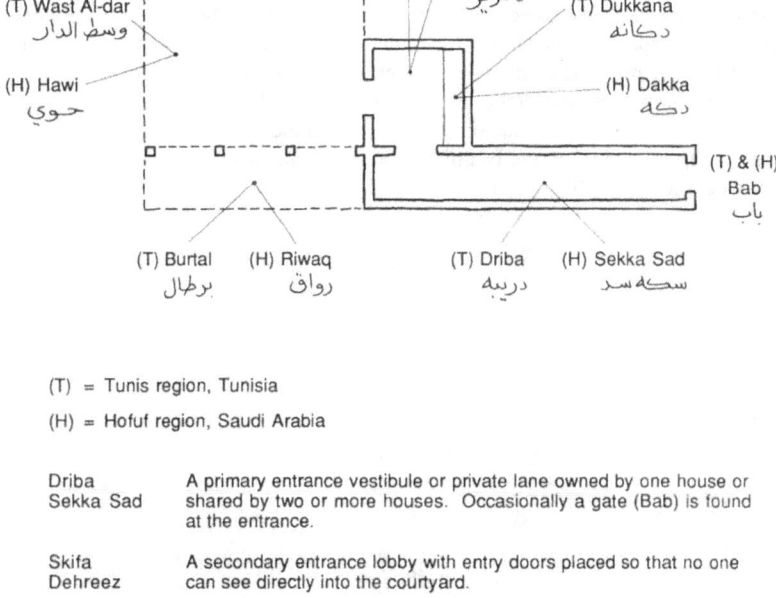

(T) = Tunis region, Tunisia
(H) = Hofuf region, Saudi Arabia

| | |
|---|---|
| Driba / Sekka Sad | A primary entrance vestibule or private lane owned by one house or shared by two or more houses. Occasionally a gate (Bab) is found at the entrance. |
| Skifa / Dehreez | A secondary entrance lobby with entry doors placed so that no one can see directly into the courtyard. |
| Dukkana / Dakka | Built-in bench. Traditionally the male owner or occupant of the house received casual visitors or salesmen. |
| Wast Al-dar / Hawi | Private courtyard open to the sky in the center of the house. |
| Burtal / Riwaq | A colonnaded gallery off the main courtyard, giving importance and sun-protection to the room behind it. This gallery could be on one, two, three, or four sides of the courtyard. |

**Figure 3.** The linguistic Urf of two regions distant from each other. The vocabulary is different but they are for the same spatial/organizational elements. However, the style and architectonics of these elements are distinct to each region. Thus we find the unity in the concepts of space and organization and the diversity in the linguistic and practical Urf which produce the specific characteristics of the region's architecture and built form.

affairs tended to perpetuate and guard the distinctiveness of local building practices and by extension the resulting built form.

Further amplification to the observations in the preceding paragraphs above is related to the issue of the relationship of Meta-principles and guidelines to localized Urf practices. Elsewhere this author has elaborated on principles and behavioral guidelines which affected the shape of the traditional Islamic city.[29] Those were general principles and could also be viewed as common Urf guidelines, i.e. Urf practice which is common to most communi-

**Figures 4A, 4B, 4C.** The distinct physical organization of Islamic cities -the initial formation of these cities followed a common concept of territorial allocation and land utilization supported by a unique system of distribution of responsibilities among all the actors involved in the decision-making process affecting building activities. This concept was spread to the far reaches of the Islamic world during the early centuries of Islam. The resulting distinct physical characteristics maintained itself despite the processes of growth and change across the centuries. This concept and its system of implementation is a prime factor which produced the phenomenon of unity among the multitude of cities in the Islamic world. A phenomenon which persisted to the early decades of the 20th century.

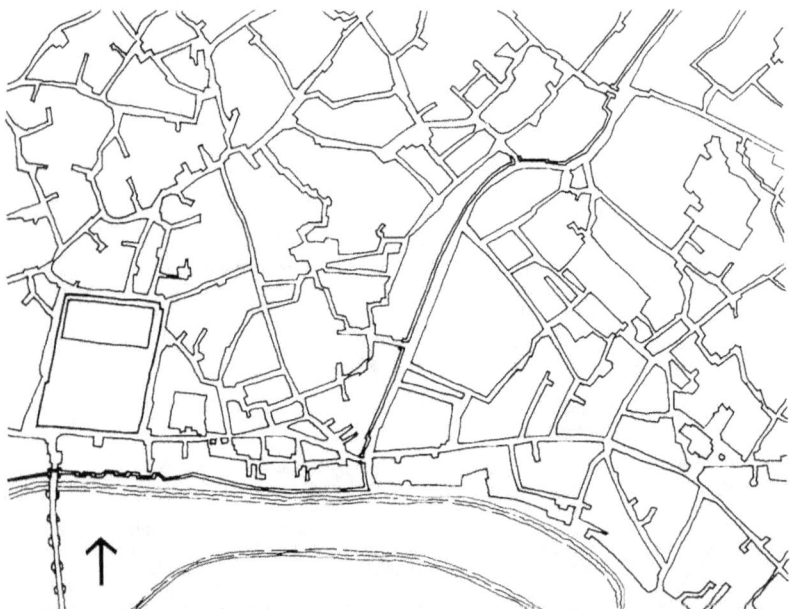

**Figure 4A.** The southern part of Cordoba in southern Spain showing the river to the south and the great mosque at the lower left corner of the sketch. After a map dated 1811 reproduced in E.A. Gutkind's *International History of City Development: Vol III, Urban Development in Southern Europe: Spain and Portugal*, The Free Press, N.Y., 1967.

ties and regions. They were followed in most Islamic cities and tended to generate the similarities we find common amongst those cities. Whereas localized Urf practices were distinct to a specific urban center or to a group of settlements within one region. Those localized practices helped to produce the distinctiveness and thus micro characteristics of each city or settlement.

An important observation can now be stated: that the nature of Islamic law when considered with its interface with the Urf and its framework for decisions – which has resulted from that interface – show the flexibility of this system of law. It is very sensitive to local conditions. It accords legitimization and protection to a locality's customs and practices and thus contributes substantially to the identity of a place through the individuality of its place-making process and its resulting built form (see Figure 2). Elsewhere the writer discussed another facet of Islamic law which further con-

**Figure 4B.** A partial map of Hofuf in eastern Saudi Arabia based on an aerial photograph dated 1935. The Al-Kut district surrounded by its own wall is shown on the upper left of the sketch. After a map by C.P. Winterhalter in his dissertation titled: *Indigenous Housing Patterns and Design Principles in the Eastern Province of Saudi Arabia*, Swiss Federal Institute of Technology, Zurich, 1981.

tributed to distinctiveness of place making. It is that guidelines for building activity and decisions emanating from this system of law are performance/intent oriented and proscriptive in nature. The ramification of this attribute alone is enormous on the quality of the built environment.[30]

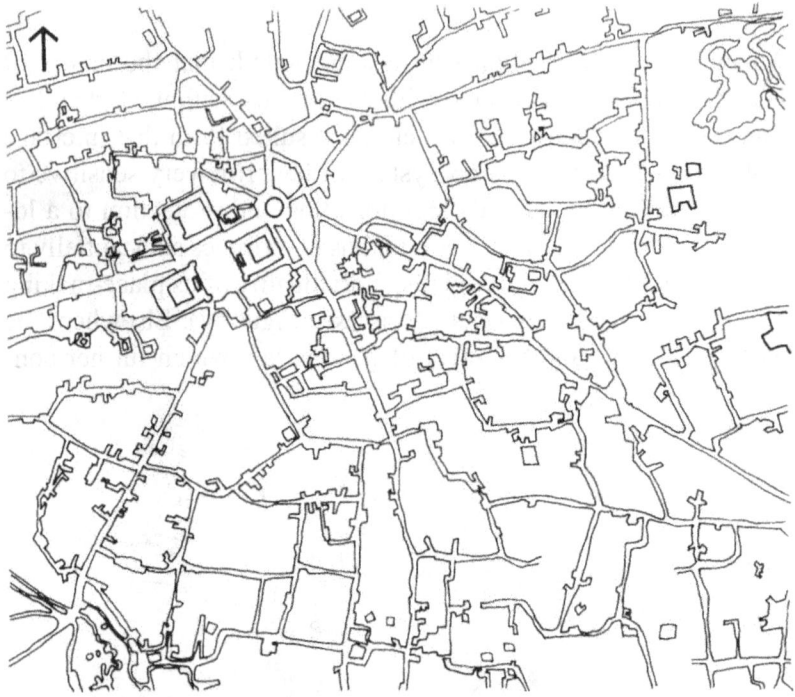

**Figure 4C.** The central part of Samarkand according to a geodesic survey of 1868, the year the city was incorporated into the Russian Empire. After the map reproduced in E.A. Gutkind's *International Histroy of City Development; Vol. VIII, Urban Development in Eastern Europe: Bulgeria, Romania, and the U.S.S.R.*, The Free Press, N.Y., 1972.

## 4 - Some lessons for contemporary urbanism and urban design

Due to the dreary sameness which resulted in our cities worldwide under the banner of "progress" and "modernism" during this century – particularly spreading after WW II, we find now that a backlash has resulted within a time frame of one generation, in just over 30 years. This is manifested under different slogans depending on the culture and country. In the Islamic countries we recognize it under the banner of demanding an "Islamic" identity

**Figures 5A, 5B.** The Sabat -an air-right structure bridging a public-right-of-way is a concept designed to provide additional space for the building to which it is attached. Islamic law recognizes this concept and there are specific guidelines governing its implementation. It is used in most Islamic cities, acting as an element of unity. The local Urf in each city shapes its architectonics and thus contributes to the phenomenon of diversity.

**Figure 5A.** View of a Sabat in Tunis. The columns supporting the structure on the left indicate that it belongs to the building on the right of the sketch. After a photograph by the author taken in the mid-1970's and published in his book *Arabic-Islamic Cities: Building & Planning Principles*, KPI, London (79) 1986.

**Figure 5B.** A Sabat in Hofuf, Saudi Arabia. Palm tree trunks are used as the main structure for support, distinctly different from the structure and building materials used in Tunis. The treatment of windows is also different. After a photograph taken by the author in early 1986.

in architecture and urban qesign.[31] Some of the Arab countries call the same thing under the banner "Arab Architecture."[32] In the West, particularly in the United States, the term "Critical Regionalism" is used for this purpose.[33] This is particularly significant because this backlash and strong feeling against sameness is occurring in a large country with a strong culture and embedded institutions, aided by the mass media and powerful advertising capabilities.

If regional identity and character is accepted as an important attribute for cities, habitat and architecture, then the strategies and methods to achieve that become an important concern. Here the careful study of the experience of other cultures, particularly in history, can be very valuable.[34] The workings of the traditional Is-

**Figures 6A, 6B.** Curving the corner of buildings which are located on public streets -a convention practiced universally in Islamic cities, towns and villages. It might have roots in pre-Islamic periods. A curved corner allows easier negotiation when turning by the rider of beast which is carrying a load, such as a camel, horse or donkey. This element contributed to the phenomenon of unity. However, its specific design and architectural treatment was governed by the local or regional Urf, contributing to diversity.

**Figure 6A.** A corner of a building in the village of Sidi Bou Sa'id north of Tunis. This example shows the enhancement of this practice by decoration, in this case with black and white inter-locking tiles. After a photograph taken in 1975 and published in *Sidi Bou Sa'id, Tunisia: A Study in Structure and Form*, edited by B. Hakim, Technical University of Nova Scotia, Hailfax, 1978.

**Figure 6B.** The corner of this building in Riyadh, Saudi Arabia is treated in a more pragmatic manner, "slicing" the building to the required height and even allowing the decoration to continue around the corner. After a photograph by John Amarantides estimated to be taken in the 1970s.

lamic city can provide us with needed insight.

It bas been over five years, from the mid-1980s, since Kenneth Frampton published ideas for designing architecture at the local level with qualities that "resist" the hegemony of what he calls 'universal civilization.' Although his suggestions are, in the view of this author, far from being comprehensive, they are nevertheless in the right direction and need to be taken seriously.[35] If we consider the last observation (in the first paragraph of this section) as addressing the 'what' of the problem and implicitly 'why'

**Figures 7A, 7B.** Design enhancement of main doors – one of the important concepts applied universally in Islamic cities is the design enhancement of the main doors of buildings, often supplemented by elaborate decoration if the owner could afford it. The main door was the primary element of the building's elevation where intentional design is applied. A clear element of unity, whereas the local Urf created the diversity, where each region developed specific design approaches and decorative motifs.

**Figure 7A.** A main door to a house in the village of Sidi Bou Sa'id, Tunisia. People in this village practiced the Urf which was predominant in the city of Tunis and its environs. The decoration is achieved by nails of two types: (i) large nails holding the door's structure together, and (ii) small nails for surface decoration of various motifs. After a photograph taken in 1975 and published in Hakim, B. (ed.) *Sidi Bou Sa 'id*, 1978.

**Figure 7B.** A main door to a house in Al-Kut district in Hofuf, Saudi Arabia. The elegant gypsum decoration above the door is typical of this region's Urf. Structural nails are commonly exposed and form part of the door's visual character. After a photograph by Mashary Al Naim taken in 1990.

it occurred, then this note on 'Resistance' should be viewed as the basis for developing a framework for working out 'how' appropriate alternative(s) may be achieved. Again the experience of the traditional Islamic city can offer us insight into an alternative framework, including the specifics of its mechanisms that was operational for over one thousand (1000) years. The following briefly addresses some of those lessons.

One of the key lessons is in the framework of the distribution of responsibilities among all actors involved in the creation, maintenance and changes in the built environment. This might be called

**Figures 8A, 8B.** Decoration of internal walls -the concept of decorating the walls of primary rooms is common in many Islamic cities. The type and nature of the decoration however was distinct to each region and sometimes to a specific town. This concept contributed to the phenomenon of unity and diversity.

**Figure 8A.** The central room of a house in the oasis town of Ghadames, Libya decorated for the occasion of marriage. The hatched areas of the sketch represent the original red color used traditionally for wedding decorations. After a photograph by Professor Intisar Azzouz of Al-Fateh University in Tripoli, Libya, as published in the illustrated presentation "Mimar Gallery" in MIMAR 1, 1981, pp. 17-23.

**Figure 8B.** A wall mural of a fruit tree with birds perched on the branches. This particular design was found in a house in Hofuf, Saudi Arabia and is a symmetrical design of an orange tree with two birds. It is approximately five feet tall. The trunk, branches and leaves are painted dark green and the oranges are in a mustard-yellow color. It is possible that this design was inspired by the Quran which mentions the abundance of fruit trees in Paradise. After a photograph taken in the 1970's, from King Faisal University 's slide collection. Photographer unknown.

the System of Production, or for short 'the System,' which involves the following questions: How is land distributed; how is space allocated; what is considered public and what is private; how do the public/private spheres interrelate; who is responsible for what? In cases of disputes, what is the mechanism of control and authority in resolving conflicts; who is responsible for land subdivision — and in design decisions: what is the role of the community and the user in the process?[36] These are the type of questions which need to be carefully studied in terms of what is occurring now and how it used to occur in the traditional Islamic city. It is only after careful analysis and understanding of the two systems that any fresh strategies can be formulated. The experience of cities in other cultures where a high level of quality in the built environ-

**Figures 9A, 9B, 9C, 9D.** The persistence of the Urf in contemporary times -examples from Dammam, Saudi Arabia. After photographs taken by the author in June 1989 in the "District 37" housing area, with the exception of photograph 9A taken in early 1986. This district was developed in the 1980s. The basis for development of this and similar housing areas in Saudi Arabia is descibed thus: municipal planners subdivide the land, the plots are then allocated to individuals who are then responsible for building their houses according to municipal regulations and requirements of the Real Estate Development Fund which loans the funds, interest free, to the owners. The system of subdivision which was earlier imposed by the govenrment divides the land into plots of approximately square shapes averaging in area of 580 square meters with a requirement of setbacks from all sides and a maximum allowable footprint area of 60% of the plot. Almost all of the house designs are based on the use of exterior windows which has resulted in overlooking problems. People have responded by developing counter measures which have evolved into contemporary customs (Urf).

**Figure 9A.** A corner of a house which shows the use of five reccent customs: (i) conversion of the garage into a shop. This is a popular Urf especially if the location is suitable; (ii) the use of the bench (dakka) near the shop for visits; (iii) the use of high perimeter walls for privacy and security; (iv) the use of colored glass panels located on top of fence and balcony walls for additional privacy protection from opposite neighbors; and (v) the use of arch motifs, in this case in the balcony, to express allegiance to Islamic culture. A prevalent linkage in the minds of the popular sector.

ment was achieved, need to be scrutinized for comparison so as to increase the sampling from which we can draw inspiration and specific lessons.[37]

As to the nature of the tools and mechanisms which directly affect the contemporary built environment – it is absolutely essential to evaluate those carefully and not take for granted their various stipulations. Sometimes it is in the details (or fine print) of these controls that the root of many of our problems reside. Elsewhere this writer has discussed the differences between contemporary Western zoning and planning tools with those that were operational in the traditional Islamic city. The impacts on the quality of the built environment of these two very different types of systems is enormous. The lessons of the Islamic city is particularly critical in this regard.[38]

The following question needs to be briefly addressed: How does the Urf apply in the case of new building types, new materials and new urban functions? The case of contemporary Saudi Arabia might illuminate the answer. Here deeply rooted social customs such as the concern for privacy persists and manifests itself in new solutions in response to the new practices of land subdivision and built form configurations resulting from imported regulations, such as the setback requirements for individual houses from plot boundaries. The illustrations in Figure 9 clearly show the ramifications – these have in turn generated new customs (Urf) in dealing with the recent changes in land use and building materials. It should be noted that the "new Urf ' is primarily the invention of

**Figure 9B.** The persistence of the Ud enhancing the front door to the house with a special design (see Figure 7). Since the front door has become part of the perimeter fence wall in the contemporary situation, people have shifted their attention to the front gate for special treatment. This has now become a strong Urf in most of Saudi Arabia, and a great variety of approaches and designs have evolved

**Figure 9C.** This example shows that the owner has responded to the visual corridors of opposite neighbors by increasing the height of his fence wall only in those locations where it is necessary. Most people however respond by increasing the height uniformly.

**Figure 9D.** With the requirement of setbacks from all sides and the necessity of opening windows for light and ventilation, people have responded by erecting lightweight walls, mainly of corrugated metal, to prevent overlooking. This is now a common Urf widely used in Saudi Arabia.

the users in the face of changes.

Unfortunately the public sector's performance is dismal in dealing with the changes brought about by new building types, materials and urban functions. It responds with negative practices and methods, facilitating the degradation of the quality of the built environment. This is primarily due to the clash resulting from imported ideas and associated regulations (dictated by the central government on the local level), with embedded deep rooted customs. Users deal with this problem on a day to day practical basis resulting in adaptations which might or might not be ideal. Whereas the public sector, comprised of appointed municipal officials with little or no experience or training, deal with such problems at a distance and in a superficial manner.

## 5 - Areas for further research

This paper should be viewed as a first draft in dealing with the Urf as an important factor in shaping the traditional Islamic city. It has covered the basic concepts of the Urf within the Fiqh and the ramification of that status on its legitimacy in the day to day decision making process as affecting building practice. The importance of both the 'linguistic' and 'practical' Urf is stressed, and how each type reinforced the other in building, thus helping to perpetuate a local system across long spans of time.

In view of the issues which the paper has covered, three important areas of research need to be undertaken so that understanding of this topic is further enhanced.

Research of traditional cases based on the Urf, both in the records of local *qadis* (judges) and in the writing of *muftis* (specialists on law). This is primarily a literature search. Urf courts were operational in North African countries during the French occupation. The records of those courts need to be carefully examined for cases related to building disputes. Some of these courts, such as in Tunis, continue to function. What is interesting to establish is the nature of the Urf rulings. How deviant, if at all, were they from the principles of the Shari'a and what was their impact on built form and the manner local identity was perpetuated? This type of research is particularly important, since the records of, say the last two hundred (200) years, will coincide closely with the on-ground situation of the built form as it stands now. Assuming that can be physically examined – without resorting to elaborate archaeological techniques – then the results will reflect very closely to what occurred within the time-frame indicated, even though some foundation outlines may date back to very early configurations. The use of successive aerial photos since the early decades of the 20$^{th}$ century is an important tool for such a study.

Field research of selected and representative traditional Islamic cities is essential. These field studies could document the design language (linguistic Urf) which was operational, and the actual physical configuration and arrangements which the vocabulary of the local design language referred to. The results will provide us with a good sampling of the local linguistic Urf which was operational in a specific time and place. As mentioned earlier in this paper, the local design language was used by the community at large and was recognized by the Shari'a in resolving local conflicts arising from building activity. Comparative study of the results of surveys of a number of cities from different regions of the Islamic World would enhance our understanding and appreciation of the built form qualities of those cities. The results of this type of research will also illuminate the design decision-making process underlying the built form and the changes that have occurred over time.

Changes brought about by increasing modernizations due to new building types, new materials, and new urban functions in contemporary times, and the impacts these changes have had on the traditional Urf, be it practical or linguistic, need to be the concern of serious study in numerous Islamic cities. Such research should address among other things, the phenomenon of the clash resulting from imported and imposed (by central authoritarian governments) land use techniques and associated regulations with embedded local practices and systems of decision-making on the culture of the people and the resulting quality of the built environment. It should also address means of modifying or changing regulations to make them sensitive to local conditions and the values shared by the population. A careful study of people's responses to modernization and contemporary changes is essential. This will illuminate the culture's priorities in the face of imposed and/or desired changes in the built environment.

If this paper has opened a new window on the workings of the traditional Islamic city and has broadened our general understanding of the processes of urbanism and urban design, then it has achieved its purpose.

## Acknowledgements

This paper was originally presented at the "International Conference on Urbanism in Islam," held in Tokyo, Japan, October, 1989. It was subsequently presented at the "Islam and Public Law" conference organized by the School of Oriental and African Studies and held in London, U.K., June, 1990.

The author is most grateful for the assistance of Mr. Yahya Al-Najjar for drawing the final illustrations, at a time when it was impossible for the author to allocate the time to undertake this task.

## Notes

[1] Abu Hamid Muhammad bin Mohammad Al-Ghazali (d. 505 A.H./1111 A.D.), *Al-Mustasfa min 'ImAl-Usul*, 2 Volumes. First printed by al-Amiriyah Press, Cairo 1322 A.H./1904 A.D.

[2] Al-Jurjani (d. 816 A.H./1413 A.D.) *Al-Ta'rifat*. The translation from the Arabic is by R. Levy from the article 'Urf' in *Encyclopedia of Islam*, 1st ed., Leiden and London, 1913-1934.

[3] Ali Haider (d. * ?) Durar Al-Hukkam: *Sharh Majallat Al-Ahkam*. (written in 1875), translated from Turkish to Arabic by Fahmi Al-Husaini, Dar Al-Kutub Al-Ilmiyah, Beirut, First Printing 1991. (*) Year of death could not be located, but if he had written this book in his 50s, then the latest date of death would be within the first decade of the 20th century.

[4] Abdul-Wahab Al-Khallaf (d. 1956 AD.) *Im Usul Al-Fiqh*. 1st ed. 1942, Dar Al-Qalam, Kuwait, 15th Printing, 1983.

[5] Mustafa Ahmed Al-Zarka (1945) *Al-Madkhal Al-Fiqhi Al-Am*. 2 Volumes, 3rd revised ed. 1952 - 10th Printing 1968 by Tarbin Press, Damascus.

[6] Abdul Aziz Al-Khayyat (1977) *Nadariyat Al-Urf*. Maktabat Al-Aqsa, Amman.

[7] Mohammad Amin Abdin, known as "Ibo Abdin," (d. 1836 A.D.), "Nashr al-Urf fi bina bad al-Ahkam 'la al-Urf," in *Majmu't Rasa'l Ibn Abdin*. 2 volumes, Printed by Dar Ihya al-Turath al-Arabi, Beirut, n.d.

[8] Ahmad Fahmi Abu-Sanah, *Al-Urf wa al-'Ada fi Ra 'yal-Fuqaha*. Al-Azhar

Press, Cairo, 1949.

[9] Part five of Volume 2 entitled "Nadariyat al-Urf" in the reference cited in note 5 above.

[10] Reference cited in note 6 above.

[11] The author has come across other sources of interest: an article "Urf and Law in Islam" by Farhat J. Ziadeh, pp. 60-67 in *The World of Islam*, edited by James Kritzeck and R. Bayly Winder, Macmillan & Co. Ltd., London 1959. It is short and useful for clarifying the semantic history of the term. There is a short section on the Urf, pp. 110-118 by Mohammad Faruq Al-Nabhan in his book *Abhath Islamiyah*, published by Mu'asasat Al-Risalah, Beirut 1986. This is particularly illuminating for the working of the Urf in North Africa. That area's Fiqh and Urf traditions is fully covered by Abdulaziz Binabdullah in *Mu'alimat al-Fiqh al-Maliki*, published by Dar al-Gharb al-lslami, Beirut 1983.

[12] This verse and many others and numerous sayings of the Prophet are fully documented as Appendix 1 in this author's book: Besim S. Hakim, *Arabic-Islamic Cities: Building & Planning Principles*, Kegan Paul International, London [1979] 1986, 2nd hardback edition 1988. Verse 7:199 appears on page 144.

[13] Although the writer has benefited from a number of sources in developing the first section of this paper, he has for the sake of being brief only made specific reference to M. Al-Zarka's book cited in note 5 above. The material in that book is divided into sequentially numbered paragraphs. Cited below are the number of paragraphs rather than the page numbers, as those differ by edition.

[14] Al-Zarka (cited in note 5), paragraph 477.

[15] For a discussion of the contrast between Urf as people's customs and Urf as dictatorial top down rulings, see F.J. Ziadah "Urf and Law in Islam," cited in note 11.

[16] Al-Zarka (cited in note 5), paragraph 479.

[17] Ibid., Paragraphs 480 and 508 to 533.

[18] Ibid., Paragraphs 484 and 486 to 490.

[19] Ibid., Paragraphs 493 to 495.

[20] Ibid., Paragraph 496.

[21] Ibid., Paragraph 502.

[22] Ibid., Paragraphs 503 to 509.

[23] The presentation in the first section is adequate for the purposes of this paper. For a fuller discussion the author refers the reader to the treatises -all in

Arabic -of lbn Abdin (cited in note 7), Abu-Sanah (cited in note 8), Al-Zarka (cited in note 5) and Al-Khayyat (cited in note 6).

[24] See Hakim, *Arabic-Islamic Cities* (cited in note 12) and the. article by this author "Islamic Architecture and Urbanism" in *Encyclopedia of Architecture*, Vol. 3, pp. 86-103, John Wiley & Sons, Inc., New York, 1989.

[25] See Hakim, *Arabic-Islamic Cities*, pp. 126 & 127, and B. Hakim (ed.) *Sidi Bou Sa 'id, Tunisia: A Study in Structure and Form*, Technical University of Nova Scotia, Canada, 1978. Updated 2009 edition available from Amazon. com

[26] For a complete discussion of the principles and behavioral guidelines which helped to unify the character of Islamic cities, see Hakim, *Arabic-Islamic Cities*, pp. 18-22. Two illustrative examples are cited here: (1) the Prophet's stipulation of 7 cubits (3.20 meters) as a minimum Right-of-Way for through public streets to allow two fully loaded camels to pass – is due to the fact that it was an implicit Urf because the camel had become the primary mode of transport about 300 years before the Prophet's time; (2) the Aqd or wall bond for the identification of ownership of walls meeting at right angles. For a full discussion of the Aqd see footnote 78 on page 174 of the author's book, first cited in note 12 above.

[27] One of the elements which established this unity was the predominant use of the concept of a building surrounding its open courtyard, especially for houses - despite the fact this plan arrangement is not suitable for cold climates experiencing heavy snowfall. But because of its legitimacy as part of the Sunnah, we find its application and use in distant cities like Kabul in Afghanistan where heavy snowfall is experienced rendering this model inefficient and cumbersome for its users.

[28] See Chapter 2 "A design language: urban and architectural elements" in Hakim: *Arabic-Islamic Cities*. Pages 98-101 are comprehensive tables of terms which were the common linguistic Urf in Tunisia.

[29] See Chapter 1 "Islamic law and neighborhood building guidelines" in Hakim, *Arabic-Islamic Cities* for a complete discussion of these principles and behavioral guidelines.

[30] See Chapter 4 "Conclusions" in Hakim, *Arabic-Islamic Cities*, and Hakim "Islamic Architecture and Urbanism" in *Encyclopedia of Architecture* (cited in note 24 above), especially pp. 97 to 102.

[31] The early 1980's (ushering the year 1400 A.D. and the 15th Islamic century) witnessed a number of conferences, such as the 'International Symposium on Islamic Architecture and Urbanism' held in January 1980 at King Faisal University, Dammam, Saudi Arabia. The first awards of the Aga Khan Awards for Architecture were given in 1980, and the seminars sponsored by the Awards Program were held in various locations. Shortly after that the King Fahd Award for Islamic Architecture was launched - for students work only. Mag-

azines appeared addressing this concern, such as MIMAR which is funded by the Aga Khan, and AL-BINA which is privately published in Saudi Arabia.

[32] The term "Arab Architecture" is not valid , whereas "Arab-Islamic" is. This author has discussed the basis for this terminology in the Introduction of his *Arabic-Islamic Cities*. The Arab League and its organizations tend to promote this designation. In Iraq a conference was held in September 1980 entitled 'International Symposium on Arab Architectural Heritage and our Contemporary Architecture.' Then in February 1981 a conference sponsored by the Arab Towns Or ganization entitled 'The Arab City' was held in Medina, Saudi Arabia. The bi-monthly journal *al-Madinah Al-Arabiya* was launched in the early 80's and is published by that organization.

[33] This term was first postulated by Alexander Tzonis and Liane Lefaivre in 1981, and subsequently codified by Kenneth Frampton into a theory (references are cited in note 35 below). Recently two International Seminars on "Critical Regionalism" were held. The first in January 1989 at the College of Environmental Design, California State Polytechnic University, Pomona, followed by the second at the Delft Technical University in Holland in June 1990. A third seminar is planned to be held in 1991 at the Milan Polytechnic.

[34] This author has been teaching an introductory course in llistory and Theory for undergraduate architecture students since 1986 at King Faisal University, Dammam, where the emphasis is on uncovering principles and patterns which have occurred in various cultures. For details refer to his paper "Teaching llistory by Searching for Emics and Ethics" published in proceedings of 77th Annual Meeting of the Association of Collegiate Schools of Architecture, held in Chicago, March 1989, pp. 167-180. It was subsequently published in *Design Studies*, Vol.12, No.I , January 1991, pp. 19-29. The course was one of three winners of the American Institute of Architects (AIA) 1990 Education Honors Award.

[35] The two pertinent articles by Kenneth Frampton on this topic are: (1) "Towards a Critical Regionalism: Six Points for an Architecture of Resistance" in *The Anti-Aesthetic*, edited by Hal Foster, Bay Press, Washington, 1983, and (2) "Place - Form and Cultural Identity" (in Italian and English) in *Domus* #673, June 1986, pp. 19-24.

[36] A number of people have addressed these issues, such as John F.C. Turner in his various articles on housing, and especially in his seminal book *Housing by People*, Marion Boyars, London 1976. More recently by N.J. Habraken in a theoretical treatise entitled *Transformations of the Site*, Awater Press, Cambridge, Mass., 1983. This author has addressed some of these issues as part of a larger framework of concerns in the article "Recycling Positive Aspects of Tradition in Contemporary Cities: Some Issues for Consideration," in the proceedings of *The Second International Conference on Urbanism in Islam*, held in Tokyo, Japan, November 1990. A revised version is published in the journal, *Cities*, Vol.8, No. 4, November 1991, pp. 274-277.

[37] Christopher Alexander and his colleagues have tried to do this by amalgamating ideas rooted in various cultures in their extensive collection of patterns as published in *A Pattern Language*, Oxford University Press, N.Y., 1977. For how some of those patterns exist in an Arab-Islamic village, see the Conclusions of *Sidi Bou Sa 'id: Tunisia* (cited in note 25 above).

[38] See the author's articles "Islamic Architecture and Urbanism" in *Encyclopedia of Architecture* (cited in note 24 above) and "Recycling Positive Aspects of Tradition in Contemporary Cities: Some Issues for Consideration" (cited in note 36 above).

# Chapter 5

# Case of 19th- c Northern Nigeria

## 1 - Introduction

A number of scholars have written about the Sokoto Caliphate, generally recognized as commencing in 1808 (with the successes of the *Jihad* of Uthman dan Fodio) and ending at the hands of the British colonists in 1903 (see Hunwick, 1995; Johnston, 1967; Kani and Gandi, 1990; Last, 1967; Smith, 1960; Sulaiman, 1987; Usman, 1979).

Although scholars interested in art history and architecture have produced studies of this period (see Bourdier and Minh-ha, 1996; Moughtin, 1985; Prussin, 1986; Schwerdtfeger, 1982), none have addressed the underlying rationale, rules, and mechanisms for decision making that shaped the cities built during this period or previously existing cities that were affected by rules reaffirmed during the 19th century. The purpose of this study is to articulate the underlying rules that were followed in the processes of decision making, which determined the layout and organization of towns and cities. To discover those rules with accuracy, we have studied the relevant manuscripts written at the outset of this period by the *Fodiawa* trio — Shehu Uthman, his brother Abdallah (known in the region as Abdullahi), and son Muhammad Bello — and, subsequently, by other scholars.[1]

The writings of the *Fodiawa* trio are rooted in the works of earlier Muslim scholars from North Africa and the Middle East. Our consultation of those works clarified the intentions of the trio, namely, to revive the *Shari'a* (Islamic law) and to establish a society that would be governed accordingly. Uthman's teachers, his family, and others who followed him were members of the Maliki *madh-*

*hab* (school of law). They affirmed their respect for the Quran and *Sunnah* of the Prophet (i.e., the Prophet's sayings and deeds), for the opinions and scholarship of the four *Imams*, and for the precedents set by the four righteous *caliphs*.[2] Whenever appropriate and necessary, they consulted the opinions of scholars from other schools of law to clarify aspects of certain rulings.

The study consists of four parts and a conclusion. Its purpose is to achieve the following:
1. understand the mindset of the founding fathers of the Sokoto Caliphate as it related to issues affecting the built environment, particularly that of towns and cities;
2. elucidate the specific issues affecting urban development and the control of change in the built environment;
3. illustrate the material by studying a city that flourished during the Sokoto Caliphate;
4. discuss the theoretical implications of the study and point the way for further research.

## 2 - Urbanization: relationship with people living outside cities and villages (primarily nomads), the role of *ribats* (fortified settlements), and the land tenure system

Shortly before the year 1230 Hijri/1815 C.E., Muhammad al-Jailani asked Muhammad Bello for advice regarding the fact that he travels a great deal, is not settled, and therefore is unable to gather his community. Bello responded by writing the treatise *Jawab shafi' wa-khitab minna kafin*,[3] in which he explained that bedouin, who know only a nomadic lifestyle, are not expected to settle down and that people who live in villages and cities are not expected to revert to the bedouin lifestyle. In general the Prophet encouraged people to live in villages and cities, except when political necessity, or *fitna*, makes it desirable to escape the city.[4] Even five households can pray together as a *jama'ah* (group); thus, living in a village is better than living as a bedouin, and living in a city is better than living in a village.[5] This relationship is reinforced by what the *Fuqaha* (Muslim jurists) have said about finding a *laqit* (abandoned child) — that it is permissible to transfer him/her from the countryside to a village or from a village to a city but not the reverse.[6]

However, the Prophet permitted the city or village dweller to live in the countryside for two months during a year, and he said that those who live in the countryside longer than that must be viewed as *A'rabi* (nomad).[7] Those who flee the city to escape *fitna* should not be viewed as reverting to nomadism, but it is preferable to stay on in the city to try to change or eliminate the *fitna*.[8] Alternatively, it is sometimes necessary for bedouin to reside in villages or cities if these are located near disputed borders and their assistance is needed to defend Muslim territories, as was the case of Basra, Kufa, Damascus, and Fustat during the reign of the Caliph Umar (r. 13-23/634-644).[9]

Building a defensive wall or moat is mandatory if the community and its leaders decide that it is needed. The example for this was set by the Prophet in Medina.[10] Bello cites other examples mentioned by Qadi Iyad and al-Maghili.[11] He also cites *al-Miyar* by al-Wansharisi, who lists five conditions that make it obligatory for residents to be directly involved in defending their town or city when there are no resources available in the *Bayt al-Mal* (treasury).[12] Bello indicates that this obligation is based on the principle that "harm must not be alleviated by an equal or greater harm, but by a lesser harm." In other words, demanding the direct involvement and assistance of the residents, although burdensome, is a lesser harm than allowing the enemy to enter or threaten the city.[13] Bello concludes his treatise by saying that he, his father, his uncle, and others have undertaken to build cities and mosques to help strengthen the Islamic community. They have also educated people in the cities on how to conduct themselves as Muslims. In addition, they have assigned various individuals to different posts and responsibilities to manage society's needs.[14] He adds that the affairs of bedouin should be considered by encouraging each tribe to designate a representative who will appoint a teacher and *Imam* for their children. The *Imam* will lead their prayers, teach them matters relating to religious observances, and teach them the proper interaction between members of their society. The Bedouin should also be encouraged to raise more camels, horses, and sheep, and less cattle, as this will strengthen their contribution to the defense of Muslim territories. In this connection, Bello cites the Prophet's sayings on the virtues of raising horses.[15]

Bello affirms the importance of living in cities and villages. He classified bedouin, who live outside of urban society, as *ra'iya* (people who are under the jurisdiction of the urbanized society in towns or cities). Bello uses the metaphor of the shepherd who is responsible for his sheep and emphasizes the importance of town or city dwellers to spend about two months per year with bedouin.[16] In this treatise Bello summarizes the views of Shehu Uthman and his disciples towards urbanization, urbanized society, and its relationship with bedouin living in the countryside, and he establishes the importance of cities and settlements for the success of *jihad*.[17]

In another treatise entitled *Kitab al-Ribat wa al-Hirasa* (the book on *Ribats* and guarding), Muhammad Bello addressed the importance of establishing *ribats* (fortified settlements for defensive purposes) located at or near the territorial boundaries of the Sokoto Caliphate. This is primarily a work of religious ethics and obligations in which the author explains the religious virtues associated with establishing and guarding *ribats*.[18]

To further understand the mindset and related concepts of urbanization in *Hausa* societies, we refer the reader to two recent studies published in the mid-1970s. Both authors analyze *Hausa* linguistic terms to develop their findings (see Dalby, 1975; Yusuf, 1974).[19]

We now turn to the land tenure system that was prevalent during the Sokoto Caliphate in the 19th century. In a manuscript entitled *Ta'lim al-radi fi asbab al-ikhtisas bi-mawat al-aradi*,[20] Abdallah Fodio delineates a number of mechanisms that affected the process of urbanization and patterns of land use. The first is *iqta*, the allocation of land to an individual or group by the *Imam*, the ruler, or by his agent. Abdallah specifies five categories of land whose allocation is controlled by the mechanism of *iqta*.[21] The second important mechanism of urbanization is *ihya al-mawat*, literally revivification of dead land, i.e., land that is not owned or utilized by anybody, as evidenced by the fact that there is no trace of a structure, markers, or signs of cultivation on it.

The status of dead land relative to its proximity to built-up areas of the city or settlement has been discussed extensively by Muslim jurists. The predominant view is that if the dead land is very close to built-up areas, then the permission of the *Imam* (religious head of the community who leads the Friday noon prayers) is required before reviving it. Otherwise, an individual can claim it for revivification. The first step is usually the delineation of the boundary with markers. Abdallah's opinion about what constitutes "near" or "far" is conditioned by the *harim*, the area surrounding a town, plot of land, or well (discussed below). If the land in question is within the *harim* of the built-up area, then the permission of the *Imam* is required; otherwise, no permission is needed. Abdallah also stipulates that if a structure or cultivation on revived land is neglected and falls into ruin, then another person can take over the land and revive it again. Abdallah outlines specific conditions for how ownership of a revived plot of land is established.[22]

The third mechanism is *harim* (the zone surrounding a property or structure), which is necessary for its function, such as pathways and roads, so that other people are prohibited from obstructing or building upon it. The *harim* also refers to a space surrounding a well that protects it from damage, maintains the well's integrity, and prevents the pollution of its water. *Harim* is effective at various levels of the built and natural environments, such as the village or city as a whole, alignment on both sides of rivers, and forests. At the neighborhood level, the term *harim* signifies the area surrounding clusters of compounds, roads and pathways between them, and access to neighborhood farms.[23]

Abdallah's fourth mechanism is sources of water. He identifies each source and specifies conditions for its utilization: public, such as rivers; private, such as wells; and water that can be collected from rainwater.[24] A fifth mechanism relates to the availability of areas for pasture in public and private lands and the conditions for their utilization.[25]

## 3 - Framework of *qawa'id fiqhiya* (fiqh principles): underlying the rationale for the scope of the *ahkam* (rules) that were developed by Muslim scholars

A survey of the literature by the *Fodiawa* trio and others who followed them demonstrates the importance of *Qawa'id Fiqhiya* (*Fiqh* principles) in establishing the basis and rationale for the suggestions and prescriptions that they have advocated for the Muslim community, including rules addressing various aspects of the built environment.

Here we briefly explain the history of the development of this branch of the *fiqh* sciences. We will then establish the framework of a hierarchy of *Qawa'id* (principles), pointing out which of the *Fodiawa* trio and their successors cited particular *qawa'id*. This method of analysis will establish the rationale for the principles as they were understood by the leaders and *fuqaha* (Muslim jurists) of the Sokoto Caliphate.

The *fuqaha* generally define the term *Qa'ida* (principle) as a "general ruling that applies to its particulars," or "a ruling addressing a general situation but that also applies to the particulars of that situation," or "an overarching rule that applies to the various levels of a situation or a problem."[26] These *Qawa'id* were not conceived and written down at a specific time by known individuals; rather, they evolved over time as the science of *Fiqh* was developing. With the exception of *Qawa'id* that can be attributed to a Qur'anic verse or a saying of the Prophet, these principles cannot be attributed to specific authors unless a link can be established to a specific text.[27]

Hanafi jurists were the first to establish the parameters for formulating *Qawa'id*. Qarafi (d. 684/1285) indicates that in earlier periods the *Qawa'id* were known as *Usul*.[28] Ibn Nujaym, in the introduction to his *al-Ashbah wa al-Naza'ir*, mentions that Abu Tahir al-Dabbas, who lived in the late third century/ninth century, was the first scholar to compile *Qawa'id*, of which he identified 17.[29] Five of those became the central *Qawa'id* for establishing *Shari'a* rulings.[30] Figure 1 displays the original Arabic and English translations.

The Shafi'i, Hanbali, Maliki, and Shi'i schools of law followed the Hanafi school in adopting and developing the science of *Qawa'id*.[31] All schools of law agree that these five *Qawa'id* constitute a framework under which other *Qawa'id* fit, covering most issues addressed by the *Fiqh* (see al-Sadlan, 1999). The central *Qa'ida*, *al-darar yuzal* (harm should be eliminated), is the most influential, and it is applied to issues relating to decisions affecting the built environment. The five central *Qawa'id* and their related sub-*Qawa'id* should be viewed as a symbiotic system in which a concept or decision related to any one of them is affected by, or affects, the others (see Heinrichs, 2002).

The *Fodiawas* viewed the articulation of judgments and rules derived from the *Qawa'id* as part of *Siyasa al-Shar'iya* (governance in accordance with the *Shari'a*). They were particularly influenced by the work of a Maliki scholar from Medina, Ibn Farhun (d. 799/1397), author of *Tabsirat al-Hukkam*.[32] The use of *Siyasa al-Shar'iya* as a distinct doctrine for organizing the content of legal scholarship is especially evident in Abdallah Fodio's treatise, *Dia al-Hukkam*.[33] The treatise is divided into five topics. The sequence of the first four topics was influenced by Uthman dan Fodio's well-known declaration of policies in his *Wathiqat ahl al-Sudan* (see Bivar, 1961). Abdallah added a fifth topic devoted to *Siyasa al-Shar'iya*, the last section of which specifically addresses issues relating to the prevention of damages to neighbors and others.

Figure 1. *Qawa'id Fiqhiya* in their original Arabic and English translations grouped by the five central *Qawa'id*. These are cited in the treaties of Uthman dan Fodio, Abdallah Fodio, Muhammad Bello, and Idris b. Khalid b. Muhammad. The author citing each *Qa'ida* is identified thus: Uthman (U), Abdallah (A, followed by the number of his treatise), Muhammad (M), and Idris (I).

Figure 1 lists the specific *Qawa'id* that affect the formulation of policy and rules relating to the management of the built environment, which are cited by the *Fodiawa* trio and by Idris b. Khaled b. Muhammad in their respective treatises. They are arranged by the five central *Qawa'id*. The author and title of his treatise, from which the *Qawa'id* are taken, are indicated below:
- Uthman dan Fodio (d. 1232/1817)
  — Treatise: *Kitab Tanbih al-Hukkam*[34]
- Abdallah Fodio (d. 1245/1829)
  — Treatise 1: *Diya al-hukkam fi-ma lahum wa-alayhim min al-ahkam*[35]
  — Treatise 2: *Jawab al-sa'il fi bina' al-husn*[36]
  — Treatise 3: *Diya al-Siyasat wa fatawi al-nawazil*[37]
- Muhammad Bello (d. 1253/1837)
  — Treatise: *Kitab al-tahrir fi qawa'id al-tabsir lil-siyasat*[38]
- Idris bin Khalid bin Muhammad (active in 1246/1830); he was *Qadi* of Gwandu during the reign of Ibrahim Khalil bin Abdallah Fodio (d. 1276/1860).
  — Treatise: *Jami ahammu masa'il al-ahkam fi qat'i al-khisam mimma ishtaddat-ilayhi hajat al-hukkam*.[39] Idris's treatise is the most comprehensive of all and, beyond the works of the *Fodiawa* trio, is a good example of a source that contains *Qawa'id Fiqhiya* of relevance to rule formulation for the management of the built environment.

There are also two other scholars who wrote short treatises and who have specified *Qawa'id* relating to Group 1, *al-darar yuzal* (harm should be eliminated): Abdul Qadir b. al-Mustafa (d. 1280/1864), in his treatise *Nubdhat bin Mustafa min kutub al-a'imma* (see Hunwick, 1995:221); and Ibn Ishaq b. Umar (d. 1303/1885), in his *Ajwiba li-ba'd al-as'ila* (see Hunwick, 1995:237).

This survey of specific *Qawa'id* touched upon and/or discussed by the *Fodiawa* trio and Idris bin Khalid are included in this study to demonstrate that the basis of the rules, which were developed for various conditions related to change and growth in the built environment, were derived from or influenced by an understanding of the intent of the *Qawa'id* as a system of overarching meta-principles affecting all aspects of societal activities, including construction and particularly the management of the built environment at the neighborhood level. It is beyond the scope of this study to demonstrate how each of the rules, discussed in the following section, was actually derived from the *Qawa'id* as a cumulative body of knowledge or from a specific *Qa'ida*. This requires a separate study with an emphasis on detailed aspects of Islamic law.

## 4 - Issues that scholars addressed while developing rules for decision making relating to the management of change and growth in the built environment

After analyzing the treatises written in 19th century northern Nigeria and the characteristics of the morphology of cities in that region, we determined that the rules developed for managing the processes of growth and change in the built environment fit under one or more of the issues in the following framework:

1. *Harim*: zone surrounding a city, town, property, or structure, which is necessary for its viability and function.
2. *Ihya al-Mawat*: revivification of dead land, i.e., land not owned or utilized.
3. *Haqq al-Irtifaq*: rights of abutting properties and rights related to access and servitude.
4. *al-Turuq al-Amma wa Haqquha*: rights of public streets.
5. *al-Marafiq wa Man' al-Darar*: preventing damages to adjacent structures and facilities.
6. *al-Daman wa al-Mas'uliyya Inda Ihdath al-Darar*: liability and the responsibility for creating damage(s).

The following are the rules for each of the above six categories:
1. Rules for the *Harim*: see note 23.
2. *Ihya al-Mawat*: Abdallah Fodio, in his treatise *Ta'lim al-Radi*, stipulates the following rules for revivification of dead land:
    i. If land is within the *Harim* of a built-up area, it can be revived with the permission of the *Imam* or his representative. If it is outside of the *Harim* of a built-up area, there is no need for permission.
    ii. Those who revive dead land acquire ownership rights to it. However, there are various rules and conditions regarding the loss of ownership of a revived land, including that another reviver of the same land may claim ownership when the first reviver allows the land in question to revert to its previous condition. Its location and distance from the

built-up area are factors that affect ownership rights when it is allowed to revert to its original condition by its initial reviver.

iii. *Ihya* is deemed legitimate when any one or more of the conditions listed in note 22 occurs.

iv. *Tahjir* signifies the boundary delimitation of a land selected for *Ihya* by using stone markers. Some scholars, such as Ibn al-Qasim, do not recognize this act as *Ihya*. Others, like Ashhab, accept *Tahjir* as an indicator of intention to revive the chosen land within a short period of time.

v. Grazing and digging a well for watering flocks is not recognized as an act of *Ihya*.

3. *Haqq al-Irtifaq*: This concerns the right to abut a neighbor's property and the right of servitude, i.e., a right that grants access through another's property. One of the earlier references to this right is found in Khalil's *Mukhtasar*, where he indicates that the owner of a structure should allow his neighbor to use the structure for inserting beams in his wall and should also give him other rights, such as access through his property or the sharing of a water source (see the section on *al-Shirka* in al-Maliki, 1995:128). Ibn Salmun al-Kinani (d. 741/1340), who lived in Granada one generation before Khalil, also explains the right of *Irtifaq* (see Ibn Farhun, 1884). He explains that such a right may be given in perpetuity or for a limited period of time. In either case, a contract or agreement should be written. Ibn Asim (d. 829/1426) of Granada also discusses the right of *Irtifaq*.[40]

Abd al-Qadir b. al-Mustafa from the Sokoto Caliphate, who was married to Muhammad Bello's daughter, Khadija, quoted his father-in-law on the issue of houses abutting a public right-of-way. Bello's views, as quoted by Abd al-Qadir, were that such streets cannot be infringed upon by the owners of abutting houses and must always be kept clean and accessible for the public. Bello uses the term *Irtifaq*, i.e., the public has the right of servitude or access on these public streets.[41]

4. *al-Turuq al-Amma wa Haqquha*: Generally the public has the right of unimpeded access on public streets.[42] Khalil b. Ishaq stipulates the following rights regarding public streets:

i. It is not permissible to build within the public right-of-way, whether or not such construction creates impediments and damage to passersby. Any infringement of this type must be demolished.
ii. Vendors who use the sides of streets to display their goods are allowed to do so if usage of such spaces is temporary and does not impinge upon the traffic of passersby. The use of a particular space on the side of a public street is determined by the person that occupies that space first, by analogy to a person who occupies a space within the confines of a mosque for the purposes of study or teaching.
iii. On a public street one neighbor cannot open a shop or a stable opposite the front door of another, as this would create a nuisance and the potential for invading the privacy of the neighbor on the other side of the street.
iv. It is permissible to build a projection, or a *Sabat* (room bridging a street), as long as it does not create harm to the passerby. A person who owns two buildings opposite each other across the street may build a *Sabat* between them.[43]

Stipulations (i) and (iii) are also mentioned by Idris b. Khalid b. Muhammad, *Qadi* of Gwandu, in his *Kitab Jami Ahammu Masa'il al-Ahkam fi Qat'i al-Khisam*, completed on August 20, 1836 (the author refers primarily to the works of the *Fodiawa* trio: Uthman, Abdallah, and Muhammad Bello). In his *Diya al-Hukkam*, written in 1221/1806 while he was visiting Kano, Abdallah Fodio clarifies a number of issues that might cause problems in public streets, e.g., digging a well in a public street is not allowed, although it is permissible to direct rain gutters onto a public street. Khalil's stipulation (iii) above is also affirmed by Abdallah Fodio. Other stipulations related directly or indirectly to public streets are also documented.[44]

5. *al-Marafiq wa Man' al-Darar*: This rule concerns preventing damage to adjacent structures and facilities. Ibn Salmun of Granada (d. 741/1340) and, two generations later, Ibn Farhun of Medina (d. 799/1397) both discussed the numerous conditions and situations that may arise between adjacent and opposite (across the street) facilities, i.e., damages of one to the other and how those potential and actualized damages may be

prevented or eliminated.[45]

Abdallah Fodio devotes the 13th section of Part 5 (*al-Siyasat al-Shari'ya*) of his *Diya al-Hukkam* to the topic of *Nafi al-darar an al-jiran wa ghayrihum* (prevention of damages to neighbors and others). Idris b. Khalid b. Muhammad's book, *Jami ahammu ...* (cited earlier), which was completed in 1836, also includes a section on *al-Marafiq wa Man' al-Darar* (preventing damages to adjacent facilities). This is followed by a shorter section on *Man ahdathah dararan umira bi-qat'ihi* (he who causes damage(s) is ordered to eliminate it).

The following are some of the issues applicable to the morphology of compounds as the nucleus of urban formation in cities of the Sokoto Caliphate. The primary justification for rules in this area, invoked by various scholars, including those from the Sokoto Caliphate, is the *hadith: La Darar wala Dirar*, which is the leading *Qa'ida* of the first category of *Qawa'id Fiqhiya* (see Part 2 and Figure 1). Abdallah Fodio's interpretation of this *hadith* follows that of al-Matiti (d. 570/1174): *Darar* is when one neighbor harms another, and *Dirar* is when both neighbors harm each other.[46] In *Diya al-Hukkam*, Abdallah Fodio provides the following list of phenomena that may create harm:
- Smoke from baths and bakeries.
- Dust from threshing wheat (*Ghubar al-Anadir*).
- Foul smell from a tanner's workshop (*Natn al-Dabbaghin*).
- Building a stable near a neighbor.
- Building a place for a grinding device, or a blacksmith workshop near a neighbor.
- An act considered to be damaging is usually viewed as being *hadith* (recent), unless it is proven to be *qadim* (old).
- Opening a window that overlooks a neighbor's private domain.
- Building a gargoyle that releases water onto a neighbor's property is not allowed even if it causes no harm, unless the neighbor grants permission.
- A door constructed in a house or structure on a public street must not face another door across the street but must be set back from it to prevent a direct visual corridor. In a cul-de-sac owned by the people who have access to it, one is not allowed to build a projection or open a new door without the consensus

of all the owners.
- It is not permissible to plaster a wall that belongs to an adjacent neighbor, from the side of the other neighbor's property.
- Maintenance of a sewer/wastewater channel is based on the principle that each user is responsible for the portion that he uses, assisted by the neighbor(s) upstream using the channel, e.g., if the channel serves four houses, then the owner of the first house cleans his portion of the channel and helps the next neighbor clean, both help the third neighbor, and so on.
- If a person owns trees on someone else's land, access must always be allowed. The owner of the land can demand that access be the shortest and most direct route to the location of the trees.
- The owner of private property cannot change the location of a path that passes through the property and is used by the public if the path has been there since the owner of the land purchased or inherited it. The owner may seek to obtain the permission of the *Imam* who, after examining the location, can determine if realigning the path is possible and beneficial to its owner and the public who use it. If the owner realigns it without the *Imam*'s permission, the *Imam*, after examining the change, may allow it or may order that it be restored to its original alignment. However, if the path is used by only a specific number of individuals, then those individuals may grant permission to the property owner to realign it.[47]

Idris b. Khalid b. Muhammad, who was active in the 1830s in Gwandu, mentioned other issues relating to the prevention of damages:
- How to determine ownership and usage rights regarding a wall between adjacent neighbors, e.g., what happens if a wall surrounding a jointly owned orchard falls into ruin and one of the partners wants to rebuild it but the other refuses?
- If a jointly owned *Rahi* (mill) falls into ruin, and one of the partners rebuilds it after the other refused, how should the revenue of the mill be shared?
- Who is responsible for a ceiling and its maintenance in a two- or three-story structure if a different party owns each level? This condition does not apply widely in towns of the Sokoto Caliphate.

Otherwise, Idris repeats information Abdallah Fodio included in his treatise. At the outset of his book, Idris lists his sources, citing the *Fodiawa* trio, Uthman, Abdallah, and Muhammad Bello. He also cites the other scholars and their specific works that he consulted.[48]

Later scholars from the Sokoto Caliphate mention cases relating to the management of the built environment, mostly repetitions of issues listed above. They include the treatise *Nubdha min kutub ala'imma* written by Abd al-Qadir b. al-Mustafa (d. 1280/1864), the son-in-law of Muhammad Bello; the treatise *Ajwiba li-Askia fi ma ashkala min al-tullab* (completed in 1285/1868) written by Uthman b. Ishaq b. Umar (d. after 1303/1885); and two short letters written by Qadi Abdullah b. al-Imam (d. 1321/1903), one to Isma'il b. Muhammad al-Bukhahri, Amir of Kebbi, and the other to Banagha, Chief of Maru.

6. *al-Daman wa al-Mas'uliyya inda ihdath al-darar*: The question of how to determine and allocate responsibility for an act creating harm and damages was addressed by scholars in the Sokoto Caliphate. In his *Kitab Tanbih al-Hukkam*, Uthman Fodio discusses the conditions under which responsibility for creating damage is determined. Part 5 (*fi al-Siyasat al-Shar'iya*) of Abdallah Fodio's treatise, *Diya al-Hukkam*, includes numerous references to the context in which responsibility is assigned for an act that has created harm. Section 12 of Part 5, entitled *fi Tadmin al-Sunna' wa Ghayrihum* (responsibility of workers and others), discusses various trades and the circumstances in which certain actions by a worker are determined to be an act of negligence for which the worker is responsible. In his book *Jami Ahammu Masa'il al-Ahkam*, Idris b. Khalid, *Qadi* of Gwandu, refers to responsibility for various deeds and under what conditions the perpetrator has to assume responsibility. He repeats some of the material in Uthman and Abdallah Fodio's works.

In a recent study, Abd al-Jabbar Ahmad Sharara discusses the theoretical and legal premises for actions that create damage and how the allocation of responsibility is determined (see Sharara, 1997:278). He quotes al-Qarafi, a Maliki scholar, who indicates three reasons for allocating responsibility: (i) *al-udwan*, or aggression, such as burning or demolishing; (ii) the result or consequence of an act, such as digging a well in a public street; (iii) the hand of the offender, or the untrustworthy hand, such as usurping someone's rights or property. Also included in this third category is the illegal abrogation of a contract, such as a renter refusing to pay the rental fee.[49]

The essential criterion for allocating responsibility is to determine if damage or harm occurred. The elimination of damage or harm becomes the responsibility of the party whose action created the damage in the first place, e.g., removing any damage that occurs in the public right-of-way of streets and paths. In a recent study, Abd al-Mejid al-Hakim observes that aggression on people's rights takes the form of aggression on a person or on assets and is the underlying basis for the principle, *Inna kulla fi'lin dar yuwajjib al-daman* (a person is liable for his/her act that is damaging to others). He bases this legal stipulation on the Prophet's saying, "*La Darar wa-la Dirar*," as interpreted by the *Fuqaha* (see al-Hakim, as quoted by Sharara, 1997:268).

## 5 - Illustrations from Zaria: the compound and neighborhood cluster — nuclei for habitat and urbanization

Due to limitations of space, we selected only one city for study: Zaria. There is sufficient information for Zaria from which data and illustrative material can be used. Although it is preferable to study as many samples as possible from different cities, the analysis presented here can be refined by applying it to other locations in future studies.

The old walled town of Zaria was the capital of the traditional Zaria emirate.[50] Formerly Zazzau or Zegzeg, this historic kingdom is said to date from the 11th century C.E., when King Gunguma founded it as one of the original *Hausa Bakwai* (seven true *Hausa* states). Camel caravans from the northern Sahara came here to trade. Islam was introduced in about 1456, and there were Muslim *Hausa* rulers from the early 16th century C.E. Muhammad I Askia, a well-known leader of the Songhai Empire, conquered Zazzau in 1512. Later in the century, Zazzau's ruler, Queen Amina, enlarged her domain by making numerous conquests. Zaria was probably founded in 1536 and later in the century became the capital of the *Hausa* state of Zazzau. Both the town and state were named after Queen Zaria (late 16th century C.E.), the younger sister and successor of Queen Amina.

In 1219/1804, the Muslim *Hausa* ruler of Zaria pledged allegiance to Uthman dan Fodio, which resulted in a *Fulani* becoming ruler of Zaria in 1223/1808. The emirate of Zaria was created in 1251/1835, retaining control of Keffi, Nasarawa, Jema'a, and Lapai to the south. A representative of the Sultan at Sokoto and the local emir governed it (see Encyclopedia Britannica, 1998).

The location of Zaria, relative to the frontier of the Sokoto Caliphate in the 19th century and the frontier of the modern state of Nigeria, is shown in Figure 2. The town map of old Zaria (Figure 3), circa 1970, shows primary streets, the built-up area within the walls, and the gates of the city. It also shows the location of the major market, the palace complex, the study area, and the location of the air photo (Figure 4).

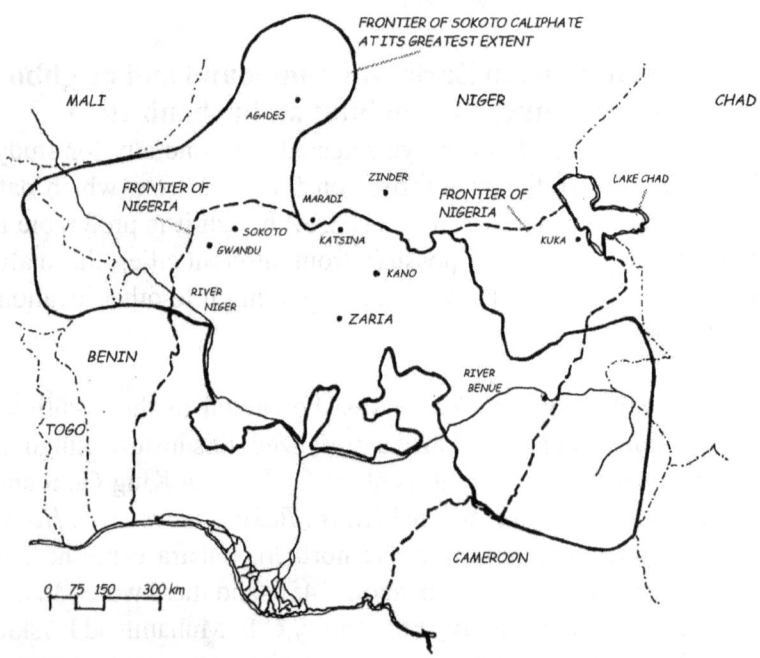

**Figure 2.** Frontier of the Sokoto Caliphate at its greatest extent, relative to the frontiers of Nigeria and adjacent countries. The frontier of the Sokoto Caliphate is based on information in Johnston (1967).

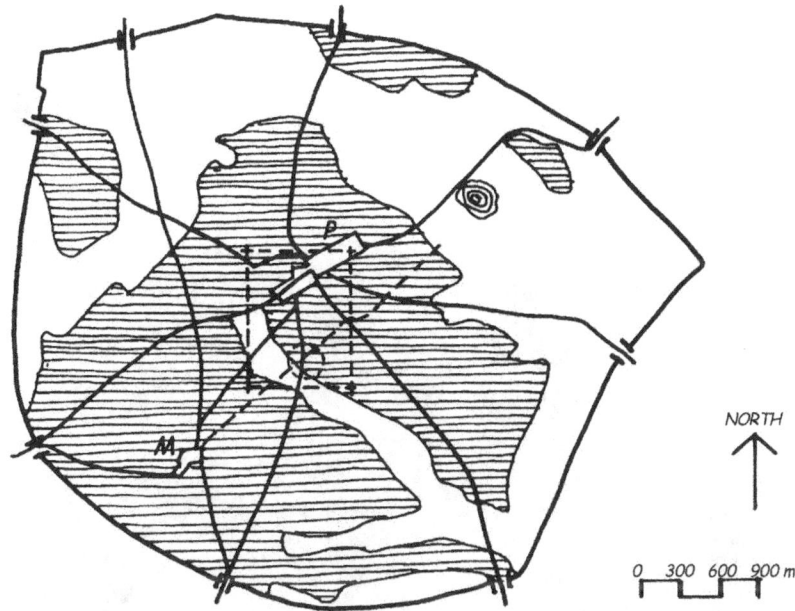

**Figure 3.** The town map of old Zaria, circa 1970, shows primary streets linking the gates of the walled town to the market area on the southwest (M) and the Friday mosque/Emir palace complex to the northeast (P). The map also indicates the location of the study area (circled) and the borders of the air photo in Figure 4. The figure is based on information in Urquhart (1977).

The study area is a cluster of 26 compounds, which may be considered a neighborhood with its common spaces and local facilities. It is located northeast of the market and south of the Emir's palace. The compounds comprising the cluster are grouped around the oldest compound in the cluster, belonging to the Chief *Imam*. Together with the small mosque and square, this forms the focal point of the cluster. The inhabitants of the compounds that make up this cluster were originally the Chief *Imam*'s sons, relatives, and relatives through marriage (see Urbanowicz, 1979).

High walls surround all compounds in *Hausa* walled cities. Their only entrance is a *Zaure*, an entrance hut that leads into the *Kofar Gida* (forecourt). To reach the central and private part of the compound, *Cikin Gida*, one has to pass through a *Shigifa,* or second entrance hut. Normally, the *Shigifa* acts as the transition space between the male and female zones (Figure 5). The area of the *Zaure, Kofar Gida*, and adjacent rooms or facilities is the men's zone, and the rest of the compound beyond the *Shigifa* is the zone for

135

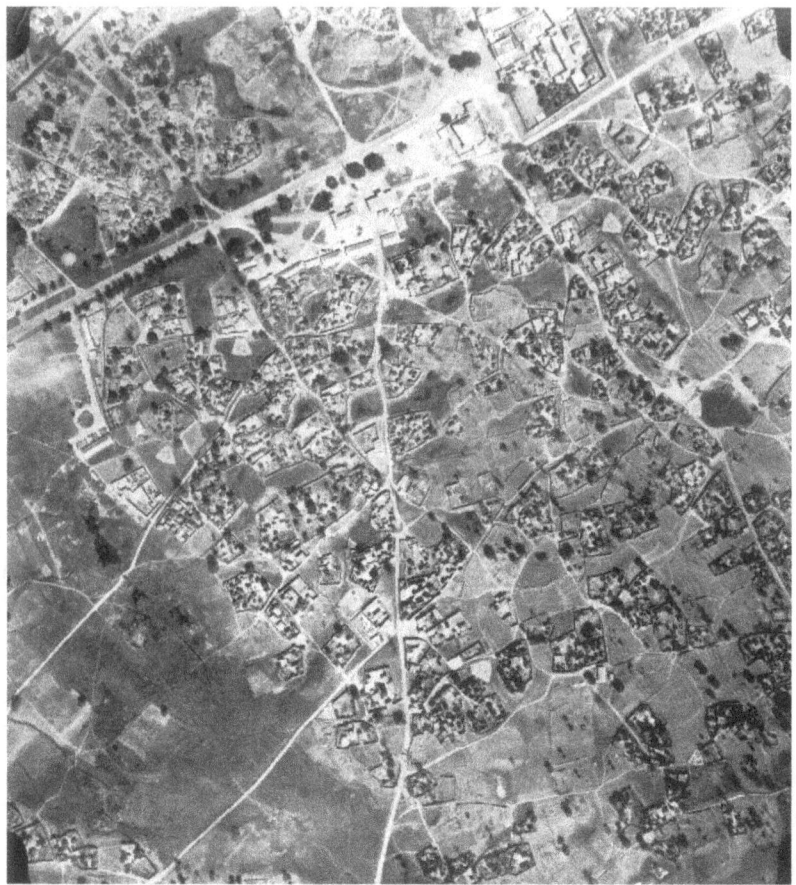

**Figure 4.** Air photo taken in 1963 showing the neighborhood cluster study area, located at the bottom of the photo. The neighborhood is linked by primary streets to Zaria's Friday mosque to the north, which is located adjacent and west of the Emir's palace complex. Also clearly visible in the air photo are small to large farm plots scattered between clusters of compounds.

the family, women, and service areas. Compounds, on a citywide basis, average 500-600 square meters in area (see Schwerdtfeger, 1972).

A detailed account by Taylor and Webb of the construction process of a compound in Zaria during the early decades of the twentieth century is available in English and *Hausa* (see Taylor and Webb, 1932:169-191). The account clearly demonstrates the involvement of the owner and builder and their mutual cooperation in decision making relating to the planning and layout of the compound. The

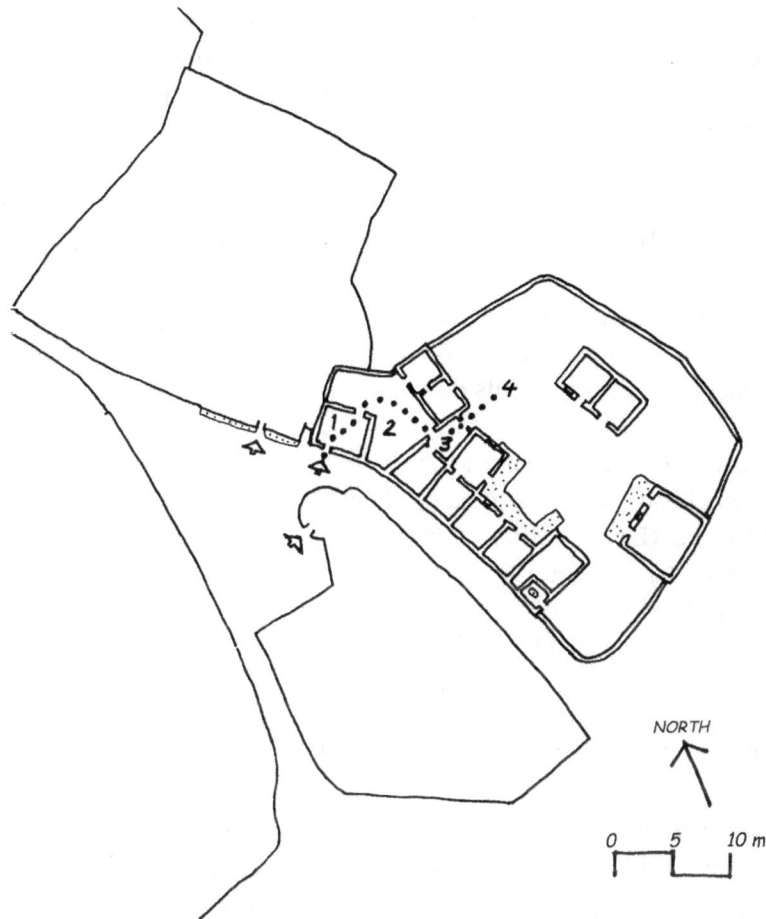

**Figure 5.** One compound located on the eastern edge of the neighborhood cluster study area, showing the route of entry from the street to the private zone of the family: (1) *Zaure* (main entrance hut); (2) *Kofur Gida* (forecourt); (3) *Shiqifa* (second entrance hut/passage), the transition space between the forecourt and the *Cikin Gida*; and (4) *Cikin Gida* (central and private area of the compound). For privacy considerations, entrances to *Zaure* do not face each other. This pattern is especially evident on narrow pathways.

magnitude of the enterprise depends on the financial resources of the owner. The account provides valuable insight into the building materials used, the stages of the construction process, and the approximate number of days that it took for a variety of construction activities. Schwerdtfeger (1982) describes the responsibilities of the compound head and the allocation of labor between members of the compound in maintaining walls, common rooms, and the construction of a new hut for a newlywed couple. The compound is named after the compound head, who, as the primary decision maker, can take independent action. Dependent or semi-dependent household heads within the compound must acquire approval of the compound head for changes in the compound.

Taylor and Webb (1932) also provide an account on farming. They observe, "If a man wants to make a farm, he chooses a place where there is good soil... ." This confirms the practice of *Ihya*, i.e., a person chooses a suitable plot to farm, and by doing so he practices *Ihya al-Mawat*. The account continues with " ...he thoroughly clears the weeds and cuts down the bushes... ."

Figures 6A-D, the plan of the study area, show (A) the neighborhood cluster of 26 compounds showing all structures and perimeter walls; (B) the pattern of growth of the cluster due to *Iqta* (land allocation) and *Ihya* (revivification); (C) the *Harim* of the compounds and *Haqq al-Irtifaq* (rights of abutting adjacent neighbors) as it is evident in 11 locations; and (D) the system of male zones comprising *Zaure* (primary entrance huts), *Kofar Gida* (forecourts), and *Shiqifa* (passages) leading to *Cikin Gida* (private areas of the compound), highlighted for all the compounds of the cluster.

The average size of compounds in Zaria is 620 square meters. On average, two-thirds of the area of the compound is open space, and one-third is built up. The population of a compound ranges between five and 19 inhabitants, with an average of 12 persons per compound. Some of the compounds studied in the late 1960s had as many as 36 persons (see Schwerdtfeger, 1982). Responsibilities within the compound are reflected in behavior and association. For example, all persons who eat together from the same *Tukunya* (pot) dwell together in one part of the compound known as *Sassa* and contribute labor, service, and/or money to the household budget.[51]

The compound model found in most of the traditional towns in Hausaland has several advantages over the prevailing model of courtyard-clustered buildings in North Africa. The average area of the footprint of houses in Tunis, for example, is about one-third of that in Zaria. In Tunis the average footprint of a house is a square 15 x 15 meters (225 square meters), and in Zaria it is 620 square meters with a variety of configurations. The one-third built-up area

**Figure 6A.** The plan of the study area — a neighborhood cluster of 26 compounds. It shows the configuration of all the structures and perimeter walls of the compounds and the location of mature trees. Entrance to the *Zaure* of each compound is indicated by a black dot. The figure is based on information in Urbanowicz (1979) and an on-site survey by coauthor Zubair Ahmed.

of the Zaria compound is approximately the size of the average footprint of a house in Tunis. This distinction has major implications for the size of walled towns in Hausaland compared to those in North Africa (Figure 7).

These are specific advantages of the compound model:
- flexibility and ease of adding new huts or enlarging older huts

139

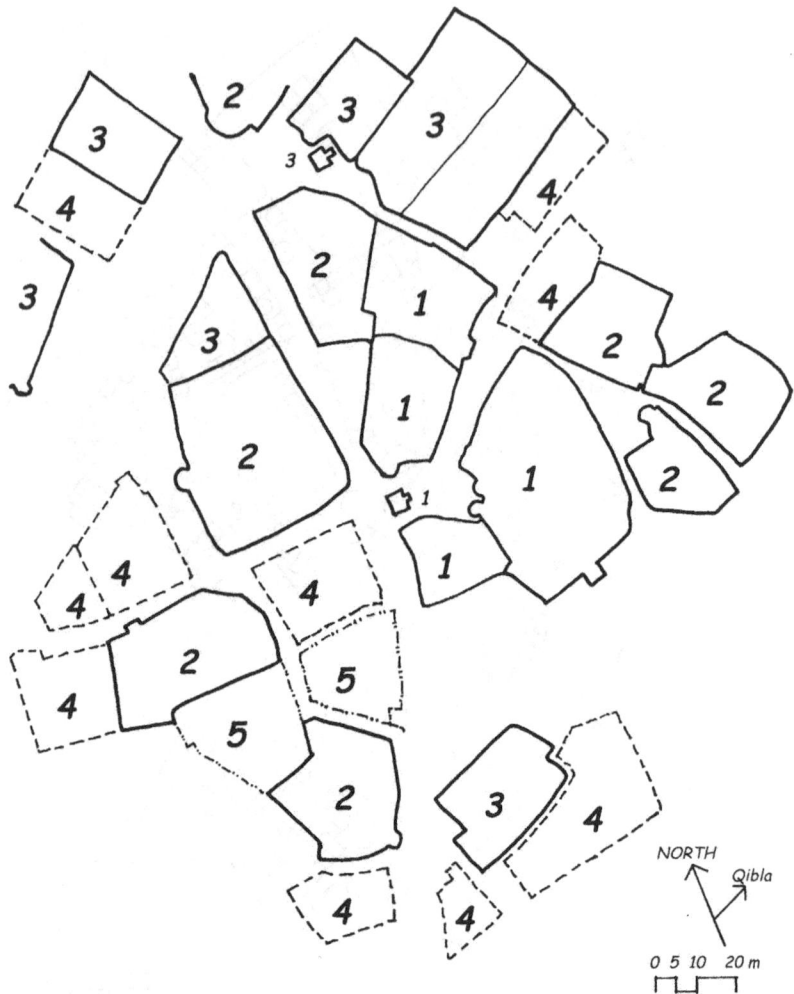

**Figure 6B.** The pattern of growth of the neighborhood cluster due to the mechanisms of *Iqta* (land allocation) and *Ihya* (revivification). The period is from inception through the late 1950s and into the mid-1970s, which is the time the cluster was studied and documented. Those compounds indicated by the numbers 1-3 are shown on maps based on air photos dated 1959, and those indicated by numbers 4 and 5 are based on information from air photos dated 1963 and the surveys undertaken in the mid-1970s.

   within the compound;
- more space between huts of various households within the compound is possible, thus reducing the potential for conflicts;
- more open space for all inhabitants, especially space for play areas for children;
- water management can occur within the compound, reducing

**Figure 6C.** The *Harim* (zone surrounding each compound whose owner is responsible for its use and maintenance) of each compound in the neighborhood cluster is shown by broken lines, and the *Haqq al-Irtifaq* (the right to abut a neighbor's property) is shown by a heavy thick line as it has occurred in 11 locations within the cluster.

potential conflicts between neighboring compounds;
- perimeter walls of the compound, which are built first, are relatively stable over long periods of time, contributing to the integrity and stability of the streets and pathways between compounds and within clusters of compounds;
- freedom to experiment with architectural design within the compound without affecting the overall character of the neighborhood; and

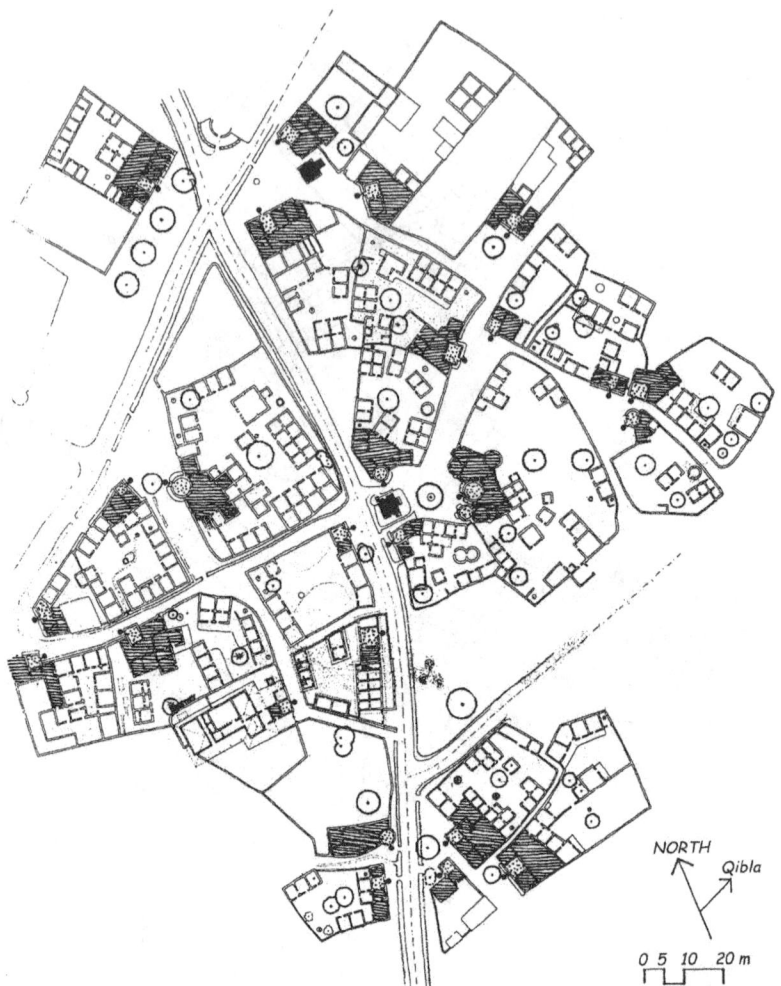

**Figure 6D.** Land use: *Zaure* (primary entrance hut shown as dotted areas); the male zone of the compound is shown as hatched areas comprising *Kofur Gida* (forecourt) and *Shiqifa* (second entrance/passage), which leads to *Cikin Gida* (private areas of the compound comprising the family and service zones). Two small neighborhood mosques are shown in black.

- there is no incentive to build higher, thus avoiding many problems associated with increase in building heights, such as overlooking neighboring compounds, obstructing breezes, and creating shadows within a compound and on neighboring compounds.

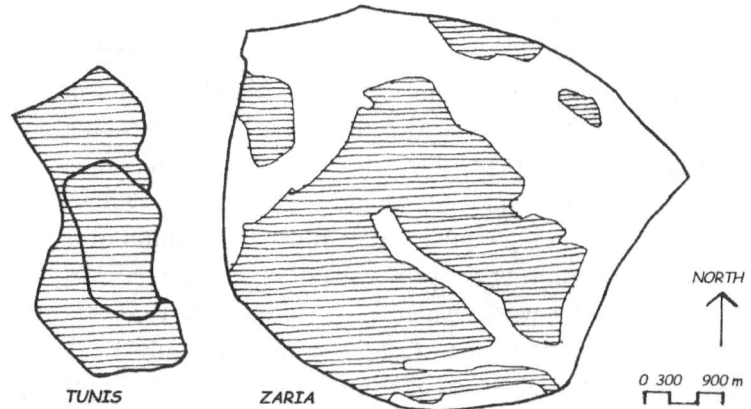

**Figure 7.** The traditional city of Tunis (capital of modern Tunisia), drawn to the same scale as the traditional walled city of Zaria. The latter has an area within its walls of over three times that of Tunis. It should be noted, however, that all of Tunis is built up, whereas only the marked areas of Zaria are built up. For details of Tunis, see Hakim (1986).

## 6 - Conclusions: the impact of Islamic law on the built environment and its theoretical implications for the disciplines of city planning and architecture

It is clear from this study that Islamic law addresses issues affecting urbanization and living in cities by covering broad considerations of the built environment and details affecting design solutions between proximate neighbors. Encouragement to live in cities, towns, and villages can be traced back to sayings of the Prophet. The *Bayt al-Mal* (treasury) was responsible for expenditures for the public good, such as defense. However, when the treasury was lacking resources, the law encouraged and expected people to pool their resources for the sake of the public good, such as building or maintaining the walls around the city.

Guidelines for the relationship of city people with bedouin are also traceable to the Prophet. Aspects of those guidelines were intended to discourage people from reverting back to a bedouin lifestyle. The building of *Ribats* (fortified settlements), their upkeep, and the constant vigilance needed for guarding them was considered a virtue. Muhammad Bello wrote a treatise on the virtues of building and serving in *Ribats*, continuing a tradition of earlier literature on this subject, which can be traced back to the 14th century C.E. in the Middle East.

There is also a rich heritage in Islamic law of detailed stipulations for land: its acquisition, individual rights associated with land and its resources, and maintaining the land's viability and usefulness. Abdallah Fodio wrote a detailed treatise on this subject and clearly defined the concepts and their mechanisms of implementation. They were simple to understand and implement, allowing flexibility without sacrificing equity. Rules for the utilization of land and its management during the processes of change and growth in the built environment were shaped by a sophisticated system of meta-principles, called *Qawa'id Fiqhiya* (*fiqh* principles), which addressed fundamental issues of equity and justice. These principles also addressed the values and code of conduct that people were expected to respect and implement in their day-to-day decisions concerning the management of their properties and buildings, particularly decisions that might have a negative impact on their proximate neighbors.

The system had few public agents to monitor peoples' compliance with the rules. The *Imam* had the traditional responsibility of *Iqta* (allocation of land) in certain parts of the city, and the *Qadi* (judge) was responsible for adjudicating cases that resulted from non-conformity with the rules. His ultimate purpose was to re-establish equity and justice between the parties of a case. By doing so on a case-by-case basis, the *Qadi* ensured that equity was maintained throughout the built environment during the processes of change and growth across time.

Traditional *Hausa-Fulani* cities, shaped to a large extent by Islamic law and local customs, share the following characteristics:
1. They are walled towns within which people live and farm.
2. The nucleus is the compound, owned by an extended family and headed by one person who controls all primary decisions affecting the compound. The built portion of the compound is about one-third of its area, the balance comprising areas for services and adequate space between households sharing the compound.
3. Farming lots are scattered between and within clusters of compounds.
4. Natural features, such as small hills, ravines, and drainage areas, are incorporated within the city walls.

The ruling authority makes only a small contribution to planning decisions for these cities. Their decisions usually affect city walls, gates, location of the palace and major mosque, the central market area, and the general alignment of the network of primary streets between the central market, major mosque/palace compound, and all gates of the city (Figure 3). The rest of the city emerges naturally as a self-regulating and adaptive system.[52] Access streets and paths are allowed to form, and their routes are delineated in response to use, the shortest distance between two destinations, and the process of revivification of land for compounds. Clusters of compounds form after lots are allocated and revived, and wealthy individuals build local mosques as a gift to the neighborhood. Revivers select their farming plots according to the principle of *Ihya*.

The urbanization process is based on the principle of *Ibaha*, i.e., one is allowed to develop one's lot without restrictions, subject to overarching proscriptive rules derived from normative principles (*Qawa'id*) that are based on Islamic values. The city emerges from decisions by the various actors involved in the processes of *Ihya* and construction activities within their immediate built environment. Thus, the analogy can be made to an organized complex system, a theory discussed in a 1948 article by Warren Weaver. The phenomenon of control and communication, which indirectly provided insight on how cities functioned, was also published that year by Norbert Wiener. Scientific thought and research activities related to complexity theory began to accelerate after the establishment in the mid-1980s of the Santa Fe Institute in New Mexico.

Jane Jacobs was one of the first observers to note the relationship between complexity theory and the city. The last chapter of her book *The Death and Life of Great American Cities* (1961), "The Kind of Problem a City Is," discusses this relationship and emphasizes an approach for comprehending the city that is relevant to our understanding of traditional cities in Hausaland and elsewhere. She says that the most important habits of thought for understanding cities are (1) to think about process; (2) to work inductively, reasoning from particulars to the general; and (3) to seek for "unaverage" clues involving very small quantities that reveal the way larger, more "average" quantities operate.

Another important concept is that of feedback. Negative feedback handles random changes in the environment. It is a way of reaching equilibrium. Positive feedback pushes the system onward, i.e., repeats the same action again and again. The relationship between adjacent compound owners depends on decisions affected by negative feedback, such as when a window from one compound overlooks the private domain of an adjacent compound. The owner of the latter reacts by demanding that the window be sealed or removed. However, if the window was there before the new neighbor built his compound, the latter would respond by laying out the compound so that overlooking would not occur.[53] The global intelligence of emergent systems, such as the traditional *Hausa-Fulani* city, depends on living within boundaries defined by rules. The system's capacity for learning, growth, and experimentation derives from its adherence to these rules (see Johnson, 2001:138, 181).

With respect to traditional *Hausa-Fulani* cities such as Zaria, we need to understand the processes of decision making relating to the construction of compounds and clusters of compounds, how day-to-day decisions are undertaken, and by what overarching values and rules those decisions are governed. We should especially note the unique conditions occurring between proximate compounds, as those will reveal the broader patterns that emerge and make up the city. As such, the traditional building experience of *Hausa-Fulani* cities, particularly as we have studied it during the 19th century, provides a good case study for the theory of complexity as it relates to urbanization.

Another important theoretical observation that impinges on politics is the question of cultural identity. Nineteenth century *Hausa-Fulani* cities are imbedded in ancient local customs, as well as Islamic values. The latter were reinvigorated by the *Jihad* of Uthman dan Fodio. Islamic values were reintroduced and reinforced in various societal activities, including the city-building process and the rules governing construction affecting the single compound and clusters of compounds. After the British conquered the Sokoto Caliphate in 1903, new concepts and procedures were introduced that affected, among other things, city building and architecture. After decades of gradual changes, we have a situation today in which most people have lost the wisdom and experience that generated the traditional fabric. The link was lost between Islamic cultural identity and its manifestation in the built environment as "modern" concepts and practices have continued to shape urbanization outside of that rich tradition.

In this study, we attempted to redress this situation by identifying some of the underlying knowledge, wisdom, and experience that created traditional cities and towns within the *Hausa-Fulani* cultural sphere in what is now the area of northern Nigeria. More studies are needed, particularly, detailed analysis of the formation of clusters of compounds, their relationships with plots of small farms, and the manner in which the street system was formed. The mechanisms of *Iqta* and *Ihya* require careful study in as many traditional towns within the *Hausa-Fulani* cultural area as possible, such as Sokoto, Katsina, and Kano in Nigeria, Agadez in Niger, and other traditional *Hausa-Fulani* towns in neighboring countries.

Studies sponsored by local governments and universities on other factors that shaped 19th century urban development in northern Nigeria will also be needed to create a larger body of knowledge, which can then be used as a framework for formulating policies for conserving historic sectors of cities, towns, and villages, as well as for developing culturally relevant policies and approaches for urbanization and architecture (for suggestions on how this can be achieved in North African countries, see Hakim, 2001).

## Acknowledgements
This study was co-authored with Zubair Ahmed, a principal partner of Triad Associates in Kaduna, Nigeria. We would like to acknowledge the following individuals and institutions for assistance in providing us with manuscript copies, publications, and other materials necessary for our research. In Nigeria, Muhammad Isa Talata-Mafara, Umar Jibril Al-Basawee, and Hamid Bobboyi for help in finding relevant Arabic manuscripts at the following locations: National Archives, Kaduna; History Bureau, Sokoto; and Northern History Research Scheme at Ahmadu Bello University, Zaria. Also, Friedrich W. Schwerdtfeger for air photos of the historic walled city of Zaria. In the United States, John O. Hunwick

and the Library of African Studies at Northwestern University, Evanston, Illinois. Portions of this study and its findings were presented by the authors at the conference titled *Islam and Africa*, Session 1C: Planning and Design of Islam, organized by the Institute of Global Cultural Studies, Binghamton University, Binghamton, New York, April 19-22, 2001.

## Notes

[1] For an explanation of the term *Fodiawa*, see Hunwick, 1995:53-55. Trio refers to Shehu Uthman, his brother Abdallah, and his son Muhammad Bello.

[2] The four Caliphs are known to Sunni Muslims as *al-Rashidun* (The Rightly Guided). They are Abu Bakr (r. 10-13 Hijri/632-634 C.E.), Umar b. al-Khattab (r. 13-23/634-644), Uthman b. Affan (r. 23-36/644-656), and Ali b. Abi Talib (r. 36-41/656-661). The four Sunni *Imams* are Abu Hanifa (80-150/699-767), Malik (96-179/715-795), al-Shafi'i (150-205/767-820), and Ibn Hanbal (163-241/780-855).

[3] On the fifth line of page 1, Bello describes this 11-page manuscript as *Jawab shafi' wa-khitab minna kafin ila Muhammad al-Jaylani* (A complete and adequate response to Muhammad al-Jaylani), listed in Hunwick, 1995:121, item 30. Al-Jaylani (d. after 1836 C.E.) was a *Tuareq* leader and *mujahid* who sought the advice of Muhammad Bello on the question of managing a Muslim community among the nomads after the *jihad*, to which this manuscript is a response. According to Last (1967:231), this manuscript is dated 1230/1815.

[4] The meaning of the word *fitna* in this context is sedition, strife, or disorder.

[5] It is generally believed that praying together as a *jama'ah* (group) is preferable to praying alone. The larger the group, the better it is.

[6] A *laqit* is an infant who does not know his parents and is abandoned due to extreme poverty or for fear of the parent being accused of adultery. See Abu Habib, 1982:332.

[7] Bello cites the Prophet's saying on this matter on p. 4 of his manuscript, *Jawab shafi' wa-khitab*: "*al-Badawa Shahran fa-ma zada fa-huwa Ta'arrab*" (a person is considered a bedouin if he lives more than two months in that lifestyle).

[8] *ibid*. Based on the Qur'anic injunction 3:104 — "*al-amr bil-maruf wa al-nahi 'an al-munkar*" (to command good and forbid evil). Bello says that if a person is able to contribute to eliminating the sedition, strife, or disorder, then he should do so; however, depending on the situation, if one group of people manages to eliminate the sedition, strife, or disorder, then the obligation on other individuals is waived.

[9] *ibid*.:5. Bello refers to the precedent established in those cities by remind-

ing al-Jaylani that during Umar b. al-Khattab's reign (13-23/634-644), people from the countryside and villages helped to build Basra, Kufa, and Fustat, and they moved to live in Damascus, where they helped to establish and strengthen those towns for defense against the enemy. He elaborates on the merits of working and living in defensive settlements in his treatise *Kitab al-ribat wa al-hirasa* (see Hunwick, 1995:123, item 44).

[10] *ibid.*:4. Bello reminds al-Jaylani that working on the defensive wall or moat of a town or city is a mandatory obligation based on the example of the Prophet. The Prophet and his companions collaborated in building the moat around Medina.

[11] Qadi Iyad (d. 544/1149) was born in Sebta (Ceuta) and became its *qadi*. Later he served as the *qadi* of Granada. He died in Marrakesh. Al-Maghili (d. 909/1503), a *faqih* (jurist scholar) from Tlemcen, travelled to sub-Saharan Africa to teach *Fiqh* and *Shari'a*. He died in Tawat, located about 400 kilometers south of Tlemcen.

[12] *Jawab shafi' wa-khitab*, 5 (full citation in note 3). Bello cites al-Wansharisi's (d. 914/1508) *al-Miyar al-Mu'rib*, 13 volumes (1981:Vol. 5, p. 33), where the *Qadi* Abu Umar b. Manzur indicates that in principle Muslims should not be asked for donations not sanctioned by the *Shari'a*. If, for instance, the *Bayt al-Mal* (treasury) has no resources for defense such as food for soldiers and war equipment, then it is lawful to ask the people to contribute, provided the following five conditions are met: (i) the need is substantiated, (ii) the donations collected are utilized justly, (iii) expenditures must be based on need and welfare of the community and not for a specific purpose, (iv) donations should be received only from those able to give and not from those who cannot afford it, and (v) these conditions should be assessed regularly based on the current resources of the treasury. When money cannot be used, then people should be required to contribute their labor for a specific cause if they are able to do so. Abdallah Fodio also addressed these issues in his four-page treatise entitled *Jawab al-sa'il fi bina al-husn* (Answer to the query about building the defensive wall), dated Dhu al-Qa'da 1230/October 1815.

[13] *ibid.*:9. This *Qa'ida*, or principle, is related to Group 1 of the five central *Qawa'id Fiqhiya* (see Figure 1).

[14] *ibid.*

[15] *ibid.*:10. Bello cites two *hadiths*: (1) "Those of my nation who have adequate horses cannot be humiliated by their enemies, yet they will be humiliated if they depend solely on cattle ... " and (2) "Being close to horses and attached to them is always a blessing ... ."

[16] *ibid.*:11. *Ra'iya* refers to subjects. It also refers to a herd of sheep. Thus, the hadith *"Kulukum ra'i wa-mas'ul an ra'iyatihi"* is a metaphor of the shepherd who is responsible for his flock. It is translated thus, "You are shepherds

and each one is responsible for his flock."

[17] We know of three scholars who have referred to this treatise (see Last, 1967:80; Prussin, 1976:8-19, 97-98; Sulaiman, 1987:117). One of the earliest treatises in the Islamic world that discusses the virtues of building cities and towns and the necessary conditions for their founding is that of Shihab al-Din Ahmad b. Abi al-Rabi' (218-272/833-885) from Baghdad, titled *Suluk al-Malik fi Tadbir al-Mamalik* (see al-Ghani, 1996).

[18] Muhammad Bello mentions at the outset of his treatise that it is an abbreviated version of a book entitled *Mashari al-ashwaq ila masari al-ushsaq*. Bello does not mention the author of this work, but it is attributed to Ahmad b. Ibrahim al-Dimashqi, known as Ibn al-Nahhas (d. 814/1411), a *Shafi'i* scholar born in Damascus who moved to Egypt and eventually lived as a guard in the *Ribat* of Dimyat, where he was martyred. A biography of Ibn al-Nahhas is available (see al-Zirkli, 1998: Vol. 1, p. 87).

[19] David Dalby was Reader in West African languages at the School of Oriental and African Studies, London University. His article has excellent air photos of the traditional sector of Kano City. In an earlier study, concentrating on the usage and meanings of the *Hausa* word *garii*, Dalby published his findings (see Dalby, 1964). The other study is by Ahmed Beitallah Yusuf. Yusuf taught in the Department of Sociology at Ahmadu Bello University, Zaria, Nigeria.

[20] The translation of the title is "On teaching about the revivification of dead land" (see Hunwick, 1995:108, item 81). Muhammad Sani Zahradeen included the study of this treatise in his Ph.D. thesis (1976). He later published an article on this treatise (see Zahradeen, 1990).

[21] There are five categories of land:

1. land taken by force, which may neither be sold nor given to anyone as a gift, but must remain as common property for use by Muslims;
2. land whose owners concluded a peace treaty with Muslims. It belongs to its owners who are free to utilize it in any form they wish;
3. land whose owners converted to Islam. It belongs to them;
4. land whose owners escaped and left it. The *Imam* has the authority to allocate its use as he sees fit; and
5. land whose owners did not convert to Islam or conclude a peace treaty with Muslims. The *Imam* may allocate it to whomever he wishes.

[22] Revivification occurs when one or more of these conditions is met: (i) finding water within the land by digging a well or opening up a spring so that it is possible to cultivate the land; (ii) removing water from a flooded land; (iii) building a permanent structure on the land; (iv) substantial planting on the land; (v) cultivation by plowing and breaking up the soil (it is to be noted that cultivation without prior plowing does not constitute revivification); (vi) removing trees from the land by cutting or burning; and (vii) breaking up

stones on the land and leveling its steep slopes.

[23] Abdallah Fodio explains how the *harim* for different entities is established and recognized:

- Village: The area surrounding it, which is usually used for gathering firewood and for grazing. The distance is based on walking back and forth in one day, which is about 10 kilometers each way for a total of 20 km. Sometimes the area for collecting firewood is beyond the grazing area; sometimes it is within the grazing area. In that situation, the *harim* includes the farther of the two.
- River: 1,000 cubits (or about 500 meters) and an area adequate for those who come to benefit from it.
- Abundant spring: 500 cubits (or about 250 meters).
- Well used for livestock: The area of land that does not inconvenience anyone who brings his flock to drink at the well.
- Well used for agricultural purposes: Space is needed to protect it from damage and to allow its users to benefit from it.
- Well used for agriculture, a house, or small tributary, or a river in land not owned by anybody: 20 cubits (or about 10 meters).
- House surrounded by dead land: Its *harim* includes the areas needed for access and egress, its built-in benches, space for accumulating soil for construction and maintenance purposes, and space for discharge of rainwater and wastewater.
- House surrounded by other houses or owned properties: No single owner is allowed to occupy an area as *harim* for his sole purpose, but rather each owner can benefit from the *harim* abutting his property without harming or inconveniencing his neighbor(s).
- Palm orchard and other trees: The *harim* is the area on the edges of the orchard and areas allowing entrances and egresses.
- Streets: Seven cubits (or about 3.5 meters). It is not allowed to sit and occupy space within the minimum width of the street, unless more space is available. If a structure is built in the street's right-of-way, it must be demolished even if it does not create harm. It is also not allowed to take space from the street's right-of-way and incorporate it within one's boundaries. Other stipulations are mentioned regarding streets.

[24] Abdallah Fodio stipulates four categories for water:

1. People have equal right of access to water that is public, i.e., it is not owned because it is in public land, such as rivers and springs. No one is allowed to have exclusive rights.
2. The owner of private land is the primary beneficiary of water located on this land, such as a well or spring. He has the right to exclude others and the right to sell the water. Although it is preferable that he provides the water without charging for it, he cannot be forced to do so unless people are desperate for water and are threatened with death. In that case, he must provide them with water, and if he refuses, they have the right to

fight him. If his neighbor's well is damaged and being repaired, causing a threat to the neighbor's crops, then he should provide any surplus water to that neighbor.
3. Water collected from rain should be shared. This is based on the principle that owners on higher ground use what they need until the water reaches their ankles, and then it must be released to the neighbor(s) at lower ground, and so on.
4. A person that digs a well in the countryside for watering livestock has first priority to use it. Once his needs are met, he cannot prevent others from using the well.

[25] People have equal rights for pasture when edible grass and shrubs are on public, i.e., unclaimed, land. If the land is owned, then its owner has priority rights for pasture. On the question of rights for selling pasture or preventing others from using it, Abdallah Fodio cites al-Kharashi, who says that it is illegal to prevent grazing rights on land left uncultivated by its owner. If, however, the owner fences his land and finds that people's livestock are trespassing and damaging his crops, then he has the right to prevent grazing. He also has the right to sell his crops.

[26] See Mustafa Ahmad al-Zarka (1989:33) in the introduction to a book written by his father, who died in 1938.

[27] *ibid.*:36. An example of a *Qa'ida* that is attributed to a saying of the Prophet is *"La Darar wa-la Dirar."* Some scholars interpret its meaning as "No infringement, whether profitable or not." Another interpretation is "Do not harm others or yourself, and others should not harm you or themselves."

[28] *ibid.*:37.

[29] *ibid.*

[30] *ibid.*:38.

[31] *ibid.*:41. It should be noted that the bulk of the intellectual activity in developing the science of *Qawa'id* occurred in the eighth century Hijri (14th century C.E.).

[32] See the third section of F. E. Vogel's article *"Siyasa"* (1997) in *Encyclopedia of Islam*, New Edition, Fascicules 159-160 (Leiden: E. J. Brill, Vol. 9, pp. 694-696). The scholars most responsible for crystallizing the doctrine were the two Hanbalis, Ibn Taymiyya (d. 728/1328) (particularly in his book *al-Siyasa al-Shar'iya*) and his student, Ibn Qayyim al-Jawziya (d. 751/1350). Their influence is clearly apparent in the work of the Maliki scholar Ibn Farhun (d. 799/1397), *Tabsirat al-Hukkam*.

[33] This treatise was written in 1221/1806 while Abdallah was in Kano. In the introduction (pp. 3-4), Abdallah indicates that he wrote the treatise after receiving many requests from friends and associates in Kano who needed a treatise on rules based on the *Shari'a*, even though Abdallah pointed out that

there was adequate information in the extant work of earlier Sunni scholars.

[34] This treatise is addressed to rulers, administrators, and others entrusted with similar administrative responsibilities. The author categorizes typical issues and problems and offers advice on how to deal with them. Not listed in Hunwick, 1995.

[35] This treatise was written to Abdallah's friends and associates in Kano who needed guidance on rules based on the *Shari'a* (see Hunwick, 1995:91, item 18).

[36] This treatise, completed in 1230/1815, was written in response to the question, "In what circumstances can the *Imam*, or ruler, require his people to assist in building a defensive wall around a settlement, town, or city?" Not listed in Hunwick, 1995.

[37] Abdallah Fodio quotes al-Maghili's response, dated 897/1492, to the Sultan of Kano (r. 867/1463- 904/1499) on pages 81-85, which includes a number of *Qawa'id* (see Hunwick, 1995:92, item 25).

[38] This treatise discusses the principles relating to the application of *Shari'a* rules in differing social and customary contexts. It contains the largest number of *Qawa'id* and draws on Shihab al-Din al-Qarafi's (d. 684/1285) *al-Ihkam fi tamyiz al-fatawi 'an al-ahkam wa-tasarrufat al-qadi wa'l-imam*. al-Qarafi, a Maliki scholar, was born, lived, and died in Cairo (see Hunwick, 1995:123, item 45). For a general study on *Urf* (customs), customary law, and its impact on the built form of traditional cities in the Islamic world, see Hakim, 1994.

[39] Completed on August 20, 1836 (see Hunwick, 1995:219, item 1). The author's objective in writing this treatise was to create a reference work for himself and also for other *Qadis* (judges). His primary sources were the works of the *Fodiawa* trio, Uthman, Abdallah, and Muhammad Bello. He also refers to well-known sources such as the *Mukhtasar* of Khalil b. Ishaq, the *Risala* by Ibn Abi Zayd al-Qayrawani, *Qawanin al-Ahkam* by Ibn Juzayy, *Kitab al-Nawazil* by Muhammad b. Salim, *al-Mi'yar* by al-Wansharisi, and others.

[40] Ibn Asim's (d. 829/1426) treatise, *Tuhfat al-Hukkam fi nakt al-uqud wa al-ahkam*, was commented on by a number of scholars, including al-Tusuli from Fez (d. 1258/1842), in his *al-Bahja fi Sharh al-Tuhfa*.

[41] Abd al-Qadir b. al-Mustafa (b. 1219/1804-d. 1281/1864), *Nubdhat Ibn Mustafa min Kutub al-A'imma* (see Hunwick, 1995:221-230).

[42] *ibid.*

[43] al-Kharashi's analysis and explanation of Mukhtasar Khalil (first published in five volumes, Cairo 1317/1900, pp. 275-278). Muhammad b. Abdallah al-Kharashi al-Maliki lived and died in Cairo (1101/1690). This book was available in manuscript form to the *Fodiawa* trio and other scholars of

the Sokoto Caliphate.

[44] The reference is mentioned in Part 2 of this study; see note 35.

[45] Ibn Salmun, *Kitab al-'qd al-Munazzam lil-Hukkam*, and Ibn Farhun, *Tabsirat al-Hukkam*. The latter was very popular among the *Fodiawa* trio and subsequent scholars in the Sokoto Caliphate.

[46] al-Matiti (d. 570/1174) was a Maliki scholar from Fez whose book, *al-Nihaya wa al-Tamam fi Ma'rifat al-Watha'iq wa al-Ahkam*, known as *al-Matitiya*, influenced many later scholars.

[47] Abdallah Fodio relied on some of the following sources in compiling the rules: Ashhab al-Qaysi (d. 204/819 in Egypt), a friend of Imam Malik (d. 179/795) from Medina; Ibn al-Majishun (d. 212/827), originally from Isfahan, lived and worked in Medina, and died in Baghdad; Asbagh b. al-Faraj b. Nafi' (d. 225/840) from Egypt; Ibn Habib (d. 238/853) from Cordoba, author of *al-Wadiha*; Sahnun (d. 240/854), originally Syrian, born and died in Qairouan, author of *al-Mudawwana al-Kubra*; Yahya b. Umar (d. 289/901) from Qairouan studied under Ibn Habib and Sahnun. His book, *Ikhtisar al-Mustakhrajah*, is known as *al-Muntakhabah*; Ibn Abi Zayd al-Qairouani (d. 386/996), one of Qairouan's great scholars, author of *al-Risala* and the multi-volume work *al-Nawadir wa al-Ziyadat*; Ibn 'Attab (d. 462/1069) from Cordoba, a scholar in the science of *al-Watha'iq*; Al-Lakhmi (d. 478/1085), originally from Qairouan, resided and died in Sfax and authored *al-Tabsira*; al-Matiti (d. 570/1174) from Fez, author of *al-Nihaya wa al-Tamam fi Marifat al-Watha'iq wa al-Ahkam*, known as *al-Matitiya*; Ibn Juzayy al-Kalbi (d. 741/1340) from Granada, author of *al-Qawanin al-Fiqhiya*; Ibn Salmun Al-Kinani (d. 741/1340) from Granada, author of *al-Iqd al-Munazzam lil-Hukkam*; and Ibn Farhun (d. 799/1397), born, raised, and died in Medina, author of *Tabsirat al-Hukkam*.

[48] *al-Risala* by Ibn Abi Zayd al-Qairouani (d. 386/996) from Qairouan; *al-Qawanin al-Fiqhiya* by Ibn Juzayy al-Kalbi (d. 741/1340) from Granada; *Mukhtasar Khalil* by Khalil bin Ishaq (d. 776/1374) from Cairo; *Tuhfat al-Hukkam* by Ibn Asim (d. 829/1426) from Granada; *Lamia fi al-Ahkam*, known as *Lamiyat al-Zaq'qaq*, by Ali bin al-Qasim al-Zaqqaq (d. 912/1506) from Fez; and *al-Miyar al-Mu'rib* by Ahmad b. Yahya al-Wansharisi (d. 914/1508) from Fez.

[49] See Sharara, 1997:262.

[50] Zaria's geographic coordinates are latitude 11°3'N, longitude 7°42'E, at an elevation of 670 meters above sea level. The direction to the *qibla* in Makkah is 67°16'NE.

[51] See Schwerdtfeger, 1982:33-35.

[52] The self-regulating aspect is a result of the decisions and actions of specific individuals in starting new compounds or small farms. In doing so,

they respond to existing conditions on adjacent properties by adjusting their planning and design decisions. Over time, changes and adaptations occur in compounds as their owners adjust and adapt to changes in neighboring and contiguous compounds. The alignment of pathways and streets will be delineated and extended in response to the creation and/or changes of farm boundaries and compound walls.

The phenomenon of self-regulating and adaptive systems has been the focus of many disciplines for at least the mid-20th century, such as in physics, biology, economics, and geography. It has been scrutinized by mathematics and has captured the imagination of social scientists whose interpretations brought the findings of these various disciplines, especially the life sciences, closer to urban planning and design.

[53] In all living systems there is a common pattern of organization. Its most important property is that it is a network pattern. Networks of communication generate feedback loops, and living systems learn from mistakes. Thus, a community can correct its mistakes, regulate, and organize itself. These observations of living systems can be applied to the manner in which the traditional *Hausa-Fulani* city self-organized in response to decisions resulting from the ongoing networking between neighbors in shaping their local built environment. For an explanation of network patterns and self-organization based on recent scientific findings, see Capra, 1996:82-83.

# References

Note: Other references and unpublished manuscripts, including those of the *Fodiawa* trio, are cited in the article and notes.

Abu Habib S (1982) *Al-Qamus al-Fiqhi*. Damascus: Dar al-Fikr.

al-Ghani AA (Ed.) (1996) *Suluk al-Malik fi Tadbir al-Mamalik*, by Shihab al-Din Ahmad b. Abi al-Rabi (d. 885 C.E.). Damascus: Dar Kinan.

al-Hakim AM (n.d.) *Al-Mujaz fi sharh al-Qanun al-Madani*. Baghdad: Matba'at al-Ani.

al-Maliki KI (1995, d. 1374 C.E.) *Mukhtasar al-allama Khalil fi fiqh al-Imam Malik*. Beirut: Dar al-Fikr.

al-Sadlan SG (1999) *Al-Qawa'id al-Fiqhiya al-Kubra wa-ma tafara'a anha*. Riyadh: Dar Belensia.

al-Zarka MA (1989) *Sharh al-Qawa'id al-Fiqhiyya*, 2nd edition. Beirut: Dar al-Qalam.

al-Zirkli K (1998) *al-A'lam*, 8 volumes, 13th print edition. Beirut: Dar al-Ilm lil-Malayin.

Bivar ADH (1961) The *wathiqat ahl al-Sudan*: A manifesto of the *Fulani jihad. Journal of African History* 2(2):235-243.

Bourdier J-P, Minh-ha TT (1996) *Drawn from African dwellings*. Bloomington: Indiana University Press.

Capra F (1996) *The web of life: A new scientific understanding of living systems*. New York: Anchor Books.

Dalby D (1964) The noun *garii*: A semantic study. *Journal of African Languages* 3(3):273-305.

Dalby D (1975) The concept of settlement in the west African savannah. In P Oliver (Ed.), *Shelter, sign and symbol*. London: Barrie and Jenkins Ltd., pp. 197-205.

Encyclopedia Britannica (1998) *Zaria*, CD-ROM standard edition.

Hakim B (1986) *Arabic-Islamic cities: Building and planning principles*. London: Kegan Paul.

Hakim B (1994) The *Urf* and its role in diversifying the architecture of traditional Islamic cities. *Journal of Architectural and Planning Research* 11(2):108-127.

Hakim B (2001) Reviving the rule system: An approach for revitalizing traditional towns in Maghrib. *Cities* 18(2):87-92.

Heinrichs W (2002) *Qawa'id* as a genre of legal literature. In BG Weiss (Ed.), *Studies in Islamic legal theory*. Leiden: E.J. Brill, pp. 365-384.

Hunwick JO (1995) *Arabic literature of Africa, Volume 2: The writings of central Sudanic Africa*. Leiden: E.J. Brill.

Ibn Farhun (1884, d. 1397 C.E.) *Tabsirat al-Hukkam* [on the margins are al-Kinani's (d. 1340 C.E.) *Kitab al-'qd al-munazzam lil-Hukkam*]. Beirut: Dar al-Kutub al-Ilmiyah.

Jacobs J (1961) *The death and life of great American cities*. New York: Vintage Books.

Johnson S (2001) *Emergence: The connected lives of ants, brains, cities, and software*. New York: Scribner.

Johnston HAS (1967) *The Fulani empire of Sokoto*. London: Oxford University Press.

Kani AM, Gandi KA (Eds.) (1990) *State and society in Sokoto Caliphate*. Zaria: Gaskiya Corp. Ltd.

Last M (1967) *The Sokoto Caliphate*. New York: Humanities Press.

Moughtin JC (1985) *Hausa architecture*. London: Ethnographica Ltd.

Prussin L (1976) *Fulani-Hausa* architecture. *African Arts* 10(1):8-19, 97-98.

Prussin L (1986) *Hatumere: Islamic design in west Africa*. Berkeley: University of California Press.

Schwerdtfeger FW (1972) Urban settlement patterns in northern Nigeria (Hausaland). In PJ Ucko, R Tringham, and GW Dimbleby (Eds.), *Man, settlement and urbanism*. London: Gerald Duckworth and Co. Ltd., pp. 547-556.

Schwerdtfeger FW (1982) *Traditional housing in African cities*. New York: John Wiley & Sons.

Sharara AAA (1997) *Nazariat nefi al-Darar fi al-Fiqh al-Islami al-Muqaran* (Theory of preventing damage in comparative Islamic *Fiqh*). Tehran: Rabitat al-Thaqafa wa al-Alaqat al-Islamiyah.

Smith MG (1960) *Government in Zazzau, 1800-1950*. London: Oxford University Press.

Sulaiman I (1987) *The Islamic state and the challenge of history*. London: Mansell Publishing Ltd.

Taylor FW, Webb AGG (1932*) Labarum al'adun Hausawa da zantatukansu* — Accounts and conversations describing certain customs of the Hausas. London: Oxford University Press.

Urbanowicz BA (1979) Selected aspects of house form in Zaria urban area with special reference to traditional forms in Zaria walled city. Unpublished doctoral thesis, Ahmadu Bello University, Zaria, Nigeria. (The author taught architecture at Ahmadu Bello University. She died in 1998.)

Urquhart AW (1977) *Planned urban landscapes of northern Nigeria: A case study of Zaria*. Zaria: Ahmadu Bello University Press.

Usman YB (Ed.) (1979) *Studies in the history of the Sokoto Caliphate*. Zaria: Ahmadu Bello University.

Weaver W (1948) Science and complexity. *American Scientist* 36:536-544.

Wiener N (1948) *Cybernetics*. Cambridge: MIT Press.

Yusuf AB (1974) A reconsideration of urban conceptions: *Hausa* urbanization and the *Hausa* rural-urban continuum. *Urban Anthropology* 3(2):200-221.

Zahradeen MS (1976) Abdallah Ibn Fodio's contributions to the *Fulani jihad* in 19th century Hausaland. Unpublished doctoral thesis, McGill University, Montreal, Canada.

Zahradeen MS (1990) The acquisition of land and its administration in the Sokoto Caliphate as provided in Abdallah dan Fodio's *Talim al-Radi*. In AM Kani and KA Gandi (Eds.), *State and society in the Sokoto Caliphate*. Zaria: Gaskiya Corp. Ltd.

## Chapter 6

## Further Studies Needed[1]

A steady growth of studies since the early 1980s, including the occasional dissertation, addressed aspects of research objectives which I set out for myself in early 1975.[2] At this time in the late 1990s, it is a valuable exercise to acquire an overview of the currently available literature for the purpose of identifying further research topics which are necessary as building blocks for structuring a theory of urban form in traditional Islamic cultures. For that purpose I have been able, through a continuous process of reading and scanning the material, to identify gaps in our knowledge. Studies designed to fill these gaps should be undertaken by individuals and institutions, and after this is accomplished we will be able to begin the task of constructing a framework for theory.

The amount of published literature in journals and books and the occasional dissertation on various aspects of the Islamic city which have appeared during the 1980s and 1990s are not focused enough to be directly useful as building blocks for the construction of theory. However, aspects of those efforts may be valuable as secondary sources. Generally the material, which was and continues to be generated, is by some MA and mostly PhD students at various universities in the Western world, with occasional relevant studies from the Arab world. Scholars undertaking research and teaching in the Western world, whether they are of Western origin or scholars whose origins are of the Islamic world, have been and continue to generate articles and occasionally books which are partly relevant for our purpose. Those efforts are usually in response to call for conference papers, invited chapters for books on thematic topics, but very rarely in response to the gaps in knowledge of this emerging field of study. This is also true of topics selected for PhD dissertations. Those are randomly chosen based on the student's awareness and interests in issues shaped by the boundaries of the discipline to which he/she belongs, and in response to the interests and expertise of the supervising professor.

What compounds this problem is the lack of leadership in the field and particularly the lack of funding for relevant research. This is further aggravated due to the strangulating effect by the discipline of art history on the majority of research activities in this field. Art history tends to encourage work and publications related to that discipline's goals and parameters; thus the resulting work is always skewed, wanting, or downright useless for the purposes of constructing theory. There are, however, rare exceptions which are valuable as indicated in the notes and references.

In an extensive review of the literature covering the period from the mid 1970s to the early 1980s (Hakim, 1990), I did point out the following observations which unfortunately continue to plague the field.

— Ernst Grube's question and answers to "What is Islamic architecture?" as it appeared in the introduction of the book *Architecture of the Islamic World* (Grube, 1978) continues to influence good intentioned upstarts in the field, particularly those whose experience was limited to the practice of architecture or whose studies was influenced by the discipline of art history.
— The continued permeation of the theme of power, which is a legacy of art historian Oleg Grabar, passed on to his students and their students. Although it is a useful analytical tool, it does have its limitations and can be counterproductive if misused.
— The concern with origins continues to be of interest but for the wrong reasons. Trying to prove that certain practices were not invented by Muslims but are a result of cultural diffusion from others is useful if undertaken for scientific purposes, but useless if used as a tool of cultural discrimination.

My earlier recommendations for the Aga Khan program and for other similar existing and future organizations are still valid today. They are:
1. develop an agenda and framework for research involving all

major disciplines, with the specific purpose for developing theory;
2. categorize all published materials according to the research framework established in the first step, and identify gaps in research for the purposes of constructing theory;
3. solicit and support top quality research from the most able and qualified people in the world;
4. create an award program for research and publications;
5. allocate adequate funds to translate key works from and to the primary languages in the Islamic world, with Arabic having the first priority.

The rest of the article will: (i) point out examples of what we currently have as building blocks for theory, and (ii) suggest a list of studies which are needed to be researched and developed for the purpose of structuring theory.

## 1 - Available knowledge for theory: some examples

Although the built environment in traditional Islamic cities, as is the situation in other societies, is an integrated system functioning at different levels with systemic linkages from one level to the other, it is helpful for research purposes to examine it in at least three levels:
1. the level of the single building, primarily buildings designed for public use, such as religious, economic, government and defense, health and water works; and private edifices built by the rich and/or powerful, such as palaces, pavilions and gardens;
2. the level of clusters of buildings within neighborhoods, such as clusters of houses, streets and the access system within clusters and quarters;
3. the level of the settlement as a whole is the level concerned with the various physical elements and spatial units which constitute a village, town, or city and how those elements relate to each other, and the rules governing their aggregation in making up the whole entity.

For illustrative purposes, I will point out examples of studies which are valuable for each of the above three levels. A thorough and extensive search will be necessary to generate a comprehensive list. Examples for the *first* level are abundant. This is primarily due to the efforts of Western scholars within the discipline of art history. In that tradition the study of the single monument, particularly its architecture and decoration as a work of art, is the primary concern (eg Grabar, 1973; El-Said and Parman, 1976; al-Faruqi, 1985). Although there is always a desire for more studies dealing with decoration and other aspects of architecture as art, what is not adequately covered at this level of the built environment are issues concerning construction systems and especially techniques of conception, design development, and on-site decision-making processes and related procedures. Nevertheless, the knowledge for constructing theory at this level of the built environment is more readily available than for the other two levels.

Examples for the *second* level is primarily the result of recent work undertaken by individuals with architectural/urban design backgrounds. My work in this area has created the impetus for others to follow.[3] This body of work provides the theoretical building blocks for the workings of the rule system, its underlying rational and how it functioned as part of the decision-making processes in shaping the built environment at this level of the settlement.

Examples for the *third* level is available through the work of historians and geographers (eg Bonine, 1979; Raymond, 1985). I have analyzed and documented the physical components of a typical city, and their relationship to each other functionally and contextually in making up the settlement.[4]

Those few references are illustrative examples of the available knowledge that can be used for constructing theory. Two books should prove valuable in identifying a large number of studies which can also be used for this purpose (Haneda and Miura, 1994; Bonine *et al.*, 1994). A more focused and thorough examination of published studies of relevance to urban form will be a prerequisite for establishing what is available for theory. However, and as an interim measure, I am indicating a group of topics which I believe will be essential to study to fill the gap in our knowledge and/or for further supporting evidence which is necessary for making generalizations, an essential necessity for constructing theory.

## 2 - Studies needed for theory: a preliminary list

The following suggestions for study and research are not exhaustive, but should be considered as an essential preliminary list of topics which are necessary to be undertaken for generating the knowledge and the building blocks, so that a serious attempt can take place in constructing a theory of urban form in Islamic cultures. The list was prepared by following a reverse order of the previous section, ie by listing topics dealing with the settlement level followed by those of relevance at the cluster/neighborhood level, and then those of value at the single building level. Some of the suggestions are of significance to all three levels combined, and some to two levels.

1. Pre-Islamic conceptions of the urban settlement and the city in the Near East and especially in the western region of the Arabian peninsula. How did the Arabs, who were converted to Islam, apply the concepts in establishing new settlements and in adapting existing towns and cities, such as the case of Damascus and Aleppo? No substantive studies, to my knowledge, are available which addresse patterns in land tenure, ownership rights, and control of space. How did those patterns affect the configurations of buildings, streets, and the alignment of shops in commercial areas and markets?

2. The process of land demarcation and subdivision in the early formation of Islamic cities. This is the initial process undertaken for allocating land to public and private uses. Did the allocation of private land precede considerations for the layout of public right-of-ways? What was the technique in undertaking this task? Or was the process in reverse?[5]

3. A detailed study of the principles and workings of land allotment (Iqta), and revivification (Ihya) of land within and on the fringes of settlements. The Prophet applied the principle of Iqta in Madina soon after he settled there. There is abundant descriptions of that example in the Arabic literature and it should be possible to reconstruct what occurred at that time using a process of simulation which is based on the available information.[6]

4. The process of territorialization of land (Ikhtitat), in the initial

and early formation of the quarter (Mahalla) or neighborhood level. After land was allotted to a group of people, they were responsible for its territorialization into clusters of plots, and allocating adequate land for access which eventually became the streets and cul-de-sacs. Since this phenomenon occurred during the early formation of most Islamic cities, it is difficult to find adequate and reliable information describing this process. Yet it is very important to develop a number of alternative scenarios for purposes of constructing theory.

5. How did the institution of Waqf function in terms of its impact on buildings and by extension on urban form? What was the impact on the processes of growth and change? There are a large number of studies on the institution of Waqf, which originates with the teaching of the Prophet. An important saying is "If you wish, retain its origin (habbasta aslaha) and provide it as charity," cited by al-Bukhari. The Hanafi School of Law defines the Waqf as: "the detention of the corpus from the ownership of any person and the gift of its income or usufruct either presently or in the future, to some charitable purpose" (Cattan, 1955). Most of the studies available deal with specific buildings designated as Waqf, but, to my knowledge, there are no studies which attempt to explain the impact of a large number of buildings and real estate on the city as a whole, its processes of growth and change, and the consequence on urban form across time.

6. What were the various types of tenure and ownership of land and buildings? What was the effect of taxation on the various types of tenure? There is a great deal of information available regarding these questions in the classical Arabic sources, and more recently in late 19th century Ottoman sources. A sketchy attempt to address these issues was published (see Serageldin *et al.* (1980), but to my knowledge no extensive studies are available which tackle these questions.

7. The institution of Hisba—what was its jurisdiction and responsibilities?—and its impact on urban management. What was the overlap and/or interaction with the judge's (Qadi) realm of jurisdiction? There are a number of well known Hisba manuals from the eastern (Mashriq) and western (Maghrib) regions

of the Islamic world which should be carefully examined for answering these questions. Further clarifications will emerge from a process of detailed study and analysis of these manuals.

8. Local customs (Urf) in design and building construction practices were a primary engine affecting decision-making and the choice of design solutions in a specific locality. Those customs were sanctioned by the School of Law (Madhab) having the jurisdiction in a locality, provided the custom did not contravene principles of Islamic law (Shari'a). Research is required for a comparative analysis of "solutions" which were generated within the umbrella of the various schools of law, and the manifestation of those solutions in physical terms, particularly noting the differences in solutions to similar problems. This research would rely on cases of rulings by customary law as was recorded by local judges (Qadis), and in the compilations of specialists on law (Muftis), aided were feasible by on-site investigations.

9. Field research of numerous cities within major regions of the Islamic world which are designed to document the design language (linguistic Urf), indicating the sources for the terms, their meaning, and the actual physical configuration and arrangements which the vocabulary of the local design language referred to, including their implication on the design of buildings and the shaping of urban form. Comparative study of the results of these surveys would greatly enhance our understanding of the built form qualities of those cities.[7]

10. Symbolic manifestations occurs at different levels of the built environment, the design and details of decorations in various locations of a building, such as part of the main entrance, around windows, and on the walls surrounding the interior courtyards. In a locality embedded in religious associations, the location of a mosque, water wells for public use, and other elements in the settlement is influenced by historical and religious associations. Comparative research of such example in various regions of the Islamic world is necessary.[8]

11. Mathematics, geometry, surveying, and engineering techniques which were used in building design and construction.

Little serious research on these interrelated aspects has been undertaken. Very recent scholarship is very encouraging; however, this area of investigation is open for a great deal of research possibilities.[9]

12. Building materials and construction techniques. What were their attributes and limitations? How and in what context were materials used separately or in combination with others? For what purposes and how was recycled material used? What were the structural limitations of materials, and how did builders innovate within those constraints?

13. Traditional energy saving practices and techniques, for example, the utilization of water, cooling devices such as wind towers, and disposal methods of human and animal excrement. Although research on these topics are mostly available on Iran, very little has been done for other regions. Comprehensive studies are needed to understand design solutions used for dealing with conditions in different climate zones and topographical features.

14. A study which focuses on the use of the courtyard in the design and planning of houses, with particular attention to its use as a customary inherited element, ie when used unconsciously as a customary practice without concern for its design potentials vs. its intentional use as a device embodied with design possibilities and opportunities for climate control.

15. An atlas of Islamic cities in various regions of the Islamic world which would document: (i) city maps drawn in the same format, using the same system of colors, and supplemented by the necessary aerial photographs; (ii) morphological patterns at the levels of the city, neighborhood, and building clusters and would include, for example, the patterns of public through streets and private cul-de-sacs, and the analysis of the typology's strengths and weaknesses. Certain peculiarities would also be studied, such as the preference for the location of a small mesjid at the strategic junction of a fork in the street system;[10] and (iii) study of building types drawn to the same scale and presented in plans, elevations, and sections.

I hope that the above list of topics will be valuable for those concerned with the lack of theory. Other topics addressing detailed aspects can be developed and added. It is important to stress that we are at a point in the development of this field which necessitates cooperative efforts to address the above issues, so as to make it possible to construct theory. Cooperation can be achieved in many ways, through (i) effective and accessible communication tools, such as through the World Wide Web pages of the Internet. Web pages can be created by individual scholars and institutions where the latest research is summarized and/or made available for downloading to personal computers; (ii) focused symposia and conferences such as those which were organized in Tokyo, Japan in 1989 and 1990 under the cosponsorship of the research project "Urbanism in Islam, a Comparative Study", which was a priority area research project supported by Japan's Ministry of Education, Science and Culture Grant-in-Aid and the Middle Eastern Culture Center in Tokyo; and (iii) testing in contemporary projects by recycling the principles underlying traditional ideas and procedures.[11] If the suggestions made in this article are carried out, then an achievement of this magnitude will not only be of immense value to the Islamic world and its numerous subcultures, but it will also be a significant contribution to our understanding of urbanism and the urban phenomenon as a cultural expression within a global context.

## Notes

[1] The completion of the preliminary draft of this article coincided with the passing away of my dear father, Dr. Selim Hakim, on 24 June 1995. This humble contribution is dedicated to his memory.

[2] I first started studying the Islamic city in the context of Arab culture in North Africa in early 1975 when I was a visiting professor during the Spring semester at the Technical Institute of Architecture and Urbanism in Tunis. The primary objective of the study as I conceived it at that time was: "To identify and record the building and planning principles which shaped the traditional Arabic – Islamic city." This evolved to include the legal and customary laws as the basis for the rule system which people respected and followed in decisions affecting their built environment. At that time material directly usable for the study was practically nonexistent, although after extensive research, some sources were uncovered which were partly and indirectly valuable. For a discussion of objectives

and related issues see pp 11–14 of the "Introduction" of my *Arabic – Islamic Cities: Building and Planning Principles*, Kegan Paul International, London and New York [1979 (1986)], and pp 15–22 for sources which were partly or indirectly valuable. See also the results of my research on customary law in Hakim (1994).

[3] For an account of the diffusion of my work see Hakim (1988) and MESA Bulletin (1992).

[4] Tunis medina, in my *Arabic – Islamic Cities*, full citation in note 2; and the village of Sidi Bou Sa'id north of Tunis medina, in Hakim (1978).

[5] J. Akbar attempted to explain this in his "Khatta and the territorial structure of early Muslim towns", in *Muqarnas* 6 (1989), pp 22–32. The effort addresses important issues and should be viewed as a good start. More extensive research is needed. Here the techniques and skills of archaeologists would be most valuable. A good example of an earlier study is by archaeologist Schmidt (1964).

[6] See the book *Wafa al-Wafa*, by Nuraldin al-Samhudi (died 1505), four parts in 2 volumes (Dar Ihya al-Turath al-Arabi, Beirut, 1955). As for the principle and implementation of Ihya, information based on the legal literature of the predominant Islamic Madahib (schools of law) aided by on site archaeological investigations of cities which were influenced by a specific school of law would clarify the workings of this principle.

[7] For a detailed discussion of what is the "design language" see Chapter 2 of my book *Arabic – Islamic Cities*, full citation in note 2 above. For what is the "linguistic Urf" see Hakim (1994).

[8] See Chapter 4, "Symbolism and form", of Hakim (1978). This chapter analyzes symbolism in the village at three levels: (i) the village, (ii) entrances, windows, and steps, and (iii) surface embellishments such as plaster carvings, stonework, and tiles. See also Abdelhalim (1978).

[9] See the articles by Chorbachi (1989) and Ozdural (1995) and the published manuscript of Efendi (1987).

[10] The utilization of this type of junction, which results from the convergence of two streets into one, within this morphological type can also be traced as far back as 2000 BC in Ur, southern Mesopotamia. See Exhibit 2 of Hakim (1982); or Figure 1 in Hakim (1989); also the street analysis in Chapter 3, "Spatial structure and built form", pp 19–56, in Hakim (1978).

[11] I have constructed a framework for action which was published in the 1991 article "Urban design in traditional Islamic culture: Recycling its successes" in *Cities*, **8**(4), pp 274–277. On 7 June 1997 I delivered a

keynote address at a Vision symposium in Riyadh, Saudi Arabia which was organized by Arriyadh Development Authority (ADA), on the occasion of the completion of phase 1 of three-phase planning process known as Metropolitan Development Strategy for Arriyadh (MEDSTAR). One of the proposals I made in that address was based on the principle of bottom – up decision-making at the neighborhood level. This principle was operational in all traditional cities and settlements in the Islamic world and was replaced, in the case of Saudi Arabia, by a top – down decision-making structure during the mid years of this 20th century as a result of Western influences and for reasons related to local political preferences. My proposal was to create neighborhood organizations whose task would be to coordinate decisions affecting the well being of a neighborhood including matters related to design and planning. This would create a situation where neighborhoods would be encouraged to compete with each other for the best ideas and designs which would alleviate or solve pervasive and common problems, such as safety in neighborhood streets, greening of streets by planting and maintaining trees and shrubs, creating pleasant pedestrian paths which would ensure the safety and protection of women and children. My other proposal was to rewrite the city's planning codes in a manner which will utilize the wisdom inherent in the traditional codes, in lieu of trying to fix codes which were formulated in the early 1980s and which have proved to be inferior as it is evident in various parts of the city. It remains to be seen if these and other suggestions will be incorporated in the process of crafting the metropolitan development strategy for Arriyadh, the capital of Saudi Arabia. I have also addressed similar issues for the context of historic towns in the Maghrib countries of North Africa in a paper titled: "Reviving the rule system: an approach for revitalizing traditional towns in the Maghrib", presented at the conference "The Living Medina: The Walled Arab City in Architecture, Literature, and History" held in Tangier, Morocco, June 1996, sponsored by the American Institute of Maghribi Studies (AIMS).

## References

Abdelhalim, A. (1978) *The Building Ceremony*. PhD dissertation, University of California, Berkeley.

Bonine, M (1979) The morphogenesis of Iranian cities. *Annals of the Association of American Geographers* 69(2), 208–224.

Bonine, M., Ehlers, E., Kraft, T. and Stober, G. (Eds) (1994) *The Middle Eastern City and Islamic Urbanism: An Annotated Bibliography of Western Literature*. Ferd. Dummlers Verlag, Bonn.

Cattan, H. (1955) The law of Waqf. In *Law in the Middle East*, eds M. Khadduri and H. J. Liebesny. The Middle East Institute, Washington, DC.

Chorbachi, W (1989) In the tower of Babel: beyond symmetry in Islamic design. *Computers and Mathematics with Applications* **17**(4–6), 751–789.

Efendi, C. (1987) *Risale -i Mimariyye: an early 17th century Ottoman treatise on architecture*, translated by Howard Crane. Brill, Leiden.

El-Said, I. and Parman, A. (1976) *Geometric Concepts in Islamic Art*. World of Islam Festival Publishing, London.

al-Faruqi, L. (1985) Appreciating Islamic art. *Arts and the Islamic World* **3**(3), 31–37.

Grabar, O. (1973) *The Formation of Islamic Art*. Yale University Press, New Haven.

Grube, E. (1978) Introduction: What is Islamic Architecture? 10–14. In *Architecture of the Islamic World*, ed. G. Michell. Thames & Hudson, London.

Hakim, B. S. (Ed) (1978) *Sidi Bou Sa'id, Tunisia: A Study in Structure and Form*. Technical University of Nova Scotia, Halifax, revised edition 2009. Available from Amazon.com.

Hakim, B S (1982) Arab – Islamic urban structure. *Arabian Journal for Science and Engineering* **7**(2), 69–79.

Hakim, B. S. (1988) *Al-Muhandis* **67**(8). Riyadh, Saudi Arabia.

Hakim, B. S. (1989) Islamic architecture and urbanism. In *Encyclopedia of Architecture: Design, Engineering and Construction*, Vol. 3, pp. 86–103. John Wiley, New York.

Hakim, B S (1990) The Islamic city and its architecture: a review essay. *Third World Planning Review* **12**(1), 75–89.

Hakim, B S (1994) The "Urf" and its role in diversifying the architecture of traditional Islamic cities. *Journal of Archtectural and Planning Research* **11**(2), 108–127.

Haneda, M. and Miura, T. (Eds) (1994) *Islamic Urban Studies: Historical Review and Perspectives*. Kegan Paul International, London and New York.

*MESA Bulletin* (1992), 26(1), 150-152.

Ozdural, A (1995) Omar Khayyam, mathematicians, and conversazioni with artisans. *Journal of Society of Architectural Historians* **54**(1), 54–71.

Raymond, R. (1985) *Grandes villes arabe a l'epoque ottomane*. Sinbad, Paris.

Schmidt, J. (1964) Strassen in Altorientalischen wohngebieten: eine studie zur geschichte des stadtebaues in Mesopotamien und Syrien. In *Deutsches Archaologisches Institut Abteilung Baghdad:Baghdader Mitteilungen*, Vol. 3, pp. 125–147. Verlag Gebr. Mann, Berlin.

Serageldin, M., Doebele, W. and El Araby, K. (1980) Land tenure systems and development controls in the Arab countries of the Middle East. In *Housing Process and Physical Form*, Proceedings of Seminar Three held in Jakarta, Indonesia, March 1979, sponsored by the Aga Khan Award for Architecture, pp. 75–88.

# Part II: Recycling Lessons

Part II addresses 1) the question of how to identify the underlying features of the traditional/historic experience that are useful as lessons to learn from, and 2) present a framework that covers issues related to the procedures of the building process, and those that are related to the organizational system and built form. The application of how to recycle the lessons pointed out in the framework is discussed in detail in chapters 8 and 9. This is followed by a discussion of how in general terms revive the rule system, applicable in many regions, with particular attention to the Maghrib countries of North Africa. Chapter 11 applies the lessons of process to a proposal for a housing project in Abiquiu, New Mexico. Followed by chapter 12 that demonstrates the application of the generic lessons inherent in the traditional physical organizational system and planning to a neighborhood test design. Part II is comprised of six chapters:

7 - Framework for Recycling ..................................... 175

8 - Recycling Experiences of Process and Form ....... 183

9 - Nature of Islamic Urbanism and its Lessons ....... 199

10 - Reviving the Rule System ................................. 245

11 - Applying Lessons in Abiquiu, New Mexico ....... 257

12 - Neighborhood Test Design ................................ 277

# Chapter 7

# Framework for Recycling

After completing extensive research and writing on the factors that shaped traditional dwellings and settlements in North Africa, culminating in the publication of the book *Arabic-Islamic Cities: Building and Planning Principles*, it was apparent that the question of what we can do with this new awareness and knowledge to improve our contemporary and future environments begged an adequate answer; this modest contribution addresses it.

The paper emphasizes the notion that we should not copy from tradition, but develop principles and lessons from a clear understanding of concepts, models and theories from man-environment studies as applied to traditional settlements. Seven sample issues and concepts are briefly discussed to illuminate this approach. A framework for viewing lessons from the past is proposed. It is divided into two broad categories of *process* and *product*, and three areas of lessons are grouped under each of those headings (Table 1).

## 1 - Motivation and objectives

My primary motivation in undertaking research on traditional Islamic environments was to derive principles and lessons from the past which can be used today to improve the quality of our contemporary built environment, regardless of location; and to learn how to develop the framework and mechanisms necessary to allow a culture's identity to be reflected in its architecture and built environment, using Islamic culture as a case study. I attempted to identify the lessons available from my research in the form of general points in lectures given since 1978 and in related publications.[1]

**Table 1.** A proposed framework for recycling relevant aspects from the experience of traditional Islamic building and urbanism.[a]

| A/Procedures of building (process) | B/Organizational system and built form (product) |
|---|---|
| **Impact of decisions by governing authority** | **Compatibility with ecology and climate** |
| Policy at highest governmental level required in centralized and autocratic systems | Excellent precedents are available for approaching building and community design passively |
| Citizens' input for policy formulation in representative democratic systems | Appropriate landscape design based on Islamic values |
| Both planning and design policies needed | |
| Coordination and experience sharing between Islamic countries called for | |
| Policies required for architecture and urban planning education to make it responsive to local and cultural conditions | |
| **Role of the *Fiqh* and its special attributes[b]** | **Physical organizational system and planning** |
| Nature of *Fiqh* guidelines and their application depended on intent and/or performance, not on prescriptive standards | Lessons in the utilization of land and the distribution of space three dimensionally, especially for residential and commercial areas |
| Unified by Koranic and *Sunnah*[c] injunction but responsive to local conditions, thus variety within a framework of unity was achieved | Impact of Islamic law on components of built environment eg ownership and maintenance of cul-de-sacs, construction of *Sabat*[d] (air-right structures) and their support systems etc |
| | Efficiency and economic advantages of traditional system |
| **Principles of the production process** | **Architectural design, style and decoration** |
| Seven questions related to production in housing.[e] | Lessons available from past, but problem is generating appropriate contemporary form which is not a direct copy from the past |
| 1. Who is in charge of building operation? | Theories required to deal with space use and articulation, use of materials and technology for contemporary Islamic environments |
| 2. How local to community is the construction firm? | How to deal with contemporary building types and functions in terms of infusing into them a local identity |
| 3. Who lays out plots and controls land between houses? | A contemporary design language – identification of certain patterns and microtypologies which are successful, and which are a result of local cultural preferences, and then developing those further |
| 4. Who lays out plans of individual houses? | |
| 5. Standard components or standard processes? | |
| 6. Cost control, how? | |
| 7. Life on construction site? | |
| Responsibilities of actors involved in all aspects of building activity and impacts on the nature of process and resulting built form | |

[a] For a discussion of this framework please refer to B. Hakim, 'Recycling the experience of traditional Islamic urbanism', paper presented at conference on the *Preservation of Architectural Heritage of Islamic Cities*, Istanbul, 22–26 April 1985. Proceedings published by the Arab Urban Development Institute, Riyadh, 1988; and to B. Hakim, 'Islamic architecture and urbanism', *Encyclopedia of Architecture: Design, Engineering and Construction*, Vol 3, John Wiley, New York, 1989, pp 86–103.
[b] *Fiqh* is the science and methodology for interpreting and applying the value system of the Shari'a (Islamic law). It was also used within processes of building and urban development.
[c] *Sunnah* is the prophet Mohammad's behaviour, deeds and sayings, as recorded in the traditional texts.
[d] *Sabat* is a structure, usually in the form of a room, which is constructed over a public right of way allowing unimpeded traffic flow beneath. A common term for this type of construction is 'air-right structure'.
[e] From C. Alexander et al, *The Production of Houses*, 1985.

**Table 1.** A proposed framework for recycling relevant aspects.

Another research objective which I set myself in mid 1974 was the recycling and testing of the principles which would be identified as an outcome of that effort. As the evidence and results began to take shape, it became clearer that testing the experience of the traditional process was more crucial than the direct testing of the physical organizational system and built form. The opportunity for undertaking such a test on a real project was not available in 1978-79 when I was in the process of completing the difficult task of documenting the results of that research, which was completed in mid 1979, and published as a book entitled *Arabic-Islamic Cities: Building and Planning Principles* in early 1986.[2]

I nevertheless decided to go ahead and at least test the traditional organizational system and built form of the housing sector to ascertain if it were compatible with contemporary amenities and requirements. That research was completed in early 1978.[3] I have been reluctant to publish the results before I had a chance first to test and use the principles generated by the research. The opportunity presented itself in the autumn 1980 when Dar Al-Islam[4] commissioned me to develop a planning proposal for their proposed village, to accommodate approximately a hundred households and the necessary community facilities. In addition, they requested a package of design guidelines for the housing sector which they intended to develop in approximate increments of five to ten houses by the families themselves. These parameters, and the desire to use a typology which allowed building to the boundaries of each plot, were the given conditions for developing the guidelines for building design decisions affecting proximate neighbours. The planning proposal for the village and the guidelines were completed in February 1981. Unfortunately events at Dar Al Islam did not proceed as intended.[5] Most of the energy and financial resources were spent on building a school, and the development of the housing sector was postponed. Thus the result of that test is incomplete. Nevertheless the guidelines were published in a shortened and more complete version.[6]

## 2 - The approach to recycling and examples of relevant issues

The writing of Amos Rapoport provides support for the thrust of my thinking on this topic.[7] Figure 1 clarifies the approach: that we should not directly copy from tradition, but develop principles and lessons from a clear understanding of concepts, models and theories from man-environment studies as applied to traditional environments. To illustrate I shall briefly discuss some examples of the relevant issues and concepts which need to be addressed, among others, in order to derive principles and lessons usable in contemporary and future design activities.

A primary concern of planning and design activity is with the environmental quality of the natural and built environments ie the *what* and *why* of planning and design. This concern relates to universal pan-human and culture specific requirements.[8] We need to stress

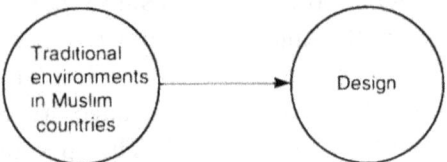

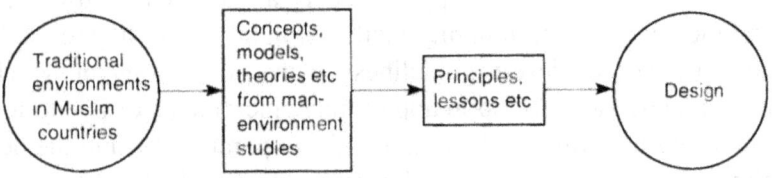

**Figure 1.** How to learn from tradition. Source: After Amos Rapoport

the latter at the local level. For example, why import international codes and standards for the arrangement of the built environment, and especially in housing areas? Why not develop control mechanisms based on local cultural requirements?

We need to look far lessons in traditional environments by studying the predominant system of arrangement at the macro- and micro-scales. This is composed of physical elements and their relationships, which contribute to the character of a place. To encourage cultural distinctiveness in contemporary environments we need to develop the planning framework and implementation mechanisms which allow this to occur. At the micro-scale I have documented examples from the history of Tunis.[9]

The framework could represent an overall typological concept and guide usage distribution. Contemporary roads, infrastructure and land-use allocation, as well as attitude to the general landscape, could be developed to represent a shared concept which does not conflict with the culture's values. This is usually associated with large capital investment and a longer time frame, whereas infill allows for change and variety and, in the case of housing, can provide the opportunity for the involvement of users in shaping their dwelling and immediate environments.[10] In this situation individuals could be guided by a set of shared building norms/rules derived from their own culture, as has happened in traditional Islamic towns.[11]

The urban environment and the character of cities can be responsive to cultural determinants if its components are manageable. The neighbourhood scale viewed as 'environmental area' can be a positive planning device for allowing local decisions to occur by the use of agreed upon and culturally sensitive control and implementation device(s).[12] This concept is related to the framework and infill concept but viewed at the macro-scale of the city. The use of the car and the differentiation of space related to it and to other uses can be culturally innovative and responsive.[13]

Images and ideals narrow the choice between possible alternatives. Governments and policy makers in many Arab and Muslim countries have purposefully encouraged the image of modernism through the media and by the example of built projects. This has had the effect of excluding the traditional environment as a repository of valuable lessons and thereby narrowing down alternatives. A reverse policy is urgently needed to educate the public through all available media means as rapidly as possible.

What people need and what they want may not be the same. Cross cultural influences affect this phenomenon. We also know that certain organizational and building typologies create more cost and investment constraints than other types, while the reverse might also be argued. This is a complex issue which requires attention at the policy level and which is affected by the level of education and awareness of people and their view of the built environment. A choice among alternatives is critical.

Conservation is predominantly viewed as conservation of existing physical cultural landscapes. Another view is that conservation of principles derived from the cultural landscape might be more critical if we want to encourage continued and dynamic use of an area ie to allow change and growth to occur while preserving its essence. I had a good opportunity of studying this problem in the case of Old Town Albuquerque, New Mexico, and proposed a revision of existing city procedures and the necessary design guidelines to be followed.[14]

**Summary**

These were only seven issues and concepts out of a large number, chosen to provide a taste of the issues at hand and the thrust of my current endeavours in this field. Table 1 attempts to classify in a clear framework areas for recycling relevant aspects from the traditional experience. It should also be viewed as a framework for research objectives and tasks. The cooperation of numerous individuals and institutions is required to achieve success in covering all the areas proposed by the framework.

It is also hoped that the proposed framework will help in identifying existing contributions, and as instigation for others to fill in the gaps, especially the numerous schools of architecture and planning in Muslim countries, who should be taking the lead in these research activities. Much needs to be done, and urgently.

**Notes**

[1] B. Hakim, 'The contemporary benefits of traditional mid-east urbanism', *Proceedings of First National Conference in Urban Design*, New York, 18-21 October 1978; B. Hakim (ed), *Sidi Bou Sa'id, Tunisia: A Study in Structure and Form*, Technical University of Nova Scotia, Halifax, Canada 1978. (Revised edition 2009, available from Amazon.com). B. Hakim, *Arabic-Islamic Cities: Building and Planning Principles*, Kegan Paul International, London, 2nd edn, 1988 (also published in Japanese by Daisan Shokan, Tokyo, 1990); B. Hakim, 'Arab-Islamic urban structure', *The Arabian Journal far Science and Engineering*, Vol 7, No 2, 1982, pp 69-79; B. Hakim and Peter G. Rowe, 'The representation of values in traditional and contemporary Islamic cities' (two papers in one article), *Journal of Architectural Education*, Vol 36, No 4, Summer 1983, pp 22-28; B. Hakim, 'Recycling a traditional housing process: a case in Abiquiu, New Mexico', *Proceedings of the 74th Annual Meeting of the Association of Collegiate Schools of Architecture* held in New Orleans, LA, March 1986, pp 109-119; B. Hakim, 'Dar Al-Islam Village, Abiquiu, New Mexico: guidelines for building design decisions affecting proximate neighbors', *REVIEW '86*, College of Environmental Design, KFUPM, Dhahran 31261, Saudi Arabia, pp 11-28; B. Hakim, 'Recycling the experience of traditional Islamic urbanism', Conference on the *Preservation Architectural Heritage of Islamic Cities*, Istanbul, Turkey, 22-26 April 1985 (proceedings published by Arab Urban Development Institute, Riyadh, Saudi Arabia, 1988); B. Hakim, 'Islamic architecture and urbanism', *Encyclopedia of Architecture: Design, Engineering and Construction*, Vol 3, John Wiley, New York, 1989, pp 86--103; B. Hakim, 'Teaching history by searching for emics and etics', *Proceedings of the 77th Annual Meeting of the ACSA: Debate and Dialogue - Architectural Design and Ped-*

agogy, held in Chicago, March 1989, pp 167-180 (also published in *Design Studies*, Vol. 12, No 1, January 1991, pp 19- 29); B. Hakim, 'The role of the *urf* (customs) in shaping the traditional Islamic city', *Proceedings of the International Conference on Urbanism in Islam*, Vol 2, 1989, pp 113-138, held in Tokyo, Japan, 22-28 October, 1989 (published in 1994 in *Journal of Architectural and Planning Research*); and B. Hakim, 'The Islamic city and its architecture - a review essay', *Third World Planning Review*, Vol 12, No 1, February 1990, pp 75-89.

[2] *Op cit*, Ref 1, *Arabic-Islamic Cities*.

[3] A test design tor a prototype neighbourhood was developed to fit in site conditions typical of arid areas in the Middle East and North African regions. The project consisted of 428 units and supporting community facilities on a typical flat site of approximately 18 hectares.

[4] Dar Al-Islam is a non-profit corporation dedicated to creating a village for a community of Muslims on land which it has purchased near the village of Abiquiu, New Mexico, USA, approximately 60 miles north-west of the city of Sante Fe.

[5] The initial intention was to start with the housing sector and then develop the other major community facilities.

[6] *Op cit*, Ref 1, 'Recycling a traditional housing process' and 'Dar Al-Islam Village'.

[7] Amos Rapoport, 'Environmental quality, metropolitan areas and traditional settlements', *Habitat International*, Vol 7, Nos 3-4, 1983, pp 37-63; and 'Development, culture change and supportive design', *Habitat International*, Vol 7, Nos 5-6 1983, pp 249-268.

[8] B. Hakim *et al*, 'Ecological systems as models for human environments', *Ekistics*, No 208, March 1973, pp 168-171; op cit, Rei 1, 'Teaching history'; and Othman Llewellyn, 'Shari'ah values pertaining to landscape planning and design', *Islamic Architecture and Urbanism*, Selected papers from a symposium organized by the College of Architecture and Planning, KFU, Dammam, Saudi Arabia, 1983, pp 31-42.

[9] *Op cit*, Ref 1, *Arabic-Islamic Cities*.

[10] John F.C. Turner, *Housing by People*, Marion Boyars, London, 1976; N.J. Habraken, *The Supports and the People: The End of the Housing Project*, Scheltema and Holkema, Amsterdam, 1961; *Transformations of the Site*, Awater Press, Cambridge, MA, 1983.

[11] *Op cit*, Rcf 1, *Arabic-Islamic Cities*.

[12] C. Buchanan et al, *Traffic in Towns*, HMSO, London, 1963.

[13] B. Hakim, 'Co-op housing, Baghdad' an evaluation and recommendations', *Ekistics*, No 196, March 1972, pp 166-172.

[14] B. Hakim, *Historic Old Town, Albuquerque, New Mexico: A Procedure for Guiding Change and Development Based on Patterns/Guidelines and Continuous Appraisal*, For Department of Community and Economic Development, City of Albuquerque, New Mexico (unpublished technical report), 1983.

## Chapter 8

# Recycling Experiences of Process and Form

A primary reason for research and study into socio-cultural aspects of traditional built environments by the environmental design professions is to understand and evaluate the factors and processes that shaped the man-made built form. This understanding can then be used in developing policies and strategies for recycling the positive and useful traditional experiences into contemporary practice. The latter objective is usually based on the assumption that it is desirable to recycle what is culturally perceived to be positive aspects of a given experience and tradition. Today most of the reasons for pursuing such policies are based on the desire for re-establishing cultural identity, and to a lesser degree in developing alternatives to unworkable contemporary solutions.[1]

In contemporary history, particularly since the twenties of the 20th century, the Islamic countries have undergone experiences and changes in the built environment that pose interesting problems and provide a valuable case study for understanding traditional and contemporary phenomenon of socio-cultural aspects of built form.

For many reasons, which are outside the scope of this paper, the trend has recently developed in most of the Islamic countries to look back on their cultural heritage, including that of building and urbanism. A primary reason for the latter is the desire for the cultural enhancement of their contemporary environments. However most attempts were confined to the building scale within the narrow framework of architectural style and aesthetics. The purpose of this paper emerged out of a reaction to this narrow view. I have attempted to summarize the larger base of traditional experiences in the area of building and urbanism from which it is possible to recycle for contemporary use.

The Islamic world today is composed of many sovereign countries at mixed levels of prosperity and development. Thus any consideration for the recycling of traditional experiences has to be of benefit to these diverse conditions.

The primary lessons offered by the experience of traditional building and planning in the context of Islamic Culture lie in (a) the procedures of building, and (b) the predominant organizational system used.[2] The former contains most of the deep-rooted, ideologically based lessons, from which it is possible to recycle. The latter is useful for generating alternative contemporary design models, particularly for the housing and commercial sectors. It also provides excellent precedence in the use of building materials, structural and construction solutions using simple technologies, design of energy conserving communities and buildings, and other related accomplishments.

I shall group selected lessons, which are of value to our contemporary time and the future, under the two categories mentioned above. They are presented briefly as a topic or issue followed by comments and suggestions of how they might be useful.

## 1 - Lessons for the Future Derived from the Procedures of Building

### 1.1 - Impacts of decisions by governing authority

Traditionally such decisions always had major impacts on the location of important buildings and the alignment of primary streets. Thus the overall framework of the city was established. However it should be noted that decisions were made within an established framework of design norms and planning/organizational relationships. Historically these were influenced by cultural values and unified by a similar approach due to the open borders and the exchange of knowledge between Islamic regions.

Today decisions by governments in the Islamic countries are more impacting, and are usually based on proposals and recommendations developed by foreign consultants. The consultant's views, however, are chiefly Western imports, and their input for the most part ignores or is insensitive to local traditions and trends. This problem is compounded by the fact that various regions of the Islamic world today are aligned to different foreign countries or systems, thus complicating the approach to city planning and building. For example in Tunisia, Algeria and Morocco, the French approach is followed, in Libya and until recently in Egypt the Soviet approach, whereas in Saudi Arabia the American Fadan approach. In Iraq and the Gulf States the British approach seems to be predominant. These foreign prototypes are usually imposed without consideration to cultural values, (Figure 1). Therefore to achieve some unity in approach, much coordination is necessary between the Islamic countries today and in the future regarding large scale planning since they all share one set of cultural norms and values.

## 1.2 - The Islamicity of traditional cities was made possible by the role of the Fiqh

A brief discussion of how this occurred in traditional settlements was presented elsewhere.[3] The central question which arises is: how can the linkage between the *Fiqh* and contemporary activities of building and urbanization occur today and in the future?

In many of the Islamic countries today and particularly since the introduction of the automobile and Western techniques of city planning, urbanization activities became gradually detached from the traditional umbrella of the *Fiqh* and the *Urf*.[4] This detachment occurred at various times in different places during the nineteenth and twentieth centuries, related to the period when European in-

**Figure 1.** View of Crash Housing in Dammam, Saudi Arabia (after Fadan)

185

fluence or colonization occurred. Thus design decisions based on quasi-technical regulations were in conflict with traditional law,[5] (Figure 2). The gradual dislocation of the *Fiqh* from building/urbanization activities under the theme of modernization is now recognized as being inappropriate. Thus the challenge and task for the future is for the re-integration of the *Fiqh* in building and planning activities. This task can be accelerated when adequate fresh approaches are developed by interdisciplinary teams of *Fuqaha* and the various disciplines involved in urbanization and building activities.[6] It would then be possible to externalize Islamic values in contemporary and future architecture. The results would be exciting and unpredictable, with potentials for unique models and approaches.

**Figure 2.** Corrugated screen erected to obstruct view into the private domain from balcony of neighbor across street, in Riyadh, Saudi Arabia (after al-Hathloul).

## 1.3 – Decision-making within a framework of performance criteria

The nature of the *Fiqh* guidelines and their application depended on intent and/or performance, and not on prescriptive standards. Thus people in the traditional setting involved in building decision-making, operated within a flexible framework of performance criteria. Each design situation could be resolved according to the conditions in the specific locality and the requirements of the people concerned. As long as the intent of the guidelines were met, the peculiar configurations of the solution would be acceptable. This approach directly influenced the three-dimensional outcome and quality of the building environment, (Figure 3).

Today the production process has changed, and the scale of projects have enlarged considerably. The time frame within which a project is to be completed is shortened. The result of this situation has fostered, for example, large scale repetitive design of housing using mostly the "turn key" approach of production. This situation has disenfranchised users from decision making affecting their future living quarters.

The challenge for the future is to develop processes of production which can be guided by performance type design criteria which are derived from the culture's value system. Methods of encouraging user participation, particularly in housing projects, should be developed. The potentially exciting results would directly contribute to the vitality and satisfaction of living and to the three-dimensional diversity of built form.

**Figure 3.** Plan of Rue Snossi in Sidi Bou Sa'id, Tunisia. The sketch view is from the location of the arrow on the plan (after Hakim's (ed.) Sidi Bou Sa'id, Tunisia: A Study in Structure and Form, 1978).

## 2 - Lessons for the Future Derived from the Organizational System and Built Form

### 2.1 - Compatibility with ecology and climate

Much has been written about traditional examples in terms of the use of natural building materials, cooling and heating devices and the behavior of compact courtyard housing and so on.[7] These techniques were historically used extensively in the Middle East, including specialized facilities such as the natural ice-maker, (Figure 4).

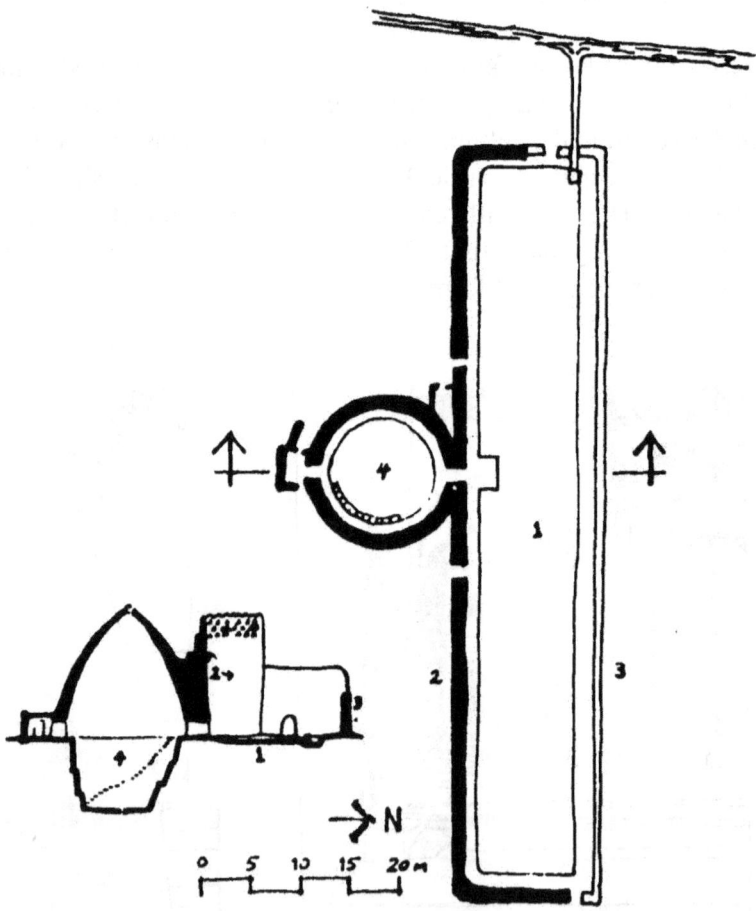

**Figure 4.** A plan and section of a typical yakh-chal (ice-house), near the city of Yazd in Iran. Ice is made in the winter and stored in the ice-pit for summer use. Legend: (1) Pool for making ice, (2) wall, (3) garden wall and (4) ice pit. For a detailed description of how ice was made, stored and used, see Living With the Desert: Working Buildings of the Iranian Plateau, by Elizabeth Beazley and Michael Harverson, 1982 (after Beazley & Harverson).

These examples provide excellent precedents and impetus for contemporary designers in approaching building and community design "passively", i.e. relying minimally on mechanical devices for cooling and heating and using minimum deletable and expensive energy and other resources for manufacturing materials and for production purposes.

As to the question of appropriate landscape design, we have some contemporary literature on the Islamic tradition of landscaping, its approach and foundations in the culture's value system.[8] For the contemporary and future landscape designer, a sensitive understanding and appreciation of the deep-rooted structure, its rational and ultimate manifestation in built form is essential for intelligent recycling.

## 2.2 - Organizational System and Planning

A study of aerial photographs of traditional towns and villages reveals the astonishing similarity in organization and clustering across the vast territory of the Islamic world.[9] Although security and defense were major determinants in maintaining the compactness of towns and surrounding them with walls, it is in the utilization of land and the distribution of space three dimensionally that interesting lessons lie for contemporary and future architects/planners. The two sectors which contain the most relevant lessons in this regard are the residential and commercial areas, (Figure 5).

The essential feature of the residential sector is the design and configuration of the typical unit. Rooms surround a courtyard open to the sky. Almost all windows open onto this interior court and the structure has one or two stories, with a basement sometimes included for summer use in some regions such as in Iraq and Iran. In other regions such as in Tunisia, a cistern is built under the court to collect winter rainwater for year round household use.

Clusters of houses are created by adjoining homes with at least three external walls of each house abutting other houses. Access to these clusters is by narrow cul-de-sacs, which branch off from a network of through streets. The cul-de-sacs are owned and maintained by the people who use them and are regarded as private property. Occasionally, rooms bridge the public through streets as

**Figure 5A.** A plan of a typical residential area in the traditional medina of Tunis, Tunisia (after plans developed by the author in 1977).

a method of creating extra space within a dwelling. Often such rooms link two properties owned by the same family, but which are across the street from each other.

What are the benefits of this form of residential design and organization? The courtyard floor and earth beneath it act as a combined radiating and storage unit. The walls on four sides, particularly if their height is greater than the width of the courtyard from the direction of the sun, will shade the court and protect it from direct sunlight during the greater part of the day. The courtyard floor, however, is left open to the sky (the zenith) to which it radiates heat during the day and particularly during the night. The earth beneath the court acts as a radiating heat sink which in turn attracts more heat from surrounding areas in contact with it.

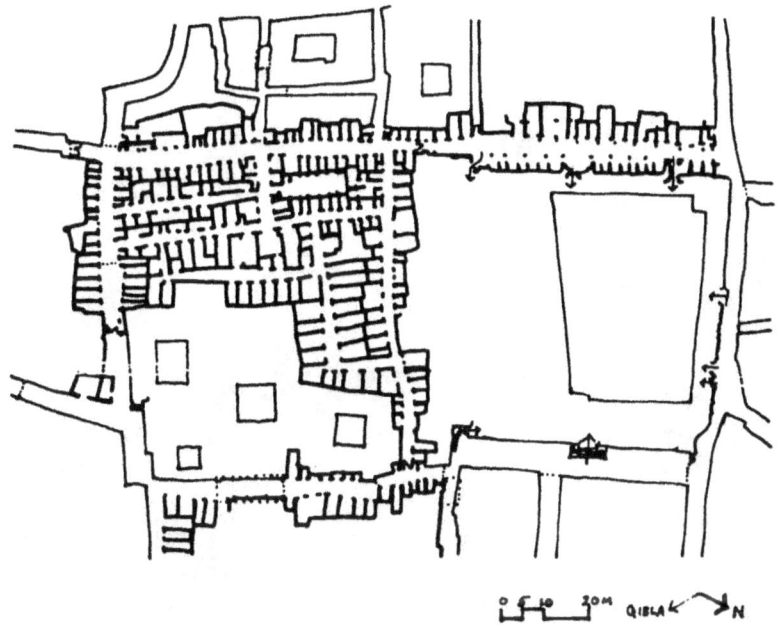

**Figure 5B.** A partial plan of the commercial area (suq) on the southern side of the Zaytuna Mosque in the traditional medina of Tunis, Tunisia (after the original sketch developed by the author in 1979 and first published on page 135 in his Arabic-Islamic Cities: Building and Planning Principles, 1986).

Other important advantages of this form of housing are: it provides high standards of privacy and security within a physical setting which could promote neighbourly social interaction if desired by the occupants. The nature of the clustering is economical due to sharing of most external walls and is a major contributor toward savings. There are, of course, alternative technical solutions to the party walls, which will solve problems of ownership, maintenance rights, acoustics and fire. It provides medium densities of between 11-14 units per acre, yet achieves large living areas within each unit. From 1345 to 1840 square feet for a single story house, to 2690 and up to 3680 square feet for a two story house. These figures were based on a prototype design which the author developed. On average the courtyard house creates 45 percent more living area than provided in the typical tract-built single-family house in the U.S., yet achieving three times the density, (Figure 6).

As for the commercial sector, the central market or "shopping center" of each traditional Islamic city is composed of a web of

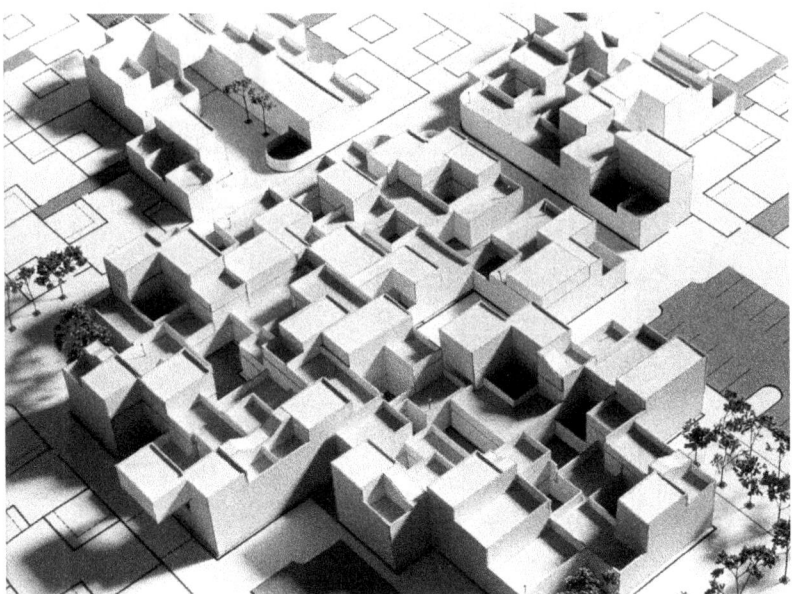

**Figure 6.** View of the model developed by the author of his Prototype Neighborhood Test Design, which seeks to evaluate and study the usefulness of the traditional organizational pattern in terms of contemporary usage.

covered pedestrian malls called "*Suq*" in Arabic, "*Bazar*" in Farsi and "*Carsi*" in Turkish. Each mall is composed of repetitive cells opposite each other and separated by a 10 to 20 foot walkway covered by vaults with skylights at intervals, creating pleasant and cool environments for shopping, (Figure 7). Security during nights and holidays is easily maintained by locking gates strategically located at entry points to the mall system. There are typically a number of other facilities adjoining the web of market malls and linked together by an overall access system. Usually the mosque is located there, as well as the public bath, hotels, individual workshops and storage facilities for the various shop owners.

## 2.3 - Architectural design, style and decoration

Much has been published in the West about Islamic architecture and decoration. For the purposes of this paper, the issue to be addressed is how can traditional building design, including its technologies prove to be of relevance to our contemporary and future building activities. The rise of post-modernism over the past decade or so, highlights the importance of this topic and the demand which some clients create for post-modernist architecture. In some

**Figure 7.** Sketch of a typical spine in the Suq adjacent to the Zaytuna Mosque in the traditional medina of Tunis, Tunisia (after a photo by the author).

Islamic countries, particularly in Iraq, this phenomenon is at least one decade older than in the United States,[10] (Figure 8).

Various criticisms have been voiced about post-modernism, nevertheless the movement is filling a vacuum which contemporary architectural design along the lines of the modern movement is unable to fill. In the Islamic countries, as well as in other cultures,

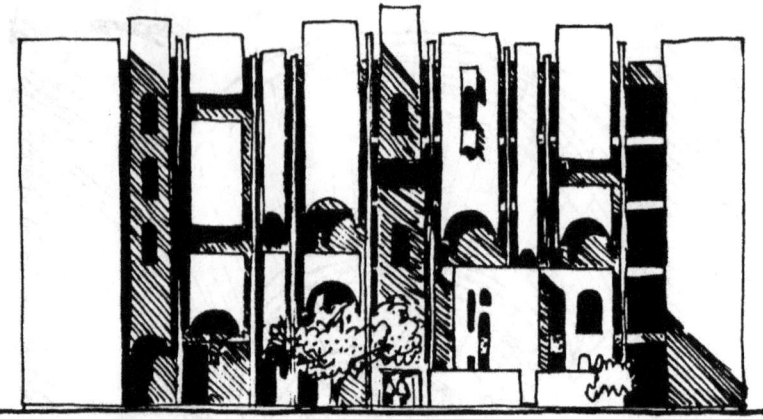

**Figure 8.** Sketch based on an etching by Rifat Chadirji of his Rafidain Bank project in Baghdad, Iraq, 1971. Etchings of Chadirji's building designs were published in MIMAR: Architecture in Development, Number 14, 1984.

the need for expressing local cultural identity through architecture is growing stronger. Thus the question of how this ought to be done without creating superficial results is paramount. Moreover the problem of contemporary and future building types which do not have historical precedence such as office buildings, airports and bus terminals requires careful study in terms of recycling traditional architectonic and decorative elements.

## 4 - Conclusions

This paper has attempted to highlight issues of significance within the experience of building and planning in traditional Islamic culture. The issues were presented in a six point framework covering aspects of procedures and built form. All six topics incorporate experiences which are worthy of study and consideration for recycling in contemporary and future practice. Most of the issues and lessons have inter-cultural benefits, and some are of local concern only.

The impacts of decisions by governing authorities, which is the first issue related to procedures of building, requires serious consideration at the policy level by national governments and local level jurisdictions. This also applies to the second issue of whether or not to reapply the *Fiqh* in planning and building activities. There is today much discussion and awareness of the former and less of the latter, primarily due to the lack of knowledge of traditional practice. It is anticipated that both issues will continue to grow in importance in the future.

The third topic concerning decision-making within a framework of performance criteria is the responsibility of government agencies and the architect. The implementation of performance type regulations in lieu of Western style prescriptive standards will require, in some instances, sophistication which might not be available in certain countries or localities. However it is the responsibility of government as the primary client, in most Islamic countries today, to instruct local or foreign consultants, when they are used, to develop such mechanisms of control. This is despite the fact that most contemporary structures and sectors of the city were built using the typical mechanisms of zoning and other prescriptive type of regulations. Yet it is not late to convert the system to performance based mechanisms of control.

The above three issues encompass most of the deep-rooted, programmatic and ideologically based sources for recycling tradition in contemporary and future Islamic environments. The lessons from the traditional organizational system and built form dealing with ecological and climatic compatibility, the nature of planning and physical organization and architectural design/ decoration includes planning, function, space, technology, building materials, problems of style, image making and the meaning of the architecture produced. The latter concerns being the most difficult to deal with, yet they are not ungraspable if intelligently derived from the careful understanding of traditional experience.

To summarize, this author believes that history and tradition provide a fertile base from which to learn and when necessary recycle experiences of process and built form. However the matrix of experiences are numerous and at different levels, part of which cannot be recycled without a total commitment by government at the policy level, others are recyclable at the cluster or building scale with few participants and decision-makers involved. Contemporary examples of the latter can be found utilizing partial aspects of traditional experience. In other words only a very small segment of the wide spectrum provided by history has so far been used in contemporary times, most of which unsuccessfully. Much must be accomplished in the future.

## Notes

[1] Various dimensions of this problem was discussed in the article: "The Representation of values in Traditional and Contemporary Islamic Cities" by Besim S. Hakim and Peter G. Row published in *Journal of Architectural Education*, Volume 36, No. 4, Summer 1983, pp. 22-28.

[2] A list of lessons was first published by the author in the article: "Arab-Islamic Urban Structure" in *The Arabian Journal for Science and Engineering*, Vol. 7, No. 2, 1982, pp. 69-79.

[3] Fiqh is the Arabic term for jurisprudence, or the science of religious law in Islam. Its impact on built form was discussed in this author's previously published articles. Op. Cit. Notes 1 and 2 above.

[4] Urf is the Arabic term for an established local tradition for how something is to be done. Foreign consultants to this day do not know of the deeprootedness of Islamic values in the traditional processes of building activities. Most of the officials in the Islamic countries who represent their government in dealing with consultants also have no knowledge of the workings of the traditional experience. This situation was compounded by the "quasi-technical" nature of master planning and architectural design packaging. In short what has and still is occurring is the implantation of an alien approach, its gradual, and occasionally sudden displacement of traditional practices as legitimized by the policies of modernization.

[5] Saleh A. Al-Hathloul in his PhD dissertation entitled: *Tradition, Continuity and Change in the Physical Environment: The Arab-Muslim City*, MIT, 1981 has analyzed some examples and has shown that in certain cases the municipal "technical" code allowed a situation to occur which the Sharia (religious) court later denied.

[6] It is encouraging to see the recent interest in building topics by Fiqh graduate students in Saudi Arabia. One PhD dissertation was completed in 1982 by Suleiman bin Wail al-Tuwaijri of Um al-Qura University in Mckka, entitled "Haqq al-Irtifag" dealing with various traditional building practices within the framework of lslamic law. Another study was undertaken for the PhD by Ibrahim al-Fayez in the Sharia College of Imam Mohammad ibn Saud Islamic University, Riyadh. It is entitled: "Ahkam al-bina fi al-Islam" or the laws of building in Islam.

[7] Two good earlier examples were by Daniel Dunham "The Courtyard House as a Temperature Regulator" in *The New Scientist* (September 1960) pp. 663-666, and M.N.Bahadori "Passive Cooling Systems in Iranian Architecture" in *Scientific American*, February 1978, pp. 144-154. Other examples were recently published in the proceedings of a symposium on Islamic Ar-

chitecture and Urbanism held in Dammam January 1980. Specifically the following authors papers are of interest, those by Miles Danby, Fuller Moore and Susan Roaf.

[8] The proceedings cited in note 7 above include two useful articles on this topic. The first by Othman Llewellyn "Shari'ah Values Pertaining to Landscape Planning and Design", and the other by Stephen Lesiuk "Landscape Planning for Energy Conservation Design in the Middle East".

[9] The use of a similar physical organizational system and architectural elements, governed by a relatively uniform regulatory code produced these results.

[10] A number of Iraqi architects experimented by using traditional motifs in contemporary design and architecture. Mohammed Makiya, Kahtan Madfai, Rifaat Chadirji and the late Kahtan Awni all of baghdad, Iraq, were probably the most serious individuals who pursued this approach since the early 1960's.

# Chapter 9

# Nature of Islamic Urbanism and its Lessons

Many people have preconceived ideas about Islamic architecture as consisting of a distinctive style. Much has been written on the development, spread, and qualities of this style, and it is suggested that the reader refer to the bibliography for information of that kind. It is more appropriate to discuss the essential underlying factors that have shaped the traditional built environment in Islamic culture. Therefore, this article is not about style, nor about buildings in isolation. It is, instead, about the interaction of societal values – which in Islamic culture are directly rooted in religion – with decision making, the production process, and the resulting built form. The context of the discussion is holistic, beyond the building scale, to produce a clear understanding of the relationship of the part to the whole, the building to its immediate surroundings and to the urban scale. An understanding of the reciprocal effects of the overall built environment and the various levels of the environment, down to single buildings and their design, is crucial to a comprehension of architecture in the context of Islamic culture.

The levels of the environment to be stressed are the city, neighborhood, clusters of buildings, and the single building. That order is not always critical to the following discussions, but the relationship between levels should be kept in mind, particularly when trying to interrelate the impact of values underlying decision making and the nature of the production and construction processes. Thus, a clear understanding of the overall system that prevailed in traditional Islamic societies, as well as the changes that have occurred in contemporary times, is fundamental.

The first part of the article is a discussion of the traditional system that produced the built environment, and is followed by a survey of the changes that have occurred in contemporary times, using the case of Saudi Arabia as a focus for discussion to illuminate why most contemporary urbanism and architecture produced in the Islamic countries cannot be described as Islamic. The third part discusses ways of learning from the past and recycling the traditional experience toward the goal of reestablishing authenticity and identity for contemporary and future architecture in Islamic countries.

## 1 - The traditional setting

Pre-Islamic settlement patterns, building typologies, construction techniques, and related decision-making processes influenced the emergent pattern of built form in Islamic cultures. One of the verses in the *Quran*, the holy book of Islam, is interpreted by some Muslim scholars as an instruction to accept local traditions and conventions, provided they do not contravene Islamic values, ethics, or codes. The applicable verse (from Surah, or chapter, 7 titled Al-A'raf, verse number 199) uses the Arabic term *urf* to refer to an established local tradition for how something is to be done.

From the sketchy evidence available, the predominant pattern of settlement in Medina, the city in Arabia where the Prophet Mohammed chose to settle during the last decade of his life, was similar to the ancient Mesopotamian model of clustered courtyard buildings.[1] Evidence of this tradition dates back to about 2500 B.C. in towns such as Ur, an ancient city in Southern Mesopotamia, (now contemporary Iraq). Archaeological digs in Ur were under taken by the architect-archaeologist Leonard Woolley in the late 1920s; his findings were published in the early 1930s.[2] Part of Woolley's discovery was the *Omen Text*, which contains various omens, some relating to building design; these may reflect some of the values of the people of that ancient time. Consider the following examples.

> If a house blocks the main street in its building, the owners of the house will die; if a home overshadows or obstructs the side of the main street, the heart of the dweller in that house will not be glad.
> If the water in the court runs to the back, expense will be continual; if the water in the court runs to the middle of the court, that man will have wealth.

Woolley published portions of the plan of Ur. Figure 1 reproduces a segment, along with, for comparative purposes, part of the plan of Tunis Medina as documented in the 1960s. Contemplation of the complex plan pattern raises the question of how the common wall problems were addressed and resolved. Later it will be shown how this and other problems related to this pattern and type of construction were addressed by Islamic law. Pre-Islamic legal precedents existed, as evidenced by the work of some scholars.[3,4]

After these brief notes on the pre-Islamic pattern, consider now the system of building and urbanism as it evolved in Islamic culture. Islam was proclaimed by the Prophet Mohammed soon after 610 A.D. in Makkah, 450 km (280 mi) south of Medina, where the Prophet finally settled in 622 A.D. That date represents year 1 of the Islamic calendar.

The next decade in Medina, which came under the guidance and leadership of the Prophet, is considered very important as a source of example and precedent for all aspects of Islamic community living, including building. A number of cases are recorded of the

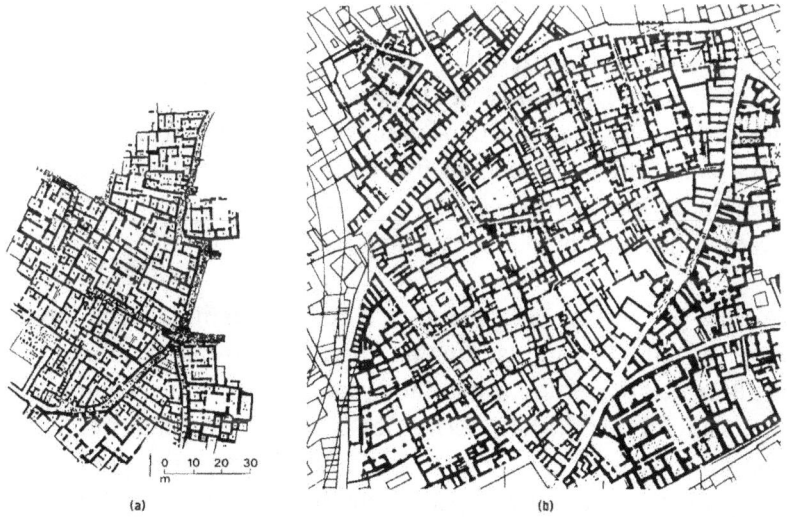

**Figure 1.** Portions from the cities of (a) Ur (2000 B.C.) in southern Mesopotamia, now Iraq[2]; and (b) Tunis Medina in Tunisia in 1960s A.D., reproduced to the same scale and compass orientation[4]. The predominant use in these plans is housing. The plan from Tunis Medina is based on sources dating from the mid-1920s to the mid-1960s, as compiled by the author.

Prophet's attitude to specific problems related to building activity. This is also true of the caliphs who succeeded him, including Omar bin Al-Khattab, the second caliph, who ruled during the period 634 to 644 A.D. This guidance concerning building proved to be particularly crucial for the Maliki School of Law, which evolved under Malik ben Anas (712-795 A.D.), who lived all his life in Medina and whose followers live to this day in the Maghreb countries of Libya, Tunisia, Algeria, Morocco, and also in Andalusia on the Iberian peninsula until the early 1500s.

During the first three centuries of Islam, a number of schools of thought and approaches to law were formulated. Under the Sunni branch of Islam, the survivors today are grouped into four schools: Hanafi, Maliki, Shafi'i, and Hanbali. Followers of Sunni Islam constitute the majority in the Muslim world, although in Iran, parts of Iraq, and some communities in Syria and Lebanon, the people are followers of Shi'ism and have their own school of law. It is important to note that the legal differences about building are minor, and result from different interpretations by the various schools of law. Thus, the discussion based on the Maliki School in North Africa would largely hold true for other regions of the Muslim world.

Eighty-three years after the Prophet's death on June 8, 632, Islam already encompassed a vast territory stretching from the shores of the Atlantic Ocean and the Pyrenees to the borders of China-an area greater than Rome's at its zenith. This was achieved under the leadership of Abd al-Malik (685-705 A.D.) from his seat in Damascus, and his four sons who succeeded him.

Across this vast geographic area, three factors influenced the nature of building and planning as it evolved within the framework of Islamic civilization. First, the urban models of pre-Islamic cultures and civilizations in territories converted to Islam influenced the evolution of the structure and form of subsequent Islamic cities. This was particularly true in the region known as the Fertile Crescent and in Iran. Second, the camel was the primary means of transportation, predominating in the Middle East between the fourth and sixth centuries A.D.[5] This important and often forgotten factor had a major impact on the street system and urban form of the Islamic city. Finally, the location of most territories of the

Islamic world between latitudes 10 and 40°, and the resulting similarity in macroclimatic conditions, contributed toward certain unifying influences in building practice.

Some historians agree that three discernible urban models evolved within the framework of Islamic civilization. These are the renewed or remodeled pre-Islamic city; the planned and designed city; and the spontaneously created and incrementally grown city. The renewed city is found most often in previously held Roman territories, and is exemplified by Damascus and Aleppo. Earlier structures and configurations were altered to suit the social requirements of the Muslim community. The pre-Islamic Southwest Arabian model of isolated multistory structures, such as Sana'a and particularly prevalent in Yemen, is also classified under this model grouping. Research is required to determine why this type did not spread beyond the few localities in which it arose.

The second type of city was preplanned and designed by Muslim rulers to be the capital of a dynasty or, more typically, as the seat of a palace complex and its related facilities. A prime example of a city constructed as a complete entity was the original round city of Baghdad, while Al-Abbasiyah, south of present Kairouan, was a palace complex; neither survives today. The model influencing the plan and design of this second type of city can generally be identified by the geographic location. In the case of the *mashreq* (eastern regions), pre-Islamic models had a distinct influence, whereas in the *maghreb* (western regions), the influences on the ruler and his experiences determined the model and approach followed. After the collapse of a dynasty, the tradition was to abandon this type of city or palace complex, with the result that today they remain as ruins or are completely obliterated and require restoration by archaeologists.

The third model of the Islamic city proved to be the most enduring and pervasive, and today most of the older areas of capitals and major towns in the Muslim world evolved out of this model (Figs. 2 and 3). The best examples of the old quarters or *medina* survive in the Maghreb countries, but in some instances are severely threatened today by the automobile.

**Figure 2.** Oblique air photo of the central portion of Fez in Morocco. The main mosque of the city and the adjacent *suq* (market) is on the upper right. Photograph by Papini, M. H. A T., Rabat.

Although the organizational principles of this model predate Islam by at least 2500 years and were particularly common in southern Mesopotamia, the strength, characteristics, and longevity of this city type reflect the manner in which building activity was pursued in Islamic society. The initial model for this building process occurred in Medina since the Prophet's arrival there in 622 A.D. Note that this article focuses on this predominant model, found most often in the Maghreb countries, and built under the guidance of the Maliki school of law.

Viewing the city as a process and a product is an effective analytical-evaluation and planning tool, and is indispensable for the study of the Islamic city. The process encompasses the decision making in building activity as guided by Islamic values. Looking

**Figure 3.** Vertical air photo of a portion of old Unayzah, located in the north central region of Saudi Arabia. The large building is one of the mosques in the city, surrounded by housing. Courtesy of Ministry of Petroleum and Mineral Resources, Saudi Arabia.

at the city as a product clarifies how a complex, heterogeneous, and sophisticated built form is achievable with a simple set of physical organizational components, and a related mechanism of verbal communication used in building decisions. The essential urban elements are the courtyard building, the street system, and the elements above the street.

### *The Courtyard Building.*
This is the basic module used for housing and public buildings. The ratio of building area to plot is 1:1 (Fig. 1). In housing, the

courtyard takes up approximately 24% of the ground coverage, and the building is one, two, or occasionally three stories in height. Public buildings differ in their ratio of courtyard size to ground coverage, and the height is one story, as in mosques, but frequently is two stories, as in a *funduk* or *khan* (hostels for merchants). It should be noted that the Prophet affirmed the use of this plan type by building his mosque residence soon after his arrival in Medina in the form of a square courtyard structure.

### The Street System.
Street systems are primarily of two types: the through, open-ended street, which was considered a public right of way and had to be wide enough for two packed camels to pass; and the cul-de-sac which, according to Islamic law, is considered to be the private property of the people living on it.

### Elements Above the Street.
The elements usually found above the street were a *sabat*, a room actually bridging the street, and the buttressing arches spanning between walls on either side of the street to provide structural strength and support (Fig. 4).

In addition to this basically simple set of organizational elements, the Islamic city evolved a sophisticated communication system in the form of a language or vocabulary of building design that operated at all scales of the built environment. At the scale of the city, it identified urban elements such as building types, public squares, and other uses. At the building scale, it identified spatial configurations and related uses, as well as details of construction, decoration, and symbolic motifs. An important attribute of this language was that it integrated a physical component's form and function into its name. This vocabulary was known and popular among most segments of society involved in building activity, and it was an effective communication device between users and builders. Regional variations in the design vocabulary existed, but the language was unified by the similarity of the built form and its constituents.

The process can best be appreciated by viewing the dynamics of building decision making as affecting two scales of the city: city-

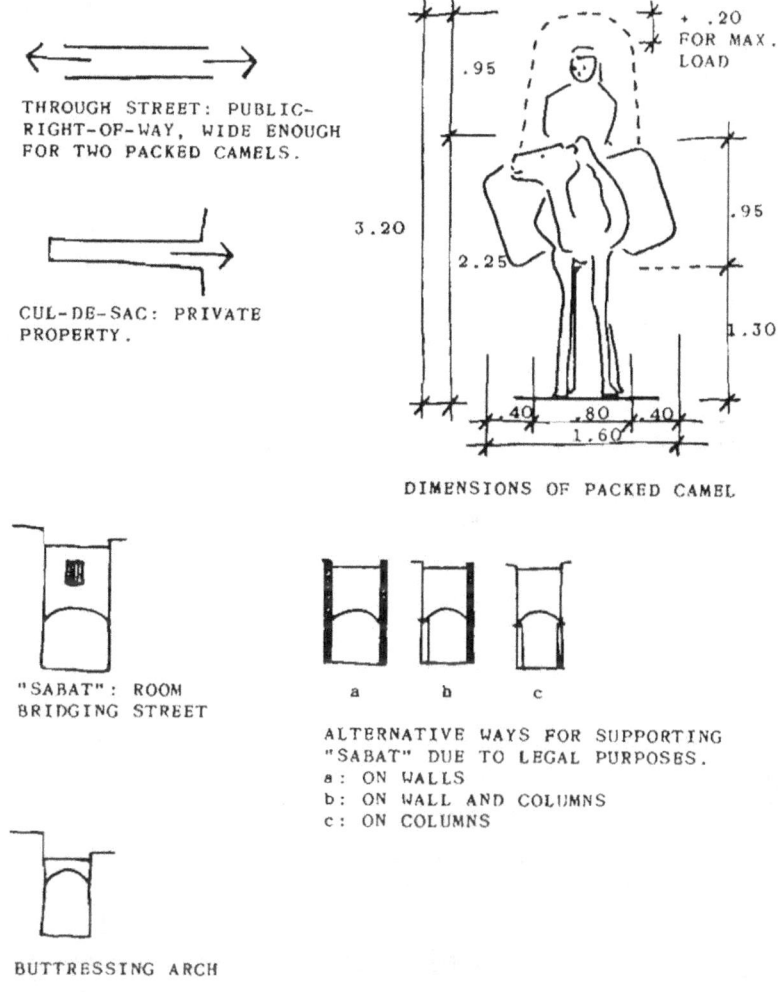

Figure 4. The street and its primary elements.[4,6]

wide and neighborhood. Decisions about the citywide scale were usually made by the ruler or government; they concerned the birth, growth, and revitalization of a city, and would include the location of the primary mosque; the distribution of the land in the projected boundaries of the city to various ethnic, familial, or tribal affiliations; and the location and configuration of the city's gates and walls. All of these are the result of decisions taken in the first few years of a city's founding.

Other typical primary decisions occurring during a city's growth involved the building of major public buildings such as mosques and public baths, or the location of new cemeteries. Revitalization activity often took place under the leadership of ambitious rulers and governments during eras marked by security and prosperity. Site conditions and the location of determining factors, such as water and natural features useful for defensive purposes, had an impact on macro decision making and, hence, the resulting urban form.

The dynamics of decisions made at the neighborhood scale tended to be of a different nature and the results were of immediate significance. The effect on urban form of numerous micro decisions by citizens of a neighborhood was indirect and usually obvious only on an aggregate basis, whereas the results of the larger decisions by rulers – such as the location of major mosques, the *suq* (market) and its configurations, and important industries – tended to be individually discernible.

Building decisions at the neighborhood scale had an impact on both the initiator and on immediate neighbors. Building activity and decisions involve the relationships and interdependence of people, and more specifically neighbors; such activity was therefore the concern of Islamic law. The development of guidelines for neighborhood building activity became the concern of the science of *fiqh* from its very early development.

*Fiqh* is the Arabic term for jurisprudence, or the science of religious law in Islam. It concerns itself with two spheres of activity: *ibadat*, dealing with matters concerning ritual observances; and *muamalat*, the legal questions that arise in social life (e.g., family law, law of inheritance, of property, of contracts, criminal law, etc.), and problems arising from building activity and related procedures . The latter were viewed by the fiqh in the same light as other problems resulting from human activities and interaction. In essence, therefore, fiqh is the science of laws based on religion and is concerned with all aspects of public and  private life and business.

The bulk of the knowledge developed by the fiqh for most aspects of human relationships, including those of building activity, appeared in the first 300 years of Islam, although subsequent generations developed and refined it. The source of most guidelines stemmed from Quranic values and from the *Hadith* which are the sayings and tradition of the Prophet particularly during the decade of his leadership and rule in Medina. (The term *sunnah* is more commonly used to mean the total traditions of the Prophet, including his deeds and life-style, as well as his sayings). Note that the recorded nature of most guidelines in the fiqh literature is implicit in the numerous cases also recorded which include the judgments of local *kadis* (judges), and the opinions of *muftis* (specialists on the law who can give authoritative opinions on points of doctrine).

A set of guidelines documented in the literature of the Maliki school of law are identified and discussed elsewhere.[6] Examples follow.
- Avoid harm to others and oneself.
- Accept the concept of interdependence.
- Respect the privacy of the private domain of others, particularly avoiding the creation of direct visual corridors.
- Respect the rights of original or earlier usage.
- Respect the rights of building higher within one's air space.
- Respect property of others.
- The rights of preemption by adjacent neighbors.
- Seven cubits as the minimum width of public through-streets (to allow two fully loaded camels to pass).
- Avoid locating the sources of unpleasant smells and noisy activities adjacent or near to mosques.

In addition, other guidelines operate as a self-regulating mechanism on the behavior of the individual and community. A prime example is the concept of beauty without arrogance, which strongly influenced the manner in which exterior facades and elevations were regarded and treated. This concept is attributed directly to the Prophet Mohammed in the form of the saying, "No person with an atom of arrogance in his heart will enter paradise." According to Muslim, the renowned Hadith scholar, a man said: "A person likes to wear good clothes and shoes." The Prophet answered: "God is beautiful and He loves beauty" (Fig. 5). By tradition, and allowing for beauty without arrogance, an owner was permitted to decorate only the front door of a building, to express his attitudes and iden-

**Figure 5.** A residential street in the city of Rabat, Morocco, showing blank exterior walls and buttressing arches. Photograph by Papini, M. H. A. T., Rabat.

tity (Fig. 6). In contrast, the interiors of buildings were decorated, particularly the facades of the courtyard. The sophistication or level of such decoration depended on the financial ability and taste of the owner (Fig. 7).

Quranic verses and sayings of the Prophet used as the source for building guidelines can be found elsewhere.[6] In most cases these verses and sayings were specifically pointed out by the author of a fiqh manuscript to back up or elaborate on the reasons and rationale behind a kadi's decision or an opinion of a mufti. A *mufti* is a specialist on law who can give an authoritative opinion on points of doctrine; his considered legal opinion is called *fatwa*.

**Figure 6.** A typical front door to a medium-size, middle-class house in Tunis. Note the studded decoration, knockers, and small inset door for daily and frequent use. Photograph by the author, 1977.

To appreciate the interaction between the mechanisms of the building process, consider the following simulation, which includes one example for each component of a five part framework devised here to represent the physical factors that shaped the traditional Islamic city, particularly at its neighborhood scale. (This framework en-

**Figure 7.** Typical decorated courtyard of a palace in Tunis. Taken in the main courtyard of the restored Dar Lasram palace. Photograph by Wisam Hakim, 1975.

compasses all building activity issues touched on in the fiqh literature of the Maliki school of law.) The components are: (1) streets, including through streets and cul-de-sacs, and related elements; (2) locational restrictions of uses causing harm, such as smoke, offensive odor, and noise; (3) overlooking elements, including visual corridors generated by doors, window openings, and heights; (4) walls between neighbors, and their rights of ownership and usage; and (5) drainage of rain and waste water.

Imagine that a man wants to build on a vacant lot or to reuse a site on which a dilapidated house stands. If the intention is to rebuild a structure for the same use, then he can proceed with no objections; if the plan is to build a public bath or bakery, however, then he will more than likely be faced with objections from the neighbors. The reasons given are that such new public uses will create harm in three ways; (1) by generating additional traffic on the street(s) providing access to the facility, thus causing the people living nearby to have to adjust to this new condition; (2) by the nuisance of the smoke generated; and (3) by diminishing the value of the adjacent houses because of the impending adjacent public uses and the nuisances that will result.

Two frequently cited sources supporting these complaints are used by the *fuqaha* (plural of *feqih*, a jurisprudence scholar), for preventing the change in use. The Quran says: "And diminish not the goods of the people, and do not mischief in the earth working corruption" (26:183). From the sayings of the Prophet comes: "Do not harm others or yourself, and others should not harm you or themselves" (cited by Ahmad and Ibn Majah).

After exploring other uses of the site, the owner decides to build a house. He asks a local builder to construct it; the two will communicate with each other about the design requirements by using the local design language. This is done by identifying each part according to its name in the design language. To illustrate, examples from the local language in the Tunis region are used: the owner requires one *skifa* (entrance lobby with entry doors placed so that no one can see directly into the courtyard from the outside), with two *dukkana* facing each other (built-in benches provided in the skifa, traditionally used by the male owner or occupant to receive casual visitors or salesmen). He specifies that the *wust al-dar* (open courtyard in the center of the house) should have under it a *majin* (cistern for the collection of rainwater from the roofs), and one *burtal* (a colonnaded gallery off the courtyard giving importance and sometimes sun protection to the room behind) off the main room. Around the courtyard he asks the builder for three *bit trida* (simple rooms) and one *bit bel-kbu u mkasar* (a primary room common in middle- and upper-middle class houses), which is usually located opposite the entrance to the court. This primary room is divided into (1) a central alcove called a *kbu*, usually containing built in seating and elaborate wall and ceiling decorations, and used to receive close relatives and friends; (2) two small rooms symmetrically located on each side of the kbu called *maqsura*, and used as bedrooms; and (3) two alcoves, constructed opposite each other, with built-in beds and/or storage. The built-in beds could be placed on one or both sides of the alcove, and are usually framed with a decorative wooden structure called *hanut hajjam*. This listing could continue on to the smallest details of decoration and finishes (Fig. 8). If the house is relatively complex, then the builder will more than likely sketch out the plan and any other details, but for

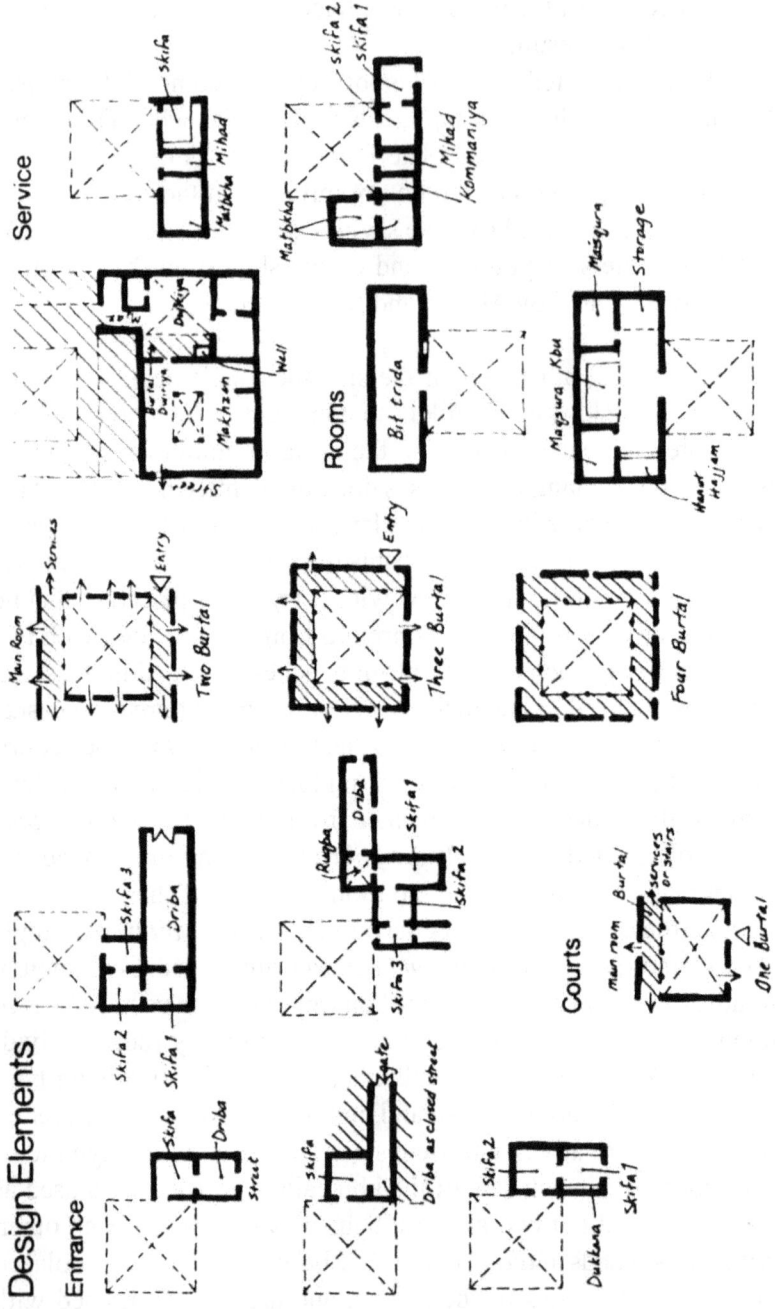

**Figure 8.** Examples of traditional housing design elements and their associated vocabulary, or design language, from the Tunis region.[7]

his own use and not to communicate with the owner. When the design language is not adequate for both owner and builder to clarify a point, then either one, but more commonly the owner, takes the other to see a house to indicate what he has in mind.

The builder is expected to know about the customs and traditions of building practice and the principles to be followed and respected. Surprisingly, the detailed implications of the building guidelines were not common knowledge among the lower ranks of builders. Often, references are made in ancient manuscripts to implemented building decisions that were violations and were later ordered by the local kadi to be demolished or corrected in response to a neighbor's complaints. It seems, however, that the more established and older builders with many years of experience, who were often hired by affluent clients, had detailed insights.

Having determined the usage of the site and using the design language for planning purposes, the builder and owner examine the likely effects on their requirements and decisions of existing surrounding buildings . If a window exists on one of the neighbor's walls, for example, then its location had to be considered out of the respect due to the principle of the earlier rights of usage. The new house had to avoid creating a direct visual corridor from the existing window into its private domain; in effect it had to block potential overlooking problems. A neighbor's wall could be used, however, to insert beams for support, rather than building another, adjacent wall. This practice was specifically encouraged by the Prophet: "A neighbor should not forbid his neighbor to insert wooden beams in his wall" (cited by Abu Hurairah ). Nonetheless, there were elaborate guidelines to be respected in using a neighbor's wall, and the associated problems of subsequent maintenance rights. For example, the ratio of the wall to be used depended on its ownership. In the case of rebuilding a dilapidated house, correct identification of the ownership of adjacent walls was therefore crucial. Careful examination of the wall was guided by criteria that determined whether ownership was single or joint. The most common of these criteria was to discover the nature of the *akd* or wall bond at the corners or junction of two walls, by examining the materials and mortar to resolve whether the two walls were built together. This practice, which was sanctioned by the Prophet, is traceable to the decade of 622-632 A.D. in Medina, and is still followed today in the older parts of Islamic cities under the local customary law, or urf.

The question of drainage of rain and waste water also had to follow certain rules and guidelines. Drainage of rainwater was a particularly delicate problem because excess water was not to be barred from others. This principle is directly attributed to two sayings of the Prophet: "If you deny excess water, you will deny the benefits of pasture" (cited by Abu Hurairah), and "Muslims are partners in three things: water, pasture, and fire" (cited by Abu Dawood and Ibn Majah via lbn Abbas).

As to the relationship of houses to streets, assume that one side of a house adjoins a through street, and the owner wants more space. One option is to build a sabat (room bridging the street). To support the structure on the opposite side the owner could acquire permission from the owner of the facing building, but the granting of such permission was not totally irrevocable and thus this alternative depended on the owner's perception of his future relationship with his opposite neighbor. More than likely the owner would choose to use columns for support, keeping the owner totally independent of his neighbor. Another option would be to use columns for supporting both sides, opening up the future possibility of being able to sell the sabat to the owner of the opposite building, and generally upgrading the marketability of the house (Fig. 4).

The preceding illustrations provide only an overview of the issues involved in the typical building process. Many other cases, some of them extremely involved, may be found elsewhere.[6] This discussion is adequate, however, to illuminate the fact that the built form was a direct outcome of the dynamics of decision making, using specific mechanisms, and as governed by fiqh guidelines derived from the Islamic values embodied in the *Quran* and the *Hadith* .

## 2 - The contemporary situation

In most Islamic countries major changes have resulted in a shift from the traditional system of construction and design to a contemporary, so-called modern system. Background, forces of change, and motivation differed from country to country, but in most instances change was the direct result of the intervention and influence of non-Muslim colonial powers, primarily the British, French, and Italians. This coincided with the introduction of contemporary technology in transportation and construction, and new building materials. Planning patterns and architectural styles introduced by these colonial powers came to be models to be emulated. The notion was that the use of modern technologies and materials meant also employing the colonials' system of planning and design. Western ideas and techniques for dealing with land subdivision, the distribution of buildings, and their design were synonymous with modernism and progress.

Unfortunately, well-documented cases of the architectural transformations of various Islamic countries is scarce, but it is very clear that, despite the differences and discrepancies in the processes of change, remarkable similarities are manifest in the end result, the contemporary built environment. To understand this phenomenon, a brief description follows of the changes that have occurred in Saudi Arabia since the mid-20$^{th}$ century.

Saudi Arabia is a mashreq country, historically considered to be part of the eastern region of the Islamic world, as opposed to the Maghreb countries, those in the western region whose traditional system was the basis of the discussion above. Although the Islamic schools of law in effect in the two regions are distinct (the Maliki in North Africa, and the Hanbali in Saudi Arabia), these and other schools of law traditionally shared more similarities than differences in matters related to cities and building. The regions' historical continuity in legal matters is supported by a comparison of the traditional morphology in North Africa with that found in central and eastern Saudi Arabia.

The case of Saudi Arabia is interesting for a number of reasons.[1,8,9]
1. The country was not under colonial rule by non-Muslims. Parts of the country, primarily the Hijaz (the western region bordering on the Red Sea) and for shorter periods Al-Hasa (in the east, bordering the Arabian Gulf), were under Islamic Ottoman Turkish rule, during which time the traditional Islamic system of building and planning continued without change.

2. The changes that occurred later were primarily instigated by the Saudis themselves, with the clear objective of creating a modern built environment, as a result of a rapid shift in the perception of what a new, good, built environment should be and how it should look. This perception was diametrically opposed to that produced by traditional settlements and their architecture.
3. Reliable information, including three valuable doctoral dissertations, is available on the changes in Saudi Arabia. The information in the second part of this article relies, to a large extent, on these sources.

Underlying the changes in Saudi Arabia's built environment was the introduction of the grid as a street pattern and of the villa as a dwelling type. Following is a brief description of how they were introduced in Saudi Arabia and the process by which they were developed and institutionalized.

## 2.1 - The introduction of the Grid Pattern

In the Eastern Province of Saudi Arabia, the development of the cities of Dammam and Al-Khobar resulted from the expansion and growth of the oil industry. The Arabian American Oil Company (ARAMCO) played a major role in the planning and development of these two cities, as well as other communities.[1,8,9] The initial growth of Dammam and Al-Khobar in the late 1930s and early 1940s was not planned in an orderly fashion. As the population grew, people took over any available land and erected basic shelters and fences from local materials. Following the traditional pattern, streets were narrow and irregular. When the physical development of the two towns increased substantially in the mid 1940s, the government felt they needed to be laid out in a controlled way. In 1947, the governor of the Eastern Province therefore requested assistance from the oil company in producing layouts for both Dammam and Al-Khobar. In response, ARAMCO's surveyors prepared land subdivision plans and actually staked out the streets and blocks. Original plans, covering only limited areas, were laid out in a gridiron pattern. For information on historical developments, see Ref. 10 (Fig. 9).

**Figure 9.** Road network of Al-Khobar (left) and Dammam (right) on the eastern coast of Saudi Arabia. The sketches are based on information from the decade 1956-1966 (8).

When Dammam was made the provincial capital of the Eastern Province, the pressure for development increased. Government offices moved from the old capital of Hofuf in 1952; by the end of that year, Dammam comprised 525 acres, plus the 400 acres of ARAMCO's subdivided plan, and its population was 25,000.[10] Engineers then engaged by ARAMCO to develop their own communities were made available to local government agencies. These engineers, in cooperation with the municipality of Dammam, developed a major street plan for the city that is still being followed today. They also developed a layout scheme for another 1000 acres, which were subdivided and sold off by the municipality of Dammam. Subsequent subdivided areas were laid out by the municipality following the earlier gridiron layout-in some areas only roughly, but in others with precisely the same dimensions [10]

Similar techniques were used in ARAMCO's planning and layout of Al-Khobar; the city was taken as a model of modern planning for many years, and its planning established numerous unfortunate precedents. Al-Khobar was the first Saudi Arabian community to be wholly planned, and to use an overall grid plan. It was also the first to start the demolition process of the traditional fabric within its boundaries. For other reasons as well[8], it led the way as a model that other Saudi cities followed from the 1950s through the 1970s (Fig. 9).

Riyadh, the capital of Saudi Arabia, was founded on the ruins of several communities around 1740, but assumed little prominence until Abdul-Aziz Al-Saud took over as its independent governor in 1902 and began his campaign for the consolidation of modern Saudi Arabia. From that time, Riyadh was the permanent residence of the king and it also eventually became the capital of the kingdom, although Makkah, the religious capital, continued to house most government agencies until the 1950s.[11]

Riyadh preserved its size during the first 30 years of Abdul-Aziz's reign. Only after the consolidation of the kingdom, however, did the king himself in the 1930s take first steps toward developing the city, which involved the construction of a number of projects outside the city core. One of the prominent later developments that had profound impact on the city is a housing complex known as Al-Malaz built in the late 1950s.

When the government decided in 1953 to move its agencies from Makkah to Riyadh and, subsequently, to build ministries along the road to the city airport, housing for the transferred government employees became necessary. The site of Al-Malaz, 4.5 km northeast of the city center, was chosen and the housing project was initiated by the Ministry of Finance. The ministry was assisted by the U.S. Corps of Engineers in the planning and design of Al-Malaz.[9] In 1957, when the transfer of the agencies actually took place, the project was under way and some parts had been completed. The project consisted of 754 detached dwelling units, or villas, and 180 apartment units in three apartment buildings; the houses were sold to employees under a long-term payment plan, while the apartments were rented on a permanent basis.

Al-Malaz contained a public garden, a municipal hall, and a public library. It also housed the buildings, originally planned as schools, for the newly founded university. It also had a race course, a football field, and a public zoo; supporting facilities such as schools, markets, and clinics were planned, although they were built by agencies other than the finance ministry.

The physical organization of Al-Malaz follows a gridiron plan with a hierarchy of streets, rectangular blocks, and large lots, which in most cases take a square shape. Thoroughfares are 30 m wide, main streets 20 m, and secondary or access streets 10 and 15 m. A 60-m boulevard divided the project into two parts. Most blocks are 100 x 50 m. The typical lot size is 25 x 25 m, but within some blocks there are a variety of widths, such as 25 m, 37.5 m, and 50 m. The depth of 25 m, however, remains constant in almost all blocks.
Comparing the new and traditional patterns, reproduced to the same scale in Figures 10 and 11, it is clear that new values in the concept of space and land use were introduced at Al-Malaz. The new pattern has a low density, one-fifth the traditional density; areas assigned to streets are three times as great, and only half of the area of the development is reserved for private lots, as compared to more than 75% in the traditional pattern.

Al-Malaz covers an area of 500 hectares and its impact on Riyadh was enormous: it was seen as a city by itself, a new town in town, and thus named New Riyadh. The project's introduction of new patterns and typologies meant the grid as a street pattern and the villa as the new house type became powerful models for the developments of the 1960s and 1970s in every Saudi Arabian city and town. Al-Malaz became a model reproduced in later developments for three main reasons. First, the project was sponsored by the government, and was a governmental statement on how a modern neighborhood should be planned. It was taken for granted by others that what is good and suitable for Riyadh must be good for other cities in the country. Second, Al-Malaz was seen as a symbol of modernity, in sharp contrast to the traditional. It was the only project at that time to use new materials and techniques, hence its subsequent imitation. Finally, in contrast to royal residences built shortly before it, Al-Malaz was constructed for government employees who were part of the public. In the 1950s and early 1960s, these employees were highly regarded by other segments of society, and their life-style admired. Almost everyone dreamed of settling into a new and similarly planned neighborhood. Riyadh

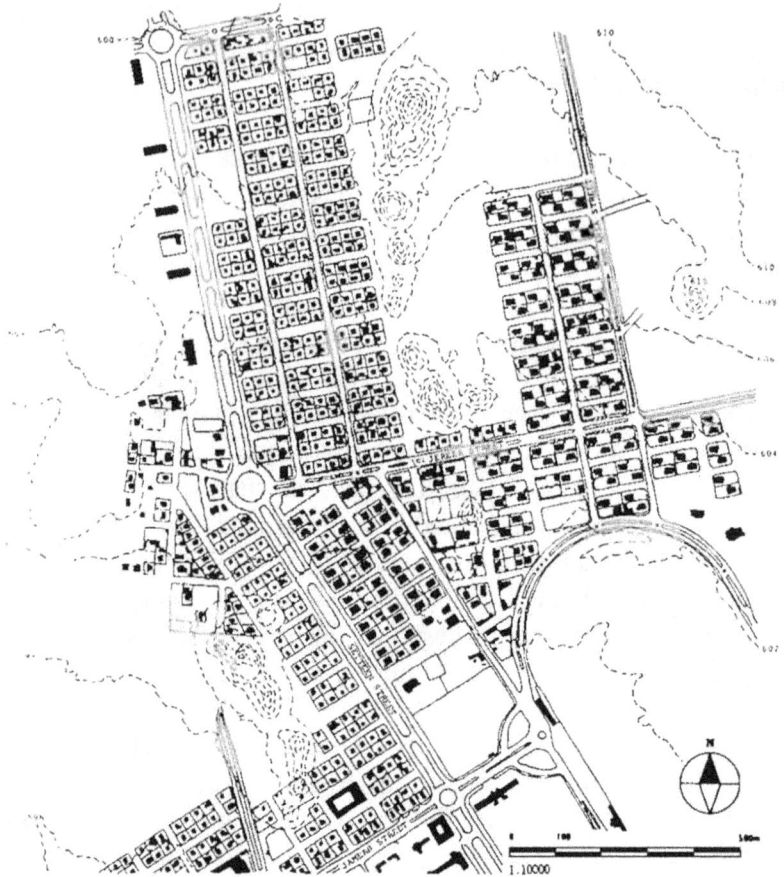

**Figure 10.** The layout of Al-Malaz, Riyadh. Located approximately three kilometers northeast of the CBD. The grid pattern predominates. Most blocks are 100 x 50 m and lot sizes have a standard depth of 25 m and a variety of widths: 25, 37, 40, and 50 m.[14]

now covers area of more than 300 km2 with an estimated density of 50 persons per hectare. Almost all of this area follows the grid pattern and has the villa as its dominant building type.

## 2.2 - Land Subdivision: Lots and Villas

The ARAMCO Home Ownership Plan, a loan program initiated in 1951[12,15], played a major role in spreading the concept of the dwelling as a detached building, and determining the subdivision of land. Under the program, the government provided the land, either as a grant or for a nominal price passed on to the employees, and ARAMCO undertook the planning and subdivision.

**Figure 11.** Al-Dira, a portion of the old city of Riyadh, Saudi Arabia. Note the traditional pattern of urbanism and recent vehicular roads cutting through the traditional urban tissue.[14]

ARAMCO also gave employees interest-free loans, the terms of which stated that the employees could choose their own designs and contractors.

To qualify for the loan, an employee had to submit a design for the house, that was to be implemented precisely, without any major changes. Due to a lack of Saudi architects at that time, employees had to rely on foreign ARAMCO architects. Employees could choose from a catalog of designs, which reflected the alien cultures and tastes of the designers. According to statistics gathered in the early 1970s, 15-25% of the houses in most Eastern Province cities are of this catalog type[13,16]. Subdivision of land, whether in Dammam, Al-Khobar, or other communities, consisted of lot sizes ranging from 400 to 900 m2, which is very large compared to traditional lot sizes. These lots tended to be roughly square in shape,

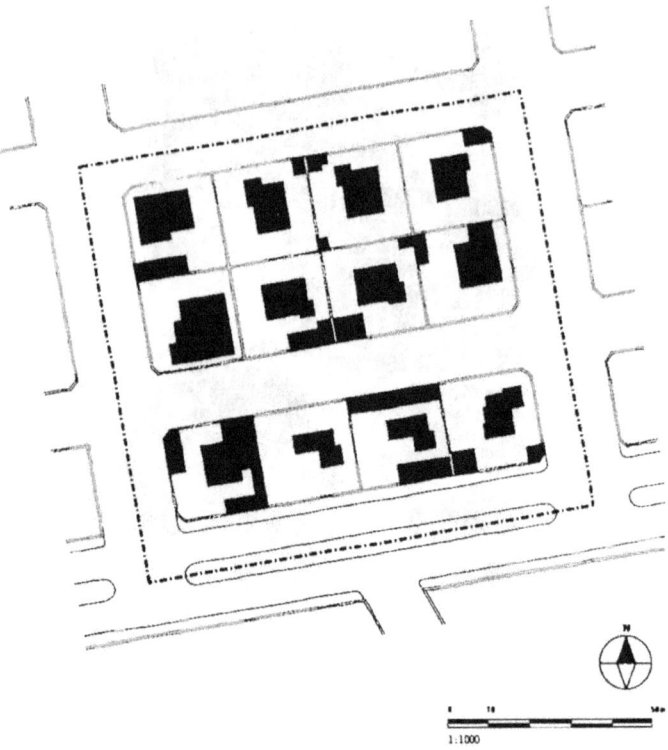

**Figure 12.** Two typical blocks from the Al-Malaz district in Riyadh, Saudi Arabia. The square Jot 25 x 25 m; later 20 x 20 m became predominant in Saudi Arabia due to its institutionalization by the government through decrees, directives, and circulars. The villa is planted in its midst through setback requirements.[14]

and the villas planted in the middle of each (Fig. 12).
Again, the Al-Malaz project and the ARAMCO Home Ownership Plan set up the pattern and shape of lots, introduced the villa as the favored house type, and became models for other developments. In fact, as early as 1938 in some cases, these models were institutionalized by the government: the square lot through decrees, directives, and circulars, and the villa through zoning regulations and related setback requirements, all of which were legitimized later by master plans that incorporated these implementation devices.

## 2.3 - The Process of Psychological institutionalization
Government media played an important promotional role in influencing attitudes toward the models of planning and design being introduced. This promotion occurred primarily through the press,

various other publications, and broadcasting, although television was not operational nationally as an effective medium until the early 1970s. Dialogue in the media was not possible, however, because of an unwritten code forbidding criticism of the government.[9]

Implementation then followed with the adoption of the system of land subdivision and related building regulations. An important note regarding cultural conditioning: It could not be expected that a conservative government and system such as that of Saudi Arabia would openly express enthusiasm for practices of Western civilization. In fact, almost all official statements for major projects or development policies stressed the conformity of the goals and policies to Islamic law and the society's cultural heritage. On the other hand, terms such as *tammadon* (civilization), *al-tatawr al-mimmari* (architectural progress), *al-imarah al-muaasirah* (contemporary architecture), and *al- taqaddom* (modernization and progress) are among the many terms used to raise the general level of aspiration and to provide a climate for national development. By associating such terms with the actual architecture and planning built and practiced in the country, there is no doubt as to the Western models to which such terms refer.

It is not surprising that Saudi Arabia, a culture that strongly adheres to Islamic traditions, has in fact, through certain events and processes, rejected the established, traditional, building and planning conventions that had strong ties to Islamic law. As a result of the prototypes initiated by the government (with the assistance of ARAMCO in the Eastern Province, the U.S. Corps of Engineers in Riyadh, and reinforced by a concerted media campaign), traditional building practices, associated forms and configurations, and traditional materials such as adobe were soon viewed by most people as substandard, and the new building conventions implemented by new technologies as superstandard.[17] A rejection of tradition resulted. Accordingly, a questionable side effect was that a concern with tradition was posited firmly against opportunities in all-or-nothing terms, without selective consideration of how new technology, building materials, and patterns of land use might be adjusted and molded to suit established conventions rooted in the society's religion and values.[18]

The scale of contemporary developments coupled with the centralization of authority and decision-making processes also had a major impact on the abandonment of the traditional system. Traditional environments had grown incrementally, over relatively adequate periods of time; the decision-making processes were decentralized. That is, the owners of property and their project builders were directly involved in the day-to-day decision making and monitoring of the building as it took shape. Another factor in the eyes of contemporary government officials and their Western consultants was the apparent inadequacy of traditional practices in coping with large-scale modern building projects, which were to be built in very short periods of time. (The experience of Turkey in the nineteenth and early twentieth centuries is illuminating for an understanding of similar changes and attitudes.[19] This was certainly not true for housing projects, yet housing also did not benefit from traditional practices, as these projects followed similar processes of implementation.

Centralization of decision making in almost all contemporary projects in Saudi Arabia meant that determinations about the configurations of large-scale developments were made by a very small group on behalf of many, and in the absence of a known user group.[20] In housing projects, this contrasted with the traditional system, in which decisions were made by owners and builders, in which neighbors were considered, and in which modifications took place through an incremental, decentralized system.

Two studies document in detail the implementation devices and procedures used by the government in Saudi Arabia to institutionalize the contemporary Western system using the grid pattern, villas, apartment and other building types, and the distribution of these citywide.[1,9] Among the devices was the drawing up of master plans, notably the plan undertaken by Doxiadis Associates for Riyadh. Statutes and other regulations are other devices that have had an impact: these include the statutes of the Makkah municipality, the Roads and Buildings Statutes, regulations pertaining to apartment buildings, and the specific zoning regulation introduced by the Doxiadis master plan of Riyadh in the 1970s. This was followed by zoning regulations proposed by the new master plan for Riyadh by SCET International in the 1980s. These proposed regulations, particularly those related to the protection of visual privacy in housing areas, are specifically worked out to suit the cultural requirements of an Arab Islamic city.[21] An evaluation of their effectiveness, assuming that they have been adopted and implemented, should stress that specific legal and implementation devices must be compatible with the values of the people for whom they are intended.

## 3 - Learning from the past

It has now been seen how the traditional system produced environments compatible with people's values and culture, so that the resulting built environment could be described as directly influenced and molded by Islamic culture. In contrast, contemporary events, such as those in Saudi Arabia, have created a situation that precludes a linkage between people's values and design and the resulting built form.

An attempt will be made now to indicate ways in which it might be possible to recycle and reintroduce traditional experiences into contemporary building and planning activities in many Islamic countries. The goal is to re-establish cultural aspirations and identity in the built environment produced today and in the future. The lessons and experiences to examine for possible recycling and emulation are grouped in two areas: those related to procedure, and those directly related to the organizational system of planning, design, and morphology.

### 3.1 - Lessons Derived from the Procedures of Building

These lessons can be grouped into the following categories: impact of decisions by the governing authority; how Islamic a traditional city is, as was made possible by the role of the *fiqh* and its special attributes; and the principles that governed the building production process.

#### *The impact of decisions by Governing Authorities.*

Traditionally, the decisions of the governing authority always had an important effect on the location of important buildings and the alignment of primary streets, thus establishing the overall framework of the city. It should be noted, however, that these decisions were made within an established framework of design norms and planning-organizational relationships. Historically, these were influenced by cultural values and unified by similar approaches arising from the exchange of knowledge among Islamic regions. Decisions by today's governments in the Islamic countries have even more impact, but are usually based on proposals and recommendations developed by foreign consultants. The input from these consultants for the most part ignores or is insensitive to local traditions and trends; foreign prototypes are usually imposed without consideration of cultural norms and values. In some cases this has been due to specific instructions from a client or his representative to ignore traditional architecture. The problem of outside influence is compounded by the fact that various regions of the Islamic world today are aligned to different foreign countries or systems, thus complicating city planning and building. For example, in Tunisia, Algeria, and Morocco, the French approach is followed; in Libya and, until recently, Egypt, the Soviet approach; and in Saudi Arabia the influence comes from the United States. In Iraq and the Gulf States, the British approach seems to be predominant.

As has been seen in the focus on housing, the traditional experience and its decentralized decision-making processes offered many positives. Yet most contemporary housing is produced as a result of decisions from the top, as opposed to grass roots decisions, and requirements drawn up without apparent consideration of the culture's Islamic values and its deep-rooted intentions. Even the design requirements that are linked to loans and mortgages preclude design preferences and significant alterations by users. Thus, the role of the individual in shaping his house and immediate environment in cooperation with neighbors is virtually eliminated-a situation diametrically opposed to that of the Islamic past.

The findings by many researchers and housing specialists in many countries concerning the significance and positive attributes of grass roots housing decisions support the urgency of changing implementation strategies in this area.

### The Traditional Islamic City and the Role of the Fiqh.
The nature of the fiqh guidelines and their application depended on intent and/or performance, and not on prescriptive standards. Thus people in the traditional setting involved in building de-

cision-making operated within a flexible framework of performance criteria. Each design situation could be resolved according to the conditions in the specific locality and the requirements of the people concerned. As long as the intent of the guidelines was met, the peculiar configurations of the solution would be acceptable. This approach directly influenced the three-dimensional outcome and quality of the built environment.

The earlier, brief discussion of the fiqh influence on traditional settlements raises a central question: how can the link be made between the fiqh and contemporary activities of building and urbanization? In many Islamic countries today, particularly since the introduction of the automobile and Western techniques of city planning, urbanization activities have gradually become detached from the traditional umbrella of the fiqh and the urf. The ignorance of foreign consultants and even government officials in Islamic countries about the deep-rootedness of Islamic values in the traditional processes of building activities is compounded by the quasi-technical nature of master planning and architectural design packaging. In short, what has happened, and is continuing, is the implantation of an alien approach, the generally gradual, but occasionally sudden, displacement of traditional practices legitimized by the policies of modernization.

This displacement occurred at various times in different places during the nineteenth and twentieth centuries, depending on when European influence or colonization occurred. Design decisions based on quasi-technical regulations came into conflict with traditional law. In certain cases, the municipal technical code allowed a situation that the *sharia* (religious) court later rejected.[1] The dislocation of the fiqh from building and urbanization activities in the name of modernization is now gradually being recognized as inappropriate. The challenge and task for the future is to reintegrate the fiqh into building and planning, which can be accelerated when adequate new approaches are developed by interdisciplinary teams of fuqaha and those involved in urbanization and building. It is encouraging to see the recent interest in building topics by fiqh graduate students in Saudi Arabia.[22,23] It should be possible to externalize Islamic values in contemporary and future architecture; the results would be exciting and unpredictable, with potential for unique models and approaches.

*The Production Process.*
The traditional building and urban production process in Islamic cultures is markedly different from that followed today, as the example of Saudi Arabia illustrates. Effectively, what has occurred in Saudi Arabia and most other Islamic countries is the abandonment of principles and practices of production that ensured quality in the built environment and the adoption of processes that render it impossible to achieve what Christopher Alexander describes as the "quality without a name".[24] Alexander has pointed out that[25]:

> The production system which we have at present defines a pattern of control which makes it almost impossible for things to be done carefully or appropriately because, almost without exception, decisions are in the wrong hands, decisions are being made at levels far removed from the immediate concrete places where they have impact . . . and, all in all, there is a colossal mismatch between the organization of the decision and control and the needs for appropriateness and good adaptation which the biological reality of the housing system actually requires.

Alexander goes on to identify seven principles that "are essential to the production of houses under all circumstances, and must be followed, whether other necessary social changes are made or not".[26]

Indeed, the traditional production process followed in most Islamic cultures over a period of more than 1000 years in large part embodied these principles. They can be reintroduced effectively in the contemporary production of houses. The initiative in the centralized and autocratic systems of government operational in most Islamic countries today must come from the responsible government agencies and their local representatives. Essentially, they must create situations in which it will be possible to recycle and reintroduce an age-old and successful tradition of production.

## 3.2 - Lessons Derived from the Organizational System and Built Form

These lessons can be grouped under three categories: compatibility with ecology and climate; organizational system and planning; and architectural design, style, and decoration.

***Compatibility with Ecology and Climate.***
Much has been written about the traditional use of natural building materials, cooling and heating devices, and the environmental attributes of compact courtyard housing.[27-29] These historically were used extensively in the Middle East, as were specialized facilities such as the natural ice-maker. These all provide excellent precedents and impetus for contemporary designers in an approach to building and community design that is passive, that relies minimally on mechanical devices for cooling and heating and uses the least possible energy and other resources for manufacturing materials and production.

Contemporary literature on the Islamic tradition of landscaping, its approach and foundations in the culture's value system can help lead landscape designers to a sensitive understanding and appreciation of the deep-rooted Islamic structure, its rationale, and ultimate manifestation in built form that is essential for intelligent recycling.[30]

***Organizational System and Planning.***
A study of aerial photographs of traditional towns and villages reveals the astonishing similarity in organization and clustering across the vast territory of the Islamic world. Although security and defense were major determinants in maintaining the compactness of towns and in surrounding them with walls, it is in the use of land and the three-dimensional distribution of space that the interesting lessons lie for architects and planners. The residential and commercial sectors contain the most relevant lessons.

Design and configuration are essential features of the typical unit in the residential sector. Rooms surround a courtyard open to the sky, with almost all windows open onto this interior court. The structure has one or two stories, and sometimes a basement for summer use in regions such as Iraq and Iran. In other regions, such as Tunisia, a cistern is built under the court to collect winter rainwater for year-round household use.

Clusters of houses are created by adjoining homes; at least three external walls of each house abut other houses. Access to these clusters is by narrow cul-de-sacs that branch off from a network of through streets. The cul-de-sacs are owned and maintained by the people who use them and are regarded as private property. Occasionally, rooms bridge the public through streets, usually to create extra space in a dwelling. Often, these rooms link two properties owned by the same family, but that are across the street from each other.

There are many benefits to this form of residential design and organization. The courtyard floor and earth beneath it act as a combined radiating and storage unit. The walls on four sides shade the court and protect it from direct sunlight during the greater part of the day, particularly if the height of the walls is greater than the width of the courtyard in the direction of the sun. The courtyard floor, however, is left open to the sky (the zenith) for heat radiation during the day and particularly during the night. The earth beneath the court acts as a radiating heat sink, which in turn attracts more heat from surrounding areas in contact with it.[27]

In addition, this form of housing provides high standards of privacy and security within a physical setting, which can promote neighborly social interaction among the occupants. The clustering of housing is economical because most external walls are shared. There are, of course, alternative technical solutions to these party walls that can solve problems of ownership, maintenance, acoustics, and fire. This housing form provides medium densities of between 11 and 14 units per acre, yet provides large living areas in each unit: from 1345 to 1840 ft2 for a single story house, to 2690 and up to 3680 ft2 for a two-story house. These figures were based on a prototype design the author developed. On average, the courtyard house creates 45% more living area than that provided in the typical tract-built single family house in the United States, yet achieves three times the density.

As for the commercial sector, the central market or shopping center of each traditional Islamic city is composed of a web of covered pedestrian malls called *suq* in Arabic, *bazar* in Farsi, and *carsi* in Turkish. Each mall is composed of repetitive cells opposite each

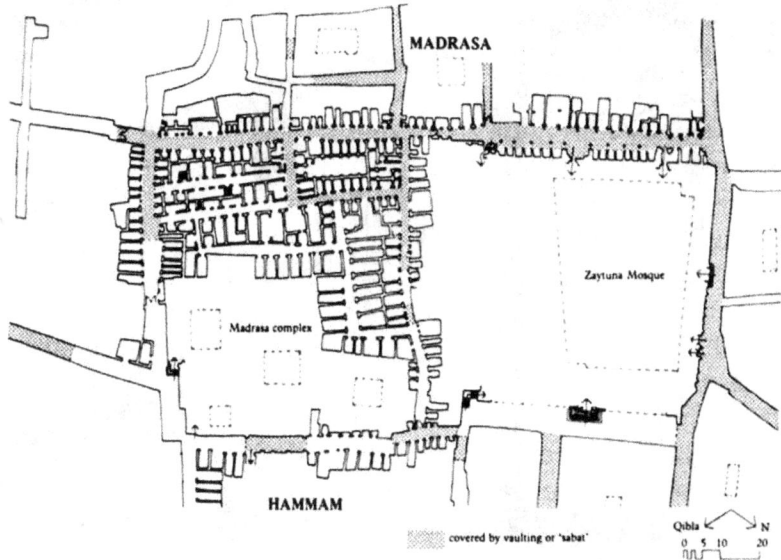

**Figure 13.** The area of the *suq* south of the main Zaytuna Mosque in Tunis. Note the manner in which the shops are inset on the west and south sides of the mosque, and on the north and west sides of the Madrasa complex. The tinted areas of the access system represent covering by vaulting or *sabat*, a room bridging over the street (6).

other and separated by a 10-20-ft walkway covered by vaults with skylights at intervals, creating pleasant and cool environments for shopping. Security during nights and holidays is easily maintained by locking gates strategically located at entry points to the mall system. Typically, various other facilities adjoining the web of market malls are all linked together by an overall access system. The mosque is usually in this area, as are the public bath, hotels, individual workshops, and storage facilities for the various shop owners (Fig. 13).

### *Architectural Design, Style, and Decoration.*
Much has been published in the West about Islamic architecture and decoration. For the purpose of this article, the issue to be addressed is how traditional building design, including its technologies, can prove to be of relevance to contemporary and future building activities. Since the early 1970s, a growing interest in tradition and historical precedents has been evident among architects in many countries, particularly in the United States. Clients have also been sympathetic and receptive. In some Islamic countries, particularly in Iraq, this was certainly evident a decade earlier. A

**Figure 14.** An early example of the work of Dr. M. Makiya of Baghdad, Iraq. This building is the Rafidain Branch Bank in Kufa, Iraq. Designed in the late 1950s and completed in 1968. The historic city of Kufa contains some of the finest brick buildings in Iraq, which has provided a source of inspiration. The walls appear as massive units emphasizing solidity and security, with the windows deeply recessed for shade. The recessed arch treatment is reminiscent of dome squinches found in early Islamic architecture. They provide a powerful formal element in the facade enhancing the solidity of the walls. Courtesy of Makiya Associates Consultants, Ltd., London.

number of Iraqi architects experimented by using traditional motifs in contemporary design and architecture. Mohammed Makiya, Kahtan Madfai, Rifaat Chadirji, and the late Kahtan Awni, all of Baghdad, Iraq, were probably the most serious in the pursuit of this approach since the early 1960s (Fig. 14).

Departure from the strict doctrines of the modern movement in architecture faced much opposition and criticism; nevertheless, the trend toward linkages with the past continues to fill a vacuum that contemporary architectural design, following the ideology of the modern movement, is unable to fill. In the Islamic countries, as well as in other cultures, the need for expressing local cultural identity through architecture is growing stronger. The question of how this ought to be done without creating superficial results remains paramount. Moreover, the problem of contemporary and future building types without historical precedents, such as office buildings, airports, and bus terminals, requires careful study in terms of recycling traditional architectonic and decorative elements.

Once again, the impact of decisions by governing authorities, which is the first issue related to building procedures, requires serious consideration at the policy level both by national governments and in local-level jurisdictions. Also an important issue is whether or not to reapply the fiqh in planning and building activities. There is today much discussion and awareness of the government's role, but less of the fiqh's, primarily due to the lack of knowledge of traditional practice. Both issues, however, will continue to grow in importance.

The question of decision making within a framework of performance criteria, addressed in the discussion of the second issue, is the responsibility of government agencies and the architect. The implementation of performance regulations in lieu of Western-style prescriptive standards will require, in some instances, sophistication that might not be available in certain countries or localities. It is, however, the responsibility of government, as the primary client in most Islamic countries today, to instruct local or foreign consultants who are retained to develop such mechanisms of control. This is true despite the fact that most contemporary structures and sectors of the city were built using the typical mechanisms of zoning and other prescriptive types of regulations. It is not too late to convert the system to performance-based mechanisms of control.

The third issue concerning the production process might be more difficult to implement, as centralized authorities are reluctant to create situations in which their influence is reduced. It is, however, possible for a government to help initiate an appropriate process on an experimental basis.

The scale of the first project(s) might be small, in order to monitor the results and ensure success. Hope of success rests in the time when powerful individuals in some Islamic countries realize that decentralization will enhance the chances of achieving a contemporary equivalent of genuine Islamic architecture and urbanism.

These three issues encompass most of the deep-rooted programmatic, production modes and ideologically based sources for recycling tradition in contemporary and future Islamic environments. The traditional organizational system and built form offer lessons on ecological and climatic compatibility, the nature of planning and physical organization, and architectural design and decoration. Broken down further, the lessons cover planning, function, space, technology, building materials, problems of style, image making, and the meaning of the architecture produced, which are the concerns that are most difficult to handle. Yet, these are not ungraspable if intelligently approached from the careful understanding of traditional experience.

History and tradition do provide a fertile base from which to learn and, when necessary, from which to recycle experiences of process and built form. The matrix of experiences are numerous and at different levels, however. Some cannot be recycled without a total commitment at the policy level by government; others are recyclable at the cluster or building scale with few participants and decision makers involved. Contemporary examples of the latter can be found that use partial aspects of traditional experience. In other words, only a very small segment of the wide spectrum provided by history has so far been used, most of it unsuccessfully. Much must yet be accomplished.

## 4 - Conclusion

The case of the traditional Islamic city as discussed in the first part of this article provides numerous critical lessons.[6] Obviously the fields of architecture and urban planning would be the ones most concerned with this knowledge, particularly as it relates to their respective values and theories. In addition, those involved in the creation and delivery of housing will also find these lessons important.

The traditional system of building and urban activities was an incremental and constantly rebalanced process of development involving the synthesis of religious and sociocultural conventions. The system was self-regulating, so that any significant departure or contravention of the principles and conventions created a situation where corrective action had to be undertaken; in the absence of such action, the intervention of the Kadi (local judge) provided the prescription for normalizing the conflict within the system, in line with the established norms and principles operational in the community.

Specifically, three experiences are valuable to the contemporary context. The first is the importance of the legal framework as the prime shaper of the urban environment, particularly environments at the scale of the neighborhood. Certainly this is also true today with zoning ordinances, subdivision regulations, and building codes. However, the nature of the legal framework is where the Islamic city can provide new experience and insight. The fiqh building guidelines were derived from societal values based on religious beliefs and were supported by adequate elaboration of the intent of each principle. Specific numerical prescriptions were not indicated and only rarely cited as an example of how a specific problem ought to be resolved. In essence, the guidelines functioned as performance criteria, as opposed to contemporary building and planning laws, which are based on standards. The former is qualitative, intent oriented, and responsive to changes in requirements or site conditions, whereas the latter is quantitative, numerically oriented, and not suitable to changes in requirements or location. Not only is the performance criteria approach more sophisticated in terms of addressing each building problem within its own context, but the aggregate results it helps to create as built environment are various and complex. Laws based on standards address all problems uniformly, with results of monotony and sameness in the built environment. The best examples are the thousands of suburbs which were developed in the West during the twentieth century and particularly since World War II.

The second lesson is the use of a building "design language" as a communication and design decision-making aid. The components of the language integrate the three dimensional form and function of the design element being communicated. This mechanism helps the user and builder to communicate with each other. It also preserves and perpetuates design configurations and forms which have proved their durability through experience without hindering diversity in the individual design solution. Recent research in architecture is rediscovering this attribute.

The third primary lesson is in the nature of the physical organization. As mentioned earlier, the system of courtyard buildings serviced by cul-de-sacs and through streets pre-date Islam; however, Islamic civilization developed and refined this system and spread it across a vast geographic area, aided by the simultaneous development and acquisition of fiqh knowledge. Some highlights of the attributes of this organizational system follow. The courtyard plan form is able to accommodate diverse uses. The densities created in housing are efficient without sacrificing the privacy of the individual unit. Streets as an access network are maximally utilized, as in the central portion of Tunis Medina. All streets take up 12.5% of the •gross built up area and only 13.3% of those are cul-de-sacs serving 28.5% of all buildings, i.e. a relatively low proportion of cul-de-sacs serving a high proportion of buildings. Sabats (rooms over streets) are used to create extra space for private users, simultaneously providing cover to the public in the streets. In the central portion of Tunis Medina, 8% of all streets are covered by sabats, in addition to 7.5% covered by vaulting, providing coverage to a total of 15.5% of the city's streets.

There are numerous attributes in addition to those mentioned above, such as the use and details of decoration and ornament in the realm of art. Another important attribute which has received some attention before is the energy saving attributes of the built form within an arid region context, aided by energy saving practices and devices such as the wind tower, air vent, cisterns for storing water and keeping it cool, and the ice maker.[28] Other practices were the collection and storage of rain water in cisterns under the courtyard of buildings, the effective use of basements as living quarters during the hot season, and the recycling of building materials.

In the second part of the article it is shown that a new, foreign system was introduced and adopted under the notion and aspiration of modernism. This modern system is based on preconceived prescriptive standards conceived and based on experiences of other cultures whose values are different from the local culture importing the system. The organizational nature of the system is legitimized by master plans and related zoning regulations. These regulations prescribe street widths, setback requirements, densities, building heights, lot sizes, and so on. They are designed to tell people what to do, thus inhibiting flexibility, responsiveness, and sometimes innovation in response to specific local constraints and conditions. In contrast, the traditional system allows for variety and innovation in response to specific local conditions of the built environment. The contemporary prescriptive system allows only for what is prescribed regardless of the unique requirements of the locality and site, thus promoting sameness, repetitiveness, and monotony. This explains the contrast in quality between traditional and contemporary sectors of Islamic cities, particularly those found in North Africa where the modern European sector was built adjacent to the medinas or traditional towns, such as in Tunis, Rabat and others.

In Learning from the Past, the possibilities of recycling aspects of the traditional experience for improving contemporary and future architecture and urbanism were examined. Although the discussion addressed Islamic environments, there are universal benefits; it is hoped that the value of this information will be of interest and use to peoples of other cultures today and in the future.

Amos Rapoport clearly points out the relevance and importance of this information, when he says[31]:

> The broader our sample in space and time, the more likely we are to see regularities in apparent chaos, as well as to understand better those differences that are significant. Thus, the more likely we are to see patterns and relationships, and these are the most significant things for which to look. Being able to establish the presence of such patterns may help us deal with the problem of constancy and change. . . . It is very important to understand constancies as well as change, since our culture stresses change to an inordinate degree. Also, if apparent change and variability are an expression of invariant processes, this is extremely important because the reasons for doing apparently different things remain the same.

## Notes

[1] S. A. Al-Hathloul, *Tradition, Continuity and Change in the Physical Environment: The Arab-Muslim City*, Ph.D. dissertation, Massachusetts Institute of Technology, Cambridge, Mass., 1981.

[2] *The Antiquaries Journal XI* (4) (October 1931).

[3] G. R. Driver and J. C. Miles, eds., *Babylonian Laws, Vol. 1: Legal Commentary*, Oxford University Press, London, 1952.

[4] B. S. Hakim, "Arab-Islamic Urban Structure," *The Arabian Journal for Science and Engineering* 7(2), (April 1982) 69-79.

[5] R. W. Bulliet, *The Camel and the Wheel*, Harvard University Press, Cambridge, Mass., 1975.

[6] B. S. Hakim, *Arabic-Islamic Cities: Building and Planning Principles*, KPl/Routledge and Kegan Paul, London, 1986.

[7] B. S. Hakim, ed., *Sidi Bou Sa'id-Tunisia:A Study in Structure and Form*, Technical University of Nova Scotia, Halifax, Canada, 1978. Revised edition 2009. Available from Amazon.com.

[8] C. P. Winterhalter, *Indigenous Housing Patterns and Design Principles in the Eastern Province of Saudi Arabia*, dissertation for D. Tech. Sci., Swiss Federai Institute of Technology, Zurich, 1981.

[9] Y. M. O. Fadan, *The Development of Contemporary Housing in Saudi Arabia [1950-1983]: A Study in Cross-Cultural Influence Under Conditions of Rapid Change*, Ph.D. Dissertation, Massachusetts Institute of Technology, Cambridge, Mass., 1983.

[10] S. G. Shiber, "Report on City Growth in the Eastern Province, Saudi Arabia," *Recent Arab City Growth*, Kuwait Government Printing Press, Kuwait, 1970.

[11] H. al-Jasir, *Madinat al-Riyadh Abr Atwar al-Tarikh*, Dar al-Yamamah, Riyadh, 1966.

[12] *ARAMCO Handbook*, Oil and the Middle East, Arabian American Oil Company, Dhahran, 1968.

[13] *Eastern Region Plan, Existing Conditions*, Candilis, Metra lnt., Dammam, June 1974.

[14] S. al-Hathloul, M. al-Hussayen, and A. Shuaibi, *Urban Land Utilization, Case Study: Riyadh, Saudi Arabia*, Urban Settlement Design Program, Massachusetts Institute of Technology, 1975.

[15] Ref. 1, p. 166.

[16] Ref. 1, p. 167.

[17] B. S. Hakim and P. G. Rowe, two articles, "The Representation of Values in Traditional and Contemporary Islamic Cities," *Journal of Architectural Education* 36 (4), 26 (Summer 1983). (The reference is to Rowe's article subtitled "Contemporary Developments in Saudi Arabia.")

[18] lbid., p. 26.

[19] Y. Yavus and S. Ozkan, "The Final Years of the Ottoman Empire," Chapter 2 in R. Holod and A Evin, eds., *Modern Turkish Architecture*, University of Pennsylvania Press, 1984.

[20] Ref. 17, p. 27.

[21] "Technical Report No. 9 of SCET International/SEDES ," in *Riyadh Action Master Plans*, Technical Reports Nos. 1-17, May 1977-March 1980.

[22] S. al-Tuwaijri, *Haqq al-Irtifag*, Ph.D. dissertation, Um al Qura University, Makkah, 1982. Deals with traditional building practices.

[23] I. al-Fayez, *Al-Bina wa Ahkamahu fi al-Fiqh al-Islami*, Ph.D. dissertation, Higher Institute for Law, University of Ibn Saud al-Islamiyah, Riyadh, 1986. Deals with laws of building in Islamic fiqh.

[24] C. Alexander, *The Timeless Way of Building*, Oxford University Press, New York, 1979.

[25] C. Alexander et al, *The Production of Houses*, Oxford University Press, New York, 1985, p. 40.

[26] Ibid., pp. 48-49.

[27] D. Dunham, "The Courtyard House as a Temperature Regulator," *The New Scientist*, 663-666 (September 1960).

[28] M. N. Bahadori, "Passive Cooling Systems in Iranian Architecture," *Scientific American*, 144-154 (February 1978).

[29] M. Danby, F. Moore, and S. Roaf in A. Germen, ed., *Islamic Architecture and Urbanism*, College of Architecture and Planning, King Faisal University, Dammam, Saudi Arabia, 1983.

[30] O. Llewellyn, "Shari'ah Values Pertaining to Landscape Planning and Design," and S. Lesiuk, "Landscape Planning for Energy Conservation Design in the Middle East," in A. Germen, ed., *Islamic Architecture and Urbanism*, College of Architecture and Planning, King Faisal University, Dammam, Saudi Arabia, 1983.

[31] A. Rapoport, "Cultural Origins of Architecture," in J. C. Snyder and A. J. Catanese, eds., *Introduction to Architecture*, McGraw-Hill Book Co., New York, 1979, Chapt. 1, p. 18.

# References

R. Holod and D. Rastorfer, eds., *Architecture & Community: Building in the Islamic World Today*, Aperture, Millerton, New York, 1983.

I. Serageldin and S. el-Sadek, eds., *The Arab City: Its Character and Islamic Cultural Heritage*, a collection of papers from a symposium held in Medina, Saudi Arabia, March 1981, Arab Urban Development Institute, Riyadh,

Saudi Arabia, 1982.

E. Beazley and M. Harverson, *Living with the Desert: Working Buildings of the Iranian Plateau*, Aris & Phillips Ltd., Warminster, Wilts, UK, 1982.

C. L. Brown, ed., *From Medina to Metropolis: Heritage and Change in the Near Eastern City*, The Darwin Press, Princeton, 1973.

N. J. Coulson, *A History of Islamic Law*, Edinburgh University Press, Edinburgh, 1964.

K. A. C. Creswell, *Early Muslim Architecture: Umayyads, early Abbasids and Tulunids*, 2 vols., The Clarendon Press, Oxford, 1932-1940.

J. D. Hoag, *Islamic Architecture*, History of World Architecture Series, edited by Pier Luigi Nervi, Harry N. Abrams, Inc., New York, 1977.

A. H. Hourani and S. M. Stem, eds., *The Islamic City*, Bruno Cassirer, Oxford, 1970.

I. M. Lapidus, ed., *Middle Eastern Cities*, University of California Press, Berkeley, California, 1969.

E. B. Macdougall and R. Ettinghausen, eds., *The Islamic Garden*, Dumbarton Oaks Colloquium on the History of Landscape Architecture IV, Trustees for Harvard University, Washington, D.C., 1976.

G. Michell, ed., *Architecture of the Islamic World: Its History & Social Meaning*, Thames & Hudson Ltd., London, and William Morrow & Co., Inc., New York, 1978.

A. L. M. T. Nijst, H. Priemus, H. L. Swets, and J. J. Van Ijzeren, *Living on the Edge of the Sahara: A Study of Traditional Forms of Habitation and Types of Settlement in Morocco*, Government Publishing Office, The Hague, 1973.

P. Oliver, ed., *Shelter and Society*, Barrie and Rockliff, London, 1969.

J. M. Richards, et al, *Hassan Fathy*, Concept Media Pte Ltd., Singapore and the Architectural Press, London, 1985.

J. Schacht, *An Introduction to Islamic Law*, the Clarendon Press, Oxford, 1964.

B. Ünsal, *Turkish Islamic Architecture : In Seljuk and Ottoman Times 1071-1923*, Alec Tiranti, London, 1959.

J. L. Abu-Lughod, "The lslamic City-Historic Myth, Islamic Essence, and Contemporary Relevance," *International Journal of Middle East Studies* 19(2) (May 1987).

A. Rapoport, *House Form and Culture*, Prentice-Hall, Inc., Englewood Cliffs, N.J., 1969.

A. Rapoport, "Environmental Quality, Metropolitan Areas and Traditional Settlements," *Habitat International* 7(3/4) (1983).

A. Rapoport, "Development, Culture Change and Supportive Design," *Habitat International* 7(5/6) (1983).

J. F. C. Turner, *Housing By People, Towards Autonomy in Building Environments*, Pantheon Books, New York, 1976.

# Chapter 10

# Reviving the Rule System

## 1 - Background

There is a great deal of literature describing traditional towns, popularly known as "Medina(s)," in the Maghrib region of the Islamic world (Tunisia, Algeria, Morocco, and including the Iberian peninsula from the eighth to the fifteenth century). Those descriptions, and the availability of aerial photos produced by the French colonial authorities during the first half of this century, have provided a clear but incomplete "image" of the patterns which make up the traditional city, known as 'Medina'. Clearly those patterns are radically different from their European counterparts that are based on the gridiron system. The difference, as I have discovered through extensive research since 1975, is due to another system of conception, implementation, and associated processes of growth and change. This is partly due to the role and the responsibilities of the people involved in decisions affecting building activities, and in the manner space is conceived, partitioned, configured for use, and controlled (Fig. 1).

The French colonialists arrived to this milieu with a different 'mind-set' about what constitutes advanced built-form attributes, coupled with an attitude of superiority, and a mission to "civilize" the North African populations. This prompted the French to build "civilized" European towns next to the Medinas, for the purpose of: (1) making it possible to live separately from the colonized people, but close enough to keep a watchful eye, and (2) to demonstrate the spaciousness of their living and working quarters relative to the dense and inward-looking attributes of the Medina. This policy has had unexpected benefits. It preserved and saved the Medina to at least the era of independence, 1956 in Morocco

**Figure 1** Aerial photo of the traditional medina of Tunis and part of its modern sector on its east side (lower part of photo), built during the French colonial period, showing the difference in the pattern of urbanization. Photo taken in 1975 – Office de la Topographie et de la Cartographie, Tunis.

and Tunisia, and 1962 in Algeria.

The outward coexistence of the Medina and the French sectors during the colonial period had bred strong desires, among at least some Arabs who had contact with the French, to imitate patterns of living in those sectors. Those usually were the well-to-do and the Western schooled segment of Arab society. Some were cultivated by the French in anticipation of independence. The use of the automobile in the colonial sectors created a compelling impression on the Arab population that the "French" town was so much better because the car could easily move around, unlike the Arab Medina that was gradually being perceived by its own inhabitants as deficient and therefore inferior. The construction of buildings by the French using modern materials and technologies also impressed the Arab population. The buildings were higher, seemed to be better constructed, and the use of modern materials such as glass, on windows and store frontages, had their share of creating a shift in the mind-set of the Arab population towards their traditional built environment.

At the time of independence most of the Arab rulers' mind-set was geared towards modernizing various sectors of societal activities. The outward manifestation of French material culture was the easiest to copy. The built environment seemed to most people the logical target for change, particularly for adapting it to the motor car. It should be stressed that in the minds of the Arab rulers and a large segment of their societies the process of change was associated with modernization, and not Westernization. This was an important distinction, because some of the Arab rulers expressed nationalism to their people, and did not want to undertake change that would subsequently be perceived as copying the French. The mind-set of the rulers and the population seemed to be in concert as far as the traditional built environment was concerned. A silent 'culture of shame' emerged about the Medina, which implied that the traditional built environment represented backwardness and was a reminder of days gone by when Islamic culture was in a state of weakness and dormancy. This perception of shame, as is well known, has been and is still very common in a large number of Arab and Muslim countries. As we shall see below, the opposite reality of the Medina is true, *ie* it embodies high qualities, and it is a result of a sophisticated process that is superior to the ones imported and implemented by the generation of Arab rulers since independence.

## 2 - Ignorance of the traditional system

The reason for this state of affairs is primarily due to the lack of knowledge and understanding of the traditional system of urbanism that was historically prevalent and active in the Near East and North Africa, and that continued to be so in the Maghrib to at least the early years of French colonial rule. This system has its roots in the pre-Islamic Near East civilizations of Mesopotamia, the Fertile Crescent region, and in the Arabian peninsula. It has a continuous history of approximately 4000 years, and because of its longevity it has achieved a high level of success and sophistication in certain aspects of its processes, particularly in its later history under Islamic culture.

If we scrutinize housing, being the predominant sector of the built environment, we find that building houses usually occurred in small increments and across a long span of time. The nature of the process, coupled with the predominant use of a compact and clustered morphological system, created certain problems and sometimes conflicts that had to be resolved by the neighbours concerned. Early Muslim jurists recognized these problems and addressed them within the framework of the *Fiqh* (the science of Islamic jurisprudence). This science is divided into two major branches: *Ibadat* that addresses matters related to religious observances, and *Mu'amallat* that addresses matters of concern and/or conflicts arising from the interactions and relationship between people. Thus the issues of minimizing damages and/or maintaining equitability as a result of building activities, particularly in housing, are addressed within the branch of Mu'amallat.

The body of knowledge and experience related to building activity, as in most other branches of the Fiqh, gradually achieved maturity within the first three centuries of Islam. By the early years of the fourth Islamic century (about 900 AD) the foundation and the essential body of knowledge in jurisprudence were attained. A great deal of the precedents and principles are rooted in the city of Medina, Arabia during the decade of 1–10 AH (622–632 AD) when it was governed under the guidance and leadership of the Prophet Mohammed.[1] Of the four Sunni schools of law, the Maliki school – which is attributed to Imam Malik (born 93 AH/712 AD, died 179/795) – is rooted most closely to the *Sunnah* (traditions) of the Prophet, and to the experience and knowledge accumulated in the city of Medina.

Since the arrival of Islam to the Maghrib, Muslims in the region became followers of the Maliki school of law. There were attempts to introduce Shi'ism by the Fatimids during the first quarter of the ninth century AD, and more than six centuries later the Hanafi school was introduced by the Ottoman Turks. Despite these attempts, Maghribis to this day observe the Maliki school. People in other regions who are at present followers of this school of law are in Central Africa, Upper Egypt, the Sudan, and West Africa. Thus the practices of urbanism and building in these regions have direct roots in the city of Medina, Arabia where most of the principles, including acceptable pre-Islamic customs (Urf), were practiced at the time when the Prophet was governing the Muslim community there.

## 3 - The traditional Rule System

As mentioned in the previous section, the roots of the traditional system can be traced back to the ancient Near Eastern civilizations. There is historical evidence to point out two types of rule system: (1) the centralized 'imposed' laws (henceforth referred to as *meta-principles*), such as the laws of Hammurabi, king of Babylon (1792–1750 BC), and (2) the localized community-based customary rules (henceforth referred to as *Urf*). There has also been a long history of central authorities in those distant civilizations respecting local traditions and customs provided those did not conflict with the intent of the meta-principles.

Both types of rule system continued in Islamic cultures and have had their impact on the traditional built environment of Islamic societies. Stipulations from the meta-principles tended to create a unity of *concepts* and *attitudes* towards the built environment in the various regions of the Islamic world, whereas the Urf tended to influence the outcome of construction details and the architectonics of the local built form. These two types of rules operating simultaneously contributed to the phenomenon of the *diversity* of settlements within specific sub-regions of the Islamic world, yet *unified* by the general concepts and attitudes that all regions shared. This resulted essentially in uniqueness at the micro-level and similarities at the macro-level.

There are certain underlying concepts and principles in Islamic law that governed the rationale of the ongoing process of growth and change. I have chosen seven Fiqh principles (*Qawa'id Fiqhiyah*) because they have had a direct effect on the traditional built environment. They are here woven together to portray their cumulative rationale: (1) The basis for action is the freedom to act, (2) stimulated and judged by the intentions for those actions, (3) which are con- strained by the prevention of damages to others, (4) however,

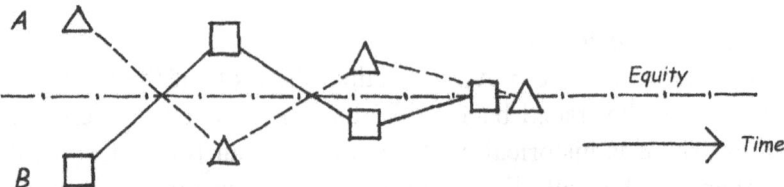

**Figure 2** Underlying concepts and principles (Qawa'id Fiqhiyah) of Islamic law that governed the rationale for the process of growth and change. The original Arabic version of these principles is included for reference. An important goal for these principles is to achieve equity between neighbours when expectations, demands, and needed change would create benefits to one owner to the detriment of his neighbour(s). Two owners (A & B) are illustrated in the diagram. The effect of these principles over time tends to equitably harmonize the competing and sometimes conflicting demands of adjacent owners.

it is sometimes necessary to tolerate lesser damages so as to avoid greater ones. (5) Older established facts must be taken into account by adjusting to their presence and conditions. (6) People's customs must be respected and followed, (7) however, time might change those customs and new solutions will be needed (Fig. 2).

When applied to the context of the built environment these principles provided the freedom to act and build, restrained by certain limits. They are thus *proscriptive* in nature, allowing the liberty to generate solutions to specific local problems in response to the site and the conditions around it (they are not prescriptive in specifying preconceived requirements and dimensions for solving problems). An equilibrium is established on the site where the 'best' solution is achieved for a specific micro condition at a specific period in time. Diversity is thus achieved in the built environment, so that every locality and street becomes unique in character and contributes substantially to its identity. This in turn contributes to the richness of the total built environment. People's customs are fully incorporated in the manner they build and they can express their world view in built form. The system also recognizes and adapts to changes in those customs across time.

I have assembled in detail the meta-principles from the various sources of the Maliki school of law including their roots in the Quran and Sunnah.[2] Some of the headings for those meta-principles are:
- Avoid harm to others and oneself.
- Accept the concept of interdependence.
- Respect the privacy of the private domain of others, particularly avoid the creation of direct visual corridors.
- Respect the rights of original or earlier usage.
- Respect the rights of building higher within one's air space.
- Respect the property of others.
- Adjacent neighbours have the rights of preemption.
- Seven cubits is the minimum width for public through streets (to allow two fully loaded camels to pass).
- Avoid locating the sources of unpleasant smells and noisy activities adjacent to or near mosques.

As for the Urf and how its impact affected the traditional built environment at the local level, and in the process contributed to local distinctiveness and identity, this was primarily due to the manner in which the Urf functioned, as in the use of local building materials and construction techniques, and especially in the design of architectural details and motifs and the use of colours. For a detailed analysis and discussion of the Urf phenomenon supported by illustrative examples, please refer to Hakim (1994). There, I proposed a theoretical concept to explain how the phenomenon of *unity* at the level of most of the Islamic world, and how localized *diversity* at the level of each town or city, was achieved. Refer to chapter 4, pages 99-101.

Unfortunately, due to the influence of the colonial period and especially after independence, the traditional system and its associated processes were gradually replaced by a system that is essentially *prescriptive* in nature, ie it is based on quantitative stipulations applied at the local level. In addition, imported concepts and techniques were adopted for the use of land and for differentiating space into separate zones at the settlement level. It should also be noted that unlike the traditional system which was controlled locally, the imported Western system is applied uniformly by the central authority, ie the government in the capital city, on all localities, reinforced by local municipal authorities. It is in the complete comprehension of differences between the two systems (ie the traditional and the imported Western), intellectually and in practicable terms, that hopes for reviving and modernizing the traditional rule system might be possible (Fig. 3).

## 4 - Suggested steps for reviving the traditional Rule System

Historical developments in this century have affected the Islamic world at large, including the Maghrib region. Those developments may be viewed in three layers:
1. The situation before dominance by the European powers. The built environment then was governed by the system that spread with Islam.
2. The direct impact of Western influence through colonial rule, or indirectly due to contacts with the West, especially by the Ottoman rulers who were infatuated by Western styles and fashions, including ideas for city planning and architecture. Changes began to take place in replacing the traditional system.
3. The post-independence period where changes, in some instances, were forcibly and rapidly brought about by Arab rulers who were convinced that these were necessary as part of the modernization process. A primary victim of those changes was the traditional built environment.

Given the above developments it would seem that the following suggested steps are necessary for reviving and modernizing the traditional rule system.[3]

Step One: A clear *policy* by the government is necessary for initiating the process of revival. This policy needs to initially address at least two objectives:
1. *Education and related research* of the workings of the traditional rule system in a particular region. This needs to be undertaken rapidly in selected villages and large towns across the country. University and college professors and students

from various disciplines need to be involved in this endeavour. Suggested disciplines are history, archaeology, anthropology, Islamic law, architecture, city planning, and art history. Expertise from other fields might also be needed.
2. *Evaluation of current laws* that affect town planning, construction and architectural design are necessary, including careful analysis of how those laws affect urban and building activities at the local level. An important issue to address is whether centralized laws are eroding local customs and practices in various regions in the country, especially at the local level of a village, town or large city. It will also be necessary to study various approaches and techniques for revising these centralized laws so as to make them responsive to the local Urf.

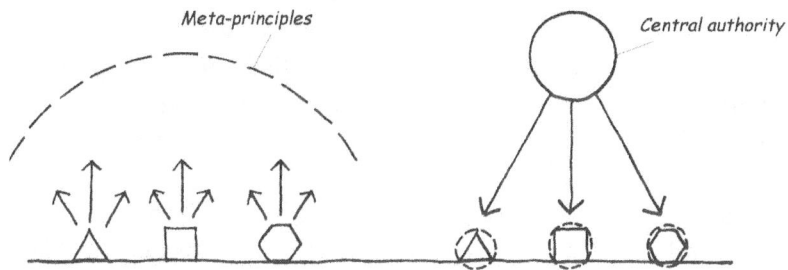

**Figure 3** Conceptual representation of the impacts on the local level (three geometric shapes denoting three settlements) by *proscriptive* meta-principles, and by *prescriptive* imposed laws. The diagram on the left represents a settlement's ability to respond freely to local conditions and requirements, but is restrained by an overarching set of meta-principles. This would result in settlements that are diverse in their physical form and exhibit distinct local identity. The diagram on the right represents how prescriptions from a central authority, which is usually far removed from a locality, inhibit creative solutions to local problems. Over time the resulting settlements would tend to be similar to each other.

Step Two: After the bulk of the work in Step One is completed, probably within a period of two to three years, areas of local jurisdictions should be organized and established. A jurisdiction would include every medium to large town and the villages traditionally associated with it. Those entities will be empowered to study and document their traditional Urf practices, followed by revisions where necessary in response to available modern technologies and to aspects of societal and community lifestyle preferences. This process needs to be undertaken democratically so that as many ideas as possible are gathered, and to provide the opportunity to as

253

many interested local citizens to participate. Essentially this process will generate a 'revised' local Urf for the community.

Step Three: Legal jurisdictions need to be re-established to adjudicate problems arising from building activities in response to the revised local Urf. It is preferable that these legal jurisdictions operate within the same boundaries as those established in Step Two above.

It is obvious that the above three steps require the initiative and full backing of the central government, and the complete co-operation of local authorities. It might be helpful for the procedure of reviving and refining the rule system to be viewed in terms of *process* (procedures relating to building activities) and *product* (the nature of the physical organizational system and related built-form attributes). I have elsewhere discussed this distinction and provided examples. That article discusses these concepts and provides extensive links to other references (Hakim, 1991). Refer to chapter 7.

The above suggestions should be viewed as open- ended, and are not intended to be final. They are to be considered as ideas and possible steps for action. An analysis of the situation in each Maghrib country will be necessary for proposing specific workable steps for reviving the traditional rule system. However, in every case a strong policy commitment to this venture is required from the highest level of decision- makers within the central government, and by all local authorities.[4] If this commitment is forthcoming and the revival of the traditional rule system is undertaken and implemented, then it will be possible to revitalize all traditional towns in the Maghrib within one generation in a manner which will maintain their integrity, cultural identity, and historical continuity.

## Acknowledgment

An earlier version of this paper was first presented in Tangiers, Morocco, June, 1996, at the conference titled: "The Living Medina: The walled Arab city in architecture, literature, and history", sponsored by the American Institute of Maghribi Studies (AIMS).

## Notes

[1] Medina is the name of the city located in the western region of the Arabian peninsula, and should not be confused with the Arabic term 'Medina' for city.

[2] See Chapter 1: "Islamic law and neighbourhood building guidelines", pp 15–54, in Hakim (1986).

[3] This approach is based on preserving the lessons and principles of the traditional system. To my knowledge it has not been considered or discussed before. Amos Rapoport confirms this by saying: "…and this is a form of preservation that has not yet really been considered or investigated." See Rapoport (1999).

[4] For a discussion of the necessary financial commitments, see Serageldin (1997).

## References

Hakim, B S (1986) *Arabic–Islamic Cities: Building and Planning Principles*. Kegan Paul International, London and New York.

Hakim, B S (1991) Urban design in traditional Islamic culture: recycling its successes. *Cities* **8**(4), 274–277.

Hakim, B S (1994) The 'Urf' and its role in diversifying the architecture of traditional Islamic cities. *Journal of Architectural and Planning Research* **11**(2), 108–127.

Rapoport, A (1999) A framework for studying vernacular design. *Journal of Architectural and Planning Research* **16**(1), 52–64.

Serageldin I (1997) Our past is our future: investing in our cultural heritage. In *Proceedings of the 4th International Symposium of the World Heritage Cities*, Evora, Portugal, 17–20 September 1997, (pp 116–125).

# Chapter 11

# Applying Lessons in Abiquiu, New Mexico

## 1 - Introduction

Dar Al-Islam, a non-profit corporation, intended to create a village far a community of Muslims on land which it has purchased near the village of Abiquiu, approximately 60 miles northwest of Santa Fe (See Figure 1). The intention in early 1981 was to develop a self-sufficient Islamic community, created out of a careful allocation of its 1000 acre property for various uses, such as agriculture, light manufacturing, handicraft industries and educational facilities. A portion of the land, a plateau of approximately 77 acres, is allocated for the construction of the village for a projected community of 100 households (See Figure 2). The village will include an educational complex, a community center, housing and parking areas (See Figures 3,4).

The Dar Al-Islam would like to plan and design the village according to principles and guidelines derived from the experience of traditional Islamic settlements, particularly in the formation of housing. Since that experience is especially valuable in terms of formulating guidelines for building decisions as it affects proximate neighbours, the Dar Al-Islam Corporation requested the author to develop appropriate guidelines for the village, which probably will be built in increments of 5 to 10 houses.

This article is in three parts, the first is a summary of the historical background followed by a brief exposition of the components which constituted the traditional building process. The third part is a condensed version of the proposed guidelines for the Dar Al-Islam housing, grouped in five categories derived from traditional considerations affecting design decisions among proximate neigh-

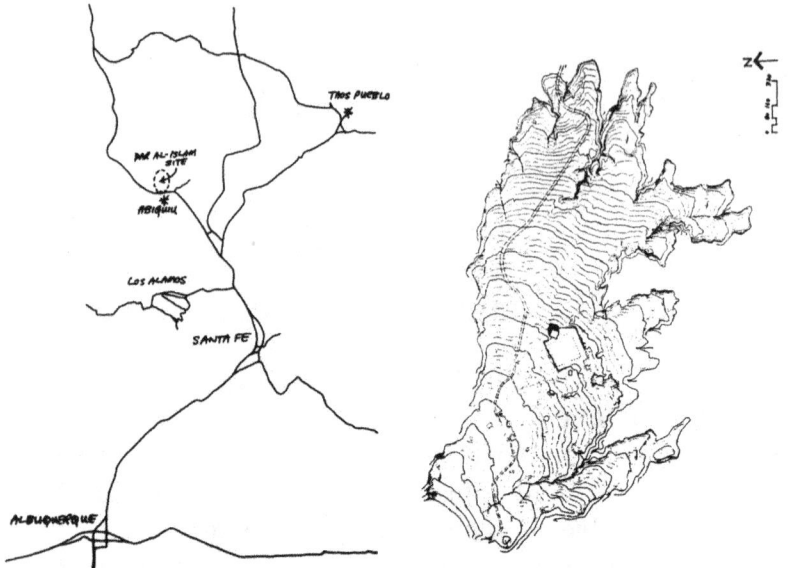

**Figure 1.** Location of Abiquiu and site of Dar Al-Islam, New Mexico.

**Figure 2.** Dar Al-Islam plateau. The area east of the mosque and south of the road is envisaged to be allocated for housing.

bours. A primary assumption in developing these guidelines rests with the understanding that the Dar Al-Islam intended to develop cluster courtyard housing where two or three exterior walls of each unit are shared with other adjacent units (See Figure 5).

## 2 – Historical background

First a brief exposition of the history and background of building guidelines in traditional Islamic urbanism. Islam encourages settlement – as opposed to maintaining a nomadic way of life – and the nurturing of a cohesive community within a physical setting which will support the necessary functions for a 'good' Islamic way of life. The primary requirements were the erection of the mosque, the necessary community facilities and housing.

As Islam spread rapidly from Arabia in the seventh century, Muslims began the process of settling in conquered towns, and with time adjusted their morphology to suit the requirements of the Islamic lifestyle. Numerous towns and villages were also created across the vast territory of the Muslim world.

**Figure 3.** Aerial view of Dar Al-Islam mosque and foundation walls far the school. These two structures are designed by Egyptian architect Hassan Fathy. Figure supplied by Professor Farouk M. Konash.

The building of housing usually occurred in small segments and increments, across a long span of time. The nature of the process, coupled with the predominant use of a compact and clustered morphological system, meant that the relationships of adjoining neighbours in matters related to building design decisions, generated certain problems and occasionally conflicts which had to be resolved. Early Muslim jurists recognized this problem and addressed it within the framework of the 'Fiqh' (The science of Islamic jurisprudence). The Fiqh, is divided into two major branches: 'Ibadat' which addresses matters related to religious observances, and 'Muamallat' which addresses matters of concern and conflicts arising from the interaction and relationships among people. Therefore, the issues of damages and/or equitability related to building activity − particularly in housing − were included in the branch of 'Muamalat'.

The body of knowledge and experience related to building activity and in most other branches of the Fiqh was crystallized within the first three centuries of Islam. By the early years of the fourth

(a)

(b)

**Figure 4.** Dar Al-Islam mosque, (a) view of main entrance facade, and (b) view of 'Qibla' wall facade, i .e. the wall which faces the directian to Makkah. Figures supplied by Professor Farouk M. Konash.

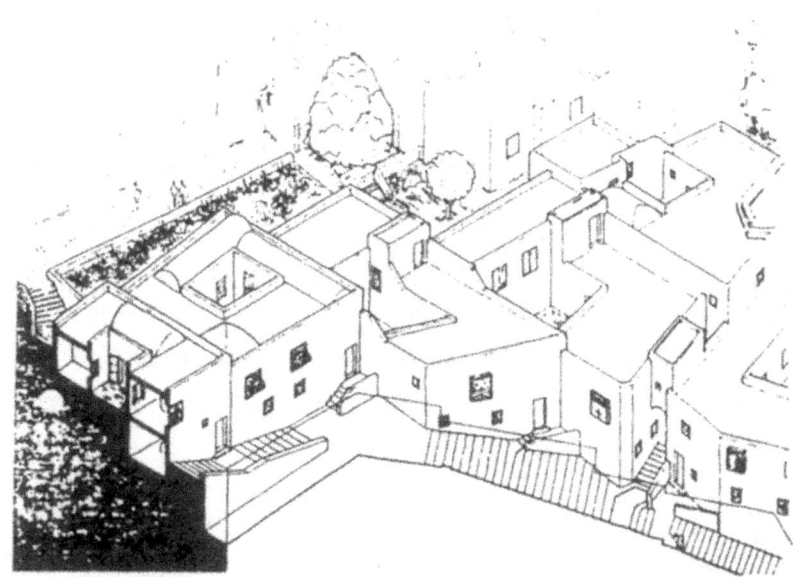

**Figure 5.** Clustered courtyard housing. It is envisaged that Dar Al-Islam will utilize a similar pattern for housing. This sketch was part of a design project located in the village of Sidi Bou Sa'id, Tunisia; undertaken in early 1976 by Mr. George Guimond, then a senior architecture student at the Technical University of Nova Scotia in Halifax, Canada. It was first published in Sidi Bou Sa'id, Tunisia: A Study in Structure and Form (For details of reference, see note 8).

Islamic century (about 900 A.D.) the foundations and the essential body of knowledge in jurisprudence was attained. A great deal of the precedence and principles are rooted in Medina, Arabia during the decade 1-10 A.H. (622-632 A.O.) when it was governed under the guidance and leadership of the Prophet Muhammad.

Of the four Sunni Schools of Law, the Maliki school, which is attributed to Imam Malik (Born 93 A.H./712 A.D., Died 179 A.H./795 A.D.) is rooted most closely to the 'Sunna' (Sayings and traditions of the Prophet) , and to the experience and knowledge generated in Medina, because Imam Malik spent most of his life in that city.

The Maghrib (or western) region of the Islamic World is the area within which the author undertook research for traditional building processes and guidelines. This area stretches from Libya in the east to Morocco in the west, and up to about 500 years ago it included most of Spain. The important point here is that Muslims in this region, since the arrival of Islam, were predominantly followers of the Maliki School of Law. There were attempts to introduce Shi'ism by the Fatimids during the early years of the third Islamic century, and more than six centuries later the Hanafi School was introduced by the Ottoman Turks. Despite these attempts, North Africa to this day follows the Maliki School of Law. People in other regions who are at present followers of this school, are in Central Africa, Upper Egypt, the Sudan and West Africa. Hence the examples and practices of building and urbanism in these regions have direct roots in Medina, where most of the principles were first founded.[1]

## 3 - Components of the building process

The following is a brief summary of the manner in which building design decisions were undertaken in the traditional setting and the methods/procedures which were utilized in the process. Essentially three components interacted simultaneously: Norms and ethical principles, Local design language, and Building rituals and ceremonies.

a) ***The norms and ethical principles*** regulating societal conduct, which are rooted in the Quran (the Holy Book of Islam) and the Sunna (the sayings and traditions of the Prophet Muhammad) . These principles are broad and their scope is general. Predominant examples are:

i. The avoidance of harming others, whether the act of infringement creating harm is profitable or not.[2]
ii. The concept of interdependence among people and avoiding selfish behaviour, i.e. The respect of one's rights and the rights of others equally, balancing out conflicting requirements equitably. This principle affects the use of common party walls, the disposition of rain water, etc.[3]
iii. Respect of privacy.[4]
iv. The right of precedence or earlier usage.
v. Respecting the rights of the neighbour, especially exercising the option of pre-emption, such as the right of buying an adjacent property offered for sale.[5]
vi. The rights of the community in public-right-of-ways by ensuring public safety and order in the streets.[6]

vii. The encouragement of individuals to behave in a responsible manner, particularly in matters affecting the welfare of the community, i.e. nurturing the sense of responsibility to the community. Examples are: maintaining the exterior walls in good structural condition, keeping the side of the street adjacent to exterior walls clean, etc.[7]

b) ***The use of a local design language or vocabulary*** in the various regions and urban centers of the Islamic world. Each term of the vocabulary embodied the form and function of the physical component which is associated with it. This vocabulary acted as a communication medium for design decisions among people involved in building, particularly among the builder or master-mason, his client and others involved in any specific project. The terms in the vocabulary related to all scales of the built environment, from the overall town scale to the ornamental and construction details of a single building type.[8]

c) ***Rituals and ceremonies*** were associated with and accompanied certain events occurring during the process of construction. This aspect of the traditional experience should be understood and appreciated, as it helps to create a form of bondage between the builder(s) and their buildings, between the owner and his building and between the builder(s) and owner. This bondage creates the extra association for the builder with the project he is constructing. There is no doubt that this would contribute to a quality product. The owner's affection for and bondage to the project, particularly if it is his house, will increase; and finally the bondage and good will generated between owner and the builder(s) working for him, a contribution to the bondage among the people of the community.

A well known example of such a ritual ceremony is the sacrifice of a sheep and the recitation of the 'Fatha' (the opening chapter of the Quran) on the site before construction begins. This ceremony is usually attended by the Imam (acknowledged religious leader) of the community, the owner and his family and some relatives. It is repeated at the completion of the project and just before the owner moves in his furniture and occupies the building. [9] It is believed that this practice has its roots in the traditional story of the Prophet Ibrahim (Abraham) and his son Ismail in Makkah; the sacrifice is inspired by the event of Ibrahim about to sacrifice his son Ismail, when God delivered to him a ram to sacrifice in lieu of his son. According to tradition this event happened some time before Ibrahim asked Ismail to help him build God's House, the origin of the Ka'bah in Makkah.

The act of building those first walls of Ka 'bah has symbolically influenced the first act of building any Islamic settlement or house. Therefore, one of the first items to be built in a town, in conjunction with the mosque, is the perimeter wall. Symbolically the act of establishing first the boundary of a house is also reminiscent of this tradition.

I would like to stress the importance of the interaction of the above three components in a way of pursuing an on-going process of building. Although the following proposed guidelines will satisfy one important component, it is up to the Dar Al-Islam community to develop aspects of the other two. At first, implementation would require the conscious effort of all involved in the building process to bring to bear the workings of this mechanism. With time it will become part of the unconscious behaviour of the community, and only then will the built environment created be truly an expression of its values and lifestyle.

## 4 - Proposed guidelines
Given the above historical sketch and outline of the major components comprising the traditional building mechanism, this author proposes a set of guidelines for design decisions affecting proximate neighbours. The guidelines are grouped under five categories which cover most considerations affecting such decisions. [10] They are concerned with: Streets, Micro Zoning, Privacy, Walls Between Neighbours and the Discharge of Rain and Waste Water.

## 4.1 - Streets
It is more than likely that there will be two types of streets in the Dar Al Islam village (henceforth DI): vehicular streets, and pedestrian streets: most of which would be accessible by a vehicle in emergencies or for other special reasons. It is also assumed that pedestrian streets will be primary and secondary. Most of the housing will be abutting pedestrian streets.

The following principles – applicable primarily to pedestrian streets - will have to be observed:

1. *A minimum right-of-way has to be maintained.*

2. *The general alignment of streets has to be maintained,* however it is not necessary to observe precise straight alignments in their ultimate formation.

3. *The application of the traditional concept of the exterior 'Fina'*: on the ground and in the air ( See Figure 6). The traditional parameters of this concept are:
    3.1. A certain width alongside the exterior walls of a house – on the street side – belongs to the owner for his benefit and use, provided such use will not create harm to the public and its right-of-way. In the absence of a public authority which maintains streets,. it will be the owner of the Fina - as defined above - who will be responsible for maintaining and keeping it clean.
    3.2. The 'Sabat' is a structure, usually a room spanning the street, commonly referred to in current building terminology as an air-right structure. Its purpose is to create more space for a house on one side of a street and/or link two houses on opposite sides of the street, or provide the potential to do so (See Figure 6).
        a. The Sabat is usually supported on the walls of the house(s) or on columns. The method of support depends on the circumstances, and intentions of the owner(s). Traditionally the Sabat is supported on the walls of the house, on the side of its owner, and on columns on the other side. This was due to legal constraints and the disadvantages of using the apposite wall, or alternatively the sequence of events precluded the use of an opposite wall. When a person decides to build a Sabat at a later date, it might be easier structurally to support it with columns on both sides.
        b. Following principle 1 above, the columns supporting a Sabat must not fall within the minimum width right-of-way of a street.
        c. The clearance height of a Sabat depends on the street

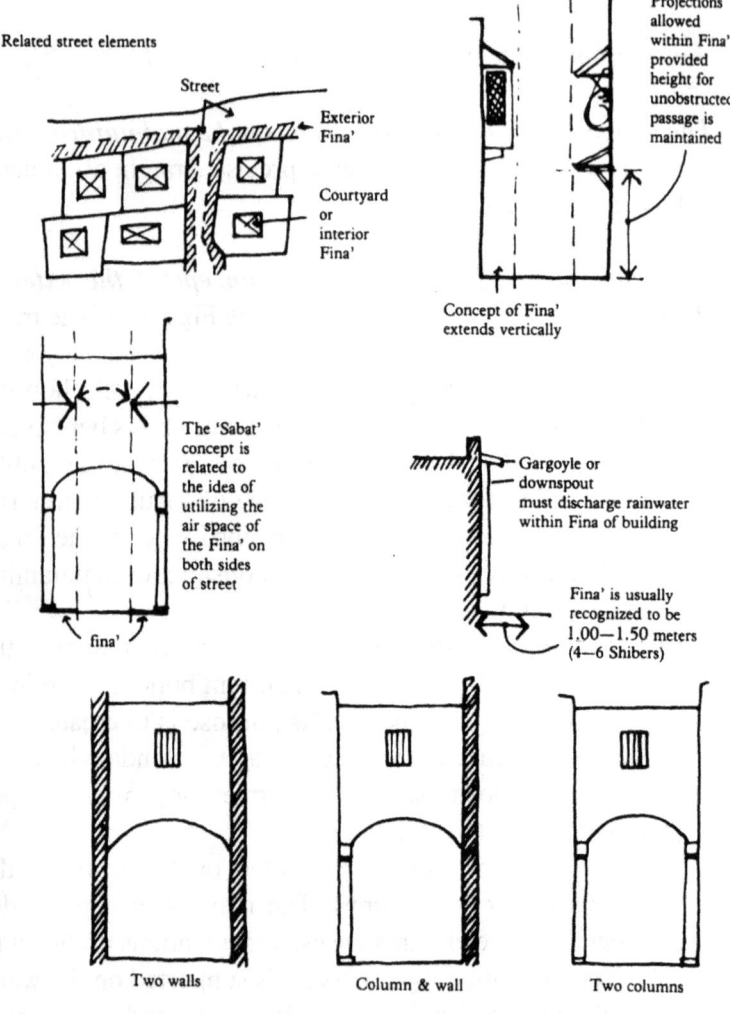

**Figure 6.** The traditional concepts of 'Fina' and 'Sabat'. This sketch was first published in the author's book *Arabic-Islarnic Cities: Building and Planning Principles*, KPI/Routledge & Kegan Paul, London, 1986.

on which it is constructed. The minimum clearance should be 2.16 meters (7 feet), which is adequate for small private cars. In addition to the seven foot stipulation, a typical average clearance should respect the height of exterior doors and other design features, and could well be more than seven feet. Where streets are designed for emergency vehicle access, such as a fire truck, the minimum clearance should be 4.10 meters (13'6").

4. *The treatment of downspouts and gargoyles on streets.* When these are used the following principles should be observed:
   4.1. Downspouts are preferred to gargoyles, because they do not cause splashing.
   4.2. When gargoyles are used they should project from a one story structure and pour within the width of the Fina of the building from which it originates.
   4.3. Gargoyles should not be allowed from structures of more than one story.

5. *Principles for street maintenance.* Traditionally street ownership affected the responsibilities and methods of maintenance. Cul-de-sacs were legally regarded to be communally owned by the people using them, and their maintenance was their responsibility. That affected cleaning and repairing its surface and the waste channel(s) which might be located under the surface. Traditionally elaborate maintenance procedures were followed based on Islamic principles of interdependence, respect and equity.[11]

## 4.2 - Micro zoning: restrictions on uses causing harm

Three sources which can create harm were recognized traditionally in the Islamic city, and they are still valid for the DI village. They are smoke, odour, and noise.

1. *Principles regarding the control of uses which generate smoke.*
   1.1. Sources of smoke should be differentiated in two categories:
      a. smoke from essential activities of a household, such as a home bakery, or heating system such as a fireplace or furnace. These are allowed and their discharge of smoke should be according to accepted practice.
      b. smoke from activities outside those of a normal household, such as building a large bakery in a house to be used for commercial purposes; or converting a house

into a public facility; or burning garbage without careful discharge of the smoke. Such activities should not be tolerated, unless there is a compelling reason for allowing them. If they are allowed, then the discharge of the smoke should be carefully considered to cause minimum nuisance to adjacent neighbours.

2. **Principles regarding the control of uses which generate odour.** Any source of offensive odour should be carefully handled and controlled, such as the location and method for garbage disposal, the location of toilets and uses which generate unpleasant odour.

3. **Principles regarding the control of uses which generate noise.** Traditionally offensive noise was usually generated by animals – from their quarters, such as a stable – or from activities such as garmet beating or wheat grinders, operated by hand or by an animal.

   Certain activities in home workshops would generate noise either directly by hearing the noise source, or indirectly by feeling the vibrations which which an activity might generate. Examples are the consistent use of power saws, hammering by a blacksmith, etc. DI should identify such potential activities and must draw clear policies for identifying which would be tolerated within the houses and others which would require allocating them outside of or adjacent to the housing areas, where noise would net disturb others.

## 4.3 - Privacy from visual infringement

1. *As a general rule windows and doors were viewed traditionally as 'old' and 'new' (or 'recent') in response to the sequence of building events.* On the whole 'older' windows and doors have a priority over 'newer' or more recent ones in terms of their right for continued existence. The consequences of this general principle are as follows: (a)When a person builds his house before his adjacent neighbours, he would have more freedom and choices regarding the location of his windows and exterior door(s). However, he should bear in mind the consequences of his decisions on future adjacent neighbours. (b) A

person who is building adjacent to existing structures must adjust his decisions according to built facts surrounding his site. Only in very special circumstances which create hardship, can a person ask that a window in an adjacent structure be permanently shut due to the harm its continued existence will create.

2. **Principles regarding the location of windows on streets and other public areas.**
   2.1. The height of a window sill on the ground level, facing a street or a public area, is determined from the exterior. It should be approximately 1.75 m (5'9"), which is above eye level of an average man. Therefore, and as a general rule, ground-level windows on the exterior walls facing streets should be designed for the purposes of ventilation and light. Measures for security should also be kept in mind in detailing such windows.
   2.2. Windows on upper levels (second and third stories) facing streets and other public areas. There is no restriction on their size and sill height. However their location should be influenced by existing windows on the other side of the street. The proper thing to do is to set them aside, but this is not as critical as the case with doors (discussed below), since exterior windows were traditionally covered by a wooden lattice to prevent visual penetration.[12]

3. **Principles regarding the location of windows facing the interior courtyard or garden.**
   3.1. There are no restrictions on the location and size of ground-level windows facing the courtyard or garden. Any constraints will be due to other design requirements.
   3.2. Upper-level windows, whether or not they are facing the interior courtyard or garden, must not be located in such a way that they would provide direct visual penetration of adjacent neighbour's courtyards or gardens. If however there are no adjacent structures, then some consideration is necessary in anticipation of the potential overlooking of future adjacent private courtyards or gardens.

4. **Principles regarding the location of doors.** The primary consideration here is the location of main and secondary doors on

the exterior walls of a house. The general principle outlined at the beginning of this section (1) regarding the status of a door being 'old' or 'new' must be observed.

4.1. Principles regarding the location of doors on streets narrower than 7 cubits, approximately 11' 6". (The distinction created by this dimension between 'narrow' and 'wide' streets is influenced by traditional practice, which also combines the width and the activity on the streets as visual distractions/barriers) . For the DI village, and depending on the plan to be adopted, it is suggested that the following principles apply to streets 11'6" feet or narrower. It is also recommended that they be followed in any other situation when direct visual corridors from opposite sides of the street are conspicuous.

4.2. A door must not be located exactly opposite another door. It should be set back from it adequately to discourage looking into the entry hall of the opposite house.

4.3. A door must not be located opposite a shop, or vice versa. They should be set back from each other so that direct overlooking will not be possible from the shop into the entry hall of the opposite house.

4.4. On the same side of a street, a door must not be located adjacent to an existing neighbour's door without his consent. This is to avoid disrupting the 'Fina' space on both sides of an existing door, in the event that such a Fina space was convenient and used by the neighbour. Examples of such uses are: the location of flower pots, loading/unloading groceries, space for temporary or emergency parking, etc.

5. ***Building height and rights of vertical airspace***. The Maliki School tradition attaches great importance to the rights of the owner within his vertical airspace. Maliki scholars sometimes suggested that even if the additional height of a structure might cause harm to an adjacent neighbour by the obstruction of sun and/or air movement, the height should be allowed. However, due to the overriding concern attached to the prevention of visual penetration, and the consistency of traditional technologies, we find that in most Islamic towns the height of residential structures is relatively uniform.

5.1. For DI village the principle of "Sun-right" or "Solar Access" should be adopted and upheld by all. That is to say any obstruction of the sun on critical areas of an adjacent property during certain hours of the day, should be considered a harmful act and must be prevented.

5.2. The other potential problem which must be addressed by the DI community is the question of distant views from upper levels and, when applicable, from roofs of the houses.

6. ***Principles for the prevention of visual infringements from roofs.*** Traditionally in towns which are located in hot dry regions of the Islamic world, people built flat roofs for sleeping on during the summer season. Overlooking from roofs and prevention from being overlooked became an important consideration. Since the climate of the Abiquiu area in northern New Mexico would net necessitate sleeping on the roof, it would be possible to use various roof configurations.

7. ***Location of shops among houses.*** As mentioned above in principle (4.3), the location of shops - or workshops open to the public - among houses should be carefully considered and the following principles observed:

    7.1. A shop must not face door(s) of apposite houses, particularly in streets 11'6" wide or narrower.

    7.2. The location of shop(s) should net generate excessive traffic in an otherwise quiet area or street. Too much activity and noise is considered harmful to adjacent houses.

### 4.4 - Walls between adjacent neighbours

In clustered and compact housing - such as the type used in traditional Islamic towns, and as suggested by the author for the DI village - the role, treatment and use of the walls between adjacent neighbours is important. In traditional situations - due to the longevity of houses on the same site, rebuilt many times over the centuries - we find that major problems which created conflict between neighbours were related to the following issues: (i) ownership verification of party walls, and (ii) when ownership is known, the rights and responsibilities of the neighbour(s) when the wall is owned by one, or when it is jointly owned by both.

In the DI village, it is suggested that careful thought be given to this problem to avoid conflicts in the future. A simple approach should be developed, and the author suggests principles (not included in this summary), derived from considerations of one of three possibilities related to the sequence of building events:

i. Wall(s) of a house are built by one owner when adjacent properties are still vacant.
This situation involves the most care, and is usually more costly to the single owner than in the other two possibilities. From an Islamic ethics point of view it would be wrong to consider design decisions which are of consequence only to the house under construction. Consideration should be given to future adjacent houses.

ii. Response to existing wall(s) by a neighbour who builds next to a house at a later date.
Just as an earlier neighbour must design his exterior walls with considerations and possible benefits to a future neighbour, the latter also has certain responsibilities and obligations regarding the use of adjacent existing walls.
In all circumstances the new neighbour must do his utmost to respect and work with the peculiarities of the existing walls. If necessary, he should undertake adequate consultation with the neighbour who owns the wall(s), to ensure that his design decisions will create no future harm to the integrity and stability of the wall(s).

iii. Wall(s) are built in joint cooperation between adjacent neighbours at the same time.
This situation assumes that two or more adjacent neighbours decide to build their houses at the same time. It is highly recommended that cooperation between such neighbours be encouraged, so that they can work out the design and potential of using the common walls jointly. This also means that the cost of these common walls be equitably divided.

## 4.5 - Discharge of rain and waste water

To begin this section it is important to clarify the distinction between rain and waste water within an Islamic framework of values and ethics. Rain water is viewed as a gift from God to be utilized and shared, whereas waste water is considered a harmful substance to be discharged appropriately.

1. ***Principles of rain water drainage***. Traditionally in Islamic towns, particularly those located in arid and semiarid regions, rain water was collected in cisterns and used for household washing requirements. Such practice had important implications on the drainage pattern of rain from roofs of houses and the impact on the responsibilities of adjacent neighbours. It is important far the DI village to decide whether or not to encourage a similar practice. This would depend on the availability of water for household use and studying the pros and cons of adopting such a practice.

2. ***Principles of waste water discharge***. Traditionally each house or building discharges its human waste into cesspools. Waste water from washing, etc. was collected from each building by a system of channels which usually run under the surface of streets. Depending on the town and its topography, surrounding natural features, the waste water thus collected will be disposed of outside the walls of the town.
In the DI village it is anticipated that human waste and waste water will be collected by a system of secondary and primary pipes which will pass through a community septic tank and then be filtered out below the plateau area. Lessons from the traditional experience cannot be used for the operation of such a contemporary system.
There are, however, lessons in the approach for cost-sharing the system and the procedures for its maintenance. Specific traditional examples exist which were developed by following Islamic principles of interdependence, respect for the neighbour and the sharing of burdens morally and materially.[13]

The above proposed guidelines for housing are a condensed version of the complete package developed for the DI community. I have presented here the material which might be of general interest and omitted the specifics, without changing the original framework for categorizing these guidelines.

## Notes

[1] According to Dr. Husain Ali Mahfoud, who is a respected scholar in Islamic studies and eastern languages from Baghdad, Iraq, minor differences due to interpretations among the various schools of law in Islam, had negligible impact on matters related to building and urbanism, as far as he can determine. Hence, the overall lessons and insights acquired from the Maliki experience would apply to most cities and settlements in the Islamic world.

[2] This principle originates in the famous Prophet's saying: "La Dharar wa la Dhirar", i.e. "Do not harm others or yourself, and others should not harm you or themselves".

[3] A good example of one of the Prophet's decrees regarding the equitable use of rain water is: That the flow of scarce water be measured to the ankles by the user of the higher ground, then sent to the lower ground.

[4] The following verse from the Quran is one of the important sources for regulating the respect of privacy: "Say to the believers that they should lower their gaze and guard their modesty, that will make for greater purity for them, and God is well acquainted with all that they do." 24:30.

[5] The following saying of the Prophet is one of the sources for this principle: "A neighbour has preemption rights over his neighbour's property. If they share common access and the neighbour is absent, then the other should wait for his return."

[6] The ultimate source for this principle is from the Quran: "You are the best nation ever brought forth to men, bidding to honour, and forbidding dishonour, and believing in God..." 3:110.

[7] Although the following saying relates to a specific act and source of public nuisance, its principle applies generally: "If a man is walking in a street and finds a branch of thorns and removes it, then God will thank him and forgive him."

[8] An example of this vocabulary - for the dwelling scale in the traditional setting of the Tunis region - is offered on pages 128 and 129 in the author's edited monograph entitled Sidi Bou Sa'id, Tunisia: A Study in Structure and Form, Technical University of Nova Scotia, Halifax, Canada, 1978. Pages 121-123 in the revised version 2009, available from Amazon.com

[9] This practice is followed to this day by most communities in the Muslim world.

[10] The author originated and developed the framework for these categories and used it for the first time in his book entitled: *Arabic-Islamic Cities: Building and Planning Principles*, KPI/Routledge & Kegan Paul, London, 1986.

[11] Ibid., pages 51-53.

[12] In traditional Islamic architecture, we find many examples of fine designs of upper-level windows, particularly those facing primary streets and public areas. The 'mashrabiyya' is the most striking example. It is basically a bay window from primary upper-level rooms, covered with wooden lattices to prevent visual penetration from the outside, but it allows the occupants to see out. Built-in benches were usually incorporated into these windows. Across the Islamic world, we find many design varieties of this basic concept and they provide excellent precedence to learn from. For examples from the Tunis region, please refer to Chapter 4 of the author's edited monograph *Sidi Bou Sa'id, Tunisia: A Study in Structure and Form*, op.cit. Note 8

[13] Op.Cit. (Note 10), pages 48-50.

# Chapter 12

# Neighborhood Test Design

From the mid-seventies of the 20th century this author was working on a project on the building and planning principles of Arabic-Islamic cities towards achieving three objectives:
1. To identify and record the building and planning principles that shaped the traditional Arabic-Islamic city.
2. To evaluate, recycle and test the traditional morphology and its organizational principles via a contemporary project to determine their validity and usefulness today and for the foreseeable future.
3. To document the findings in a systematic and clear format so that others may benefit directly.

A manuscript for a book titled *Arabic-Islamic Cities: Building and Planning Principles* was completed in early 1979 and the book was eventually published in early 1986. It documents the research and findings for objectives (1) and (3). This study is a summary of the work for achieving objective (2). The long hiatus of three decades has been an advantage, primarily to benefit from the insight of this author's and the work of others that was published in the interim. The hesitation to publish this material since then was to avoid giving the impression that the primary benefit was to emulate the traditional morphology. It is a simplistic pursuit by many architects and urban designers that continues to this day. In fact this author has come to the conclusion that essentially the processes underlying the traditional system are the level from which to draw the primary lessons.

In a short earlier study by this author a framework was developed for recycling relevant aspects from the traditional experience of

**Figure 1.** Ariel view of a part of Fez medina, Morocco, 1982, showing the compactness of the urban tissue. Photo by Georg Gerster.

building and urbanism. That framework was divided into aspects related to the procedures of building, i.e. *process*, and to aspects related to the organizational system and built form, i.e. *product* (Hakim, 1989, 1991). Those related to the former considerations are by now reasonably covered by this author and the publications of others (Hakim, 2001, 2007), (Alexander, 1987). Three areas of design enquiry were identified within the latter segment of the framework: (i) compatibility with ecology and climate, (ii) physical organizational system and planning, and (iii) architectural design, style and decoration. Adequate studies have been published that relate to areas (i) and (iii). With the exception of a few studies (Petruccioli, 1998, 2007), (Kropf, 1996), very little is published

**Figure 2.** A wonderful street in the village of Sidi Bou Sa'id, Tunisia, 2005, showing the high quality of the street environment. Photo by Bojan Stankovski.

about the second area of design enquiry: the physical organizational system and planning. This paper is a contribution to fill this void.

Housing is the predominant sector in towns and cities, and it is usually comprised of neighborhoods. Thus it was decided that this is the level at which a useful test design should be undertaken. The aim therefore of this test is to evaluate its outcome, a product resulting from addressing the issues and possibilities posed by the following two questions:

**Figure 3.** The compactness of the village of Sidi Bou Sa'id, Tunisia that shows narrow shaded pathways, roof terraces and other features that can be achieved using this morphology. Photo by Kahia, Tunis in the early 1970s.

1. Is it possible to design a contemporary built environment that achieves and embodies the best qualities (both qualitative and quantitative) evident in traditional environments located around the Mediterranean basin and especially those in North Africa? (Figures 1 and 2).
2. What aspects of the traditional experience and/or achievement the designer can explore in order to achieve a working knowledge of the principles governing the spatial and physical organizational system?

This exploration and a reflective design approach is a pre-requisite for re-creating the desired built-form qualities and ambience found in most traditional environments of North Africa (Figures 3 and 4). The test design was undertaken outside of a specific site, although a geographic area and cultural parameters were assumed as indicated below. The test design can thus be described as being generic and prototypical in its results.

Extensive research undertaken by this author clearly demonstrated that one of the major lessons offered by the understanding of the processes of traditional cities and settlements, found in the region mentioned above, was in the user's role in the decision-making process which affected his/her immediate built environment. Fur-

**Figure 4.** A simple and delightful courtyard somewhere in Morocco. Photographer and date of photo unknown.

thermore this role necessitated that decisions taken by users had to respect a framework of rules which the culture at large established, and which embody its commonly shared values and aspirations. It is thus obvious that to be able to test this aspect of the workings of the traditional environment would require a live project (Hakim, 2007).

Certain lessons from the morphology of the traditional system can be explored and tested by the individual designer. It is these lessons that this test design attempts to address (Figure 5). They are concerned with the quality, characteristics and subtleties of the physical organization, planning and design aspects of those traditional environments. This is also an essential task if we are serious in our desire to recycle and recreate those positive qualities and lessons offered by centuries of experience. To undertake this test design certain assumptions had to be made and design parameters established for the design of a Prototype Neighborhood. These are summarized below.

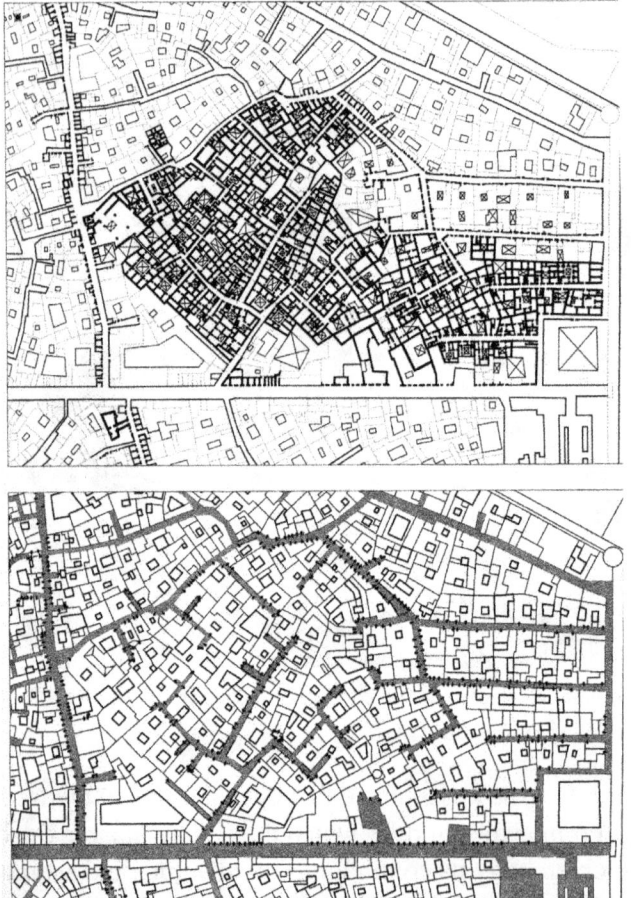

**Figure 5.** The morphology of the town of Essaouira, Morocco, located on the Atlantic Ocean. The drawing shows the manner the access system of through streets and cul-de-sacs provide access to the buildings within a compact morphology. Drawing by students of Professor Attilio Petruccioli as published on page 163 in *After Amnesia*, 2007.

## 1 - Assumptions
1. It is assumed that the inhabitants would share similar values due to their adherence to Islam (Hakim, 1986). This assumption provides the historic linkage to the users of traditional environments in North Africa, which is the precedent used for this test design.
2. The location was assumed to be somewhere in North Africa close to the Mediterranean coast between southern Tunisia and the area west of Alexandria, Egypt.
3. The site was assumed to be flat.
4. Local building construction practice and materials are to be utilized. These include the use of load bearing brick walls and simple reinforced concrete technology for roofing and foundation footings.

## 2 - Design Parameters
These are established at various levels of the project, comprising:
1. Dwelling Types
2. Dwelling Groups
3. Neighborhood Segment
4. Community Center
5. Prototype Neighborhood.

The following are the parameters at each of the five levels.

### *Dwelling Types*
Three generic types were used (Figure 6), these are (i) the square shape with the courtyard in the center, (ii) the U-shape with the courtyard on one side, and (iii) Z-shape with two courtyards in opposite corners. Dimension of plots for all three types is 14x14 meters and the primary courtyard is usually 5x5 meters. These dimensions are derived from the study of traditional settlements and towns, with adjustments to take into consideration contemporary life style and its requirements. Although these three generic types can generate, in principle, unlimited plans within the system's parameters, however only four types were developed and are designated for testing (Figure 7). This is because the test was designed to be undertaken manually. If a sophisticated computer program and the skill to run it were available, it would have been possible to undertake the test with customized house plans in response to simulated individual household requirements. The following sta-

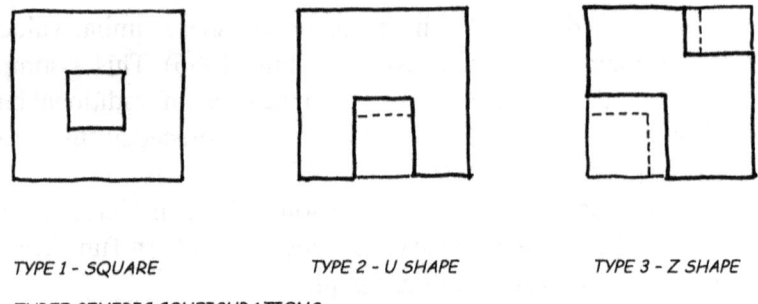

TYPE 1 - SQUARE   TYPE 2 - U SHAPE   TYPE 3 - Z SHAPE

THREE GENERIC CONFIGURATIONS

**Figure 6.** The three generic courtyard configurations that were used to design the four courtyard dwelling types used in the test design.

**Figure 7.** The four dwelling types that were used in the test design. The drawing assumes that each dwelling is built up to its maximum three stories.

tistics relate to this level of the project:
i. Ratio of plot to the ground coverage of each unit (including its courtyards) is 1:1.
ii. Ground coverage of the largest unit, type B including the courtyards, is 196 square meters.
iii. Ground coverage of type B, excluding its courtyards, is 156 square meters.

iv. Assuming that up to 2.5 stories is built up, based on the four house types used in the test design and excluding courtyard areas at the ground and upper levels, the average maximum area of all units is 340 square meters.

***Dwelling Groups*** (Figures 8 and 9)
The following are two critical rules that were used in design decisions at the Dwelling Group scale. They are:
a. Avoidance of creating visual corridors into the private domains of adjacent dwelling units, especially into courtyards and the roof terraces/gardens that are designed to be used by the occupants.
b. Avoidance of creating a tight sense of enclosure. The nature of the morphological system encourages configurations that might, in aggregate, create a tight sense of enclosure, such as within courtyards due to high walls on most sides, or tunnel effects within streets due to high walls and fences abutting them.

***Neighborhood Segment*** (Figures 10, 11, 12 and 13)
Each segment consists of approximately 3.4 hectares that includes circulation, parking and open spaces. The following are highlights of the design parameters used at this scale of the test design:
i. Ratio of dwelling unit to parking is 1:1.2.
ii. Separation of parking from the front door of the dwelling unit: maximum distance allowed is 50 meters. Most front doors of dwelling units are within shorter distances. Grocery pushcarts are provided for every household at the parking cluster locations.
iii. Maximum distance from any dwelling to a play area is 40 meters.
iv. Vehicular access is restricted within the segment, allowing only emergency vehicles, such as fire trucks, to penetrate the area. A maximum distance of 20 meters is allowed from a fire truck and its wheeled escape ladder to a face of a burning building.
v. Infrastructure lines are along streets and cul-de-sacs, and not allowed to pass under buildings.
vi. Orientation - it is assumed for the test design that undesirable winds in the summer are from the south. Dwellings are rotated against this wind direction. This orientation of buildings will provide a balance of sun/shade within courtyards and the

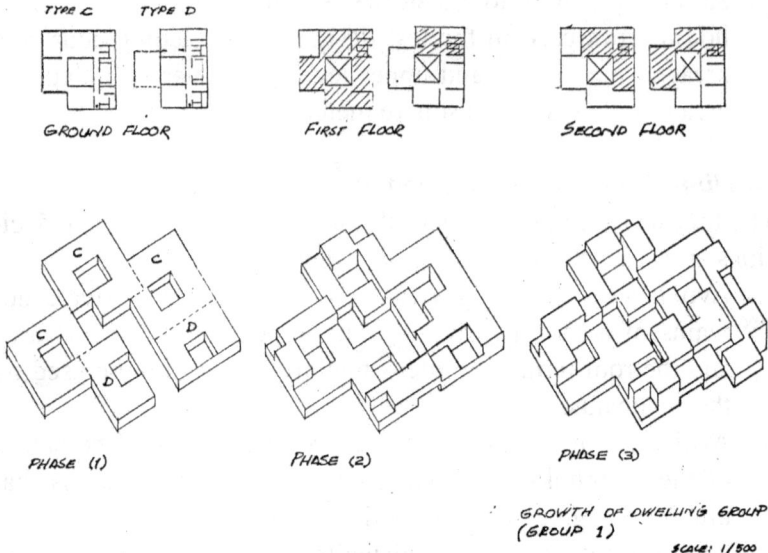

**Figure 8.** One of the dwelling clusters comprising 3 units of type C and two of type D in phase one of construction. Owners of each dwelling unit can later increase the area of their house incrementally in two additional phases.

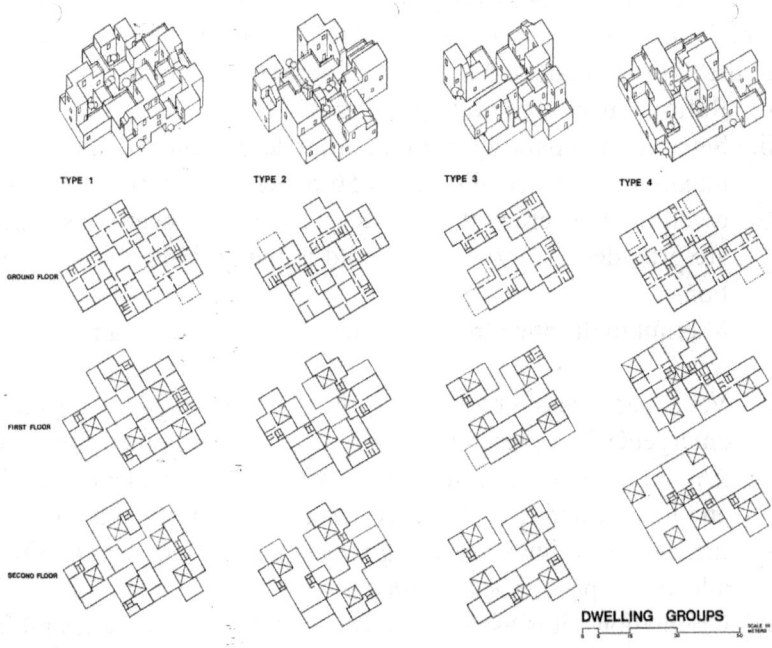

**Figure 9.** Four types of dwelling clusters show the increase in the area of each dwelling upwards to two additional floors for a total of three floors. The axonometric drawing for each cluster assumes the maximum built up area for each dwelling.

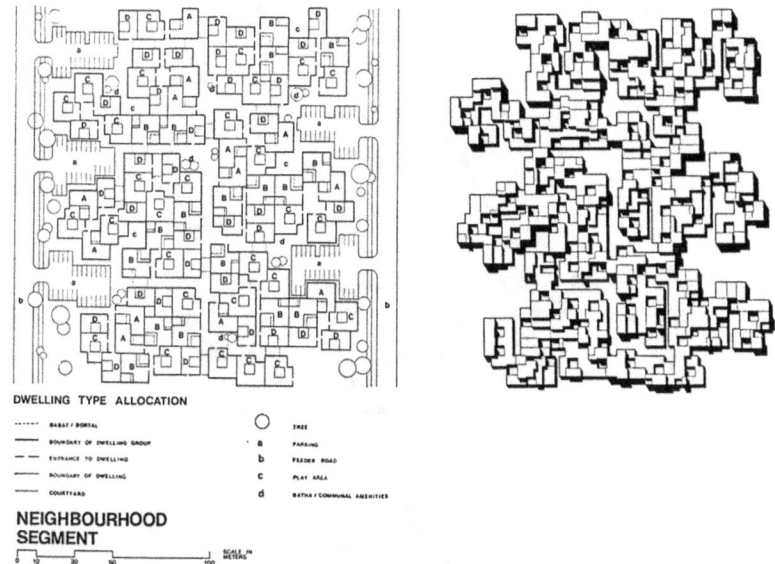

**Figure 10.** Neighborhood Segment: Dwelling Type Allocation shows how the dwelling clusters are grouped that comprise the distribution of the four dwelling types within them and the whole neighborhood segment shows how it is accessed by streets and pathways and the location of parking.

**Figure 11.** Neighborhood Segment built form. This drawing is based on the segment and dwelling type allocation in figure 10 and assumes the maximum built up of the dwellings.

    public domain. The *Qibla* (direction to Makkah) is taken as 19 degrees east to south, which affects the planning and design of the mosque.

vii. The concept of the *Fina*, which was operational in traditional built environments of North Africa, is the abutting areas to external walls up to about 1 meter in width and was the responsibility of the adjacent owners or tenants. This concept was utilized to encourage the maintenance of a landscaped strip along the side(s) of pedestrian pathways (Figure 14).

### *Community Center* (Figure 15)

The layout is directly influenced by the intricate and interesting physical configurations and mixture of uses found typically in the central areas of traditional towns and settlements. The orientation of the mosque and its *Qibla* vs. the general alignment of major streets, which affect the planning of the neighborhood as a whole, provides a challenge to create interesting spaces in this area. Major

**Figure 12.** Partial architectural model of the neighborhood segment. View form the top showing the buildings, their courtyards, terraces and parking areas.

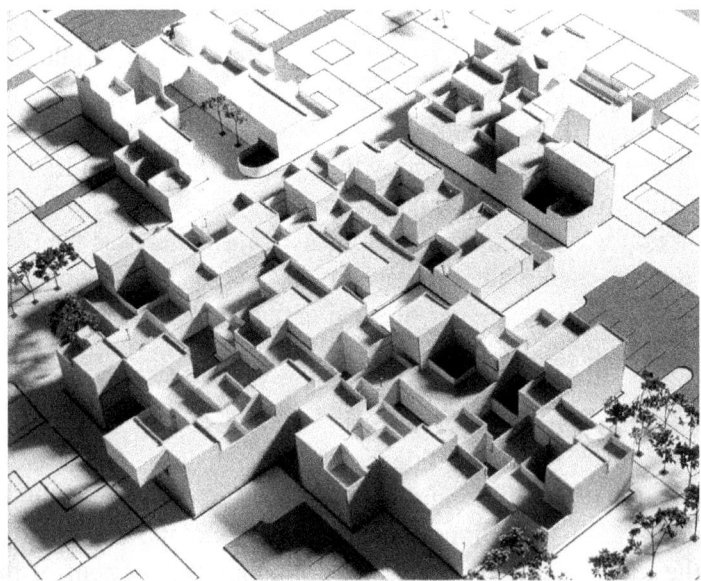

**Figure 13.** Oblique view of the architectural model of the neighborhood segment. The view shows how the dwelling units cluster together creating terraces for each unit that are designed not to overlook the private areas of adjacent units.

facilities include the mosque for the whole community, a public bath/health facility, shops of various sizes, a restaurant, two separate primary schools for girls and boys (assumed to be the preference in some communities), each can accommodate 200 pupils in six classrooms and adjacent open play fields. The Community Center covers an area of 2.5 hectares, including parking, vehicular access, open spaces and play areas. Its design was governed by a number of considerations including for example the stipulation that the maximum distance from any shop to its service parking area is 50 meters.

**Figure 14.** Street in the village of Sidi Bou Sa'id, Tunisia, 2007, showing the use of the *Fina* for planting vegetation in the trough that enhances the quality and ambience of the street. Further down the street the *Fina* is used to place removable plant pots. Photo by Beschreibung.

*Prototype Neighborhood* (Figures 16)
The concept as presented comprises four neighborhood segments and a community center, covering an area of 17.6 hectares that includes 428 dwelling units, traffic and pedestrian circulation, parking and open spaces. Vehicular circulation is based on a hierarchy of four types: Arterial roads, Collector roads, Feeder roads and Access streets. Other streets are primarily for pedestrians and also follow a hierarchal concept as evident in the plans. The neighborhood as a prototype is responsive to repetitive growth in a variety of ways and in response to different contextual site requirements such as those found in the suburbs, in urban fringe areas or urban areas. The gross density of the whole prototype neighborhood, including its community center, is 24 dwelling units/hectare. The density without the ground coverage of the community center is 28 dwelling units/hectare. The public domain is 55% of the total area of the prototype neighborhood and it includes all streets, parking, community center, playgrounds and open spaces. The private domain is 45% of the total area and it includes all dwelling units and cul-de-sac access only.

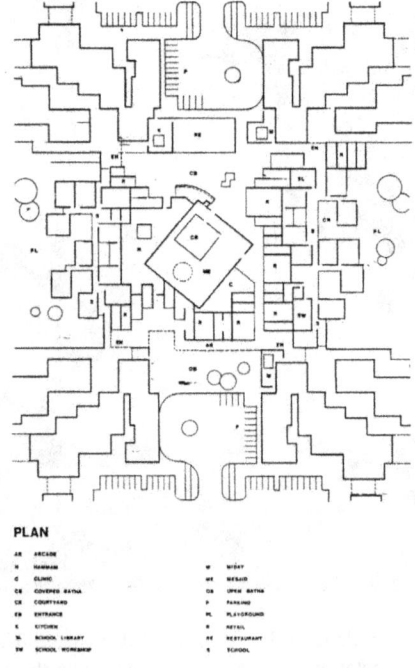

**Figure 15.** Community Center plan showing the distribution and location of the various facilities that are included.

## 3 - Conclusion

The purpose of this test design, as was mentioned at the outset, was to find out through design inquiry whether or not we can recreate the desired qualities of traditional environments as those found in most regions of the Mediterranean. Every year those locations attract vast numbers of tourists from many countries. The evidence seems to suggest that there is a unanimous feeling among most visitors, regardless of cultural background, that those traditional built environments do offer an attractive setting for an alternative life style, and conjure up a strong feeling for a sense of place not easily found or experienced in contemporary environments.

This test design, therefore, can provide us with the opportunity to evaluate rationally its results in terms of qualitative and quantitative attributes and accordingly be able to consider its outcome, or its possible derivates, as an additional viable alternative to our contemporary habitat and settlement patterns.

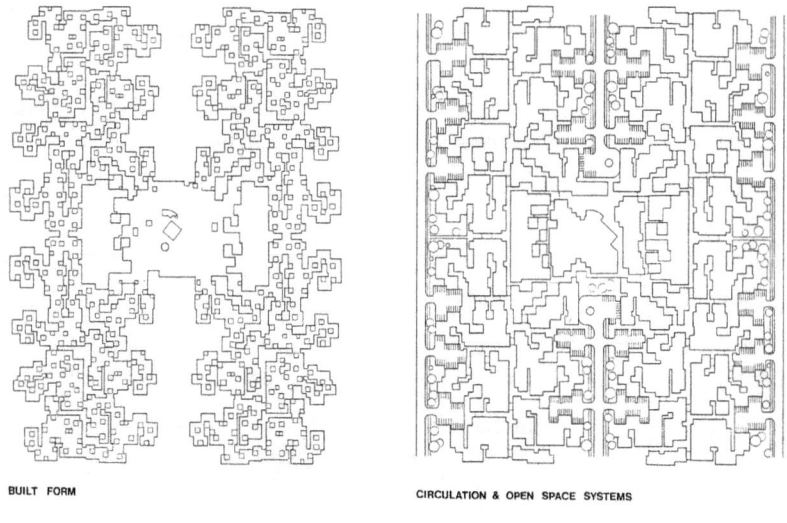

**Figure 16.** Prototype Neighborhood: (a) circulation and open space system that also shows parking locations, and the footprint of the built up areas, and (b) roof outline of the built form.

# References

Alexander, C. et al. (1987) *A New Theory of Urban Design*. Oxford University Press, NY.

AlSayyad, N., Bourdier, J-P. (eds.) (1989) *The Courtyard as Dwelling*, Center for Environmental Design Research, Vol. 6, IASTE WP06-89, University of California, Berkeley.

Amadouni, Z. (1994) *Courtyard Housing: A Typological Analysis*, M.Arch. Thesis, School of Architecture, McGill University, Montreal.

Bianca, S. (2000) *Urban Form in the Arab World: Past and Present*, Thames and Hudson, London.

Blaser, W. (1985) *Atrium: Five Thousand Years of Open Courtyards*, Translated by D.Q. Stephenson, Wepf and Co., Basel.

Dunham, D. (1960) 'The courtyard as a temperature regulator', *The New Scientist*, 8: 663-666.

Gallotti, J.(1924) *Moorish Houses and Gardens of Morocco*, William Helburn Inc., New York (text in French).

Hakim, B. (ed.) (1978) *Sidi Bou Sa'id, Tunisia: Structure and Form of a Mediterranean Village*, Technical University of Nova Scotia, Halifax. Redesigned paperback edition, 2009.

Hakim, B. (1986) *Arabic-Islamic Cities: Building and Planning Principles*, KPI, London. Paperback edition with additional material, 2008.

Hakim, B. (1989) 'Islamic architecture and urbanism'. *Encyclopedia of Architecture: Design, Engineering and Construction*, Wiley, volume 3, 86-103.

Hakim, B. (1991) 'Urban design in traditional Islamic cultures: recycling its successes'. *Cities*, 8: 4, 274-277.

Hakim, B. (2001) 'Reviving the rule system: An approach for revitalizing traditional towns in Maghreb', *Cities*, 18: 2, 87-92.

Hakim, B. (2007) 'Generative processes for revitalizing historic towns or heritage districts', *Urban Design International*, 12: 2-3, 87-99.

Hakim, B. (2008) "Mediterranean urban and building codes: origins, content, impact, and lessons", *Urban Design International*, Vol.13, No. 1, Spring 2008, pp. 21-40.

Kropf, K. (1993) *An enquiry into the definition of built form in urban morphology*. PhD dissertation in 2 volumes, Department of Geography, University of Birmingham.

Kropf, K. (1996) 'Urban tissue and the character of towns', *Urban Design International*, 1:3, 247-263.

Macintosh, D. (1973) *The Modern Courtyard House: A History*, AA paper number 9, Lund Humphries, London.

Nijst, A. et al. (1973) *Living on the Edge of the Sahara: A Study of Traditional Forms of Habitation and Types of Settlement in Morocco*, Government Publishing Office, The Hague.

Petruccioli, A. (1998) *Typological Process and Design Theory*. Aga Khan Program for Islamic Architecture and MIT, Cambridge, Massachusetts.

Petruccioli, A. (2007) *After Amnesia: Learning from the Islamic Mediterranean Urban Fabric*. ICAR, Department of Civil Engineering and Architecture, Polytechnic University of Bari, Italy.

Reynolds, J. (2002) *Courtyards: Aesthetic, Social and Thermal Delight*, Wiley, New York.

# Part III: Generative Processes

This third part of the book presents the underlying generative processes that comprise the backbone of the manner in which the procedures of building activity took place in traditional / historic societies in most locations and cultural settings. It is a dynamic process that has attributes of complex adaptive systems and sustainability. Three case studies are presented, two in chapter 13 and the third in chapter 14. Chapter 15 uses the concept of eco-urbanism as an overarching theme, that includes generative processes and its components, by recommending principles and policies for repairing and re-building Iraqi cities and towns after many years of war. The content of this last chapter is useful and applicable to other countries that underwent similar traumas.

13 - Generative Processes and its Components ........ 297

14 - Applying Generative Process in Al-Ain ............. 317

15 - Eco-Urbanism for Iraqi Cities ........................... 329

# Chapter 13

# Generative Processes and its Components

## 1 - Introduction

What is a generative process? The goal of this study is to clarify what it is, and by doing so shed light on how it is different from the common processes of development currently used in many parts of the world. Although the study addresses the context and problems of historic towns or heritage districts in cities, the insight gained is applicable to new development projects as well as it is valuable for formulating policies and appropriate codes for projects that incorporate generative processes in their implementation.

Two maps from Bahrain (Figures 1a and b) visualize the difference of the built environment that resulted from a generative process and a pre-planned and designed one. The latter type is based on a static plan in the form of a blueprint, commonly known as a 'master plan' that describes what needs to be done and which generates a fabricated structure. Whereas a generative program is one that creates built environments that are guided by a step-by-step procedure within a reasonable time frame. In essence a generative process tells us what to *do*, what *actions* to take to build or revitalize buildings, rather than detailed drawings that tells us what the *end*-result is supposed to be[1].

Historic towns in many parts of the world were initially built following a generative process.[2] When confronted with the task of revitalizing such historic towns today we must create the conditions that will allow a generative process to function and thrive.[3]

## 2 - Generative system and its components

I will put forward the essential components of a generative system. This is adapted from my insight of how traditional towns

**Figure 1a** (top) and **1b** (below) are from the city of Muharraq, Bahrain. The map is a part of the traditional fabric resulting from a generative process. Located below is a partial map of a housing subdivision from the mid-1990s, a result of a ‹master plan› blueprint. Both maps are dated 2005, from MoMAA, Bahrain.

emerged from such a system and from my experience in designing programs for revitalizing historic towns. It is therefore an amalgamation from both sources.

A generative program must be composed of the following components:

***I – Meta-principles comprised of ethical/legal norms that is derived from the history and value system of the society for which such a program is proposed***
To provide a concrete example of such principles I will use those that were predominant in Islamic societies. Similar principles were also predominant in non-Islamic societies around the Mediterranean. The following seven meta-principles are a part of ethical norms:

i. Good intentions are the basis for sound decisions.
ii. The basis for action is the freedom to act within one's property, constrained by the ethical norm of 'Beauty without Arrogance,' and by avoiding creating harm as stipulated in the following norms.
iii. Harm to others and oneself should be avoided, and if two damages should occur then, and only if necessary, accept the lesser of the two.[4]
iv. Respect the rights of older established conditions on the ground including existing buildings, and by extension accepting the idea of interdependence and cooperation between neighbors.
v. Respect the privacy of others, particularly avoiding the creation of direct visual corridors into private domains. In addition, in traditional Greek societies, avoid blocking the views of harbors and the sea.
vi. Do not debase the social and economic integrity of adjacent properties by changes or the use of one's property that would create such harm.
vii. Local customary practices must be respected and followed, although with the passage of time changes to those customs might be necessary.[5]

***II – Private and public rights are fairly and equitably exercised***
In a generative bottom-up system most of the decisions affecting the built environment are made by the people living in their neigh-

**Figure 2.** A view of a street from the island of Paros, Greece. The *Sabat* belongs to the house on the right because the left side is supported by columns independent of the structure on the left. Photo by Constantin Papas from the early 1950s.

borhoods. Rights that affect those decisions have to be clearly articulated and understood by the public. They are:
1. Right for abutting an adjacent neighbor, and the right of servitude and access. This will depend on the specific configurations of the site and buildings.
2. Privacy rights – their protection and maintenance.
3. Rights of original and earlier usage. This means that subsequent decisions and acts have to take into account existing conditions.[6]
4. Rights for the full utilization of one's property that include the right to increase useable areas such as building a *Sabat*(room bridging the right-of-way without creating obstructions to traffic, as the example in Figure 2), or increasing the height of a building within stipulated restrictions if those exist for a specific locality or site.
5. Right for using a part or all of one's property for generating income, provided such use does not create damage to the neighborhood.
6. Right of pre-emption of an adjacent property. This right provides the first option for purchasing an adjacent property by the neighbors.
7. Right of *Waqf* property. The Waqf is an Islamic institution that allows owners of property to endow their property and the income it generates for charitable purposes.
8. Right of inheritance by taking into consideration the impact it might have on division of a property.

Public rights relate to transportation, infrastructure, and certain public facilities. The public authorities have to implement and maintain them.

### *III – Private and public responsibilities are properly allocated and implemented*
Historically, the responsibilities of private citizens and institutions in generative systems that were clearly evident in societies and cultures located around the Mediterranean basin were:
1. Utilizing the exterior *Fina* when needed and the responsibility for keeping it clean. (The *Fina* is a longitudinal space along the exterior wall of buildings about one meter wide. It has many useful purposes as the example in Figure 3 shows.)[7]

**Figure 3.** A street scene in the Albaicin quarter, Granada, Spain. The *Fina* is fully utilized in the structures by projections from the upper levels and by its use by the people without obstructing the public-right-of-way. The result is a dynamic built and social environment. Photo by Arthur Erickson from the early 1960s.

2. Informing the public authorities of any danger to the public realm from within private properties so that corrective action is taken. A typical example is the leaning wall that might pose a danger to passersby on the street.
3. Each individual and family is responsible to maintain peace and tranquility with their surrounding neighbors.

Responsibilities of public authorities were:
1. Protecting the rights of the public.
2. Building and maintaining public streets and sewer lines, water and electricity distribution and maintenance, garbage collection, and insuring that the public realm – streets and open spaces – are always kept safe.
3. Protecting the integrity of local customs that are related to change and growth in the built environment.
4. Resolving equitably problems and disputes that may arise be-

tween property owners, particularly between adjacent neighbors.

## IV – Control and Management

It is important to establish a system of control and management that will be guided by the meta-principles and that would ensure private and public rights are fairly and equitably exercised, and that responsibilities are properly followed by private and public parties. Such a system of control and management should be based locally and must have legitimacy to the people living in the area or who will live there in the near future. One effective method that was predominant in many traditional societies was the system of neighborhood representatives, that is, one person is elected or selected/identified by the majority residents of a neighborhood to represent them at a council of representatives. If a council system were not used, then each representative would have direct access to the ruling authority. In some traditional Greek communities a council of elders was responsible for the day-to-day affairs of a community including matters that related to building activities.

That was all that was needed in traditional societies to correctly control and manage the built environment. However, with changes that occurred in many societies since the first half of the 20th century plus the introduction of the municipal system in countries that traditionally did not have them, an intermediary became necessary. This role can take the form of the Office of Arbitrator and his/her technical and secretarial assistants. It can be a small office or a large one depending on the size of the community that it serves. Ideally a council of neighborhood representatives should select the Arbitrator. His/her primary responsibility would be to liaise between neighborhoods and the municipal central authorities. This is necessary to maintain a healthy generative process controlled by the people, that is, keeping it a bottom-up system. The Arbitrator will also be responsible for ensuring that all parts of a generative program function properly, and that the rights and responsibilities of private and public parties are respected and followed.

## V – Rules and codes

Another important component of a generative system are the necessary rules and codes that can be followed during the process of growth and change and for resolving unforeseen conflicts between neighbors. It is preferable that such a system of rules and codes is compatible with the ethical/legal norms, the rights and responsibilities of private and public parties, and should also be linked in content to traditional local customs that are still viable socially and technically. They should also be proscriptive in nature and their intention clear, that is, what is to be achieved must be understood by everybody involved in the generative process. They are to be open for interpretation in response to the peculiarities of each location and condition. Prescriptive codes that do not allow localized interpretation must be discouraged unless they are absolutely necessary. For examples of such codes developed for the Bahrain project discussed below, see Figures 4, 5, 6 and 7.

**Figure 4. Heights of Buildings.** (continued on the next page)
*Background:* In traditional Arab-Islamic cities, we notice that the heights of buildings tend to be uniform. The reasons for this are:

1. 1. Roof terraces are potential locations for people to overlook the private domains of adjacent neighbors. Thus the custom (*Urf*) was not to build appreciably higher than adjacent buildings.

2. 2. Owing to limitations of traditional construction methods and building materials, constructing a building higher than two or three stories was discouraged and in some cases was impractical. This was also the case in the heritage areas of Muharraq and Manama. With the availability of modern building materials and technologies, it is now possible to build very high buildings. Such open-ended freedom will destroy the heritage characteristics of both towns.

*Implementation:*
1. In both Muharraq and Manama it is necessary to undertake a study to establish the average height of traditional buildings in the area. That average can be established as a benchmark for building heights. Certain exceptions might be allowed on a case by case basis. For example, if the average height of a two story building and its terrace parapet is 3.5 m +3.5 m +1.5 m+1 m (for the floor thicknesses) = 9.5 m, then for exceptional cases a 10 or 15% additional height might be allowed. That will make the building height between 10.5 and 11 m.

2. It should be noted that the height of a building should be the primary measure and not the number of floors, as those can vary between 2.5 and 3.5 m or higher. Thus the average allowable height of buildings may allow within their dimension up to three floors: 3 floors @ 2.5 m/floor = 7.5 m +1.5 m for the terrace parapet +1.5 for the floor thicknesses = 10.5 m, which is within the average range for buildings with an allowable 10% increase in height.

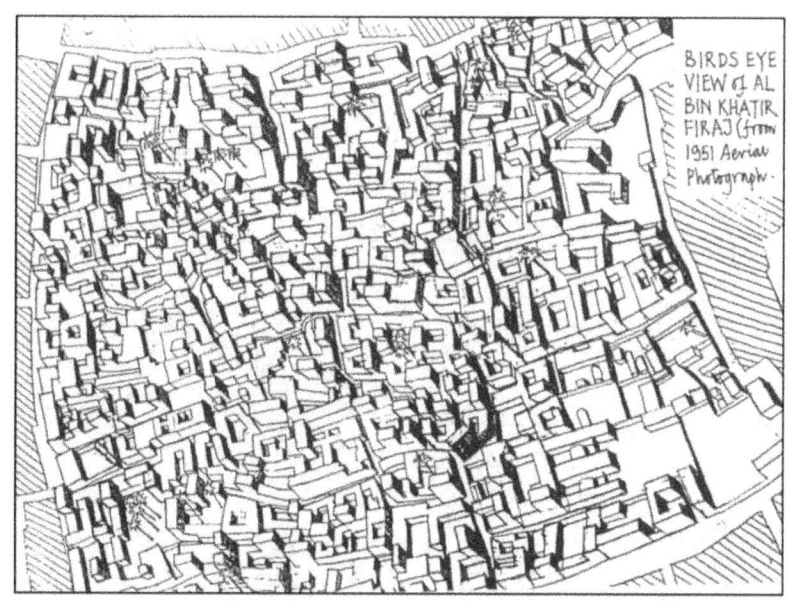

THIS BIRD'S EYE VIEW SHOWS THAT BUILDING HEIGHTS RANGED BETWEEN ONE, TWO, AND OCCASSIONALLY A PARTIAL THIRD LEVEL WAS ADDED. THE LOCATION OF THIS AREA OF MUHARRAQ IS SHOWN ON THE MAP BELOW. Drawing by John Yarwood, 1980s.

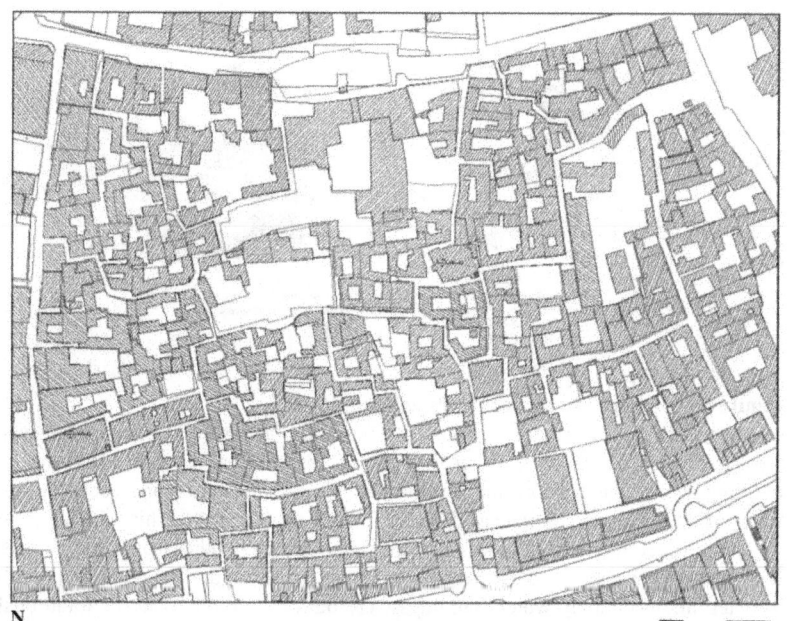

2005 MAP FROM MoMAA, BAHRAIN. THE LOWER PART OF THIS MAP ALSO SHOWS ON THE TOP OF FIGURE 1a.

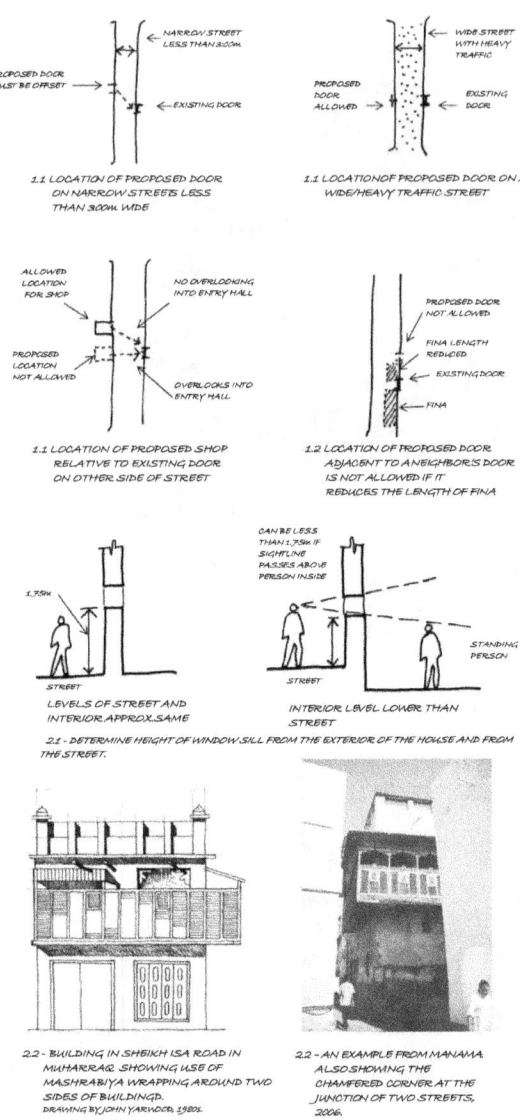

**Figure 5. Location of exterior doors and windows.**
***Background:*** As a general rule doors and windows facing the public-right-of-way were traditionally viewed as either ‹old› or ‹recent,› as a result of the sequence of building events. Older doors and windows have a priority over more recent ones in terms of their right to continue as they are. This is related to the Ethical/Legal norm 4 ‹ ... to respect the rights of older established buildings.› In other words, the ‹recent› door or window has to adjust to the conditions of the ‹older› ones. It is difficult to determine accurately which buildings were built before others in the traditional fabric of Muharraq or Manama; however, the principle can still be followed today. For example, if an owner of a house which is in a very bad state decides to tear it down and re-build it, he should respect the existing conditions of adjacent and

opposite buildings in locating the exterior door(s) and window(s) of his proposed new building.

*Implementation:*
1. The following rules should be followed for any changes to door locations:
   1.1. A door must not be located exactly opposite another door. It should be offset from it adequately to discourage looking into the entry hall of the opposite house. However, this stipulation might be relaxed if the street between opposite buildings is wider than usual and has a higher pedestrian activity than other streets in the vicinity. A door must not be located opposite a shop, or vice versa. They should be offset from each other so that direct overlooking will not be possible from the shop into the entry hall of the opposite house. However, this stipulation might be relaxed if the street between opposite buildings is wider than usual and has a higher pedestrian activity than other streets in the vicinity.
   1.2. On the same side of a street, a door must not be located adjacent to an existing neighbor's door without his consent. This is to avoid disrupting the *Fina* space on both sides of an existing door, in the event that such a Fina space was used by the neighbor. Examples for such uses include space for flower pots, unloading groceries, and temporary or emergency parking if cars are allowed in that area.

2. The following rules should be followed for any changes to window locations:
   2.1. The height of a window sill on the ground level for residential buildings, facing a street or a public area, is determined from the exterior, that is, from the street. It should be approximately 1.75 m from the surface of the street or public area. This dimension is above eye level of an average man. It can be less if the sightline from the window into the interior would pass above head level of a standing person(s) inside. This condition would occur when the interior floor level is appreciably lower than the outside street level. Therefore as a general rule, ground level windows on exterior walls facing streets should be designed for the purposes of ventilation and light. Measures for security should also be kept in mind for the design of such windows.
   2.2. Windows on upper levels (ie first and second floors that are above the ground level) facing streets or other public areas have no restriction on their size and sill height above the street. However, their location should be influenced by existing windows on the other side of the street. The proper thing to do is to offset, that is, set them aside, but this is not as critical as the case with doors discussed above, because exterior windows were traditionally covered by a wooden lattice to prevent visual penetration. This treatment is commonly termed *Mashrabiya*, and its use should be encouraged. The specific design should be influenced by traditional models found in Muharraq and Manama.

3. Location of windows facing the interior courtyard or garden:
   3.1. There are no restrictions for the location and size of ground level windows that face a courtyard or garden. Any constraints will be due to other design requirements.
   3.2. Upper level windows, whether or not they face an interior courtyard or garden, must not be located so they would provide direct visual penetration of an adjacent neighbor's courtyard or garden.

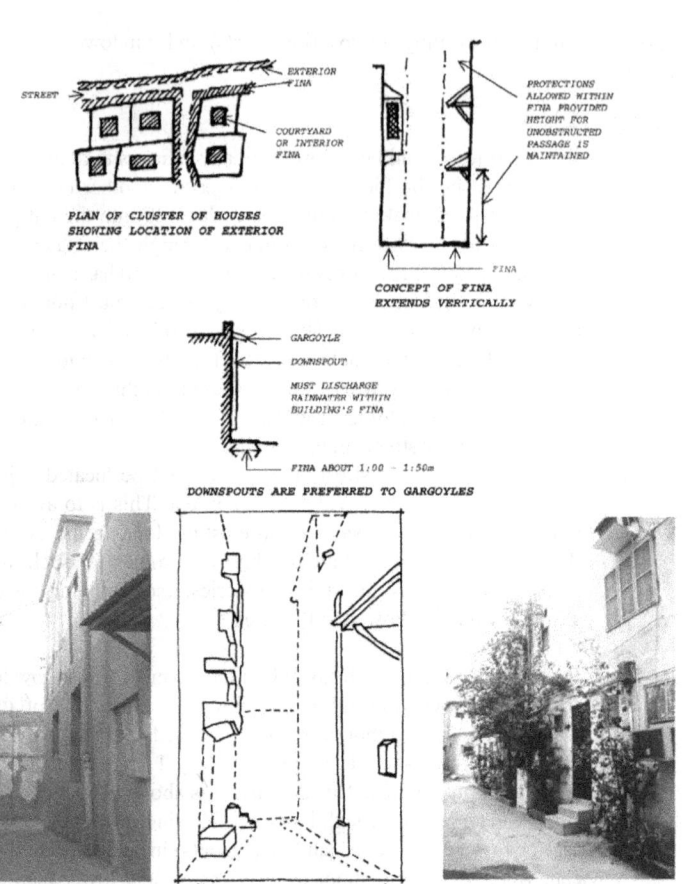

**Figure 6. Rules for the utilization of the *Fina* on the ground and vertically.**
***Background:*** The Fina is an Arabic term that refers to two types of spaces. The internal courtyard of a building is named Fina in some parts of the Arab world. It also is synonymous with the term *Harim* which refers to an invisible space about 1:00 to 1:50 m wide alongside all exterior walls of a building that is not attached to other walls, and primarily alongside streets and access paths. It extends vertically alongside the walls of the building. The owner or tenant of the building has certain rights and responsibilities associated with the Fina. He has the right to use it for temporary purposes provided such use will not impede the traffic in the street, and he has the responsibility to keep his part of the Fina always clean and safe from any obstructions. The Fina extended vertically allows high-level projections in the form of balconies, enclosed bay windows, and rooms bridging the public-right-of-way which are called *Sabat*.

***Implementation:***
In the past, before the era of municipal government, the historic sectors of Muharraq and Manama fully utilized the Fina as in other Arab-Islamic cities. Therefore:
1. The Fina should be recognized as a generative principle.

2. As it is evident in the attached photo from a street in Muharraq, projections at the upper level were allowed as well as steps to front doors within the space of the Fina. This practice should be encouraged to continue so that the traditional character of the built form within streets will continue.

3. Although the municipal system took over the responsibility of cleaning streets, it never manages to keep them always clean. Therefore, owners or tenants of buildings are responsible to:
   3.1. clean the Fina adjacent to the exterior walls of their building at least once/week.
   3.2. Placing any kind of item within the Fina that will impede access in the street is not allowed, except for dire necessity and only for a few hours.
   3.3. If the public-right-of-way is determined to be wide enough for vehicular access (depending on the location in the town) and particularly if wide enough for emergency vehicular access, then it is allowed to use the Fina for planting vines and flowers, and to locate *a Sabil* – which is a privately donated and maintained drinking fountain for public use.
   3.4. Any projections from the upper floor(s) of a building are allowed provided its base is at least 4.60 m higher than the street level. The height may be lower if that part of the street is determined not to allow emergency vehicles to go through. The width of the projection must not exceed the width of the Fina, keeping in consideration the nature of use of the Fina on the other side of the street. One set of steps to the front door are allowed for each building.
   3.5. The treatment of downspouts and gargoyles for rainwater evacuation onto streets should observe the following rules:
      i. Downspouts are preferred to gargoyles, because they do not cause splashing.
      ii. When gargoyles are used they should project from the roof of a one-story structure and pour within the width of the Fina of the building from which it originates. It is preferable to build the spout at a 45° angle from the surface of the wall so that rainwater will fall within the Fina and thus avoid splashing the wall of the opposite neighbor, particularly in narrow streets.
      iii. Gargoyles are not allowed from structures of more than one story.

# 3 - Highlights of two cases: Old Town Albuquerque, New Mexico, and the historic districts of Muharraq and Manama, Bahrain

The earlier case developed for the city of Albuquerque, New Mexico in 1983[8] was essentially based on two tools of a generative program: the appraisal process, and planning principles and guidelines that are to be used as necessary in specific parts of old town after a careful assessment and appraisal is made of a specific site and its surroundings. In other words, the generative program

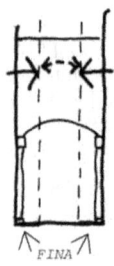  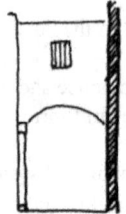 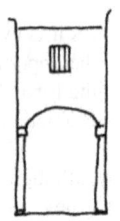

THE SABAT CONCEPT IS RELATED TO UTILIZING THE AIR SPACE OF THE FINA ON BOTH SIDES

ALTERNATIVE SUPPORT SYSTEM FOR A SABAT

Sketches taken from the book: Arabic-Islamic Cities: Building & Planning Principles, London, 1986, by B. Hakim.

VIEW OF A SABAT IN TUNIS.

A SABAT IN HOFUF, SAUDI ARABIA. PALM TREE TRUNKS ARE USED FOR THE MAIN STRUCTURE FOR SUPPORT.

EXAMPLES OF TWO SABATS: ON THE LEFT FROM TUNIS, ON THE RIGHT FROM HOFUF IN EASTERN SAUDI ARABIA. ALTHOUGH THE CONCEPT IS THE SAME, THE CHARACTER AND SENSE OF PLACE IS RELATED TO THE CONTEXT.
Both sketches are from the article by B. Hakim titled: "The Urf and its role in diversifying the architecture of traditional Islamic cities". Journal of Architectural and Planning Research, 11:2, 1994, pp. 108-127.

**Figure 7. Rules for building a *Sabat*.**
***Background***: The possibility of bridging the public-right-of-way is an extension of the concept of the Fina. It is an element that allows the creation of additional space attached to a building. The tradition of building Sabats was not a part of the local Urf (customs) in Muharraq and Manama. However, it is widely used in most traditional Arab-Islamic cities. It is an effective method for creating additional space and its use provides shade for pedestrians in the street and can be an excellent cover for front doors of buildings if they are built above them.

***Implementation***:
1. Sabats are allowed to be built when one or more of the following conditions arise:

- 1.1. When opposite buildings on both sides of the street are owned by the same person or family.
- 1.2. When a house is small in area and whose height is within the maximum limit allowed, and the owner can demonstrate that some or all of his requirements for additional space can only be met by building a Sabat.

2. The design and structural requirements of Sabats are:
    - 2.1. Ideally a Sabat should be supported on both sides structurally independent of the walls of the buildings on opposite sides of the street. This allows change of ownership easily. The supports have to be built in such a manner that they touch the walls of the building, so that no space, however small, is not taken from the right-of-way.
    - 2.2. The support of one side of the Sabat can be on the building whose owner wishes to build it. The other side has to be supported by columns built adjacent to the wall of the opposite neighbor provided careful design is made to ensure no damage occurs to the wall or its foundation.
    - 2.3. The technical aspects of the support has to be determined on a case by case basis with the aid of a qualified structural engineer who will ensure that no damages will occur to the walls that are adjacent to the supports.

was designed for changes in the built fabric of an existing historic area that traces its history and its founding to 1706. The planning principles and guidelines were developed to ensure that results from change would maintain the character and sense of place of the historic district. To ensure authenticity the Spanish Laws of the Indies, that date back to 1573 comprising 148 rules and codes, were carefully consulted. These laws influenced the physical parameters of old town at the time of its founding.

The other part of the generative program that was proposed is the Coordination Process between the city authorities and residents/users of the area. In the case of Old Town Albuquerque it was made up of three components: (i) certificate of appropriateness, (ii) city investment in public improvement projects due to the large amount of land owned by the city in the area, and (iii) user participation for projects initiated by the private sector. A number of steps for implementation were suggested as a part of the generative program that was specifically worked out for this project.

The case of the historic districts of Muharraq and Manama, Bahrain was developed in early 2006.[9] The generative program for this project, as it should be for every project, was developed from a careful understanding of the history and traditional processes of the two historic districts.[10] Although the case of old Muharraq and Manama has similarities to other towns in the greater Islamic world, they also have certain unique attributes.[11] The generative program, which I developed for revitalization of these historic districts, was designed to ensure that the changes that will occur would maintain the character and sense of place of each district. This is a similar goal that was established for the Old Town Albuquerque project described above. The general approach that I have used is similar to the outline of a generative program explained above in this study. It remains to be seen if the centralized authorities of Bahrain will adopt a generative program that is based on a bottom-up decision-making structure. In other words, are the authorities willing to revert to a system similar to the one that created those historic districts in the first place? If they do, then it will demonstrate serious intention to revitalize those areas following a generative program.

## 4 - Conclusions and the future of generative processes

In the past generative processes were the norm in most cultures, that is they were the type of processes that shaped the morphology and form of what we currently refer to as 'vernacular architecture.' They were very different from current 'modern' processes that have spread to many parts of the world.[12] It is difficult to imagine that generative processes will make a comeback soon. However, they can at least be used for revitalizing historic towns and heritage districts within cities. This will ensure that authenticity will be maintained when revitalization is undertaken by a generative process that is derived from the uniqueness of a particular site and a thorough understanding of its history. Such an approach can embrace the use of modern materials and technologies were necessary or appropriate. It will also encourage residents of such places to maintain, improve, or renew their buildings, knowing that these activities will ensure the continuity of the general character and sense of place of their neighborhoods.

To summarize, the following are the attributes that must be present in a generative process:
1.  Agreed upon ethical meta-principles, derived from a locality's

history and customs, must be articulated. They have to be respected and followed by the residents.
2. Private and public rights and responsibilities must be clearly assigned so that all actors and parties making decisions know what is expected from them, either as individuals or as public entities.
3. Control and management: this must be worked out and established based on a locality's history and customs as it relates to the function of the traditional generative process, including the interface between residents and the various public authorities.
4. Traditional rules and codes must be identified and refined, revised if necessary, to be compatible with contemporary building materials, technology, and infrastructure requirements including transportation. New rules and codes might also have to be devised to ensure maintaining the character and sense of place of the historic area or district.

## Acknowledgements

The work on the Bahrain project, during January and February 2006, was undertaken with the collaboration of all employees of the Research and Development Department and its director, Dr. Falah al-Kubaisy, of the Bahraini Ministry of Municipalities and Agricultural Affairs (MoMAA) and all the consultants for the project who were present during that period. It was my pleasure to work with all of them. I would also like to acknowledge the assistance of Dr John Yarwood, from the UK, for providing me with valuable information from the work he did for Muharraq during the mid-1980s.

## Notes

[1] To my knowledge this approach was not considered or discussed until the early years of the first decade of the 21$^{st}$ century. Amos Rapoport confirmed this – by saying ‹ ... and this is a form of preservation that has not yet really been considered or investigated.› – in his article ‹A framework for studying vernacular design,› *Journal of Architectural and Planning Research*, vol. 16, no. 1, 1999, pp. 52–64.

[2] For the analysis and findings of how this occurred in towns around the Mediterranean basin since antiquity including areas under Byzantine control or influence and later as a part of the Islamic world. Refer to chapters 1 and 2.

[3] The analogy is very clearly described by Lewis Wolpert in his book *The*

*Triumph of the Embryo*, 1991, page 17 under the sub-heading – A Developmental Programme: 'If the cells in the embryo "know" where and when to change shape, contract, or move, then it begins to be possible to envisage a program for the development of form.' And 'We can think of this pattern of cell activities as being part of the embryo's developmental program. It is a program that contains the instructions for making the shapes. A key feature of a generative program is that it can be made up of quite simple instructions, yet generate very complex forms.' From the same author in his *Principles of Development*, 1997, page 21: 'All the information for embryonic development is contained within a fertilized egg. So how is this information interpreted to give rise to an embryo? One possibility is that the structure of the organism is somehow encoded as a descriptive program in the genome, which contains a program of instructions for making the organism – a generative program. Consider origami, the art of paper folding. By folding a piece of paper in various directions, it is quite easy to make a paper hat or a bird from a single sheet. To describe in any detail the final form of the paper with the complex relationships between its parts is really very difficult, and not of much help in explaining how to achieve it. Much more useful and easier to formulate are instructions on how to fold the paper. The reason for this is that simple instructions about folding have complex spatial consequences. In development, gene action similarly sets in motion a sequence of events that can bring about profound changes in the embryo. One can thus think of the genetic information in the fertilized egg as equivalent to the folding instructions in origami: both contain a generative program for making a particular structure.'

[4] The Golden Rule of reciprocity is very ancient. A number of websites, available on the internet, discuss it. Socrates, Greek philosopher from the 5th century BCE, wrote: ‹Do not do to others that which would anger you if others did it to you.›

[5] Refer to note 11 below, and to chapter 4..

[6] Refer to the discussion in note 12 below.

[7] For a detailed description of the *Fina* and how it is to be used, and the rights and responsibilities of the residents to their *Fina*, see my *Arabic-Islamic Cities: Building and Planning Principles*, London, 1986, pp. 27–31.

[8] *Historic Old Town: Albuquerque, New Mexico – A Procedure for Guiding Change and Development Based on Patterns/Guidelines and Continuous Appraisal*. For the Department of Community and Economic Development, City of Albuquerque, NM. Besim S. Hakim, Consultant, March 1983. Sixty-one page technical report plus appendices. Available at: historiccities-rules.com.

[9] This project was undertaken by the United Nations Development Program and the Bahraini Ministry of Municipalities and Agricultural Affairs,

titled: *Capacity Building for Enhancement of Urban Governance.* I developed the Control, Management and Coding aspects of a generative program. My report was completed at the end of February 2006.

[10] When developing a generative program for a specific site, it is imperative to do so based on the locality's history and customary practices that formed that built environment in the first place. Thus, such a generative program becomes unique to that particular project.

[11] For a detailed study of how customary laws and practices in each locality within the Islamic world achieved distinct architectural and urban form qualities, refer to chapter 4.

[12] For example the temporal priority issue is very different from current practice. If someone has built something, then the person who comes later must legally pay attention to what is there and respond to it. This process is akin to weaving, that is, the next act always responds to the previous act and completes it. Compared to current law, in most US cities, that provides each person the same rights, regardless of the temporal sequence. Thus each project, and each lot, becomes an isolated island, with no significant relation to the whole, and is unable, for the same reason, to intensify the context in which it is located. A fundamental principle that was explicit in traditional generative processes is that a new construction shall not do harm to its surroundings. This is in reverse to the current approach of zoning law that is followed in most US cities, which implicitly accepts that each case is different, by applying strict geometrical regulations blindly. Another important practice in traditional generative processes is negotiating decisions that may cause harm to the surroundings and the means to avoid them.

# Chapter 14

# Applying Generative Process in Al-Ain

Al-Ain in the UAE is seeking to establish its identity and image by exploring the possibilities that are available for this goal. It has launched for this purpose an extensive planning study that is titled "Al-Ain City Image Management". An essential aspect of identity and its resulting image is the underlying system of decision-making and related allocation of responsibilities to the various parties in the day-to-day management and control of the built environment.

There is a rich traditional heritage in the Islamic world that can inform us today about the processes that were operational in the past in shaping the built environment —from small villages, to towns, and to cities (Hakim, 1986). See figures 1 and 2. Even the Bedouin that relied on mobile tents shared in this tradition (Dickson, 1949). The earliest settlements in the UAE, including Al-Ain, also shared in this tradition incorporating the particulars of the local (Urf) customary practices that gave shape and identity to the community. See figures 3, 4, and 5.

Learning from the heritage of the region has to essentially draw from two sources: the procedures of building construction (process), and the physical organizational system that is reflected in built form (product). The process is the essential source from which to draw valid lessons for contemporary implementation. The product also has valuable lessons. In fact most contemporary architects, urban designers and planners have drawn wisdom from the product. However, what is emphasized and suggested here as a part of the future image of Al-Ain is to draw lessons from the pro-

**Figure 1.** Sidi Bou Sa'id, Tunisia. A village that was shaped by a generative process.

cess, particularly the generative process that shaped housing and communities in the past that constituted the bulk of the traditional built environment. Therefore, a generative process and its related rules and codes is suggested to gradually replace the current system as it affects the Emirati housing sector particularly the single family pattern of "villas" that constitutes about 61 % of the city's area.

## 1 - The Concept of Generative processes

What is a generative process? If we look at a typical recent subdivision development of single family housing in Al-Ain - see figure 6 - we find that it is a result of a static plan in the form of a blueprint, commonly referred to as a "master plan", generated by a master planner, that describes what needs to be done by following very strict codes that control what the owner can or cannot do on his plot. Whereas a generative process is one that is guided by a step-by-step procedure for implementation within a reasonable time frame. In essence, a generative process tells us what *actions* to take to build, rather than a strict prescriptive code that tells us what the *end*-result is supposed to be (Hakim, 2007). For the analogy with the human embryo and origami, see figure 7.

**Figure 2.** Tunis Medina, 1975. A major Arab-Islamic city that was shaped by a generative process. It is immediately adjacent to the more recent development that was shaped by French colonial urbanism.

## 2 - Generative Process in Islamic Law

The built environment of Muslim towns and cities was determined in the past largely by the manner in which responsibilities were allocated and individual behaviors were affected by the notion of rights (*huquq*). In the early period of Islamic history the predominant customary practices (Urf) of the Arabian Peninsula in particular and the Near East in general were assimilated by the early Muslims (Hakim, 1994). These practices were adapted and changed as necessary to bring them into conformity with the practice and experience in Medina following the hijra in 622 C.E. Through his statements and actions, the prophet Muhammad affirmed customary practices that were consistent with Islamic values and clarified the purpose of other practices that he encouraged. Thus was es-

**Figure 3.** Abu Dhabi in 1959. This photo is of a model that is currently displayed at the Abu Dhabi Cultural Foundation building. The aggregation of family compounds is a result of a generative process. The alignment of streets between compounds is a result of decisions that determined the configurations and boundaries of the compounds.

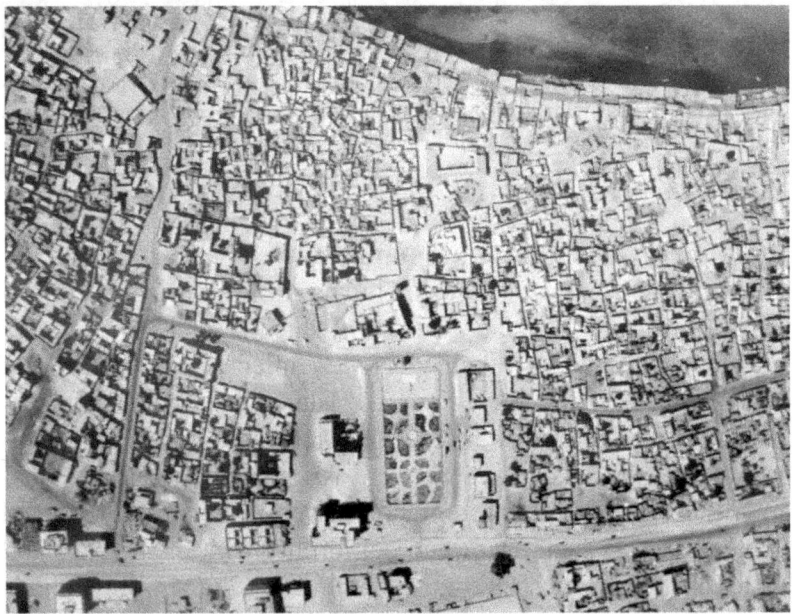

**Figure 4.** Sharjah before the oil era. Note the aggregation of walled housing compounds clustering together as a result of following the rules of a generative process.

**Figure 5.** Dubai courtyard housing model. This area in Dubai is currently being conserved following this traditional pattern that was shaped by a generative process.

**Figure 6.** Zakhir Suwaifi district, Al-Ain. A typical master-planned development that has a pre-determined end-result where people have no say in shaping their houses or the Fareej community.

The analogy is very clearly described by Lewis Wolpert in his book *The Triumph of the Embryo*, 1991, page 17 under the sub-heading- A Developmental Programme:
"If the cells in the embryo 'know' where and when to change shape, contract, or move, then it begins to be possible to envisage a program for the development of form." And "We can think of this pattern of cell activities as being part of the embryo's developmental program. It is a program that contains the instructions for making the shapes. A key feature of a generative program is that it can be made up of quite simple instructions, yet generate very complex forms."
From the same author in his *Principles of Development*, 1997, page 21:
"All the information for embryonic development is contained within a fertilized egg. So how is this information interpreted to give rise to an embryo? One possibility is that the structure of the organism is somehow encoded as a descriptive program in the genome, which contains a program of instructions for making the organism – a generative program".

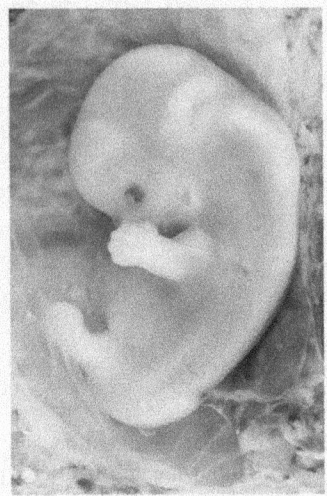

9-week human embryo

## ORIGAMI

"Consider origami, the art of paper folding. By folding a piece of paper in various directions, it is quite easy to make a paper hat or a bird from a single sheet. To describe in any detail the final form of the paper with the complex relationships between its parts is really very difficult, and not of much help in explaining how to achieve it. Much more useful and easier to formulate are instructions on how to fold the paper. The reason for this is that simple instructions about folding have complex spatial consequences. In development, gene action similarly sets in motion a sequence of events that can bring about profound changes in the embryo. One can thus think of the genetic information in the fertilized egg as equivalent to the folding instructions in origami: both contain a generative program for making a particular structure."

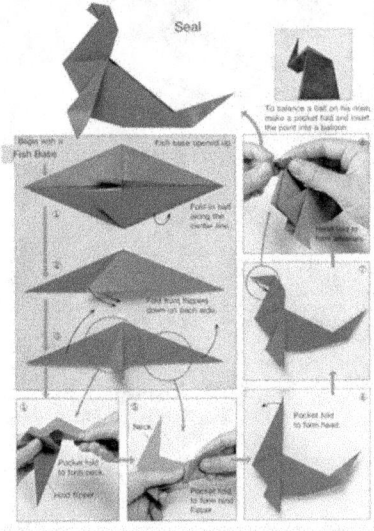

**Figures 7.** The generative process has an analogy in the human embryo and origami, the art of paper folding.

tablished the basis for practice that subsequently was elaborated upon and expanded by Muslim jurists from different schools of Islamic jurisprudence. In general, it can be said that there are more similarities than differences in the positions adopted by the various schools of Islamic law relative to the built environment.

At the level of neighborhood formation, change in the urban environment was regulated by *qawa'id fiqhiyya*, overarching legal principles that formed the framework within which the Muslim community set out rules that people understood, respected, and followed in making decisions that affected the design of their houses and the manner in which those decisions affected adjacent buildings. Muslim jurists define the term *qa'ida* as a "general ruling that applies to its particulars," or "an overarching rule that applies to the various levels of a situation or a problem" (al-Zarka, 1989). The two *qa'ida* that directly affected the built environment are: (1) do not harm others and others should not harm you (*lā ḍarar wa-lā ḍirār*), and (2) custom has the weight of law (*al-'āda muhakkima*). Additionally, there are rights (*huquq*) and conditions that operated at the level of a single unit of a community, the house:

1. Freedom to act within one's property, on the condition that harm is not inflicted on adjacent properties or facilities (Madkur, 1963). This freedom, known as *ibāha*, is defined as "freedom that is constrained by what is forbidden" or "permission to act as desired by the actor" (*al-idhn bi-ityān al-fi'l al-kayfa sha'a al-fā'il* -- al-Jurjānī, 1983).
2. Precedence: those who follow must respect realities on the ground created by buildings of earlier owners. Thus a person who builds a new structure adjacent to or across from an existing structure must situate and design the new building—especially its windows and doors—so that no visual corridor is created between the two buildings (Hakim, 1986, and 2007).
3. The person who builds first has the right to exercise "control over potential damage" (*hiyāzat al-ḍarar*, Ibn Farḥūn, 1884). That is to say, the earlier building or facility exercises control over what a subsequent builder can or cannot do when building next to it.
4. A neighbor has the right to abut his building against the wall of an existing structure, provided no harm is done to the pre-existing wall or structure. Because houses in many regions of the

Islamic world were built around inner courtyards that provided light and air, this right facilitated the clustering of buildings adjacent to one another on more than one side.

5. Access to a structure is through a space called a *finā'* (or *ḥarīm*) that is approximately 1-1.5 meter wide and runs alongside all exterior walls of a building. This space also extends vertically alongside the walls of the building. The owner or tenant of a building has the right to use the *finā'* for temporary purposes provided such use does not impede traffic in the street, and he is responsible for keeping his part of the *finā'* clean and safe from any obstructions. The vertically extended *finā'* allows elevated projections in the form of balconies, enclosed bay windows, and rooms bridging the public right-of-way (called *sābāṭ*), as well as temporary usage at the ground level and evacuation of rainwater, provided it is not allowed to accumulate and pose a hazard for pedestrian traffic.

## 3 - Generative Process in Nature and Science

The emergence of the built environment that results from a generative process resembles any organized complex system. One of the earliest studies on the science of complexity was by Warren Weaver (Weaver, 1948). Scientific thought and research activities related to complexity theory began to accelerate after the establishment in the mid-1980s of the Santa Fe Institute in New Mexico. Jane Jacobs was one of the first observers to note the relationship between complexity theory and the city. The last chapter of her book *The Death and Life of Great American Cities* (1961), "The Kind of Problem a City Is" discusses this relationship and emphasizes an approach for comprehending the city that is relevant to our understanding of traditional villages, towns and cities in the UAE and elsewhere. She says that the most important habits of thought for understanding cities are (1) to think about process, (2) to work inductively, reasoning from particulars to the general, and (3) to seek for "unaverage" clues involving very small quantities that reveal the way larger, more "average" quantities operate.

The relationship between the owners of adjacent houses depends on decisions affected by negative feedback, as when a window in one house overlooks the private domain of an adjacent house: the owner of the adjacent house reacts by demanding that the window be sealed or removed; if the window existed before the new neighbor built his house, the new neighbor must respond by designing his house in such a way that no visual corridor is created. In all living systems, feedback loops generated by communication among its members make it possible for a community to correct mistakes and to regulate itself (Capra, 1996). These features of living systems help explain how the local built environment developed in the traditional Islamic city as residents interacted with one another. The emergence of the city is thus best understood as a product of a system of rules that created conditions that were observed by residents. The system's capacity to accumulate and internalize experience by growth and experimentation derives from its adherence to these rules (Hakim, 2007, and 2008).

## 4 - The Benefits to Al-Ain by Using Generative Processes

When thinking about the benefits of introducing and applying the generative process in Al-Ain, the first thing to consider is where in the urbanization pattern of the city it should be applied. Clearly it is the Emirati Communities (Plan Al-Ain 2030, pp. 112-113) that should adopt the generative process and related codes. The "Fareej" in the past was built up following a generative process and it can now adopt a similar system that is informed by our current knowledge of the workings of generative systems supported by the advantages and limitations of contemporary construction and infrastructure technology. Working with the levels identified in the Al-Ain 2030 planning study: the Fareej, then the local cluster, and upward to the neighborhood level, we can anticipate the following benefits:

*At the Fareej level:* nineteen units are indicated that make up a population of 125 persons (at 6.6 persons/household). This means that there would be 19 individuals each representing their household. These people can form a committee that would explore various possibilities for the distribution and allocation of plots. These plots might not be equal in size or shape. The group would also decide upon the sequence, or timeline, for building out their houses (i.e. who builds first and who follows after) that would depend on each family's commitments and financial situation. Each household might not build up their house all at once, but might start with a minimum area depending on its family size and financial ability.

This latter condition will also affect how banks or lending agencies work out their loans. In addition, a set of simple rules and related specific codes for the generative process will be worked out for the particular conditions in the city of Al-Ain, taking into consideration successful historical and contemporary local (Urf) customary practices such as architectural features that are now associated with the image of the city.

*At the Local Cluster level:* Each Fareej would potentially evolve into its own distinctive character and identity and would look and feel different from others that shape the local cluster of 150 units (per the suggestion on p. 113 of Plan Al-Ain 2030). Further rules will be necessary for ensuring that the eight Fareej knit well together, i.e. the generative process will have its own dynamics at the cluster level, especially taking into consideration which Fareej is built up first. The facilities for each cluster might not occur in the geometric center of the cluster but would evolve in response to the manner the numerous Fareej coalesce together.

*At the Neighborhood level:* we can imagine very different neighborhood patterns emerging from a generative process that will constitute whole districts of the city. The process of the grouping of clusters will involve input from the Al-Ain municipality for the design of streets that are necessary to tie together the clusters that make up the neighborhood. At the neighborhood level it is essential to establish macro pedestrian and bike paths that have to be accommodated during the process of the formation of the neighborhood, and the micro pedestrian/bike paths that can be responsive to the manner the local cluster is shaped following the coordination between the various Fareej that make up the cluster.

In conclusion the generative process will achieve the following benefits for the city of Al-Ain:
• It will empower each household to shape its house within the Fareej according to its desire to build within a given time frame. It can configure the size of the first stage of the building according to its financial ability.
• The households that will generate the Fareej will establish strong neighborly relations and this will be the basis for the pride in their community. This is fully encouraged by Islamic ethics (Hakim,

1986). The number of households in each Fareej can be studied and established based on traditional practice in Islamic cities and the social conditions in Al-Ain.

• The generative process can be applied to a number of housing typologies that would result in different configurations and densities. The possibilities of housing typologies can include the detached villa type, attached houses on one side only, and the clustered housing that are attached on more than two sides and that might utilize a system of enclosed or partly enclosed courtyards.

• The generative process will open up many possibilities for the emergence of local clusters that will have the attributes of being uniquely responsive to the alternative grouping patterns of the Fareej.

• The clusters might take on different layouts and shapes including different densities that are the result of the housing typology used. They would coalesce to form distinct neighborhoods which would result in a city that would have a unique identity relative to other cities in the region and in turn that will be a major boost for the image of Al-Ain.

• Al-Ain will be the first modern Arab city that would utilize the traditional generative process in an innovative manner. It will be an example that will inspire other cities in the region and internationally to emulate and learn from. Just as the Masdar project in Abu Dhabi will be an experiment for utilizing modern technology to achieve a carbon-free built environment that will endow Abu Dhabi with a specific brand and image, so will Al-Ain be known for its application of the generative process and its sophisticated dynamic coding being the more serious link to the heritage of the region and the wider Islamic world.

## References

Abu Dhabi Urban Planning Council (2009). *Plan Al-Ain 2030: Urban Structure Framework Plan*, Abu Dhabi (Arabic and English).

Capra, Fritjof (1996). *The Web of Life*, London and New York.

Dickson, H.R.P. (1949). *The Arab of the Desert*, London. Revised edition 1983. (See especially chapter 5 "The tent and its furnishings").

Hakim, Besim S. (ed.) (1978). *Sidi Bou Sa'id, Tunisia: Structure and Form of a Mediterranean Village*, Halifax, Nova Scotia. Revised paperback ed. 2009.

---------- (1986). *Arabic-Islamic Cities: Building and Planning Principles*, London. Paperback edition 2008, with a Postscript dated June 2008.

---------- (1991). "Urban design in traditional Islamic culture: recycling its successes", *Cities*, 8/4, pp. 274-277.

---------- (1994). "The Urf and its role in diversifying the architecture of traditional Islamic cities", *Journal of Architectural and Planning Research*, 11/2, pp. 108-127.

---------- and Zubair Ahmed (2006). "Rules for the built environment in 19th century Northern Nigeria", *Journal of Architectural and Planning Research*, 23/1, pp. 1-26.

---------- (2007). "Generative processes for revitalizing historic towns or heritage districts", *Urban Design International*, 12/2-3, pp. 87-99.

---------- (2008). "Mediterranean urban and building codes: origins, content, impact, and lessons", *Urban Design International*, 13/1, pp. 21-40.

Hamouche, Mustapha Ben (1999). "Incremental Housing in Al-Ain", *Housing Science*, 23/3, pp. 193-202.

Ibn Farhun, Ibrahim b. Ali (1884, died 1397 C.E.). *Tabsirat al-hukkam* (on margins of al-Kinani (died 1340 C.E.), *Kitab al-aqd al-munazzam lil-hukkam*), Beirut (Arabic).

Jacobs, Jane (1961). *The Death and Life of Great American Cities*, New York.

Al-Jurjani, Ali b. Muhammad (1983, died 1413 C.E.). *Kitab al-Ta'rifat*, Beirut (Arabic).

Madkur, Muhammad Sallam (1963). *Al-Hukum al-Takhyiri aw Nazariyyat al-Ibaha inda l-Usuliyyin wa-l-Fuqaha*, Cairo (Arabic).

Weaver, Warren (1948). "Science and Complexity", *American Scientist*, 36, pp. 536-544.

Al-Zarqa, Mustafa Ahmad (1989, 2nd ed). *Sharh al-Qawa'id al-Fiqhiyya*, Beirut.

# Chapter 15

# Eco-Urbanism for Iraqi Cities

## 1 - Introduction

This paper addresses the current situation in Iraq and is intended to be broad in its consideration by using the term Eco-Urbanism, which is an encompassing concept that is relevant at all levels of the built environment. The paper will address issues that are directly linked to society's values and the policies that are necessary for implementation to achieve desired goals and objectives.

The following are some of the issues that Iraq faces in rebuilding its communities in a sustainable fashion:
- Overcoming the recent traumatic experiences that most people have endured either directly or indirectly, and the opportunity that reconstruction provides as a therapeutic process.
- Rebuilding, in a sensible and economical way, by recreating the sense of place of localities that were the victim of destruction, thereby reaffirming the sense of communities that were traumatized.
- The opportunity exists to deal with the phenomenon of globalization by avoiding its negative aspects, particularly as it affects the reshaping of the built environment.
- The possibility is open during the reconstruction process to recycle the positive aspects of traditional Iraqi indigenous design and practice at the levels of neighborhoods, building design and construction practices.

I will discuss principles that relate to the following: sustainability and ecology; society's values and ethics; decision-making and management including rules and codes for planning and construction; and suggestions for formulating policy. Principles related to all of these areas are of direct relevance to the issues outlined above.

## 2 - Sustainability and design principles

There are numerous definitions in the current literature for sustainability. I find the following valuable

> "... the ability of the community to utilize its natural, human, and technological resources to ensure that all members of present and future generations can attain high degrees of health and well-being, economic security, and a say in shaping their future while maintaining the integrity of the ecological systems on which all life and production depends."
> *Tufts University Consortium for Regional Sustainability* (Krizek and Power, 1996).

It is important to understand basic principles of ecology as it relates to the built environment and the manner in which people ought to intervene in the shaping of their cities, towns and villages. The following are five important general principles (Van der Ryn and Cowan, 1996):

### *Solutions Grow From Place*
Ecological design begins with the intimate knowledge of a particular place. Therefore, it is small-scale and direct, responsive to both local conditions and local people. If we are sensitive to the nuances of place, we can inhabit without destroying. A bottom-up decision-making process is necessary.

### *Everyone Is A Designer*
Listen to every voice in the design process. No one is a participant only or a designer only: Everyone is a participant-designer. Honor the special knowledge that each person brings. As people work together to heal their places, they also heal themselves.

### *Ecological Accounting Informs Design*
Trace the environmental impacts of existing or proposed designs. Use this information to determine the most ecologically sound design possibility.

*Design With Nature*
By working with living processes, we respect the needs of all species while meeting our own. Engaging in processes that regenerates rather than deplete, we become more alive.

*Make Nature Visible*
De-natured environments ignore our need and our potential for learning. Making natural cycles and processes visible brings the designed environment back to life. Effective design helps inform us of our place within nature.

Seven specific principles related to city design and development must also be added to the above:
1. The city should strive to learn from the efficiency and resiliency of nature by relying on cyclical rather than linear systems.
2. Integration of housing, energy, food, work and recreation are made possible by their proximity to one another.
3. Neighborhoods are favored where people can live, work, shop, and play within a small radius.
4. The city should support a thriving, vibrant, culturally diverse center with convenient, accessible public transportation linked to bicycle and walking routes.
5. The city should be compact with a defined edge, so that residents have easy access to surrounding rural and natural areas.
6. Incrementalism should be encouraged at the level of the house plot to the level of the city center. In other words do not only think of completed projects, but rather of a first step in an ongoing process of growth and change as resources and needs dictate.
7. Encourage conversion of building uses instead of demolition and replacement.

The diagrams on next page, from (Rogers, 1997), reinforce the above principles:

**Linear** metabolism cities consume and pollute at a high rate

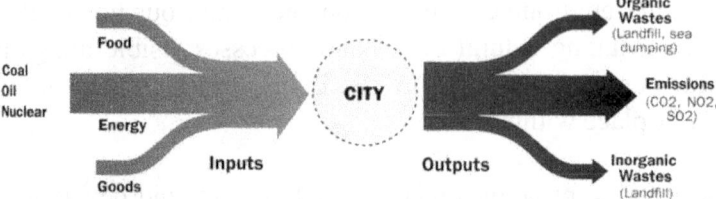

**Circular** metabolism cities minimise new inputs and maximise recycling

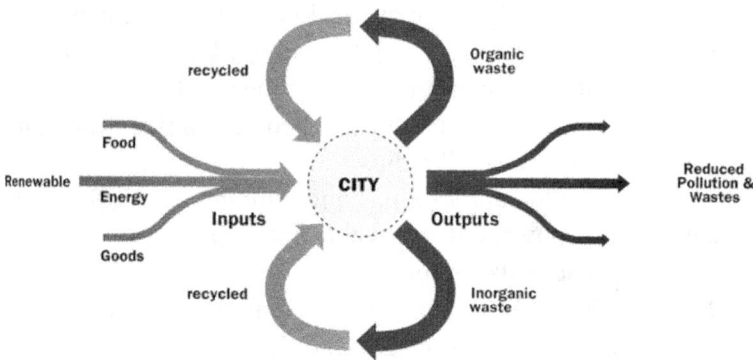

## Compact mixed-use nodes reduce journey requirements and create lively sustainable neighbourhoods

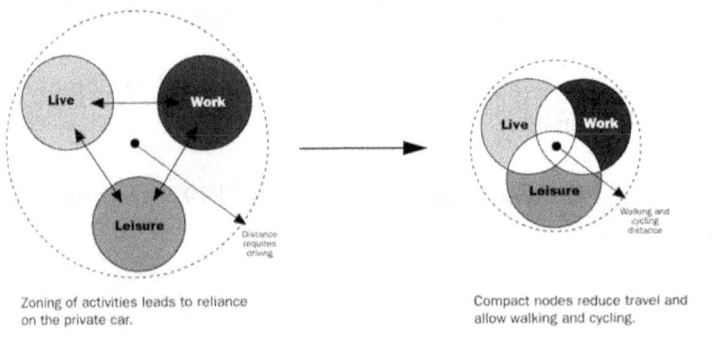

Zoning of activities leads to reliance on the private car.

Compact nodes reduce travel and allow walking and cycling.

The following are three quotes that are very relevant for creating a mindset conducive for absorbing the concept of eco-urbanism (Krizek and Power, 1996):

> "If we change the way we make decisions, we will change the decisions we make."
> *Jim MacNeil*
> *Secretary General, U.N. World Commission on Environment and Development*

> "We have created a regulatory system of command and control, that limits choice and says No, instead of one that sets goals and encourages innovation."
> *Lawrence R. Codey*
> *Public Service Electric and Gas Co*

> "Tell me, I forget.
> Show me, I remember.
> Involve me, I understand."
> *Chinese proverb*

The Charter of Calcutta was formulated as a result of the International Conference and Exhibition of Architecture of Cities that was held in Calcutta, India on 20 November 1990. Here is the wording that was adopted in the Concluding Session of that conference (Ecopolis and Downton, 1993):

> *"We are at a turning point in history.*
> *Our planetary environment is severely damaged.*
> *Desertification is spreading, the globe is warming.*
> *Entire ecosystems are under threat.*
> *And the City is at the center of the storm of destruction.*
> *But that is the key!*
> *We must cease seeing the City as a problem.*
> *We must see the City as the solution.*
> *For the City is our home.*
> *It is what we make it to be.*
> *It is where we live.*
> *If we fail to seize the Future, We will be consumed by the past.*
> *The Future begins NOW!*
> *Let the Charter of Calcutta be simple and clear,*
> *To be heard by all,*
> *And filled with hope and vision*
> *The City Can Save the World!"*

The Hannover Principles – developed by William McDonough & Partners for EXPO 2000 World's Fair at Hannover, Germany – is an excellent start for an evolving set of principles that can be fine-tuned with more knowledge and experience. These nine principles were assembled after extensive consultation with representatives from the design, environmental, and philosophical communities-(available from http://www.mcdonough.com/principles). They are adaptable to the concerns of different cultures and countries.

1. Insist on rights of humanity and nature to co-exist.
2. Recognize interdependence.
3. Respect relationships between spirit and matter.
4. Accept responsibility for the consequences of design decisions.
5. Create safe objects of long-term value.
6. Eliminate the concept of waste.
7. Rely on natural energy flows.
8. Understand the limitations of design.
9. Seek constant improvements by the sharing of knowledge.

## 3 - Society's values and ethics

These are meta-principles comprised of ethical/legal norms that are derived from the history and value system of society. To provide a concrete example of such principles I will use those that were predominant in Islamic societies.[1] Those were embedded in the Quran and Sunnah of the Prophet. Elsewhere I have documented a large number of pertinent verses and hadith (Hakim, 1986). They clearly articulate the importance of thinking in ecological terms about our intentions and actions related to decisions affecting the built environment. Thus the concept of Eco-Urbanism is clearly sanctioned by those sources. The following seven meta-principles are a part of Islamic ethical norms:

i. Good intentions are the basis for sound decisions.
ii. The basis for action is the freedom to act within one's property, constrained by the ethical norm of 'Beauty without Arrogance', and by avoiding creating harm as stipulated in the following norms.
iii. Harm to others and oneself should be avoided, and if two damages should occur then, and only if necessary, accept the lesser

of the two.
iv. Respect the rights of older established conditions on the ground including existing buildings, and by extension accepting the idea of interdependence and cooperation between neighbors.
v. Respect the privacy of others, particularly avoiding the creation of direct visual corridors into private domains.
vi. Do not debase the social and economic integrity of adjacent properties by changes or the use of one's property that would create such harm.
vii. Local customary practices must be respected and followed, although with the passage of time changes to those customs might be necessary.

For a thorough analysis and discussion of the articulation of Islamic values, principles and related institutions that are pertinent to the environment at large, see (Bagader, et al. 1994).

## 4 - Decision-making and Management

*I - Private and public rights are fairly and equitably exercised.*
In a generative bottom-up system, as found in most traditional cities and towns in the Islamic world, most of the decisions affecting the built environment are made by the people living in their neighborhoods.[2] Rights that affect those decisions have to be clearly articulated and understood by the public. They are:
1. Right for abutting an adjacent neighbor, and the right of servitude and access. This will depend on the specific configurations of the site and buildings.
2. Privacy rights--their protection and maintenance.
3. Rights of original and earlier usage. This means that subsequent decisions and acts have to take into account existing conditions.
4. Rights for the full utilization of one's property that include the right to increase useable areas such as building a *Sabat* (a common practice in traditional cities was to build a room bridging the right-of-way without creating obstructions to traffic), or increasing the height of a building within stipulated restrictions if those exist for a specific locality or site.
5. Right for using a part or all of one's property for generating income, provided such use does not create damage to the neigh-

borhood.
6. Right of pre-emption (*Shufa'a*) of an adjacent property. This right provides the first option for purchasing an adjacent property by the neighbors.
7. Right of *Waqf* property. The Waqf is an Islamic institution that allows owners of property to endow their property and the income it generates for charitable purposes.
8. Right of inheritance by taking into consideration the impact it might have on division of a property.

Public rights relate to transportation, infrastructure, and certain public facilities. The public authorities have to implement and maintain them.

## *II - Private and public responsibilities are properly allocated and implemented.*

Historically the responsibilities of private citizens and institutions in generative systems that were clearly evident in societies and cultures located in the Islamic world and around the Mediterranean basin were:
1. Utilizing the exterior *Fina* when needed and the responsibility for keeping it clean. (The *Fina* is a longitudinal space along the exterior wall of buildings about one meter wide. It has many useful purposes. See example 1 in section IV-Rules and Codes).[3]
2. Informing the public authorities of any danger to the public realm from within private properties so that corrective action is taken. A typical example is the leaning wall that might pose a danger to passersby on the street.
3. Each individual and family is responsible to maintain peace and tranquility with their surrounding neighbors.

Responsibilities of public authorities are:
1. Protecting the rights of the public.
2. Building and maintaining public streets and sewer lines, water and electricity distribution and maintenance, garbage collection, and insuring that the public realm- streets and open spaces- are always kept safe.
3. Protecting the integrity of local customs that are related to change and growth in the built environment.

4. Resolving equitably problems and disputes that may arise between property owners, particularly between adjacent neighbors.

### III - Control and Management.
It is important to establish a system of control and management that will be guided by the meta-principles and that would ensure private and public rights are fairly and equitably exercised, and that responsibilities are properly followed by private and public parties. Such a system of control and management should be based locally and must have legitimacy to the people living in the area or who will live there in the near future. One effective method that was predominant in many traditional societies was the system of neighborhood representatives, i.e. one person is elected or selected/identified by the majority residents of a neighborhood to represent them at a council of representatives. In Iraq this person was the *Mukhtar*, literally translated as the selected one. If a council system were not used, then each representative would have direct access to the ruling authority. In some traditional communities a council of elders was responsible for the day-to-day affairs of a community including matters that related to building activities. That was all that was needed in traditional societies to correctly control and manage the built environment. However, with changes that occurred in many societies since the first half of the 20th century plus the introduction of the municipal system in countries that traditionally did not have them, an intermediary became necessary. This role can take the form of the Office of Arbitrator and his/her technical and secretarial assistants. It can be a small office or a large one depending on the size of the community that it serves. Ideally a council of neighborhood representatives should select the Arbitrator. His/her primary responsibility would be to liaise between neighborhoods and the municipal central authorities. This is necessary to maintain a healthy generative process controlled by the people, i.e. keeping it a bottom-up system. The Arbitrator will also be responsible for ensuring that all parts of a generative program function properly, and that the rights and responsibilities of private and public parties are respected and followed.

### IV - Rules and codes.
Another important component of a generative system are the nec-

essary rules and codes that can be followed during the process of growth and change and for resolving unforeseen conflicts between neighbors. It is preferable that such a system of rules and codes is compatible with the ethical/legal norms, the rights and responsibilities of private and public parties, and should also be linked in content to traditional local customs (*Urf*) that are still viable socially and technically. They should also be proscriptive in nature and their intention clear, i.e. what is to be achieved must be understood by everybody involved in the generative process. They are to be open for interpretation in response to the peculiarities of each location and condition. Prescriptive codes that do not allow localized interpretation must be discouraged unless they are absolutely necessary.

Two examples of codes that were followed in traditional Arab-Islamic towns are indicated here.[4] The first is about the *Fina* and its utilization on the ground and vertically. The second example is about the location of exterior doors and windows. By studying these two examples it is hoped that this type of *dynamic* codes is understood and especially how it differs from *stasis* codes that orders people exactly what to do regardless of the micro- conditions of their location in a neighborhood.
Refer to the descriptions and illustrations for Examples 1 and 2 in Chapter 13, Figures 6 and 5.

**Example 1: Rules for the utilization of the *Fina* on the ground and vertically**
Refer to Figure 6 in chapter 13.

**Example 2: Location of Exterior Doors and Windows**
Refer to Figure 5 in chapter 13.

## 5 - Suggestions for policy makers
Beyond the abundant traditional examples from the Islamic world and from other traditional societies, we need to learn from the various ideas and suggestions made by numerous individuals and organizations worldwide. These date back primarily to the decades of the 1980s and 1990s.[5] The following are a list of some of those ideas that can be the basis for formulating sustainable policies for

the future of rehabilitation and reconstruction of Iraqi cities, towns and villages:
- Cities should be based on a circular metabolism system. The distinctions between the circular and linear systems are:
  - Linear metabolism cities consume and pollute at a high rate; whereas
  - Circular metabolism cities minimize new inputs and maximize recycling.
- Reduce the ecological footprint. This is an accounting tool that enables us to estimate the resource consumption and waste assimilation requirements of a defined human population or economy in terms of a corresponding productive land area.
- Build or retrofit to achieve compact mixed-use nodes that reduce journey requirements.
- Compact nodes that make up the city can be linked by mass-transit systems.
- Local transportation can rely on bicycles, small one or two person vehicles, and delivery vans.
- The compact city should rely on its own local power generation and waste recycling, not on distant power sources.
- Use water resources sensibly, and recycle rainwater for sustaining local plants and trees.
- People should have the option of establishing small local farms within or near their neighborhoods.

Other principles, mentioned and discussed in this chapter, can be added to the above as an arsenal and basis for policy formulation.

## Notes

[1] For numerous articles that discuss these principles, please visit: http:/historiccitiesrules.com

[2] A generative bottom-up system is one that is based on local control where citizens have the freedom and ability to articulate and implement their rights. Those rights are constrained by overarching meta-principles that are derived from the values and ethics listed in the previous section.

[3] For a detailed description of the *Fina* and how it is to be used, and the rights and responsibilities of the residents to their *Fina*, see my *Arabic-Islamic Cities: Building and Planning Principles*, London, 1986, pp. 27-31.

[4] These two examples, and others, were developed by the author as a consul-

tant for the UNDP sponsored project titled *Capacity Building for Enhancement of Urban Governance* for the revitalization of the historic towns of Muharraq and Manama in Bahrain. The author was responsible for the aspect of the project titled "Control, Management, and Coding". This consultant's report was completed in late February 2006.

[5] Girardet, 1999; Hakim and Ahmed, 2006; Register, 2002; Rogers, 1997; Wackernagel and Rees, 1996.

# References

Bagader, et al. (1994), *Environmental Protection in Islam*, IUCN Environmental Policy and Law Paper No. 20, 2nd revised edition, Gland, Switzerland, and Cambridge, UK.

Barton, Hugh (ed.). (2000), *Sustainable Communities: The Potential for Eco- Neighbourhoods*, London, UK.

Ecopolis and Downton, P. (1993), *The Halifax EcoCity Project*, Adelaide, Australia.

Girardet, H. (1999), *Creating Sustainable Cities*, Devon, UK.

Girardet, H. (2004), *Cities, People, Planet: Liveable Cities for a Sustainable World*, Chichester, West Sussex, UK.

Grant, Jill, et al. (1996), "A Framework for Planning Sustainable Residential Landscapes", *Journal of the American Planning Association*, 62 (3): 331-344.

Hakim, B. (1986), *Arabic-Islamic Cities: Building and Planning Principles*, London, UK.

Hakim, B. (1991), "Urban design in traditional Islamic culture: Recycling its successes", *Cities*, 8 (4): 274-277.

Hakim, B. (1994), "The 'Urf' and its role in diversifying the architecture of traditional Islamic cities", *Journal of Architectural and Planning Research*, 11 (2): 108-127.

Hakim, B. (2001), "Reviving the Rule System: An approach for revitalizing traditional towns in Maghrib", *Cities*, 18 (2): 87-92.

Hakim, B. and Ahmed, Z. (2006), "Rules for the built environment in 19th century Northern Nigeria", *Journal of Architectural and Planning Research*, 23 (1): 1- 26.

Krizek, K. and Power, J. (1996), *A Planners Guide to Sustainable Development*, Planning Advisory Service Report # 467, American Planning Association, Chicago.

Register, R. (2002), *EcoCities: Building cities in balance with nature*, Berkeley, California.

Rogers, R. (1997), *Cities for a Small Planet*, London, UK.

Van der Ryn, S. and Cowan, S. (1996), *Ecological Design*, Washington, D.C.

Wackernagel, M. and Rees, W. (1996), *Our Ecological Footprint: Reducing human impact on the earth*, Gabriola Island, B.C., Canada.

# Appendices

## Appendix 1

Synopsis of the author's four books

344 - 347

## Appendix 2

Postscript for the book Arabic-Islamic Cities

348 - 352

## Appendix 3

The Author

353 - 378

# Appendix 1

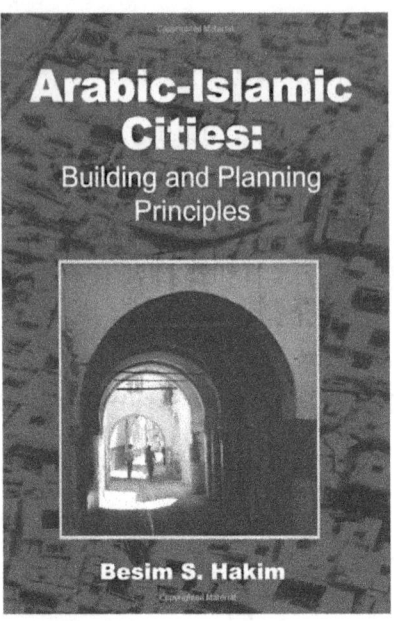

**Arabic-Islamic Cities: Building and Planning Principles**
Kegan Paul International, London, 1986. Second revised edition, 1988. ISBN 0-7103-0094-8. U.S.Library of Congress catalog No. HT147.5.H35 1986. Paperback edition, with a Postscript and an additional appendix, was published 2008 by EmergentCity Press, ISBN: 978-0-968318423. Available from Amazon.com.

This is a pioneering study of how traditional towns and cities were conceived, organized, and developed over long periods of time following simple rules that were based on religious and ethical values. Sources were used that date back to the fourteenth century and earlier. Although the study is embedded in the Arab-Islamic culture of North Africa and the Middle East, its implications are universal particularly in light of scientific discoveries of natural processes and the underlying principles of complexity theory and the processes that bring about emergence. Generative processes that shaped urban form are clearly demonstrated in the book. The study also sheds light on the implications of responsibility allocation to the various parties who are involved in the development process and the resulting patterns of decision-making that affects change and growth in the built environment. All of these issues are of significance when trying to understand the concepts that relate to various aspects of sustainability, the future potential of eco-cities, and the nature of policies and programs that are required for the immediate present and for the future. This work is a major contribution for enhancing the theories and practice of urban planning and design.

## Sidi Bou Sa'id, Tunisia: Structure and Form of a Mediterranean Village

A revised and reformatted paperback edition was published in 2009 by EmergentCity Press. ISBN: 978-0-968318416. U.S. Library of Congress Control Number: 84204583. Available from Amazon.com

This book, profusely illustrated with original drawings and photographs, is an important case study of traditional towns and their processes of urbanization. Professor Besim Hakim undertook a landmark analysis of the village of Sidi Bou Sa'id, located on the Mediterranean in northern Tunisia, working with a team of talented students in 1975. He notes that their findings echo recent scientific developments in the theory of complexity and the processes of emergence -- phenomena that can be observed and studied all around us in nature, and in social systems and urbanization processes. The case study demonstrates how a small village is in fact an outcome of similar processes, resulting in a well-ordered, high-quality built environment. This book offers important lessons for contemporary and future processes of building and urbanism.

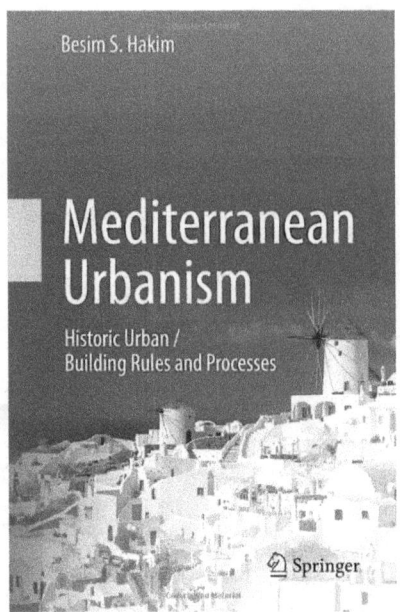

## Mediterranean Urbanism: Historic Urban / Building Rules and Processes

Springer, Dordrecht, Heidelberg, New York, London, 2014. Hardcover edition ISBN: 978-94-017-9139-7, eBook ISBN: 978-94-017-9140-3. Library of Congress Control Number: 2014946288. Available from Springer.com and Amazon.com.

This book brings together historic urban / building rules and codes for the geographic areas including Greece, Italy and Spain. The author achieved his ambitious goal of finding pertinent rules and codes that were followed in previous societies for the processes that formed the built environment of their towns and cities, including building activities at the neighborhood level and the decision-making process that took place between proximate neighbors. The original languages of the texts that were translated into English are Greek, Latin, Italian, Arabic and Spanish. The sources for the chapter on Greece date from the 2nd century B.C.E. to the 19th century C.E. Those for the chapter on Italy date from the 10th to the 14th centuries C.E. and for the chapter on Spain from the 5th to the 18th centuries C.E. Numerous appendices are included to enhance and elaborate on the material that make up the chapters. This book provides lessons and insights into how compact and sustainable towns and cities that are greatly admired today were achieved in the past and how we and future generations can learn from this rich heritage, including the valuable insight provided by the nature of the rules and codes and their application through centuries of continuous use.

## Rules for Compact Urbanism: Ibn al-Rami's 14th Century Treatise

Edited and Introduced by Besim S. Hakim. Translated from the Arabic by Mohd Dani Muhamad. EmergentCity Press, March 2017. ISBN 978-0-9683184-4-7. U.S. Library of Congress Control Number: 2017901407. Available from Amazon.com.

This is a translation from the original Arabic of a treatise that dates back to the early fourteenth century, written by a builder and master-mason. It presents rules for building and address change and growth within built environments that were compact and typical of the majority of towns and cities located in regions surrounding the Mediterranean basin. Walls between proximate neighbors posed a challenge that was resolved by intricate rules, which were designed to ensure that the rights of all parties involved would be respected and protected. An underlying principle that was always observed was to ensure no harm or damage occurs to owners of properties during the on-going processes of change and growth. The rules also assumed and were designed to protect the freedom of property owners to exercise their full rights within their property. They were compatible with the nature of a dynamic process that relied on the timeline and sequence of built facts that had to be respected and which ensured subsequent decisions would be compatible. Feedback between proximate neighbors was a part of the system that promoted balance and equity. Our contemporary low density built environments that are manifested in the suburban landscape were questioned and criticized since a number of decades ago. Recent efforts to create compact neighborhoods friendly to pedestrians can be inspired by the rules and solutions of historic compact towns and cities which are discussed and presented in this treatise.

# Appendix 2

## Postscript to the 2008 paperback edition of *Arabic-Islamic Cities: Building and Planning Principles*

Since completing the research and writing for this book in 1979, a number of dissertations have appeared on various aspects of this area of study, in addition to several books and articles. I am happy to report the present work was instrumental in influencing the direction of some of those studies.[1] Reviews of this book have appeared in numerous languages, and several authors have made extensive use of material from the book. A Japanese, Farsi, and Arabic translations were published.[2] Yet only few of those works have addressed the processes and the system of rules that were followed in making decisions affecting various levels of the built environment. One of the reasons for the rarity of such studies might be the difficulty in finding reliable original sources; the language barrier and difficulties in reading handwritten manuscripts might be another. Yet without employing such sources and meticulous research, nothing of significance can be achieved. Happily more original manuscripts are being verified, edited, and published in their original Arabic, which should make it much easier for future researchers to use this material.[3]

One of the objectives of my work, mentioned in the Introduction, is the challenge of recycling and testing traditional principles in contemporary and future urban design and architecture. This is an issue of cultural continuity in the built environment. I took this matter up again in early 1981 and have continued to examine it since then in a number of published studies.[4]

I have used the essential material and core arguments presented here in a number of articles.[5] Other aspects of this field of study were not covered in the book; I have subsequently published complementary material, such as the role of customary practices (*Urf*) and their impact on the identity of towns and cities.[6] Other important aspects of research related to the Islamic city await study; I have published an annotated list of studies needed to develop a comprehensive theory of urban form in traditional Islamic cultures.[7]

As my research has progressed in this field, it has become increasingly evident that the *processes* underlying the traditional system are the level from which to draw meaningful and practical insights. We should not place undue priority on typologies of the traditional system, as most people involved in the field of architecture and urban design tend to do, since those are in turn controlled and configured by the process and rule system governing decisions in space design and building activities. Thus if we recycle the essence of the process, we can apply it to any typological system and achieve the high quality results associated with the traditional system.[8] For example, the typology utilized in the Hadramaut region in southern Yemen, as well as in the northern part of the country (as at San'a) and in the architecture found in the major Hijazi cities of western Saudi Arabia, is dramatically different from the predominant typology found in most other parts of the Islamic world, as illustrated by the examples in this book. Yet in all these locations the underlying process and its mechanisms were similar, resulting in the same high quality and sophistication found elsewhere. In other words the process is flexible and dynamic and not tied to a specific typology.[9]

During the mid-1990s I allocated time to uncover the rule system related to the built environment in the early centuries of the Byzantine era, so as to provide an intelligent basis for studying the built environment of Greece before independence in the early nineteenth century, and other non-Islamic Mediterranean countries.[10] The knowledge gained from such an investigation will assist in the further formulation of theory, because the case of Greece, Italy, and Spain represents high-quality achievement in the traditional built environment. The similarities and differences between cultures will sharpen our tools for constructing theory and for developing techniques for maintaining the cultural continuity of built environments, with lessons useful for other cultures. The world will be a much richer place for it.

*Besim S. Hakim*
June 2008

## Notes

[1] My lectures and personal interaction with academics and their students during the period 1977-1986 have influenced the content and outcome of a number of Ph.D. dissertations. The earliest that I am aware of, which cited a 1977 draft of chapter one, is by Mahmoud Daza dated 1982 from the University of Pennsylvania. A brief history of events associated with the research

and preparation of this book was published in the Saudi engineer's magazine *al-Muhandis*, no. 8, (Dhu al-Hijja 1408/ July 1988): 67. Additional details can be found in the "Communication" published in *MESA Bulletin*, 26/1 (1992): 150-52.

[2] Some of the reviews in English were published in the following journals: *Housing and Planning Review*, 41/4 (1986); *Mimar 22* (1986); *Third World Planning Review*, 8/4 (1986); *Progressive Architecture*, 68/1 (1987); *The Geographical Review*, 77/2 (1987); *Cities*, 4/2 (1987); *MESA Bulletin*, 21/1 (1987); *Journal of Architectural Education*, 41/2 (1988); and *Journal of Architectural and Planning Research*, 6/1 (1989). At least two books that I am aware of have used extensive material from the present work:A.E.J. Morris, *History of Urban Form*, 3rd Edition,1994, and G. Broadbent, *Emerging Concepts in Urban Space Design*, 1990. A Japanese edition was published in Tokyo, December 1990, a Farsi translation was published in Tehran, 2002, and an Arabic translation was published in Cairo in 2015.

[3] For example: Ibn al-Rami's manuscript was not available in published form when I worked with it. The first unverified edition was published in Morocco by *Majallat al-Fiqh al-Maliki wa al-Turath al-Qada'i bil-Maghrib*, 2/ 2,3,4 (1982): 259-490. This was followed by a reliable scholarly verified edition by Abdul-Rahman al-Atram in 2 volumes, *al-Ilan bi Ahkam al-Bunyan* (Riyadh, 1995). A more recent edition using the same title was published by Ferid ben Slimane (Tunis, 1999). Another important manuscript by Ibn al-Imam, Isa ben Mousa al-Tutaili (mentioned on p. 23 ), was verified and published in Saudi Arabia by Ibrahim ben Mohammad al-Fayez, *Kitab al-Jidar*, (Riyadh,1996). It was also verified by Muhammad al-Numainij and published by ISESCO, (Rabat, 1999). Four years later by Ferid ben Slimane and al-Mukhtar al-Tulaili (Tunis, 2003).

[4] A framework suggesting how to learn from the past was first published in the *Proceedings of the conference on the Preservation of Architectural Heritage of Islamic Cities*, Istanbul, Turkey, 1985, published in Riyadh, 1988, pp. 305-17. It was further developed and published in *Al-Muhandis* (Ibid., note 1, pp. 2-6, in English), and then further refined and presented at the *Second International Conference on Urbanism in Islam*, November 1990, Tokyo, Japan, available in the proceedings volume (1994 ), pp. 377-84. Its final form was published in *Cities*, 8/4 (1991): 274-77, which also includes detailed citations of my other published work in this field. The components of the framework were further elaborated with examples in the encyclopedia article cited in note 5 below, and on page 171 of this book. The rules and design guidelines that were developed for the Muslim community in Abiquiu, New Mexico, in early 1981 were published in *Proceedings of the 74th Annual Meeting of the Association of Collegiate Schools of Architecture*, New Orleans, March 1986, pp. 109-19. An expanded version followed in *Review 86*, UPM, Dhahran, Saudi Arabia, November 1986, pp. 11-28. That project represented an attempt to recycle the rules and know-how of the traditional

system and adapt it to contemporary conditions on location in Abiquiu, New Mexico. In early 2006 I was hired by the United Nations Development Program and the Bahraini Ministry of Municipalities and Agricultural Affairs to work on a project for revitalizing the historic districts of Muharraq and Manama in Bahrain. I developed the Control, Management, and Coding aspects of a generative program. Parts of that work was published: "Generative processes for revitalizing historic towns or heritage districts", *Urban Design International*, 12/2-3 (2007): 87-99. I have drawn on the insight of the traditional experience in developing the proposals for that project.

[5] "Arab-Islamic urban structure," *The Arabian Journal of Science and Engineering*, 7/2 (1982): 69-79; "The representation of values in traditional and contemporary Islamic cities" *Journal of Architectural Education*, 36/4 (1983):22-28; and the article "Islamic Architecture and Urbanism," *Encyclopedia of Architecture,* vol.3 (New York,1989): 86-103. The case study of Saudi Arabia is used in this encyclopedia article to analyze the changes that occurred due to the abandonment of the system that created the traditional built environment and the consequent adoption of imported Western values and techniques to create new settlements and cities in that country. This was followed by "Rule systems: Islamic," *Encyclopedia of Vernacular Architecture of the World*, vol. 1 (Cambridge, UK, 1997): 566-68. All of these articles summarize and/or elaborate on the essential findings in this book and also address contemporary and future issues of cities in the Arab and wider Islamic worlds.

[6] The results of my research on the *Urf* were first published in the *Proceedings of the International Conference on Urbanism in Islam*, Tokyo, Japan, October, 1989, vol. 2 (Tokyo, Japan), pp. 113-38. A revised version was subsequently published as chapter 7 of the book *Islam and Public Law*, ed. by C. Mallat (London, 1993). A further revised, expanded, and illustrated version was published in *Journal of Architectural and Planning Research*, 11/2 (1994):108-27. Due to the importance of this topic it should be viewed as an extension of this work, and I have attached it at the end of the book.

[7] See B. S. Hakim "Urban form in traditional Islamic cultures: further studies needed for formulating theory," *Cities*, 16/1 (1999): 51-55. Of the fifteen topics, there are three that I would like to see investigated very soon. They all deal with the processes of land demarcation and subdivision in the early formation of Islamic cities: the study of the principles and workings of land allotment (*Iqta*), the revivification of land (*Ihya*) within and on the fringes of settlements, and the processes of territorialisation of land (*Ikhtitat*), particularly at the neighborhood and building cluster levels. For my views on the state of scholarship concerning the Islamic city and its architecture to the early 1980s, see my review essay in *Third World Planning Review*, 12/1 (1990): 75-89.

[8] For suggestions on how the traditional rule system can be revived and used as a mechanism to revitalize and preserve the character of the traditional

sectors of towns and cities in the Maghrib countries of Libya, Tunisia, Algeria, and Morocco, see my article: "Reviving the Rule System: An approach for revitalizing traditional towns in Maghrib," *Cities*, 18/2 (2001): 87-92. The substance of this article was first presented in Tangiers, Morocco, June 1996, at the conference entitled: "The Living Medina: The walled Arab city in architecture, literature, and history," sponsored by the American Institute of Maghribi Studies. The same approach suggested there could be used in other regional / cultural contexts.

[9] This is corroborated by the findings of a study I undertook with Zubair Ahmed of the traditional rules and their manifestation in the unique neighborhood clusters found in Northern Nigeria and illustrated by examples from Zaria. The results of our work titled "Rules for the built environment in 19th century Northern Nigeria" was published in *Journal of Architectural and Planning Research*, 23/1 (2006): 1-26.

[10] See my article "Julian of Ascalon's treatise of construction and design rules from sixth-century Palestine," *Journal of the Society of Architectural Historians*, 60/1 (2001): 4-25. For a comparison of the treatises of Julian of Ascalon and Ibn al-Imam Isa ben Mousa al-Tutaili and the significance of generative processes see my: "Mediterranean urban and building codes: origins, content, impact, and lessons", *Urban Design International*, 13/1 (2008): 21-40.

Appendix 3

# BESIM S. HAKIM, FAICP, AIA

Town Planner/Architect
Former Professor / Independent Scholar
Albuquerque, New Mexico

www.historiccitiesrules.com
www.archnet.org

# Contents of Curriculum Vitae

## Education

## Professional Experience
- Urban Planning Research
- Urban Planning Practice
- Architectural Practice
- Teaching Urban Planning and Architecture

## Publications
- Articles resulting from research published in journals, conference proceedings, encyclopedias & book chapters
- Books
- Reviews of *Arabic-Islamic Cities: Building and Planning Principles*
- Articles on Urban Futures Studies undertaken at Harvard
- Articles on Urban Planning Practice
- Books reviewed by Besim Hakim
- Technical Reports of Urban Planning Practice

## Lectures and Paper Presentations based on Research Results

## Public Service

## Honors, Awards, and Recognitions

## Membership in Professional and Allied Organizations

# EDUCATION

Two Years (1969-71)
**Masters of Architecture in Urban Design (M. Arch. U.D.)**
Graduate School of Design, Harvard University
Cambridge, Massachusetts, USA

Five Years (1957-62)
**Bachelor of Architecture (B. Arch.)**
School of Architecture, Liverpool University
Liverpool, England

# PROFESSIONAL EXPERIENCE

## Urban Planning Research

Research activities while undertaking studies at Harvard University and Massachusetts Institute of Technology. Primary topic of interest was the impact of technological growth and social change on physical design and planning. The lessons from the science of ecology to urban planning/ design theory and practice. Techniques for generating future scenarios in urban development. A number of articles and technical reports resulted from this work. (See Publications: Articles on Futures Studies undertaken at Harvard).

Applied Research dealing with the factors that shaped traditional/vernacular towns and villages in North Africa with the goal of identifying criteria and processes of relevance to contemporary practice. This was undertaken while a member of the Faculty at the Technical University of Nova Scotia, Canada. The work involved numerous trips to North Africa, particularly Tunisia. Substantial material was generated for articles and books. A Citation for Applied Research was awarded for the book resulting from this work by *Progressive Architecture* in January 1987. Lectures on the research findings were delivered in U.S. universities and international conferences. (See Publications and Lectures & Paper Presentations based on Research Results).

Starting September 1994, on an ongoing part/ full time basis, work on two research projects. They are:

(a) The rule system and the customary laws which governed construction activities in Greece, particularly during the period 15-19th centuries. The Byzantine heritage will be carefully studied. The architecture and urbanism of the Cyclades islands in the Aegean will be used for analysis. Initially this project started in mid-1992, and a 22,000-word article comprising extensive analysis of a 6th century manuscript by an architect Julian of Ascalon in Palestine during the Byzantine period, published in 2001 (See publications). This publication was selected for the 2002 International Poster Session of Recent Research, established as a joint effort of the Association of Collegiate Schools of Architecture (ACSA), The American Institute of Architects (AIA), and the Architectural Research Centers Consortium. This joint effort is known as the Initiative for Architectural Research (IRA).

(b) The building rules and customary practices associated with the planning and design of towns and buildings by the Hausa and Fulani peoples during the 19th century and up to the mid-twentieth century in Northern Nigeria. This project started in Fall 1998 and completed in 2004. Results published in 2006 (See Publications).

Starting in mid-2005, on an ongoing basis, working on generative processes as manifested in traditional towns and cities, and how we can learn from that experience. Results published since 2007 (See Publications). A book that brings together the results of this research was published by Springer in 2014 titled: *Mediterranean Urbanism: Historic Urban / Building Rules and Processes.*

## Urban Planning Practice

Organizations and clients include:
- City of Halifax, Nova Scotia, Canada;
- City of Albuquerque, New Mexico;
- Dar Al-Islam Corporation, Abiquiu, New Mexico;
- City of Phoenix, Arizona;
- UNDP and Bahrain's MoMAA.

For Halifax's downtown core, an area of 115 acres, developed:
- An urban design concept and planning framework.

- A detailed urban design and development plan for a 10-acre historic area within the downtown core.

- The legislation to protect visual corridors from Citadel Hill (a historic fort-castle overlooking downtown and the harbor). This zoning by-law, that limits heights of structures in the downtown, was adopted in March 1974.

For Albuquerque developed:
- Coors Corridor Study, which is a design and development control plan for a 10-mile parkway strategically located in Albuquerque on the west side of the Rio Grande. The plan elements include: Ecological Conservation of sensitive lands, View Preservation of foreground and distant views of mountains from the roadway, Design Guidelines for development, Movement and Access plan. Directed project for over a year and coordinated input of professionals. Authored design guidelines, view preservation system and the legal/ implementation approach. *The Coors Corridor Plan* is the result of modifications by other staff after my departure, and was adopted in May 1984.

- Historic Old Town, Albuquerque: An urban design framework and related recommendations for amending the text of the Historic District and its guidelines. It also includes other design suggestions for enhancing the area's historic and cultural character.

- Participant: Downtown Albuquerque Planning Charrette held at the Downtown Alvarado Station, June 18, 2002.

- Invited participant for the one-day event, July 10, 2010, that was organized by the Mayor's office of the City of Albuquerque to discuss the 2010 City's Goals Forum.

For Dar Al-Islam, Abiquiu, New Mexico:
- Preliminary plan for village, and detailed rules and design guidelines for the housing sector.

For Phoenix, Arizona:
- Recommendations for establishing an approach to ensure quality in the built environment.

For the United Nations Development Program (UNDP) and Bahrain's Ministry of Municipalities and Agricultural Affairs (MoMAA):
- A project titled: "Capacity Building for Enhancement of Urban

Governance". Work undertaken during January and February 2006. Results of Hakim's contribution to the project published in 2007 titled: "Generative processes for revitalizing historic towns or heritage districts" (See Publications for full reference).

Sub-consultant to Roberts Day Pty Ltd. of Perth, Australia to provide City Image Management consultancy for the Municipality of the city of Al-Ain, United Arab Emirates. Results of Hakim's contribution published as "Generative Processes and Coding for Emirati Housing in Al-Ain", in the report titled: *Al-Ain: City Management Strategy*, July 2010, pp. 98-103. Also published in *2A:Architecture & Art*, as "Generative Processes for Housing: A bottom-up approach illustrated by the case of Al-Ain, UAE", double issue No. 25/26, Autumn 2013/Winter 2014, pp. 37-42.

## Architectural Practice

Worked for firms in the U.S., Canada, and Mid-East, and for myself as sole proprietor.

Experience ranged from client contacts and recruitment to providing a broad range of services: schematic design, design development, construction documents, site supervision, and liaison with engineers.

Built projects include: 11 custom-built houses, an eight-story office building, hospital renovation/additions, apartment buildings and a religious facility. These buildings are located in the U.S., Canada and the Mid-East.

Other accomplishments include: award winning designs, design studies for low-rise medium-density housing, user needs specifications as related to manufactured housing.

Provided consulting services to Skidmore, Owings & Merrill - Architects/Engineers, Chicago; Keith Graham & Associates - Architects, Halifax, Nova Scotia; and to other architectural firms.

Undertook design testing by exploring the application of findings from urban design research. Prototype Neighborhood comprising 428 units and its supporting community facilities, on a typical flat site of 44 acres (18 hectares). The test explored the potentials of clustered courtyard housing for contemporary use in arid regions.

Worked for one year (1983/1984) as an architect/planner for the then newly constructed King Khaled International Airport in Riyadh, Saudi Arabia. Involved in a variety of studies and projects.

In-house consultant to Gulf House Engineering/Architects & Engineers, Bahrain, June 2005.

Consultant to The Prince's Foundation for The Built Environment, London, UK, during the period mid to late 2007. The project was titled: "Saudi Traditional Village Project" that was located within the city of Jizan, in the Asir region of Saudi Arabia. The task was to provide input and advice regarding the Form and Process aspects for the project.

Sub-Consultant to Hyder Consulting Middle East Ltd for the project: "Development of Planning Standards and Guidelines for Mosque Developments in the Emirate of Abu Dhabi" in the United Arab Emirates. Duration of sub-consultancy from November 2010 to December 2011.

## Teaching Urban Planning & Architecture

Experience in teaching since 1967. A faculty member at the Technical University of Nova Scotia, Halifax, Canada from 1967-1980. Assistant Professor for the first seven years, which included a two-year leave to study urban design at Harvard University; and the latter six years were as Associate Professor with tenure. Resigned effective 9/80, to move to the U.S. I continued my affiliation with Halifax from 1980-83 as Adjunct Research Professor. TUNS merged into Dalhousie University in 1997.

Boston Architectural Center (part time/1 year: 1969/70).

McGill University, Montreal (Visiting Professor/short visit: 3/74).

Technical Institute of Architecture & Urbanism in Tunis, Tunisia (Visiting Professor/1 semester: 1-3/75).

Massachusetts Institute of Technology (short visit: 4/77 and Aga Khan Program (AKP) Visiting Scholar: 2/81).

University of New Mexico, Albuquerque (Adjunct Associate Professor/1 year: 1982/83).

King Saud University, Riyadh, Saudi Arabia (Visiting Professor/short visits: 1/82, 4/87, 6/89, 5/92).

University of Jordan, Faculty of Engineering & Technology, Department of Architecture, Amman, Jordan (External Examiner for thesis projects of B.Arch. candidates: 5/88).

King Faisal University, College of Architecture and Planning, Dammam, Saudi Arabia (Visiting Professor/8 years: 1985/93). Resigned effective 9/93 to return to home base in the US. The college is now a part of University of Dammam that was established in 2009.

Cornell University, Departments of Architecture, City & Regional Planning, and Near East Studies (Visiting Scholar/ 2 weeks: 3/95).

My overall teaching experience involved teaching urban design/planning and architecture at the undergraduate and graduate levels, including advising doctoral students from Saudi Arabia, Egypt, Nigeria, Norway and Italy on detailed aspects of their PhD dissertation work.
Gave courses in history and theory, urban design/planning and the impacts of cultural values and processes on the built environment. I have also been involved in developing studio instructions, course materials and evaluation procedures. Responsibilities for coordinating design studio classes. Teaching individually and as part of a team. Taught studio at all levels of undergraduate programs. Undertook administrative duties, and member of various faculty committees.

Awarded the American Institute of Architects (AIA), Education Honors Award in 1990 for "Teaching History by Searching for Emics & Etics - A significant achievement in the formulation, implementation, and outcome of instruction", signed by AIA President, dated March 21, 1990. The 73-page AIA booklet that documents the 1990 Education Honors was published in mid-1991. Hakim's contribution was republished with more detail in *Design Studies* Vol. 12, No.1, January 1991, pp. 19-29.

One of five international experts that were invited to review the proposed curriculum for the Master of Islamic Urban Planning and Architecture degree administered by the Qatar Faculty of Islamic Studies of Qatar University. November 2010.

# PUBLICATIONS

## Articles resulting from research published in journals, conference proceedings, encyclopedias and book chapters

"The Contemporary Benefits of Traditional Mid-East Urbanism", [Abstract] *Proceedings of First National Conference on Urban Design*, New York, October 18-21, 1978.

"Arab-Islamic Urban Structure", *The Arabian Journal for Science and Engineering*, Volume 7, No. 2, 1982, pp. 69-79.

"Values and the Built Environment: The Case of Islamic Culture". *Proceedings of the 71st Annual Meeting of the ACSA: Architectural Values and World Issues*, held in Santa Fe, New Mexico, March 1983, pp. 46-55.

"The Representation of Values in Traditional and Contemporary Islamic Cities." Two papers by Besim S. Hakim and Peter G. Rowe combined in one article. *Journal of Architectural Education*, Volume 36, Number 4, Summer 1983, pp. 22-28.

"Recycling the Experience of Traditional Islamic Urbanism." *Proceedings of the Conference on the Preservation of Architectural Heritage of Islamic Cities*, held in Istanbul, Turkey, 22-26 April, 1985, pp. 305-317. Published by AUDI, Box 6892, Riyadh 11452, Saudi Arabia.

"Recycling a Traditional Housing Process: A Case in Abiquiu, New Mexico. "*Proceedings of the 74th Annual Meeting of the ACSA: The Spirit of Home*, held in New Orleans, Louisiana, March 1986, pp. 109-119. Re-published with more information in *Review 86*, KFUPM, Dhahran, Saudi Arabia, pp. 11-28.

"Recycling the Experience of Traditional Islamic Built Environments: A Proposed Framework and Notes for Generating Principles." *Al-Mohandis*, Vol. 1, No. 8, July/August 1988, pp. 2-6. Published by the Engineering Committee, Box 85041, Riyadh 11691, Saudi Arabia. Also in the same issue on p.67 is a synoptic history of events associated with research for Hakim's book *Arabic-Islamic Cities*.

"Islamic Architecture and Urbanism." *Encyclopedia of Architecture: Design, Engineering and Construction*, Volume 3, John Wiley & Sons, Inc., New York, 1989, pp. 86-103.

"Teaching history by searching for emics and etics", *Design Studies*, Vol. 12, No. 1, 1991, pp. 19-29.

"The Role of the 'Urf' (Customs) in Shaping the Traditional Islamic City." *Proceedings of the International Conference on Urbanism in Islam*, Vol. 2, pp. 113-138. Held in Tokyo, Japan, October 22-28, 1989. Revised version published as Chapter 7 in the book *Islam and Public Law*, edited by Chibli Mallat, Graham & Trotman, London, 1993. A further revised, expanded and illustrated version is published as "The 'Urf' and its role in diversifying the architecture of traditional Islamic cities", *Journal of Architectural & Planning Research*, Vol. 11, No. 2, Summer 1994, pp. 108-127.

"Recycling positive aspects of tradition in contemporary cities: Some issues for consideration." *Proceedings of the 2nd International Conference on Urbanism in Islam*. Held in Tokyo, Japan, November 27-29, 1990, pp. 377-384. Revised version titled "Urban design in traditional Islamic culture: Recycling its successes", published in *Cities*, Vol. 8, No. 4, November 1991, pp. 274-277.

"Rule systems: Islamic", *Encyclopedia of Vernacular Architecture of the World*, (3 vols.), Edited by Paul Oliver, Cambridge University Press, 1997, Vol.1, pp. 566-568.

"Urban form in traditional Islamic cultures: Further studies needed for formulating theory." *Cities*, Vol. 16, No. 1, 1999, pp. 53-58.

"Julian of Ascalon's treatise of construction and design rules from 6th-c. Palestine". *Journal of the Society of Architectural Historians*, Vol. 60, No. 1, March 2001, pp. 4-25.

"Reviving the Rule System: An approach for revitalizing traditional towns in the Maghrib". American Institute for Maghrib Studies (AIMS) conference on "The Living Medina, held at Tangier, Morocco, 5/29 - 6/4, 1996. Published in *Cities*, Vol. 18, No. 2, April 2001, pp. 87-92.

"Byzantine and Islamic Codes", Congress for the New Urbanism/ *Council IV Report, On Codes,* Santa Fe, New Mexico, October 2002. Report published in 2003, pp. 42, 43, 63.

"EcoCities Embedded Locally: Learning from Tradition and Innovating Now", *Proceedings of the International Conference on Heritage, Globalization, and the Built Environment, Bahrain*, December 6-8, 2004, pp. 17-28.

"Rules for the built environment in 19th century Northern Nigeria", with Zubair Ahmed. *Journal of Architectural and Planning Research*, Vol. 23, No. 1, Spring 2006, pp. 1-26.

"Hakim's Work on Traditional Islamic and Mediterranean Urbanism", *International Journal of Architectural Research*, Vol. 1, No. 2, July 2007, pp. 100-105.

"Revitalizing Traditional Towns and Heritage Districts", *International Journal of Architectural Research*, Vol. 1, No. 3, November 2007, pp. 153-166.

"Towards Eco-Urbanism for all Iraqi Cities, Towns, and Villages", Chapter 6 of the book *Rebuilding Sustainable Communities in Iraq: Policies, Programs and International Perspectives*, Edited by Adenrele Awotona. Published by Cambridge Scholars Publishing, 2008, pp. 101-116.

*The City in the Islamic World* (2 volumes), Edited by Jayyusi, Holod, Petruccioli and Raymond, Brill, 2008. Contributions by Besim S. Hakim in volume 1: "Law and the City", pp.71-92, and "The Sub-Saharan City: Rules and Built Form" with Zubair Ahmed, pp. 663-676. Illustrations for both articles in the Plates section of volume 2.

"Generative processes for revitalizing historic towns or heritage districts", *Urban Design International*, Vol. 12, No. 2/3, June/September 2007, pp. 87-99. Corrigendum in Vol. 13, No. 3, Autumn 2008, p. 210. Re-published in the book: *Current Challenges for Patterns, Pattern Languages & Sustainability*, Edited by Hajo Neis and Gabriel Brown, published by PUARL Press, Portland, Oregon, 2010, pp. 122-131. Revised version in *Journal of Biourbanism*, Vol. 5, No. 1&2, 2016, pp. 99-107, titled "Generative processes for revitalization and development".

"Mediterranean urban and building codes: origins, content, impact, and lessons", *Urban Design International*, Vol.13, No. 1, Spring 2008, pp. 21-40.

"Built Environment, in Law", *Encyclopedia of Islam Three*, 2009, pp. 176-179.

"The Generative Nature of Islamic Rules for the Built Environment", *International Journal of Architectural Research*, Vol. 4, No. 1, March 2010, pp. 208-212.

"Neighborhood test design based on historic precedents", *International Journal of Architectural Research*, Vol. 6, No. 2, July 2012, pp. 135-148.

"Generative Processes for Housing: A bottom-up approach illustrated by the case of Al-Ain, UAE", *2A:Architecture & Art*, double issue No. 25/26, Autumn 2013/Winter 2014, pp. 37-42. Initially published in July 2010 by the Australian consultant Roberts Day Pty Ltd. in their report titled: *Al-Ain: City Management Strategy,*pp. 98-103.

## Books

*Rules for Compact Urbanism: Ibn al-Rami's 14$^{th}$ Century Treatise.* Edited and Introduced by Besim S. Hakim. Translated from the Arabic by Mohd Dani Muhamad. EmergentCity Press, March 2017.
ISBN 978-0-9683184-4-7. U.S. Library of Congress Control Number: 2017901407. Available from Amazon.com.

*Mediterranean Urbanism: Historic Urban/Building Rules and Processes.* Springer, Dordrecht, Heidelberg, New York, London, 2014.
Hardcover edition ISBN: 978-94-017-9139-7, eBook ISBN: 978-94-017-9140-3. Library of Congress Control Number: 2014946288. Description of content and reviews posted on Springer.com and Amazon.com.

*Arabic-Islamic Cities: Building and Planning Principles.* Kegan Paul International, London, 1986. Second revised edition, 1988. ISBN 0-7103-0094-8. U.S.Library of Congress catalog No.HT147.5.H35 1986. Copy of typescript and illustrations were deposited and registered in 1979 with the Copyright Office in Washington, D.C. This book received a Citation for Research from *Progressive Architecture* in their 34th Annual Awards Program, January 1987. Results of the Awards were published in the January '87 issue of *P/A*. The Japanese edition was published by Daisan Shokan Publishers, Tokyo, in December 1990. A Farsi edition was published in Tehran, 2002. An Arabic edition was published in Cairo, 2015. Paperback edition, with a Postscript and an additional appendix, was published 2008 by EmergentCity Press and available from the online bookseller: Amazon.com, ISBN: 978-0-968318423. Library of Congress Control Number: 82074252.

*Sidi Bou Sa'id, Tunisia: A Study in Structure and Form.* Technical University of Nova Scotia, Halifax, Canada, 1978. A 186-page illustrated monograph, the edited work of ten senior architecture students under the supervision of Professor Hakim, undertaken in Tunisia during the Fall Term of 1975. U.S. Library of Congress catalog No.NA1591.2.S56.S56 1978. A revised and reformatted paperback edition titled: *Sidi Bou Sa'id, Tunisia: Structure and Form of a Mediterranean Village*, was published in 2009 by EmergentCity Press and available from the online bookseller: Amazon.com, ISBN: 978-0-968318416. Library of Congress Control Number: 8204583.

## Reviews of *Arabic-Islamic Cities: Building and Planning Principles*

(Following are some of the reviews published in English. Reviews in other languages are not listed).

Ian Haywood, *Housing and Planning Review*, Vol. 41, No. 4, August 1986, p.26.

Naima Chabbis, *Planning Outlook*, Vol. 29, No. 2, 1986, pp. 99-100.

Jim Antoniou, *The Architect* (RIBA Journal), October 1986, p.34.

Brian Brace Taylor, *MIMAR #22*, October-December, 1986, pp. 80-81.

Miles Danby, *Third World Planning Review*, Vol. 8, No. 4, November 1986, pp. 371-372.

Michael E. Bonine, *The Geographical Review*, Vol. 77, No. 2, April 1987, pp. 253-255.

Muhammad A. Al-Hammad, *Cities*, Vol. 4, No. 2, May 1987, pp. 182-183.

Janet Abu-Lughod, *MESA Bulletin*, Vol. 21, No. 1, July 1987, pp. 29-31.

Amos Rapoport, *Journal of Architectural Education*, Vol. 41, No. 2, Winter 1988, pp.60- 61.

Brian W. Beeley, *Planning Perspectives*, Vol. 3, 1988, pp. 121-122.

Paul Oliver, *Journal of Architectural and Planning Research*, Vol. 6, No. 1, Spring 1989, pp. 88-90.

Extensive use of material from Hakim's book *Arabic-Islamic Cities* in:

Geoffrey Broadbent, *Emerging Concepts In Urban Space Design*. Van Nostrand Reinhold (International), London, New York, 1990. In Part 1, pp.11-15

A.E.J. Morris, *History of Urban Form*. Longman Scientific & Technical, U.K./ John Wiley & Sons, New York, 3rd edition, 1994. In Chapter 11, pp. 365-401

## Articles on Urban Futures Studies Undertaken at Harvard

"Theory of Conversion", World Future Society, Washington, D.C., 1973. Co-authored with Leland Cott and Thomas Nelson. On technology, citizen participation and generating future scenarios for urban development.

"Ecological Systems as Models for Human Environments", *EKISTICS #208*, March 1973, pp. 168-171. Co-authored with Leland Cott and Thomas Nelson. The lessons derived from the principles of ecology and their relevance to planning and design.

"The Impact of Technological Growth and Social Change on Physical Design and Planning. Illustrative Application: Lysander New Community, New York." *School of Architecture Report Series #14*, March 1972, Technical University of Nova Scotia, Halifax. Co-authored with Leland Cott and Thomas Nelson.

## Articles on Urban Planning Practice

"A Systems Framework for Examining Growth Policies of Metropolitan Halifax, Nova Scotia", *School of Architecture Report Series #17*, November 1972, Technical University of Nova Scotia, Halifax. Co-authored with Gary Hiscox.

"Protecting the View: Citadel Hill, Halifax, Nova Scotia," *EKISTICS #232*, March 1975, pp. 186-191.

"Halifax: Downtown Development Activity", *EKISTICS #243*, February 1976, pp. 94-95.

Juli Chase, "Housing Lesson from the Mideast". *Scottsdale Daily Progress*, May 15, 1979, page 13. (Article about Hakim's ideas and proposals for clustered courtyard housing for the U.S. Southwest).

Joseph R. La Plante, "Future May Be in the Past", *The Arizona Republic*, June 24, 1979. Sun Living Section, page 1. (Article about Hakim's proposals for clustered courtyard housing for the U.S. Southwest).

"Urban Design by Climate Zones", *Phoenix Magazine*, October 1979, pages 106, 108, 118, 119, 132, 143.

"Urban Design Plans for 'Urban Villages' Suggested", *Arizona Planning*, January 1982, pages 2, 3.

## Books Reviewed by Besim S. Hakim

"The Islamic City and its Architecture: A Review Essay" (State of Knowledge to the Early 1980's). A 6000 word essay that reviews seven books, two of which in depth. They are *Architecture of the Islamic World*, edited by George Michell, [1978]84 and *Architecture and Community*, edited by Renata Holod and Darl Rastorfer, 1983. *Third World Planning Review*, Vol. 12, No. 1, 1990, pp. 75-89.

Jamel Akbar. *Crisis in the Built Environment: The Case of the Muslim City*. Concept Media, Singapore, 1988. *MESA Bulletin*, Vol. 23, No. 1, 1989, pp. 45-46. Also in *Third World Planning Review*, Vol. 12, No. 2, 1990, pp. 197-198. Follow up 'Communications' in *MESA Bulletin*, Vol. 26, No. 1, 1992, pp. 150-152.

Christopher Alexander, et al. *A New Theory of Urban Design*, Oxford University Press, New York, 1987. *Journal of Architectural Education*, Vol. 44, No. 2, February 1991, pp. 120-123.

Nezar AlSayyad. *Cities and Caliphs: On the Genesis of Arab Muslim Urbanism*, Greenwood Press, Westport, CT, 1991. *Cities*, Vol. 9, No. 4, November 1992, pp. 318-320.

Alex Krieger (ed), *Andres Duany and Elizabeth Plater-Zyberk: Towns and Town-Making Principles*. Rizzoli International Publications, New York, 1991. *Cities*, Vol. 11, No.1, February 1994, pp. 73-74.

Pierre von Meiss, *Elements of Architecture: From Form to Place,* Van Nostrand Reinhold, 1990. *Journal of Architectural Education,* Vol. 47, No. 3, February 1994, pp. 182-183.

"Redesigning the American Dream", a review essay of four books: Solomon, D. *Re-Building*, 1992; Sorkin, M. *Local Code*, 1993; Calthorpe, P. *The Next American Metropolis*, 1993; Nelessen, A. *Visions for a New American Dream*, 1994. *Journal of Architectural Education*, Vol.49, No.2, November 1995, pp. 129-131.

Masahi Haneda and Toru Miura (eds.) *Islamic Urban Studies*, Kegan Paul International, London and New York, 1994. *Yemen Update: Bulletin of the American Institute for Yemeni Studies*, No.38, Winter/Spring 1996, pp. 31-32.

Michael Bonine, et al (eds.) *The Middle Eastern City and Islamic Urbanism: An Annotated Bibliography of Western Literature*, Ferd. Dummlers Verlag, Bonn, 1994. *Islamic Law and Society* , Vol. 4, No.2, 1997, pp.244-246.

Amir Pasic. *Islamic Architecture in Bosnia and Hercegovina*, Research Center for Islamic History, Art, and Culture, Istanbul, 1994. *Journal of Architectural Education*, Vol.50, No.4, May 1997, pp.289-290.

Catherine Saliou, *La Trait d'Urbanisme de Julian d'Ascalon,* De Boccard, Paris, 1996. *Journal of Roman Archaeology*, Vol. 11, 1998, pp. 680-682.

N.J. Habraken, edited by J. Teicher. *The Structure of the Ordinary: Form and Control in the Built Environment*, MIT Press, Cambridge, MA, 1998. *Cities*, Vol. 15, No. 6, 1998, p. 473.

Chris Wilson, *The Myth of Santa Fe: Creating a Modern Regional Tradition*, University of New Mexico Press, Albuquerque, NM, 1997. *NM Chapter of the American Planning Association Newsletter,* July 1999, pp. 4-5.

Paul Oliver (editor), *Encyclopedia of Vernacular Architecture* (3 volumes), Cambridge University Press, 1997. *Journal of Architectural Education*, Vol. 52, No. 4, May 1999, pp. 246-247.

Howard Davis, *The Culture of Building*, Oxford University Press, New York, 1999. *Journal of Architectural Education*, Vol. 54, No. 2, November 2000, p. 117.

Stefano Bianca, *Urban Form in the Arab World: Past and Present*, Thames and Hudson, London and New York, 2000. *Cities*, Vol. 18, No. 6, December 2001, pp. 426-427.

John S. Reynolds, *Courtyards: Aesthetic, Social, and Thermal Delight*, John Wiley & sons, Inc., New York, 2002. *Journal of Architectural Education*, Vol. 56, No.4, May 2003, p. 83.

Hisham Mortada, *Traditional Islamic Principles of Built Environment*, Routledge, London, 2003. *Cities,* Vol. 21, No. 1, 2004, pp. 84-85.

Douglas Farr, *Sustainable Urbanism: Urban Design with Nature,* John Wiley & Sons, Inc., NJ, 2008. *Urban Design International*, Vol. 15, No. 3, Autumn 2010, p. 183.

Galina Tachieva, *Sprawl Repair Manual,* Island Press, Washington, DC, 2010. *Urban Design International,* Vol. 16, No. 4, Winter 2011, p. 297.

The following five reviews are posted online at: http://www.intbau.org/resources/documents:

Christopher Alexander, *The Nature of Order* (4 Books), Center for Environmental Structure, Berkeley, California, 2002-2004.

James Steele, *The Architecture of Rasem Badran*, Thames and Hudson, London, 2005.

Andres Duany, et al. *Smart Code and Manual, version 8.0*, New Urban Publications, Ithaca, NY, 2006.

Julie Campoli and Alex S. MacLean, *Visualizing Density,* Lincoln Institute of Land Policy, Cambridge, Massachusetts, 2007.

Jenny Quillien, *Delight's Muse: On Christopher Alexander's The Nature of Order*, Culicidae Architectural Press, Ames, Iowa, 2008.

## Technical Reports of Urban Planning Practice

HALIFAX, NOVA SCOTIA

*What Kind of Downtown Do We Want?* Prepared for the Downtown Committee, Halifax, Nova Scotia, December 1972

*Development Plan for the Granville Street Building Moratorium Area*, 1972, and *Urban Design Principles and Elements Used in the Preparation of the Development Plan for the Granville Street BMA*, 1973. This is an urban design plan for a 10-acre site within downtown Halifax, Nova Scotia, Canada.

*Views from Citadel Hill: Halifax, Nova Scotia, Proposed By-Law*. Prepared for the City of Halifax, Nova Scotia, June 1973. Adopted in March 1974.

Elizabeth Pacey, *The Battle of Citadel Hill*, Lancelot Press, Hantsport, Nova Scotia, 1979. This book documents and analyzes this issue, and devotes Chapter Six to "The June Report" cited above.

ALBUQUERQUE, NEW MEXICO

*Coors Corridor Study*, Draft report February 26, 1982, and condensed draft of August 2, 1982. Planning Division, Municipal Development Department, City of Albuquerque, New Mexico.

*Historic Old Town, Albuquerque, New Mexico. A procedure for guiding change and development based on patterns/guidelines and continuous appraisal*. For Department of Community & Economic Development, City of Albuquerque, New Mexico, March, 1983.

## LECTURES AND PAPER PRESENTATIONS BASED ON RESEARCH RESULTS

*I have been active since the late 1970's in delivering numerous* **lectures** *and later as* **Keynote speaker**, *based on my research work, at universities, symposia and conferences delivered at the following institutions in response to invitations:*

Keynote lecture for the summer school of the International Society of Biourbanism, July 2014, located in the historic town of Artena, Italy. Lecture title: "Generative Processes of Mediterranean Cities and Towns". PowerPoint presentation and interview of Besim Hakim by Antonio Caperna, president of the society, posted on the society's web page: biourbanism.org.

Harvard University, Kennedy School of Government, Dubai Initiative Conference and Workshop on "Urbanism in the Middle East: A Search for New Paradigms", April 8-9, 2011. Two presentations: (1) Urban Sustainability, and (2) Architecture and Urban Planning Education.

University of New Mexico, School of Architecture and Planning, March 1, 2011. Presentation as a part of a panel that explored the implications on open space design by the revolutions in Tunisia and Egypt.

University of Notre Dame, School of Architecture, South Bend, Indiana. Public lecture on September 29th, 2010 titled: "Historic Byzantine and Islamic Building Rules and Processes".

University of Oregon, Portland. International Symposium on "Current Challenges for Patterns, Pattern Languages and Sustainability", October 30 – November 1, 2009. Presentation on generative processes, that was published in the proceedings book (See Publications).

Arizona State University, Tempe, AZ, October 10, 2008. Lecture co-sponsored by the Late Lessons from Early History project and by the School of Geographical Sciences. Consultations with researchers of the project Late Lessons from Early History. Title of public lecture: "Eco-Policies and Generative Programs for Sustainable Cities".

American University of Sharjah, Sharjah, UAE in cooperation with the Center for the Study of Architecture in the Arab Region (CSAAR). Keynote speaker at the conference titled "Instant Cities", April 2008. Followed by another Keynote address at the University of Sharjah's conference titled "International Forum on Islamic Architecture and Design (IFIAD)". Followed by lectures at Ajman University of Science and Technology, Ajman, Al-Hosn University, Abu Dhabi, and at Dubai Municipality's Historical Buildings Section, Dubai, UAE.

University of Massachusetts, Boston, College of Public and Community Service. Keynote speaker at the conference titled: "Rebuilding Sustainable Communities in Iraq: Policies, Programs and Projects", July 22-29,

2007. Presentation was published as a chapter in the book that resulted from the conference (See Publications).

Congress for the New Urbanism, Smart Code Workshop, Austin, Texas, March 29-31, 2007. Presentation titled: "Dynamic Coding in History".

Urban Design Forum of Albuquerque, September 29, 2005 meeting. Presentation on the visit to Poundbury, undertaken in July 2005. Poundbury is the urban extension to Dorchester, Dorset, UK. It was planned by architect Leon Krier for the Prince of Wales.

International Conference on Heritage, Globalization, and the Built Environment, Bahrain, December 6-8, 2004. Keynote speaker (for the topic presented see Publications). Presentation was later repeated at the Shaikh Ebrahim Bin Mohammed Al Khalifa Center for Culture and Research, sponsored by Mai Al Khalifa.

La Ciudad en el Occidente Islamico Medieval: First conference, of a series of conferences, titled: La Medina Andalusi, November 2004, held at the Escuela de Estudios Arabes in Granada, Spain. Presentation on Mediterranean traditional urbanism and codes.

Congress for the New Urbanism (CNU), Council IV On Codes, Santa Fe, NM, October 18-20, 2002. Presentation on "Byzantine and Islamic Codes", published in the *Council Report III / IV*, 2003.

Binghampton University, Broome County, NY. Institute of Global Cultural Studies conference on "Islam and Africa: Global, Cultural and Historical Perspectives", April 19-22, 2001. Chaired a session on "Planning and Design of Islam: Urbanism, Architecture and Art". Presented a paper at this session with Zubair Ahmed on "Rules for the Built Environment in 19th Century Northern Nigeria", subsequently published in 2006.

University of New Mexico, Fine Arts Building. "Eco-City Practices: Learning from the Past". Sponsored by the Permaculture Institute of Santa Fe, New Mexico-Albuquerque Chapter, April 17, 1998.

Arriyadh Development Authority (ADA), Riyadh, Saudi Arabia. Participant and Keynote speaker during the ADA Visioning Symposium for the future of the capital, June 1997.

## Lectures and Presentations at the Following Institutions

Department of Architecture at University of Strathclyde, Glasgow, Scotland, September 2017.

Bibliotheque Generale et Archives, Rabat, Morocco, June 1996.

Agency for de-densification and rehabilitation of Fes medina (ADER), Fes, Morocco, June 1996.

Departments of Architecture, City & Regional Planning, and Near East Studies, Cornell University, Ithaca, New York, March 1995.

College of Architecture and Planning, University of Arizona, Tucson, April 1994.

Dubai Municipality, Dubai, United Arab Emirates, February 1993.

Faculty of Architecture and Planning, School of Technology, Aristotle University of Thessaloniki, Thessaloniki, Greece, June 1992.

Faculty of Architecture and Planning, National Technical University of Athens, Greece, April 1992.

Faculty of Architecture and Planning, Istanbul Technical University, Istanbul, Turkey, March 1992.

Department of Architecture, Faculty of Engineering & Technology, University of Jordan, Amman, Jordan, May 1988.

College of Architecture and Planning, King Faisal University, Dammam, Saudi Arabia, November 1985, April 1986, April 1988, May 1991, April 1993.

College of Environmental Design, King Fahd University of Petroleum and Minerals, Dhahran, Saudi Arabia, December 1983, April 1989, May 1990, May 1992.

College of Architecture, King Saud University, Riyadh, Saudi Arabia, January 1982, April 1987, June 1989, May 1992.

School of Architecture and Planning, University of New Mexico, Albuquerque, New Mexico, May 1981.

Architects Collaborative at 46 Brattle Street, Cambridge, Massachusetts, February 1981.

Department of Architecture, Massachusetts Institute of Technology, Cambridge, Massachusetts, February 1981; and in April 1977 seminar with two Saudi Ph.D. students, whose final dissertations are based on various aspects of my research work.

Department of Anthropology, University of Texas at Austin, Texas, July 1980.

College of Environmental Design, University of California, Berkeley, California, November 1979.

*Papers* were presented at the following symposia and conferences in response to invitations to proposed paper topics based on my research results. Papers selected for the Annual Meetings of the Association of Collegiate Schools of Architecture (ACSA) are by a process of anonymous competition.

American Institute for Maghrib Studies (AIMS) conference on "The Living Medina", Tangier, Morocco, June 1996.

AIA Committee on Design conference "The search for the American place: Southwestern cross-cultural", Santa Fe, New Mexico, July 14-17,1994. Panelist on Round table: Santa Fe growth and planning.

Western Social Science Association (WSSA) 36th Annual Conference, Albuquerque, New Mexico, April 20-23,1994. Paper presented within the "Urban Studies" group.

International Conference on "Urbanism in Islam", organized by the Institute of Oriental Culture, University of Tokyo, Japan, October 1989. Also the Second International Conference held in Tokyo, November 1990.

"Quality in the Built Environment" (Public and Private Responsibilities in Housing Design and Settlement Planning), University of Newcastle Upon Tyne, U.K., July 1989.

ACSA Annual Meetings of 1983 (Santa Fe, New Mexico), 1986 (New

Orleans, Louisiana), 1989 (Chicago, Illinois), 1990 (San Francisco, California). Attended the ACSA/EAAE Conference in Athens, Greece, 1990.

"Built Form and Culture Research" Conference, The University of Kansas, Lawrence, Kansas (could not attend, but paper was distributed), October 1984.

International Symposium on "Islamic Architecture and Urbanism", held at King Faisal University, Dammam, Saudi Arabia, January 1980.

"First National Conference on Urban Design", New York, October 1978. Could not attend, but abstract of paper was published in the conference proceedings.

## PUBLIC SERVICE

Civic Affairs Committee, Halifax Board of Trade, Halifax, Nova Scotia, Canada, 1971-78.
As a member of the Civic Affairs Committee I was responsible for evaluating technical planning documents for submissions made by the Board to the City of Halifax, NS.

"Scottsdale 2000 Directions for Tomorrow" Town Enrichment Program, Scottsdale, Arizona, 1979-80. Active participant and contributor to the program as a community service. Certificate of Participation presented by the Mayor and City Council.

Shared Vision: Building a Great Community, Town Hall Meetings, Albuquerque, New Mexico. These are meetings for community dialogue among citizen participants who are working to shape a future direction for Albuquerque. Active participant in the June 1994 and October 1995 meetings.

Member of the 1000 Friends of New Mexico, from 1996-2008 upon its shut down.

Member of the Board of Directors of the Green Alliance of Albuquerque (6/2001 – 8/2002)

# HONORS, AWARDS, AND RECOGNITIONS

Research for the book *Arabic-Islamic Cities* won a Citation in National Competition sponsored by *Progressive Architecture* magazine in the 34th Annual P/A Awards program, January 1987. Twenty three winners were selected from 805 entries. The following is a quote from the P/A News Release:
"Published by Routledge & Kegan Paul as a book entitled *Arabic-Islamic Cities: Building and Planning Principles,* the research shows how traditional Arabic cities, long admired for their visual unity, are the outgrowth of planning principles stipulated by Islamic law. What most impressed the jury about the research was the clear connection that it made between a culture and the built environment. The jury also praised its use of history to develop planning principles for the future growth of these cities."

American Institute of Architects 1990 Education Honors for an undergraduate history/theory course: "Teaching History by Searching for Emics & Etics - A significant achievement in the formulation, implementation, and outcome of instruction." Signed by AIA President, dated March 21, 1990. Selected jury comments from the booklet by the AIA titled *AIA 1990 Education Honors, 1991,* p. 24:
 - "The question of cultures is central today. This submission is one of the very best in this regard. It makes sense and the material is thoroughly addressed", and
 - "It also has an excellent construct --looks at constant factors as well as culturally determined variables. Both constancy and variability have excellent applicability to our present situation. Emphasis on principles reinforces memory. Tremendous applicability of construct.", and
 - "There are fascinating things about learning what the differences and the constraints are in cultures . . . . 
this course addresses a construct which is useful across cultures ... this idea could be used in any part of the world."

The Marquis Who's Who Publication Board selected Besim S. Hakim to be a subject of biographical record in *Who's Who in America* and *Who's Who in the World* (first inclusion in the 1997 editions). The inclusion of the biography "is limited to those individuals who have demonstrated outstanding achievement in their own fields of endeavor and who have, thereby, contributed significantly to the betterment of contemporary society": from the certificate signed by the Publisher.

Elected to the College of Fellows of the American Institute of Certified Planners on April 15, 2000.

"Election to the College of Fellows is one of the highest honors that the American Institute of Certified Planners, the professional institute of the American Planning Association, bestows upon a member. This honor recognizes the achievements of the professional as a model planner with significant contributions to planning and society.
Fellowship will be granted to planners who have been members of AICP and have achieved excellence in professional practice, teaching and mentoring, research, public or community service and leadership".
Quote from the APA web site: http://www.planning.org/faicp/. The following quote is about Hakim's induction in 2000:
"Besim S. Hakim is the first town planner/architect who has authoritatively researched the ethical principles, customary practices of planning and building, their related codes and the rule systems which shaped traditional built environments in Islamic and other societies surrounding the Mediterranean. He has published an internationally acclaimed book and numerous scholarly contributions based on his research results. Professor Hakim practiced with city planning authorities and taught planning and architecture at a number of universities in Canada, the United States, and the Middle East, applying unique insights from research to practice and teaching".

Green Alliance plaque presented June 15, 2002 for friendship, leadership, and service on the Board of Directors of the Green Alliance.

Honorary Membership bestowed by the International Society of Biourbanism (ISB), November 2017.

Member of Advisory and Editorial Boards of the following journals:
- Editorial Board: *Urban Design International*; *Journal of Urbanism.*
- Advisory Board: *International Journal of Architectural Research; Journal of Biourbanism.*

## MEMBERSHIP IN PROFESSIONAL AND ALLIED ORGANIZATIONS

- Fellow: American Institute of Certified Planners
- Member: American Planning Association - New Mexico Chapter
- Member: American Institute of Architects
- Member: American Institute of Architects - Albuquerque Chapter
- Member: Urban Design Forum of Albuquerque since its inception in the early 2000s.

- Member: 1000 Friends of New Mexico from 1996-2008 upon its shut down.
- Member of the Board of Directors of the Green Alliance of Albuquerque (6/2001 – 8/2002).
- Member: Civic Affairs Committee, Halifax Board of Trade, Halifax, NS, Canada (lapsed).

# Acknowledgements

Earlier versions of the chapters in this book were published previously as indicated below. Changes to each chapter were made as necessary to fit the purposes of the book. The chapter numbers are indicated sequentially as they appear in the book.

## Part I: Historic Precedence

Chapter 1 - "Mediterranean urban and building codes: origins, content, impact, and lessons", *Urban Design International*, Vol.13, No. 1, Spring 2008, pp. 21-40.

2 - "Julian of Ascalon's treatise of construction and design rules from 6th-c. Palestine". *Journal of the Society of Architectural Historians*, Vol. 60, No. 1, March 2001, pp. 4-25.

3 - "The generative nature of Islamic rules for the built environment", *International Journal of Architectural Research*, Vol. 4, No. 1, March 2010, pp. 208-212.

4 - "The 'Urf' and its role in diversifying the architecture of traditional Islamic cities", *Journal of Architectural & Planning Research*, Vol. 11, No. 2, Summer 1994, pp. 108-127.

5 - "Rules for the built environment in 19th century Northern Nigeria", with Zubair Ahmed. *Journal of Architectural and Planning Research*, Vol. 23, No. 1, Spring 2006, pp. 1-26.

6 - "Urban form in traditional Islamic cultures: Further studies needed for formulating theory". *Cities*, Vol. 16, No. 1, 1999, pp. 53-58.

## Part II: Recycling Lessons

7 - "Recycling the experience of traditional Islamic built environments: A proposed framework and notes for generating principles", *DAAR 1988*, pp. 10-13. Republished in *Cities*, Vol. 8, No. 4, November 1991, pp. 274-277.

8 - "Recycling the Experience of Traditional Islamic Urbanism." *Proceedings of the Conference on the Preservation of Architectural Heritage of Islamic Cities* held in Istanbul, Turkey, 22-26 April, 1985, pp. 305-317.

9 - "Islamic Architecture and Urbanism." *Encyclopedia of Architecture: Design, Engineering and Construction*, Volume 3, John Wiley & Sons, Inc., New York, 1989, pp. 86-103.

10 - "Reviving the Rule System: An approach for revitalizing traditional towns in the Maghrib". *Cities*, Vol. 18, No. 2, April 2001, pp. 87-92.

11 - "Recycling a Traditional Housing Process: A Case in Abiquiu, New Mexico." *Proceedings of the 74th Annual Meeting of the ACSA: The Spirit of Home* held in New Orleans, Louisiana, March 1986, pp. 109-119.

12 - "Neighborhood test design based on historic precedents", *International Journal of Architectural Research*, Vol. 6, No. 2, July 2012, pp. 135-148.

## Part III: Generative Processes

13 - "Generative processes for revitalizing historic towns or heritage districts", *Urban Design International*, Vol. 12, No. 2/3, June/September 2007, pp. 87-99. Corrigendum in Vol. 13, No. 3, Autumn 2008, p. 210.

14 - "Generative Processes and Coding for Emirati Housing in Al-Ain", in the report titled: *Al-Ain: City Management Strategy*, July 2010, pp. 98-103.

15 - "Towards Eco-Urbanism for all Iraqi Cities, Towns, and Villages", *Proceedings of an International Conference on Rebuilding Sustainable Communities in Iraq: Policies, Programs and Projects*, July 23-26, 2007, pp. 179-193.

www.ingramcontent.com/pod-product-compliance
Lightning Source LLC
Chambersburg PA
CBHW070716160426
43192CB00009B/1208